Property of
FAMILY OF FAITH
LIBRARY

W9-AON-372

Family of Faith Library

# SECONDARY EDUCATION IN THE UNITED STATES

**HARL R. DOUGLASS**

University of Colorado

Property of
FAMILY OF FAITH
LIBRARY

SECOND EDITION

THE RONALD PRESS COMPANY · NEW YORK

Copyright © 1964 by

THE RONALD PRESS COMPANY

Copyright 1952 by

THE RONALD PRESS COMPANY

*All Rights Reserved*

No part of this book may be reproduced
in any form without permission in writing from the publisher.

Library of Congress Catalog Card Number: 64–13942
PRINTED IN THE UNITED STATES OF AMERICA

373.73
D73∂2

May 19, 1964 · Pub 5.84

# Preface

The Second Edition of *Secondary Education in the United States* reflects the author's many years of working with students and includes advice and help received from teachers who have used the previous edition for more than a decade.

The book's principal aim is to provide an understanding of the various types of secondary schools and their relation to national and local problems, culture, and trends. Throughout, specific attention is given to developments such as team teaching, teaching machines, and programed learning.

Comprehensive in scope, the book offers an overview of the place in secondary education of each of the subjects for all of the students in the class, regardless of subject field of specialization. Treatments in the various chapters are written from a modern eclectic point of view.

The discussions of guidance and extrasubject activities are intended to furnish an understanding of the basic philosophy in these areas, to introduce fundamental principles, and to examine the major responsibilities of, and the better techniques used by, the classroom teacher. Material on the history of education and on comparative education is distributed throughout the book in connection with the various topics.

Suggestions for supplementary reading avoid as far as possible duplication of material. The questions and problems at the end of the chapters have been carefully thought through so as not to restrict the instructor in his teaching but to make suggestions that he may wish to employ.

HARL R. DOUGLASS

Boulder, Colorado
January, 1964

PROPERTY OF
OKLAHOMA BAPTIST UNIVERSITY
LIBRARY

# Acknowledgments

The author is indebted to many who gave suggestions, including the following: Dr. F. Gordon Foster, Arizona State College, Flagstaff; Dr. Hazlett Wubben, University of Colorado, and his wife, Betty, who read the entire manuscript and made suggestions; Dr. Richard C. Schettler, University of Colorado, who offered valuable suggestions relative to content and organization; Professor Hubert H. Mills, of the University of Colorado, with whom the author has worked for many years in the areas included in this volume and from whose writings a number of important quotations were made. The author is especially indebted to Dr. James G. Umstattd, of the University of Texas, and Dr. John E. McAdam, of the University of Iowa, each of whom read the manuscript carefully and made valuable criticisms and suggestions with reference to content and organization, and to Dr. Albert I. Oliver, of the University of Pennsylvania, who made suggestions for the general outline of content. The author is also indebted to many instructors in courses in secondary education who made suggestions directly or indirectly, including the following: Dr. Milton J. Gold, of Hunter College of the City University of New York; Dr. Daniel C. Neale and Dr. William E. Gardner, of the University of Minnesota; Dr. Florence H. Lee, of Rutgers—the State University of New Jersey; Dean Vernon Anderson, University of Maryland; Dr. Bob G. Woods, University of Missouri; Dean Paul Jacobson, University of Oregon; Professor John D. McNeil, University of California at Los Angeles; Dr. Brantley Edwards, University of California; Clarence Samford, University of Southern Illinois; and Dr. Derwood Baker, New York University.

# Contents

## Part III:  TEACHING AND LEARNING MATERIALS

## Part IV:  STIMULATING AND GUIDING LEARNING

## The Competent Teacher

The competent teacher is a student . . .

1. OF THE WORLD IN WHICH HE LIVES. He is constantly seeking a more rational *Weltanschauung*, into which he incorporates the findings of science, as evaluated by his own reason.

2. OF THE SOCIETY IN WHICH HE LIVES. He is constantly seeking to interpret the *Zeitgeist* as reflected in literature, art, and music, in customs, politics, and economics; and to balance this against his rational *Weltanschauung*. He is able, therefore, to compare what is with what he thinks ought to be.

3. OF HUMAN NATURE. He is constantly seeking to expand his understanding of human behavior and the learning process.

4. OF EDUCATION. He is constantly reviewing and/or conducting experimentation in the field of education, so that his understanding of the process may be fuller and more mature.

5. OF THE PARTICULAR SUBJECTS HE TEACHES. He is constantly expanding his knowledge, understanding, and appreciation of these fields through research, reading, and creative professional activities of many kinds.*

* James M. Hanlon, Director of Teacher Education, University of Detroit.

# I

## *THE MAGNIFICENT CHALLENGE*

# The Current Challenge to American Secondary Education

## IN THE BEGINNING

Sela was afraid. For several months now he had been noticing signs about his body indicating that he was passing from the stage of a boy to the stage of a man. And now the expected and feared was about to happen.

Tomorrow Sela and a number of other boys in this very ancient tribe would be taken away from the camp and village into the wilds which were referred to as "the bush." Here he and the other pubescents would be given a series of lessons and tests by selected older men of the tribe. He looked forward to this with great curiosity and pride. He would soon be a man, but he was afraid. In the bush he would be given painful physical tests to try his nerve and his muscle. Body markings would be made on him—tattooing, incisions, cicatrizing, and tooth breaking.

For several nights now he had not been able to sleep well and he had noticed that there had been a guard around the structure that his family called home and one around that of each of the other boys to be trained and initiated into the manhood of the tribe. He knew that this was to prevent any of them from running away to escape the painful training and preparation. During a week to two weeks spent in the bush, he would be taught a great variety of things, following the education that he had received by watching, and participating with, the others of the tribe.

Indeed, this training would continue after he had been made a male citizen of the tribe.

In a way, his education and that of his fellow pubescents would seem to be composed of types of subject fields similar to those of the secondary schools of today. For example, these boys were given facts and trained in skills that would be of the nature of vocational education. In other words, they were trained in the obtaining of food and what was used for clothing and in the construction of shelters. They were given training in the types of wooden and stone tools that were useful for these purposes as well as in battle.

They were given training in religion, such as it was, consisting largely of animism and superstition, particularly as it might relate to his appeasing the gods for obtaining rain for the crops, a good catch of fish, good results of hunting trips, or protection from lightning, severe windstorms, disease, and his enemies. There were dozens of gods, each with a special field of operation.

These primitive youths were taught literature in the form of an abundance of folklore—proverbs, aphorisms, riddles, fables, legends, astronomical fables and myths, war songs, hero tables, and tales about migrations, battles, and love affairs. These stories were transmitted orally, largely by the older men of the tribe but also by wandering minstrels.

They were trained in arts of the types that would be useful and pleasurable, including drawing and carving, particularly figures of animals and men.

They were given training in science, as a matter of fact—what we call today nature facts. Much of this knowledge was useful, but much of it was superstition invented to fill the vacuum of ignorance in the areas of science. This science consisted principally of (1) facts about the animals that could be obtained for food and clothing, (2) facts about foods, natural plants and animals, and about their production and harvesting, and (3) facts about the weather and simple facts about the sun, the stars, the night, the day, and the seasons. Some of the "scientific" knowledge and what passed for it had to do with the human body and its care and strengthening.

In mathematics, their training was limited, but at least they were taught to count to five, usually to ten, and sometimes in groups of five, for example, five, ten, and fifteen. People in the tribe measured time by so many moons, and they measured distances by how far they could reach with outspread arms and by paces. They measured months by the cycle of the moon and years by the number of summers and winters. Usually, they did not know their own age, so initiation into the tribe did not come at a certain age but at the onset of pubescence, which varied from thirteen to sixteen years of age for the boys.

Music was of a very simple type; the rhythmic chanting and beating of very simple drums was used primarily in connection with war dances and other ritual dances that occurred at different times of the year, particularly in connection with harvests and religious ceremonies.

History, of course, was taught through folk tales and "literature" ordinarily given by elders of the tribe and was not particularly accurate but was employed as a means of developing loyalty to, and enthusiasm for, the tribe and a belief in its superior powers in warfare.

They received a great deal of physical education in connection with the activities of hunting, swimming, fishing, preparation for war, religious rituals, dancing, etc.

This learning resulted from observation of the elders, imitation, practice, and participation, although much was given orally by the older people of the tribe.

Shortly after Sela returned from the bush, he would participate in "graduation exercises." Before the rest of the tribe, he would exhibit the results of his training; in other words, there would be a sort of final examination and commencement. There were athletic events of various kinds, dances, religious rituals, and, most prominent, the exhibition of the development of the power to bear pain, so that he would not be classified as a weakling and, if captured in war, would not reveal any secrets about his tribe. Some of the body mutilations of the pubescents were made at this time.

Sela happened to belong to a tribe in which the boys also learned a "foreign language." It was a language that was developed for the men only, so that they might converse with one another and not be understood by enemies or the women and children of the tribe who might be captured by enemies.

**The Education of Girls.** Sela's sister did not receive special education during pubescence or adolescence. She began her education as soon as she was able to get about well, by helping her mother and her younger brother and sisters. She was trained for life as a wife and mother in the tribe.

**General Characteristics of Primitive Secondary Education.** The foregoing is indicative of the typical education of prehistoric peoples as we are able to reconstruct it from various types of folk tales that have been handed down through hints in the early literature of the ancients and by inference and analogy from the primitive tribes of today in Australia, the South Pacific islands, and Africa.[1]

[1] Edgar Lee Hewett, *Ruling Races of Prehistorical Times;* Découlanges, *Ancient City;* Walter Baldwin Spencer and Francis J. Gillen, *Native Tribes of Central Australia* (London: Macmillan & Co., Ltd., 1918).

Secondary education is the education of adolescents. Certain note-worthy characteristics of the secondary education of primitive peoples may be noted:

1. It was definitely associated with pubescence and adolescence.
2. It was primarily for boys.
3. It was not selective but was for all boys.
4. It centered on the preparation for various areas of life activities.
5. The materials and activities of education were not separated logically into subjects such as literature, science, history, and so on, but they were interrelated or integrated around the problems and needs of life. For example, many of the stories and activities were literature, history, social studies, and religion all combined so as to focus upon certain types of life problems.

## SECONDARY EDUCATION IN EARLY CIVILIZED TIMES

As time went on and civilization began, people tended to become members of class societies. The rulers and the warriors were able to impose upon the people the idea that they were entitled to special privileges. In the early societies around the Mediterranean, the adolescents were given special training. The education and training that the boys and girls of the common people received could hardly be called *secondary education* in the sense in which that term is used today, but it bordered on secondary education for life situations. They were trained to do the hard work in agriculture and in elementary manufacturing, and they were also trained for warfare. The boys of the ruling classes were given special education so that they might become government officials, professionals with respect to medicine or law, or merchants.

**Secondary Education in Greece.** The first people to move more definitely into higher types of secondary education were the Greeks. In their city-states of Athens, Sparta, Corinth, etc., they developed different types of education. A very simple primitive education was given boys who would be warriors and workers, and there was a higher level of intellectual education for the sons of the citizens of Greece (about one-sixth of the population). This not only prepared them for higher duties including professional work but also gave them knowledge and culture that would enable them to lead and enjoy enriched and more comfortable lives and, therefore, to have status among their fellow citizens.

In later times, especially in Athens, the men of outstanding intellectual knowledge, such as Socrates, Plato, and Aristotle, would gather about them a group of abler young men from the upper class and would teach them things that today would be called geometry, science, social studies, religion, and literature. This was all referred to under the general heading of "philosophy."

**Secondary Education in Rome.** In the early days of Rome, the education of boys was very simple, consisting of preparation for the great masses of them to be soldiers and workers. Those who were the sons of "citizens" of Rome were educated to be officers in the armed forces and to be members of the legislative and ruling bodies, in other words, to be military leaders or politicians.

However, after the Romans conquered Greece and came into contact with the cultural development in that land, they brought well-educated Greeks to Rome and employed them as tutors for their boys and, indeed, for themselves, and Rome began to develop a higher type of secondary education, although it centered largely upon oratory—speech writing in both the classical Ciceronian Latin and the common Latin. This was vocational education for the sons of Roman citizens.

For several centuries after the Roman Empire was broken up and overrun by the Huns, Visigoths, and other barbarian hordes, secondary education did not advance materially, although throughout Europe there were what might be called secondary schools. These existed particularly at the courts of the rulers of cities, and of very small states, around certain cathedrals or religious centers where there were some monks or priests who delighted in intellectual thinking and in giving intellectual training to adolescents. Such centers were also established in the cities of central Europe for boys of well-to-do parents, and in certain cities in England and France, particularly as fostered by religious or guild organizations.

In the next few pages, we will make a quick survey of how our present-day high schools in the United States came to be what they are. We will also review the major criticisms of our secondary schools and take a look at the current challenge.

## PREDECESSORS OF THE AMERICAN HIGH SCHOOL

**The Influence of the Renaissance.** In the fifteenth and sixteenth centuries, there was what has been called a "rediscovery" of the manuscripts of the Greeks and the Romans, which contained a very large part of the scientific and literary knowledge of the civilization of that time. These documents became to a very large degree the curriculum of the secondary schools of the various countries in Europe.

Among these schools was an outstanding one reorganized by Johann Sturm at Strassburg, Germany. Sturm, who had been a well-known professor of Latin at the University of Paris, was brought to Strassburg to reorganize the school, which was not appealing to the sons of the German merchant traders. The other secondary schools in Europe tended to become like the *Gymnasium* in Strassburg, and they set the pattern for early secondary schools in the United States. Since then, secondary education has struggled against discouraging odds in efforts to meet the needs of the times.

**The American Latin Grammar School.** When the Pilgrims and others came to settle in New England, their thoughts turned immediately to education for their children, particularly their sons, so that they might not lack educated ministers and, indeed, educated men in various professional walks of life. At Boston (in 1635) and elsewhere, they soon after set up secondary schools similar to those they had known in Europe. The curriculum consisted largely of Latin and Greek, since much of the important knowledge of civilization existed in Greek and Latin manuscripts.

These schools took boys at about the onset of pubescence, or even earlier, and kept them on through adolescence until they were thought to be prepared for Harvard College, established in 1636, or some other college or university. In these secondary schools, in which the day was long and arduous, the teaching was very largely of the authoritarian type and there was much insistence upon religious conformity. The Latin grammar schools were for boys, although, later, girls were admitted to some schools.

Emphasizing greatly the study of Latin and Greek, these schools did not prepare well for the beginning of a new life and new occupations on the rocky soil of New England, and they did not spread to the rest of the United States. In the South there were tutors, and to the west of the original colonies there was no secondary education except as passed on in a few instances by fathers and by ministers.

**The Academy.** Back in the Middle Ages there had been much justification for emphasizing Greek and Latin in the curriculum of secondary schools. In the first place, most the printed knowledge was in those languages; secondly, Latin was the international language of the courts; and thirdly, it was the language of the Catholic church. However, as time went on, these conditions changed and much knowledge came to be printed in local languages; international communications were also carried on in languages other than Latin; and Protestant church services were conducted in the local languages. Many thinking people in Europe and in the United States protested against the narrow curriculum of these Latin grammar schools, called "*Gynmasia*" in Austria, Germany, and the Scandinavian countries, "*lycées*" and "*collèges*" in France, and "public schools" in England.

There developed several groups of people who believed that a more practical and realistic type of education was needed. They believed in (1) less dependence upon the learning of words and (2) instruction in the native language, with a greater use of words in the native language as opposed to Latin and Greek. In Germany, there were developed what were called Ritter academies, and a little later in other leading European countries secondary schools with more useful curriculums were developed.

The academies did to some extent get away from excessive emphasis upon instruction in Latin and Greek, and some new subjects were offered in many, including somewhat more science, history, and English. Some academies offered courses in surveying, navigation, bookkeeping, or music and art, and some gave special courses for girls, so that the academy might serve as a finishing school for girls who were about to make their social debuts or get married.

At that time, there happened what has occurred so constantly in connection with progress in education. Educational conservatives opposed to the new subjects insisted that the older subjects were more respectable, that they possessed unusual values for training the mind, and that knowledge of them gave social status. For the most part, the 5,000 academies existing in 1850 were narrowly academic schools that emphasized religious education, mind training, and preparation for college.

Most academies were not publicly controlled, and, in general, they were not publicly supported. Most of them became coeducational, although for a long time most of the academies enrolled either boys or girls but not both. Ordinarily, the earlier academies took students at about the age of twelve and graduated them at about eighteen. Unlike the Latin grammer schools, the academies eventually spread into the South and into the states west of the Appalachian Mountains.

## DEVELOPMENT OF THE AMERICAN HIGH SCHOOL

**The First High Schools.** In the United States, dissatisfaction with the academies soon developed on many points, particularly with reference to the following:

1. They were not publicly supported, but, rather, they charged tuition.
2. They were not publicly controlled.
3. The curriculum had retrogressed toward the Latin grammar school type.
4. They combined religion with education in a way that was contrary to both the melting-pot idea of the United States and the fundamental American doctrine of separation of church and state.

5. They admitted youngsters at too early an age.
6. They did not prepare the sons and daughters of the large middle class to earn a living.

As a result of this dissatisfaction, a new secondary school, the public high school, was to develop and eventually replace the academy as the prevailing institution of secondary education. Beginning with the English High School in Boston in 1821, high schools began to appear throughout New England and New York; they spread very, very slowly in the South, but rather rapidly later in the Middle West and still later in the Rocky Mountain and Pacific Coast regions, as towns and populated areas large enough to support a high school sprang up.

**The Curriculum of the Early High Schools.** Partly because of the expense involved and partly because of the opposition of those interested in positions for themselves, the high schools in the early decades of their existence did not develop a curriculum for the great mass of young people or for all areas of life. However, it was much broader than Latin and Greek. There were few, if any, vocational courses in most high schools, no courses in health and physical education, and practically no extracurricular activities or counseling, the latter being supervised in a very amateurish and incidental manner by teachers and principals with no appropriate special training.

With the spread of the public high school, those opposed to broadening and modernizing secondary education employed arguments based on the special advantages of traditional subjects, particularly Latin and mathematics, for the training of the mind, and on the doctrine of formal discipline or transfer of training. Also developed was the argument that the accumulation of credits in certain preferred secondary school subjects would ensure, or at least contribute heavily to, the success of the graduate in achieving good marks in college.

**Coeducation.** Almost from the beginning, the great majority of public high schools, except in southern states, were coeducational. This may be partly attributed to the fact that it was much cheaper to establish one high school for both boys and girls than to establish two separate high schools. In conservative areas and in areas more densely populated, particularly in New England and the South, coeducation came about only after it had become standard in the rest of the country

**Education of Negroes.** In northern states, the public schools have always been open to all youngsters, regardless of race or citizenship. In the South and in the border states there was, prior to the emancipation of the slaves, hardly a thought of providing secondary education for Negroes. Throughout the first half of the twentieth century, separate secondary schools for Negroes were established in many places in the South. At first they were in very cheap and overcrowded buildings with very poorly prepared teachers and large classes. But later on, particularly since 1930, secondary schools for Negroes in the South improved greatly. There had come to be many more graduates of Negro colleges with considerable subject-matter training for teaching in secondary schools. In many communities much better buildings were built (indeed, in some places better buildings for the Negroes than for white students), and except in a few of the most conservative and poorer states—Mississippi, South Carolina, Alabama, Louisiana, and Arkansas—salaries of Negro teachers began to approach the average of teachers in white secondary schools. Classes still remain large in most Negro secondary schools, the teaching load high, and the facilities for transportation varying from good to non-existent.

With the Supreme Court decision in 1954 declaring segregation unconstitutional, there began a very slow trend toward desegregation. Before 1964, no progress has been made at all in secondary schools in Alabama, South Carolina, or Mississippi. In most other states, at least token desegregation had taken place, and, in the border states, desegregation has been very largely accomplished; among the latter states, Missouri, Kentucky, and Oklahoma have made much progress.

**Broadening of the Curriculum.** Since 1880, enrolments in the American secondary schools doubled every ten years until 1930, and, by 1960, 90 per cent of the young people of secondary school age were attending secondary school, and 65 per cent of them were graduating. It was only logical that, beginning in the 1880's, new subjects were introduced, particularly in the fields of business education, physical education, music, art, social studies, agriculture, manual training (woodworking), and home economics. The requirements for graduation became more flexible, and in a number of ways the secondary school became a school for all the children of all the people. These developments were opposed and delayed by the conservatives, and their proponents were embarrassed by some of the mistakes made by the early experimentalists, particularly superficialists and faddists.

**Milestones in the Development of Secondary Education in the United States.**

> 1635—The Latin grammar school, the first American secondary school, was organized to provide preparation for college. It established the college domination of the secondary school and a reverence for classical subjects.

> 1751—The first academy was established. The idea of preparation for life as well as preparation for college made its appearance.

1821—The first public high school was opened. Preparation for life, which the academy had in a large measure forsaken in its desire for respectability, was reaffirmed as its principal aim. American social and economic life had continued to change, and the democratic ideal of equality of opportunity brought new demands which the academy as a private enterprise could not meet.

1827—The Massachusetts law of 1827 required each urban community to provide opportunity for secondary education. This preceded a series of similar enactments in other states, legalizing the high school.

1870—The accrediting of the high school by the state university began in Michigan and then spread to other states. This move substituted inspection and accreditation of the high school by the university for the examination of high school graduates and strengthened the authority of the college over the schools.

1874—The Kalamazoo Case resulted in a decision by the Supreme Court of the State of Michigan legalizing the expenditure of public funds for the support of the high school. Similar legislation followed in other states.

1885—The first of the present six regional accrediting associations was organized. The requirements that were set up improved physical standards and raised the qualifications of teachers.

1890—Beginning in 1890 and lasting through 1930, enrolments in grades nine through twelve doubled every decade, and they increased 5 per cent between 1930 and 1941.

1893—The Committee of Ten of the National Education Association claimed that secondary education was for the few who could profit by it, and declared college preparatory subjects good for all students.

1899—The Committee on College Entrance Requirements of the Nation Education Association contributed the system of computing secondary education in units of credit.

1900—The philosophy of John Dewey began to make an impression on the educational attitude of the more liberal educators.

1902—The first junior college (at Joliet, Illinois), beginning the extension of secondary education to include the thirteenth and fourteenth grades, was established.

1909—The opening of the first junior high school marked the beginning of the administrative reorganization of public secondary schools.

1917—The Smith-Hughes Act marked the appearance of the federal government in the promotion of vocational education.

1918—The Commission on the Reorganization of Secondary Education set forth the famous Seven Cardinal Principles of Secondary Education, affirming the idea that secondary education must aim at nothing less than complete and worthy living for all youth.

1919—The Progressive Education Association was organized by a group of educators and interested citizens, for the purpose of uniting those who were experimenting with the newer schools.

1932—The Pennsylvania Study uncovered evidence showing wide variations in intelligence and achievement of students in different schools and further weakened the justification for the admission of students to college on the basis of school marks.

1933—The Eight-Year Study of the Progressive Education Association was begun: Is the study of certain subjects essential to college success? Findings eight years later showed that there are no inherent values in certain subjects that make their study indispensable in preparation for college.

1934—The Cooperative Study of Secondary School Standards, involving the six regional accrediting associations, began work in the development of new principles and practices for accrediting secondary schools. Standards evolved were democratic and qualitative and had much to do with liberalizing secondary education.

1937—The George-Deen Act extended the principle of the Smith-Hughes Act to new areas of vocational education.

1942—Results of the Eight-Year Study began to appear. The first volume, *Adventure in American Education,* reported no discoverable relationship between the pattern of subjects taken in school and student success in college.

1945—The Prosser Resolution, made at a conference on vocational education sponsored by the Office of Education, pointed out that the vocational program and college-preparatory courses provided for about 40 per cent of the high school students, leaving 60 per cent who received no adequate life-adjustment education. This resolution became the basis for extended study by the National Commission of Life Adjustment Education for Youth.

1947—Beginning in 1947 and continuing through 1950, numerous studies were made of the holding power of secondary schools, such as those by W. H. Gaumnitz and Ellsworth Tompkins (*Holding Power and Size of High School*) and H. J. Dillon (*Early School Leavers in New York*). Illinois and California made extensive studies of causes for students' leaving school.

1949—With the establishment of a National Citizens Committee, there began a great increase in the use of citizens' advisory committees. This year was also marked by a great increase in the use of audio-visual aids, to continue for many years.

1954—The Supreme Court of the United States decided that segregation of races in public schools was unconstitutional.

1956[2]—Stimulated by the White House Conference report and FBI statistics, greatly increased attention began to be given to juvenile delinquency and its rapid increase.

This year marked the beginning of rapid increase in consolidated districts and the disappearance of the small school.

1957—There began an accelerated increase in the offering of college courses in high school (often called advanced placement courses), for students in senior high school with superior academic capacity.

The Greater Detroit Study began—an experiment in better programs, guidance, and community relations in slum areas, for culturally deprived students.

There was marked acceleration of the trend to replace the 8-4 plan of organization with 6-3-3 plans in large communities and 6-6 plans in smaller ones.

1958—The National Defense Education Act was passed, marking an excursion of federal influence into local schools. The Act provided funds for schools following the patterns set forth for improving instruction in mathematics, science, and foreign languages.

A trend began toward a longer school day in many schools, principally by addition of an extra, "early bird" period for volunteers.

The launching of Sputniks I and II stimulated much criticism of American high schools, especially with respect to the provisions for the bright child and programs in mathematics, science, and some foreign languages.

Team teaching, especially the Trump plan set forth by the Committee on Utilization of Staff of the National Association of Secondary Principals, began to be employed in larger numbers of schools.

Enrolments in junior high school began a great increase as the postwar babies began to reach the seventh grade.

Conant's report of his investigation of the American high school was published, supporting the comprehensive high school, bet-

---

[2] More detailed discussion will be made in later chapters of recent important events and developments.

ter provisions for abler students, and a greater place for general academic education.

1959—There began a marked acceleration of provisions for special classes and special teachers for students with physical and mental handicaps, and for students of superior ability.

Stimulated by the Sputnik furor and the consequent great increase in criticism of the schools, journals, newspapers, and book-publishing houses increased greatly the publication of materials relating to public education.

The use of teaching machines and programed textbooks increased, precipitating a national controversy as to their value and place in secondary schools.

1960—There was a marked increase in cities requiring five years of college preparation for high school teaching positions. Several states began to require five years for certification.

The shift to a seven-period day accelerated, especially in junior high schools.

There was a marked acceleration in the attention given to history and cultures of other peoples and to instruction in Russian and other languages.

There was an increase in the feeling of the general public and college professors and officials that more adequate provision should be made for the ablest and the least able students.

Greatly increased attention was given to the plight of the student who does not finish high school—the "dropout."

1961—Enrolments in senior high schools began a great increase.

Much stimulated by studies by R. J. Havighurst, of the University of Chicago, and J. B. Conant's "Slums and Suburbs," considerably more attention was being given to education programs, guidance, and close contacts with parents in areas populated by people of the lowest cultural and economic levels.

1962—Desegregation in the Deep South began to take place on a substantial scale.

Following experimentation at Pittsburgh, Chicago, and elsewhere, plans of having students attend public schools part of the day—the "shared plan"—began to spread and receive much more attention.

Stimulated by a national committee on economic education, there began a great increase in the attention given to instruction in economics in high school.

A large number of secondary schools introduced courses in Russian, and more students took third- and fourth-year courses in foreign languages.

Many secondary schools introduced courses in world cultures, world geography, and history of non-Western nations. More attention began to be given to Latin American nations in many schools.

## THE CURRENT EXTRAORDINARY CHALLENGES TO SECONDARY EDUCATION[3]

**The International Situation.** It is very fortunate that secondary education is reaching so large a percentage of our people and that its program is so much improved. The very important problems facing our nation in this troubled world have become so complicated and so numerous that the ability of the great mass of citizens to understand them and to identify and follow safe and sound leadership is very limited. At least until tens of millions of new citizens are poured out from the high schools and colleges with better and more appropriate education, it will hang in the balance whether a nation so dedicated to free enterprise and democracy can endure.

A most fundamental, far-reaching, and critical challenge to American secondary education lies in the struggle between the Free World and the totalitarian countries and rulers involving half of the world's 3 billion living people on the issues of whether or not we shall be governed by some sort of totalitarian regime such as obtains in the U.S.S.R., Czechoslovakia, Romania, Bulgaria, Poland, Yugoslavia, Albania, China, and Cuba, which substitutes communism for free enterprise and the ownership of property. The American people must be sufficiently educated and oriented to be able to identify and follow the leadership that will enable them to preserve their way of life and to protect themselves against attack without precipitating nuclear war. Even if the Russians and the Free World reach an enforceable agreement to keep the peace, there still would be more than 400 million Chinese who apparently are determined to head toward a nuclear war if and when they become able to participate in one on equal terms with the United States.

In this rivalry, which is both military and economic, and which is so deadly in its possibilities, the basic resource in the United States is education. Neil McElroy, formerly Secretary of Defense, stated at the Thirty-second Annual Conference on Educational Administration, at Harvard University, on July 14, 1960, that "in this struggle with its military rivalry, with ideological competition, with economic competition, education is the ultimate and the deciding weapon."

[3] These challenges and their educational implications are discussed at greater length in later chapters.

**The Economic Challenge.** It has been rather obvious that leaders of Communist and totalitarian countries have entertained the hope that the United States with its expenditure of some 40 billion to 60 billion dollars a year for defense and military purposes would bankrupt itself and therefore become impotent in world affairs. This is what Premier Nikita Khrushchev probably had in mind when he said, "We will bury you." While we have succeeded so far in avoiding economic disaster, we have not been far from it at times, and we are not yet out of the woods. The American dollar has been in serious danger in that we do not have a sufficient amount of gold to constitute adequate security against our indebtedness. There is a very serious problem of unemployment which has increased in recent years. These problems are but a few of the many that illustrate the need for maintaining a healthy economic system.

**Problems Created by Technological and Scientific Advances.** At a greatly accelerating pace, America has made progress in science and in technology, which enables it not only to keep up with, but in many respects to surpass, the striking Communist advances. Americans have increased their ability to produce goods to a point much beyond the needs of the people. Huge surpluses of crops and goods have piled up, and the work week has been shortened in order that there might not be a dangerous surplus of goods (as has already developed in farm products, costing hundreds of millions of dollars annually for storage).

The problems resulting from these technological and scientific advances, affecting our types of employment, our economics, our international relations, and our financial system, are serious and require very careful thinking and education of the masses. Among the problems is that resulting from our obvious capacity for producing far beyond our needs while half of the people in the world have insufficient food, very primitive shelter, little or no medical service, and limited clothing and protection from the elements; their envy constitutes a very fertile breeding ground for communism and anti-Americanism when appealed to by Communists and others who will promise them a greater share in the worldly goods and worldly comforts.

## RECENT CRITICISMS AS A CHALLENGE

In recent years, a powerful challenge has existed in the vigorous and widespread criticisms of secondary education in the United States. These criticisms have rendered very valuable service in connection with the problem of improving the selection of materials and the learning activities related to them.

**Lack of Emphasis upon Intellectual Attainments.** Some outstanding educators[4] have protested vigorously against what they believe to be neglect of the intellectual values in education. They are concerned with the lack of mastery on the part of high school graduates of factual materials of history, science, and the contents of the great books of all times, and with the lack of abilities among high school graduates in mathematics, foreign languages, and English grammar.

Many of these critics are very much opposed to such ideas as "education for all aspects of growth," including preparation to earn a living, character and morality, personal and emotional adjustments, and they particularly oppose what they call "progressive" education and "education for life adjustment."

**Lack of High Standards.** Many critics protest that the secondary school curriculum and the standards for passing courses and making grades are too easy and do not require the effort or the attainment that is possible and desirable. There are teachers and courses that do not require much effort of students and are not insistent upon a sufficiently high standard of attainment.

**Too Few Students Are Failed.** Some critics are evidently disturbed because of the lowered failure rate in secondary schools. The high school diploma does not appear to stand for that for which it once stood. Here is involved a question of fundamental philosophy. Some of the most widely read critics advocate that secondary education in the United States should be a selective process weeding out those of less than average ability and that, therefore, more students should receive failing grades.

**Inadequate Preparation for College.** For at least 200 years, there have been college professors who have complained that students are not properly prepared to do college work. One of the popular means of working to attain academic respect has been to point one's finger at "low standards." Many investigations made in recent years of the ability of high school graduates to do college work show that, even though a larger proportion of young people are being graduated from high school, they enter college with greater subject-matter mastery and achieve better grades once they are in college than did college students of previous decades. In fact, many college professors, deans, and advisers have said recently that the upgrading of the standards and materials of college freshman courses to meet the increased ability of entering freshmen

---

[4] See references at end of chapter.

In Memphis, Tennessee, as elsewhere, girls mature a little sooner than boys.

Improving reading speed—Grosse Pointe, Michigan.

A king-sized slide rule can be used effectively to bring home mathematical principles (Dwight D. Eisenhower High School, Blue Island, Ill.).

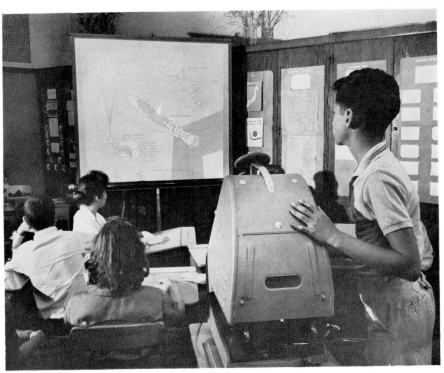

Audio-visual presentation in a Chicago junior high school.

should be continued.[5] It seems certain, however, that preparation for college can be much improved.

**American Secondary School Students Do Not Learn as Rapidly as Russian Secondary School Students.** This criticism of the American secondary schools is to some extent true. In Russia, students do not enter school until the age of seven, and then, seven years later, when secondary education begins in earnest, they are very carefully selected, as, of course, is true in practically every other country except the United States. Furthermore, the Russian secondary school student attends school six days a week and ten months a year.

There is enormous motivation for the Russian secondary school student, because he may not be permitted to enter secondary school or may even be eliminated from it once he has entered it, in which case he would be destined to belong to the lower class. Furthermore, the curriculum of the Russian secondary school is much narrower, providing very little time and space for extracurricular activities.

In Russia, young people cannot be spared in large numbers from the labor force for as long a period as in the United States. There great pressure, therefore, has been put upon teachers and students, to push students along so that they may, in certain fields, learn as much as would be learned in secondary schools in other European countries and in junior colleges in the United States.

**Inadequate Provision for the Bright and Creative Student.** A very frequent criticism, particularly on the part of intellectuals, is the protest that American secondary schools do not provide for the talents of bright and creative children. Without question, there is truth in this statement. Although very much progress has been made along this line, very few schools make adequate provision for the complete development of the talents and potentialities of gifted students. The facts that we have such a heterogeneous student body and that teachers are so heavily loaded make it almost impossible to achieve this goal.

**Inadequate Provision for the Less Able Student.** By parents particularly, and by very careful students of education, the protest has been frequently made that our secondary school curriculums do not provide adequately for the students of lesser talent, but discourage their continuance in school, fail to prepare them for life, and contribute to juvenile delinquency and to emotional illness. In American schools, it is obvious that the curriculums and methods of teaching must be better adapted to

[5] See "College Freshmen Are Better Than Ever," by President Lee A. Du Bridge, Massachusetts Institute of Technology, in the October, 1962, issue of *National Education Journal,* pp. 10–12.

students of all levels of ability. As in the case of provision for the bright student, great strides have been made in many schools, particularly in formation of classes for the less able, preparation and assignment of teachers to them, and better guidance services.

**Too Little Emphasis upon Development of Ideals, Morals, and Character.** Particularly in recent years, there has been a growing and severe criticism of the schools for their failure to give adequate attention to the development of character, morals, and ideals. This comes not only from people who are strongly religious but also from many others who see, in the great trend toward materialism and in the greatly increased incidence of juvenile delinquency in the United States and the world in general, a distinct challenge to all education and character-forming agencies including the home, the church, and the school.

**Inadequate Preparation for Earning a Living.** The fact that there have been on the labor market for several years an increasing number of unemployed young people between the ages of sixteen and twenty-four (more than 2 million in 1963) has given impetus to the criticism that the schools do not provide adequate preparation for earning a living. The great amount of juvenile delinquency among the dropouts and graduates who do not go on to college is attributed to inability to earn enough to satisfy the most powerful desires. There is criticism of the character of the courses in vocational education, on the basis of their being somewhat out of date and on the basis of the lack of provision for vocational training for many new types of occupations. Many economists, however, believe that the real problem is a shortage of jobs and that older, experienced heads of families are given preference in employment. Nevertheless, there has begun an increasing amount of vocational retraining of unemployed workers.

**Inadequate Preparation for Understanding People and Cultures of Other Nations.** The schools have been criticized for failing to provide better for teaching about peoples of other countries. This criticism has arisen and increased in scope and vigor as a result of the recognition of the fact that, for at least several decades, Communist and democratic groups will probably carry on a struggle for the good will and cooperation of nations and peoples throughout the world.

**Failure To Improve Mastery of the Fundamentals.** A century-old criticism of the schools is the claim that there is insufficient attention to, and mastery of, the fundamentals—the "three R's." It seems to serve the purpose of giving status to the critic if he claims that the schools are not what they used to be, particularly with reference to the fundamentals. Nevertheless, it is quite true that the secondary schools have never done all that they could in improving the mastery of fundamentals.

**Inadequate Education for Mental and Physical Health and Physical Vigor.** Among the critics on this point was the previous President of the United States, who was alarmed by the fact that, in tests of physical vigor and fitness, a much larger percentage of young people of other countries met the minimum standards of the test than was the case with our young people of comparable age. The criticism goes further than this. In spite of the increased availability of physical and medical inspections and the reporting of results to students and parents, there has been an increase in the number of students and young people not many years out of high school who have developed heart defects and other serious ailments.

Perhaps the most important area is that of mental health. The number of young people who have developed mental illness, serious emotional disturbance, or other evidences of a lack of mental health has greatly increased in recent years. Whatever the causes may be, there is definite challenge to the schools here, since so few, though an increasing number, are doing much about this.

**Excessive Verbalism.** Even going back to Comenius, Pestalozzi, and Rousseau in the seventeenth and eighteenth centuries and to other early critics of education, there have been criticisms of the emphasis upon the learning of phrases and sentences to be repeated orally upon examination without complete understanding of their meanings and without ability to make use of them in application to problems of life. Current critics insist that failure to retain a great deal of what is learned and learning of less than would be desired may be attributed to the failure of teachers to provide learning activities which ensure understanding and retention.

**Dull and Uninteresting Nature of Secondary Education.** More recently, critics have been articulate with reference to the belief that the materials of instruction and, indeed, the methods of instruction could be definitely improved in the direction of causing youngsters to be more interested in applying themselves to learning.

Studies of the reasons why boys and girls have withdrawn from high school before graduation and the reasons for student vandalism in the schools have revealed that a large minority of American youth is very much bored with materials and the methods of instruction, is not greatly challenged, and does not have much faith in the utility for the student himself of what is taught. This condition has become worse as the percentage of young people atending high school has increased. Formerly, those who disliked the schools or lost faith in them dropped out and went to work. This possibility no longer is available to a great many of them, and they stay in large numbers to lower the morale and interest of others.

PROPERTY OF
OKLAHOMA BAPTIST UNIVERSITY
LIBRARY

**Inadequate Emphasis upon Education for Leisure and Home Living.**
Many people are appalled at the greatly increased amount of leisure in
sight for the next few years, as well as disturbed by the degree to which
leisure time today is employed in ways not conducive to the physical,
mental, and moral health of the individual or the benefit of the nation.
Critics are prone to express dissatisfaction with the excessive relative
emphasis in schools upon preparation for college, vocational education,
and decorative learning, to the neglect of cultivating good interests and
habits for expenditures of leisure time.

Also, there are critics who insist that problems of marriage and parent-
hood, as well as those of consumer buying, have been increased and
complicated without appropriate extension of secondary school programs
in the field of family living. These critics are prone to point out the
increase in divorce, the increase in the mishandling of youngsters in the
home, and the increased tendency for both parents to be working and
spending less time with their children.

## QUESTIONS, PROBLEMS, AND TOPICS FOR FURTHER STUDY

1. Criticize the curriculum for adolescents in primitive times.
2. Compare and contrast secondary education in early Greece, later Greece,
   and Rome.
3. Be able to explain to the class why the curriculum in the Later grammar
   schools and the academies constituted inadequate preparation for life.
4. What new ideas and advantages did the early high schools have that the
   academy and the Latin grammar school did not have?
5. How do you account for the fact that only a few new subjects were introduced in high schools generally until toward the end of the nineteenth
   century or the beginning of the twentieth?
6. What do you think American secondary school teachers can do to combat
   the spread of totalitarianism and communism? Be prepared to give a seven-
   or eight-minute talk on this subject in class.
7. State the principal criticisms of the secondary school curriculum, and give
   your opinions of the validity of these criticisms.
8. With recent criticisms in mind, what changes do you think should be
   made in secondary education?

## SUPPLEMENTARY MATERIALS

### Selected Readings

ADLER, IRVING. *What We Want of Our Schools.* New York: John Day Co., Inc.,
    1957. Chapter 7, "Progressive Education: Boon or Bane?"; Chapter 8,
    "The Critics of Progressive Education."
BECK, ROBERT H., MRS. ROLLIN BROWN, HAROLD L. CLAPP, and BENJAMIN C.
    WILLIS. "The Meaning of Quality in Education—a Symposium," *North
    Central Association of Secondary Schools Quarterly,* Summer, 1961.
BENJAMIN, HAROLD. *The Sabre Tooth Curriculum.* New York: McGraw-Hill
    Book Co., Inc., 1939.

BEREDAY, GEORGE Z. F. "Selective Education Versus Education for All," *Teachers College Record,* LVIII (January, 1957), 198–206.

BURKETT, L. A., D. C. MANLOVE, B. S. MILLER, and J. E. RUSSELL. "Implications of the Conant Report for Quality Education in the Comprehensive Secondary School," *Bulletin of the N.A.S.S.P.,*[6] XLIV (April, 1960), 219–25.

CREMIN, LAWRENCE A. "The Revolution in American Secondary Education, 1893–1918," *Teachers College Record,* LVI (March, 1955), 295–308.

CREMIN, LAWRENCE A. "What Happened to Progressive Education?" *The Education Digest,* XXV (January, 1960), 48.

"Good Reasons for Doing Nothing," *The Education Digest,* XXVI (April 1961), 32–35.

HAND, HAROLD C. "Myths Which Hoodwink the Public," *The Education Forum,* XXIII (November, 1958), 19–38.

HARRIS, RAYMOND P. *American Education.* New York: Random House, Inc., 1962. Chapter 11, "The Legend of Anti-intellectualism"; Chapter 12, "The Grand Illusion of Progressive Education"; Chapter 13, "Those Maligned Education Courses."

"Is European Education Better Than Ours?" *Saturday Evening Post,* CCXXIII (December 24–31, 1960), 60–76.

LAMBERT, SAM M. "Investing in Quality Education," *Phi Delta Kappan,* XLIII (December, 1961), 110–18.

LEE, GORDON C. *Education in Modern America.* New York: Holt, Rinehart & Winston, Inc., 1957. Part II: Chapter 5, "Traditionalist Approaches to Education"; Chapter 6, "The Experimentalist Approach to Education."

LUND, KENNETH W. "It's Time for a Breakthrough," *The Education Digest,* XXV (December, 1959), 18–20.

ORTON, DON A. "Issues Raised by Changes in Secondary Education," *The School Review,* LXIX (Spring, 1961), 1–11.

"Public Schools in the Decade Ahead," *The Education Digest,* XXVI (May, 1961), 1–5.

SNOW, ROBERT H. "The Forces of Miseducation—How Can We Combat Them?" *The Education Digest,* XXV (December, 1959), 9–13.

THAYER, V. T. *The Role of the School in American Society.* New York: Dodd, Mead & Co., Inc., 1960. Chapter 16, "Public Education Under Fire."

"The Proposals of Dr. Conant," *The Education Digest,* XXVI (April, 1961), 15–19.

TRACY, J. P. "Issues in Catholic Secondary Education," *Catholic School Journal,* LX (September, 1960), 462.

VAN TIL, WILLIAM. "Is Progressive Education Obsolete?" *The Education Digest,* XXVII (May, 1962), 4–7.

## AUDIO-VISUAL AIDS

### Film

*How Good Are Our Schools? Dr. Conant Reports.* National Education Association, Public Relations. Washington, D.C. 28 minutes, 16 mm., black and white or color, sound.

---

[6] These initials will be used throughout this volume to designate the National Association of Secondary School Principals.

# 2

# Secondary Education in a Democratic Society

## EDUCATION AS AN INSTRUMENT OF SOCIETY

**Education for the Nation's Welfare.** There have always been in the United States, and in increasing proportions in recent years, those who have felt that the content and procedures of education should be so selected and organized as to prepare young people for effective participation in the more important areas of life.

While there have been differences of opinion as to what are the more important areas of life for which the public schools should prepare future adults, practically all of the serious students of education have felt that in American democratic society the major function of education should be to prepare young people to perform as intelligent and dedicated citizens. Even among those splinter groups who held that education is primarily for some such purpose as preparation to earn a living, preparation for college, or preparation to participate in polite society, the objective of preparation for intelligent citizenship has ranked high.

**Education and the Type of Society.** It has been characteristic of every nation that the purposes, content, and procedures of its education have been designed to contribute to the advancement of the particular type and philosophy of the prevailing society, government, and economic system. In Hitler's Germany, Mussolini's Italy, Shinto Japan, and today's Communist and totalitarian Russia, China, and satellite states, the purposes, program, and content of education were and are to indoctrinate future adults with the credo of the society and economic system existing

24

in those countries, and to provide strong sinews for the advancement of the people along the established line of organization. In Russia, for instance, great stress has been placed upon the preparation of scientists, particularly in the fields that would contribute to Soviet military strength.

**Education for Intelligent Citizenship.** The United States, being a republican form of government and having democracy as its ideal, must develop an educational system that prepares not only for intelligent citizenship but also for leadership. Unlike the situation in a totalitarian regime in which the basic thinking about social, economic, and political affairs is done by a selected minority, in a democracy such as ours the entire population must be given an education in economic and political affairs, complicated as the problems in these areas have become.

From the beginning there have been outstanding leaders who have recognized the importance of this basic principle. For example, John Adams, the second president of the United States, urged the Congress to adopt a farsighted and sensible social and educational policy. He said, "Among the first, perhaps the very first instrument for the improvement of the condition of men is knowledge, and to the acquisition of much of the knowledge adapted to the warmth, the comfort, and enjoyments of human life, public institutions and similar areas of learning are essential."

There were many including Gouverneur Morris and Alexander Hamilton who did not believe that the common people could possibly participate in government effectively and who were either uninterested in or opposed to the extension of public education, believing that the masses should leave matters of state to "their betters." But other outstanding leaders, with more democratic and hopeful points of view, insisted upon extension of education. For example, Thomas Jefferson said, "I hope that education of the common people will be attended to; convinced that on their good sense we may rely with the most security for the preservation of a new sense of liberty."

It was principally because of his belief in the importance and necessity of education of the public for the purpose of democracy that he established in Virginia a state system of education, including a university, for the motto of which Jefferson chose "Ye shall know the truth, and the truth shall make you free."

Education as an instrument does not consist only of materials and methods for preparing students as citizens. The welfare of American society depends also very much upon the preparation of people for effective participation in other types of activities.

**Education for Cultural and Economic Health.** The welfare of American society depends greatly upon the effectiveness of its economic system and activity. It depends upon the degree to which we are able to produce all of the desirable food needed by our people and indeed enough surplus so that we can trade for other goods not produced in sufficient quantity in our nation.

The welfare of the nation depends upon our ability to provide effectively and economically goods and services in many other areas including shelter, furniture, means of transportation, highways, drugs, clothing, and household appliances for heating, lighting, cooking, and cleaning.

Furthermore, our national welfare depends upon preparation, through education, of competent individuals to perform many important services including, among the professions, medicine, engineering, teaching, law, dentistry, journalism, and science, and, among the non-professions, skilled work of a large variety of types involved in manufacture. While a large part of the preparation of individuals for service in these areas is the responsibility of institutions of higher education, the secondary school plays a very prominent part, for example, in the preparation of young people for study in the professional school of the university.

The welfare of the nation also depends greatly upon the education of people in various aspects of culture and arts in living—music, sculpture, painting, creative writing, and other, similar fields of activity.

**National Needs vs. Individual Needs.** There is considerable confusion in the thinking of some people including many teachers and administrators and perhaps a majority of parents. They seem to feel, at least at times, that school exists almost entirely for the benefit of the students attending. Their thinking about what should be taught and other educational problems seems to depend almost entirely, if not completely, upon the fundamental premise that these things must be decided on the basis of what will contribute to the personal, individual ability of those receiving education.

The thoughtful students and leaders in American education recognize that this is a shortsighted and unfortunate basic idea.

In the first place, except on the basis that the schools exist primarily for the benefit of society and people in general, one could not justify taxation of all of the people for the education of some, taxation for education on the basis of wealth or income instead of on the basis of the number of children, or taxation of individuals who send their children to non-public schools or of those whose children are no longer in the schools. Furthermore, if the aims, subject matter, and procedures of education were chosen solely on the basis of the personal welfare of the individuals educated, the very important interest of the nation—our democratic way of life—would suffer.

Because the children are present in the classroom and the parents in the community, it is only natural that teachers and administrators may tend to neglect the social purposes of the schools and to emphasize the benefits accruing to the individuals who are being educated. It is therefore incumbent upon the education profession—teachers and administrators—to see that the stake of American society in its public schools is protected.

It must develop talented leaders in every field of activity. We shall need many people prepared to guide the evolution of an expanding economy: able, thoughtful, dedicated educators, writers, politicians and diplomats, clergymen, businessmen, labor leaders and legislators. All will be essential, and all will be capable to the extent of the quality of the educational system that will have produced them.

There is actually little conflict between the needs of society and the needs of the individual. At the outset one will readily see that what benefits one benefits the other. But it is an important and truthful corollary that the failure to benefit one also brings about a failure to benefit the other. Over and above what is necessary to enable the student in school to earn a good living, to enjoy life, to participate well in home and family activities, to enjoy good physical and mental health, there is the necessity for education of each individual along lines that will contribute to the welfare and the progress of the nation and its people. Likewise, educating the child for the benefit of society alone, a practice that conforms with the theories of totalitarians who believe that the individual exists for the state rather than vice versa, does not conform with the thinking of American people.

**American Faith in Education.** It is an inspiring historical fact that from the beginning, soon after the landing of the Pilgrims, our people have had a strong belief in the value of, and the necessity for, education. In Massachusetts and other New England colonies, laws were passed compelling the establishment of schools and the support thereof.

Our people have long believed that schools are necessary for preservation and development of our way of life. As a consequence of this belief there is in every state a legal requirement of school attendance.

Because of this faith in the public schools, reinforced by their operation and their products for more than 300 years, the American public not only has supported but has insisted upon maintaining its public school system, which now enrols more than 90 per cent of all the young people between the ages of five and eighteen, carrying 95 per cent through elementary school and 70 per cent through high school, with nearly half the graduates going on for some college work and one in four graduating from a college or university. The percentage of youths enrolled in American secondary schools is several times the percentage enrolled in secondary education in any other country.

The faith of the people in the public schools has also been eloquently evidenced by the amount of money they have been willing to spend upon them. In the United States, in 1962, the total expenditure for schools at all levels exceeded 20 billion dollars, or about 160 dollars for every adult and nearly 400 dollars for every family—and this in spite of the vigorous criticisms of the schools, regardless of the extent to which they could be satisfied.

**The Supplementary Character of the School.** Young people do not get all of their education from the school; it is but one sector in their complex and varied educational environment. Most valuable education is received in the homes, where the young people acquire a language, a great many of the fundamental motor and social habits and skills, interests and attitudes, and much important information about many areas of life. Much of their education also comes from such sources as the church, the press, the radio, the movies, the television, friends, and other people with whom they are associated.

The program of the school, therefore, must be planned in the light of what contribution is made toward education by other agencies. It should be so planned as not to duplicate to a wasteful extent. It must be planned to reinforce and to be in harmony with the desirable education received from other sources in the environment. In some instances, it must counteract, and must assist in solving problems created by, unfortunate educational influences from the other sources.

The supplementary character of secondary schools necessitates changes in program appropriate to changes in the rest of the environment of young people, sometimes taking over areas in which the home or other agencies are no longer functioning well, providing education for dealing with problems created by new developments in the environment, and diminishing its efforts where outside agencies function more effectively than formerly.

It follows naturally and inevitably that educators must be informed and must maintain contact with society and the child's environment in general and must be able to adapt the educational program as required by changes in the society in which he lives and will live. It is necessary not only to understand the conditions that exist in life today but to be able to discern trends, to picture life as it will be lived by today's boys and girls ten, twenty, or more years from now, and to develop definite educational programs adapted so as to prepare them for the future.

## THE IMPACT OF SOCIAL CONDITIONS, TRENDS, AND PROBLEMS UPON SECONDARY EDUCATION

**The Problem of International Security.** A distinct challenge to American education lies in the situation that has developed since 1915 in our relationships with governments of other countries. Prior to World War

II, the United States was more or less isolated from other nations, protected on the east and west by oceans and on the north and south by the presence of friendly and relatively weak countries. Beginning with the Spanish-American War, at the close of the nineteenth century, the relationships of the people and government of the United States to those of other countries began to shift and change. The change was accelerated by World War I. It was not, however, until World War II that the situation became critical. Prior to the conclusion of that war, the leading powers and influences in international relations were France, Germany, and England, with Russia, the United States, Italy, Spain, China, Austria, and other nations occupying important positions. At the end of World War II, there were left only two major powers, the U.S.S.R. and the U.S.A., all others having become distinctly secondary. These two powers were relatively uninitiated and inexperienced in international relations; furthermore, the tension was increased by the fact that the governmental and economic systems of these two powers were diametrically opposed and of a nature that encouraged the belief that neither could exist safely as long as the other existed.

Intense opposition and rivalry had developed between the two nations, an animosity which made very difficult any type of international relations, since any American statesman advocating any type of concession would be immediately labeled by opposing politicians as pro-Russian, pro-Communist, or a "no-win" advocate.

**Technological and Business Changes.** The development of technological processes and business structures based upon them has gone on at a rapidly accelerated rate, not only in connection with atomic energy but in many other fields, particularly in the field of machinery for computation and production. This development not only increased old problems but created new ones in the problems of distribution of increased income to capital and to workers. It has created unemployment and, indeed, in some areas has created great surpluses involving problems of exports and imports, tariffs, etc.

**Urbanization.** In 1900, only 30 million, or approximately 35 per cent, of the people in the United States lived in the cities. By 1940, 75 million, or approximately 60 per cent, lived in cities and, in 1960, 125 million, or 70 per cent, were city dwellers. There is no reason to believe that this trend will not continue, with eventually all but a very small percentage of the people living in urban or suburban areas. This concentration of people has created many social problems of increasing importance, the solution of which calls for immediate appropriate education.

Among the more important of these are the problem of encouraging wholesome leisure pursuits, particularly those involving outdoor activities; the health problem, which is aggravated by the ease of spreading contagious diseases; and the necessity for adequate water-supply and sewage systems. Without any question, crime and immorality flourish better in cities, and political machines more greatly influence elections and government. The problem of transportation becomes critical. One of the problems that is most significant to education is the fact that there have been developing in recent years slum areas in which underprivileged people live and in which children are brought up in the midst of unfortunate environmental influences, and their attitudes toward education and their behavior in school are very unwholesome.[1]

**Problems Resulting from the Population Explosion.** The very great increase in population in recent decades—from approximately 125 million in 1940 to about 180 million in 1962, and certain to increase to 200 million by 1970—has created a considerable number of problems that are a challenge to education and that must be solved by educated people. Professor Philip M. Hauser, of the University of Chicago, lists the following as the important ones:

1. Lowered quality of the schools
2. Strained job market and increased unemployment of young people
3. Increased racial tension, particularly in the larger cities
4. Increased crime
5. The creation of new slums
6. Very serious water problems
7. Very serious transportation problems[2]

**Problems of Physical and Mental Health.** As a result of changes in conditions in life and in ways of living, there has been a very noticeable increase in the incidence of certain types of illness, particularly those relating to the heart and to the nervous system. In addition, mental illness and emotional disturbance are becoming much more common in people of all ages, although this increase may be in part only an apparent one, resulting from more accurate diagnosis made possible by increases in psychiatric knowledge and in the number of physicians whose specialty is psychological illness.

Among other things, these developments seem to indicate the necessity for conducting education under less stressful conditions and for teaching young people about the importance of keeping stress under control in later life. The situation also seems to call for increased medical, psychological, and psychiatric service to be made available for students and teachers.

[1] See James B. Conant, *Slums and Suburbs.* McGraw-Hill Book Co., Inc., 1960.
[2] Philip M. Hauser, "America's Population Increase," *Look,* Vol. 25, No. 24 (November 21, 1961), pp. 30–31; and No. 25 (December 5, 1961), pp. 21–27.

**Consumer Problems.** With the meteoric development of advertising and with the increasing tendency to purchase rather than to produce food, clothing, and other necessities of life, there is a growing necessity for education of young people relative to the selection and purchase of various types of goods and services. For example, such education might provide guidance in choosing safe, effective drug products and nutritious foods.

**Labor Problems.** Accelerated very much during the great depression of the 1930's, there have developed very powerful labor organizations with greatly increased power over the lives of a large segment of the population in the United States. These organizations control and limit entrance to, and training in, many occupations. To a limited but important extent, the same situation has developed with respect to entrance to the medical and legal professions, especially the former.

Furthermore, labor organizations in a considerable number of industries and occupations include such a large percentage of the workers that labor leaders may call strikes that have very crippling effects upon the national economy. In addition, some of the more powerful labor organizations' officers are not selected or held responsible in a democratic manner, and various abuses have developed, including those related to hundreds of millions dollars collected from members of unions. Unions have become such a powerful factor in American life that they are approaching the government in the extent of their influence.

**Home-Living Problems.** There have developed in recent decades various challenging changes in the American home, the basic unit of our society. The American home has materially disintegrated as a work unit group, as a social unit group, and as a religious unit group. Contributing to this disintegration, along with the decreasing self-sufficiency of the home in the production of food, clothing, and other goods, has been the greatly increased incidence of homes from which both parents are absent to be at work a great deal of the time. Among other problems created by this development are lack of contact of the parents with children, the tendency for young people to become involved in unsocial if not immoral leisure activities, and the lack of opportunity for parents to pass the cultural heritage on to their children.

Among other unfortunate results of this trend are the very greatly decreased opportunity and responsibility of boys and girls for participation along with their parents in work experience in the home. Great educational benefits that result from such participation include the development of a sense of responsibility and the acquisition of knowledge, skills, and habits related to different types of work activities.

**Leisure Problems.** Recent decades have almost seen the disappearance of non-sedentary leisure pursuits, especially outdoor play and group activities centering around the home and the church. Instead, young people have come to spend more and more of their time in such activities as viewing television programs and cruising in automobiles. The current types of leisure activities, especially movies and TV programs, are planned with little or no concern for educational values. This development constitutes a challenge and responsibility for the schools in connection with education and guidance that will lead to fortunate selection of programs and activities as well as the development of morals and standards which will prevail against the temptations of unwholesome leisure activities.

**Problems of Foreign Trade.** In the past, the United States occupied a favored position with respect to the export not only of food and other raw materials but also of the finished products of its factories. In recent years, other countries have increased their capacity to produce food and to become independent of imports, and, in many parts of the world, industrialization has occurred to such an extent as to reduce very materially needs for imports. The development of the European Common Market and the loss of our trade with China and Russia and their satellite countries have cut sharply into our exports.

There are serious problems of tariff rates, of shifting in the volume of our products at least in some areas, and of developing friendly commercial relations with large nations with which they do not now exist. Among other things, the position of the American dollar has in recent years been threatened, as had not been the case for a very long time.

These developments call for increased attention in the schools to various related aspects of study, particularly in the field of economics.

**Changes in Mass Communications.** In recent years, American people have spent a much greater amount of their time in listening to radio and viewing television, without increasing the amount of time spent in reading. Naturally, what they think and how they feel about many important matters depend somewhat upon the nature of these programs. Practically all the radio and television programs are commercially sponsored and make very skilful appeals to the pocketbook of the American consumer. Likewise, practically all the magazines and newspapers that are read are supported largely by advertising and contain skilful sales appeals for which highly developed talents in art and composition are employed.

Furthermore, these mass communications are in very large part owned and operated by individuals and corporations constituting a small segment of the population whose economic and political interests are relatively homogeneous.

These developments present a real challenge for educating the consumer to develop habits and skills of careful and critical reading and propaganda analysis.

**Increasing Acceleration of Change.** It has been noted by several keen observers of the American scene that the world, particularly America, changed more between the years 1945 and 1960 than it did in the first 45 years of this century, that it changed more in the first 60 years of this century than it did in the preceding 500-year period, and that in the last 500 years it has changed in more important ways than it did in the preceding time since the birth of Christ. At any rate, it is quite clear that tremendously important, challenging, shocking, and critical changes have taken place that call for a large variety of important adjustments in American life, and probably most important of all are adjustments in educational programs which will prepare future citizens to adapt appropriately and safely to these changes and to control them in the future for the common good.

# THE UNIQUE CHARACTER OF SECONDARY EDUCATION IN AMERICAN SOCIETY

Far more than most Americans and even many teachers realize, secondary schools in the United States are quite different in many important respects from those in any other country, although, since the close of World War II, the secondary schools of most countries have become somewhat more like those in the United States. In the majority of those countries, however, the gap has been lessened only a bit, and the differences are still very great and important. In large part, our schools reflect the nature and fundamental philosophy of American society.

**Fundamental Differences.** The principal differences are the following:

1. Secondary schools in the United States are planned for all the boys and girls who complete elementary school, while in other countries they are admitted usually only after written examinations.

2. The program of the American secondary school is very comprehensive, including in the same school vocational and academic subjects as well as new subjects not offered in foreign schools at all.

3. A great many parents do not believe as strongly in hard study for a long school week and a long school year as do parents in European countries.

4. The American secondary school is controlled almost entirely by elected officials in the local community.

5. The American secondary school is a democratic social institution, and employed in connection with it are various types of democratic

rather than authoritarian procedures, affecting lay people, students, teachers, and administrators.

6. The objectives of the American secondary schools are much broader, including preparation for various areas of life, and are less concentrated upon preparation for college. Also, they are concerned with developing all aspects of human growth and not merely the intellectual asset.

7. The teaching and administrative staffs in American secondary schools are quite differently prepared, have less professional preparation, and are composed about equally of men and women, as contrasted with the great majority of men in secondary schools in other countries.

8. School housing and equipment for secondary education in the United States are much more modern, are better adapted to the program of instruction, and include not only many new features of room and building construction but also special rooms and equipment rarely found in secondary schools elsewhere.

In the rest of this chapter these differences will be discussed in some detail, and, through the book, differences between American secondary education and secondary education in other countries will be pointed out.

**Universal Attendance.** In practically all other countries, students are admitted to secondary school only after having passed a rather thorough written examination at about the age of eleven or twelve. In Great Britain it is called the "eleven-plus" examination.[3] Secondary education in other countries is selective and intended only for a minority of the young people. Although boys and girls who fail this examination may later be admitted to secondary schools, this happens only in rare cases where the superior ability of the individual has become very obvious.

Also, in other countries, by reason of the examinations and other factors, secondary education is somewhat selective. Students in secondary schools come very largely from the upper classes, and the very great majority are males. Only in the United States, as yet, has the economy developed to the point where all young people can be spared from the labor force until the age of seventeen or eighteen.

In all other countries, there still exists, regardless of what claims may be made, a class society which is perpetuated by the fact that, while only the educated may become rulers, the selective secondary school system tends to favor the children of the upper classes. This has been particularly true of Latin American, Mediterranean, and Asiatic countries, although even in Great Britain it has only been in the last twenty years that any substantial progress has been made toward democratization of the opportunity for secondary education.

[3] Winston Churchill failed the eleven-plus examinations twice.

In the United States, approximately 90 per cent of young people of ages fourteen through seventeen and 95 per cent of those twelve or thirteen years of age are enrolled in schools. Two-thirds of American youths graduate from high school, as compared to 12 per cent in England, 17 per cent in Sweden, 31 per cent in France, 10 per cent in West Germany, and 11 per cent in Russia.

This trend toward completion of high school by all young people has gone on at various paces in different sections of the United States, being of course much slower in the southern states, where the percentage of Negroes has been much greater and where the economic level of both races is much lower than in other sections of the United States. It has also gone on much more slowly in areas in which a considerable portion of the population were immigrants, particularly from the southern-European and Latin American countries.

When American secondary schools are compared with those of Russia, England, France, and Germany, as they are by those who are unfriendly to American public schools or ignorant of the nature of European secondary schools, it is often charged that graduates of secondary schools in European countries are further advanced in academic subjects by from one to two years. It should be remembered that students graduate from European secondary schools at least a year older and are definitely a very select group. The only practical comparison that could be made would be to compare the achievements of the graduates of European secondary schools with those who have finished at least one year of academic study in the better colleges and universities in the United States, or with the graduates of junior colleges.

**The Comprehensive Nature of American Secondary Schools.** In view of the facts that American secondary schools are for all American youth and that in the United States we have been committed to democratic thinking, which opposes the division of people, especially in the schools, into religious, social, economic, or other types of groups, it is perfectly natural that a very comprehensive program would be developed. For example, in the United States the number of subjects offered in the secondary schools is much greater than that in secondary schools in other countries and includes vocational subjects and modern subjects such as speech, journalism, economics, space science, and electronics.

Likewise, in our schools there are programs of extracurricular activities— clubs, sports, musical organizations, etc.—in which students spend much time. Programs of guidance are very commonly found in American secondary schools and are more advanced than in secondary schools in other countries.

**Local Control and Support of American Secondary Schools.** In the American colonies the Latin grammar school was not truly a public institution; it was supported largely by tuitions, special taxes, and gifts, though it was controlled by committees of the town government, or the town board, or of a religious organization.

The academy was controlled and supported by local or regional religious groups and by tuition. In neither instance was the control on a statewide or a national basis as is education in practically all foreign countries.

With the development of the public elementary school and later the public secondary school, there came to be what is known as the "district" form of organization. The district was originally and still is to a very large extent a geographical unit—a community establishing, supporting, and controlling a system of local elementary and secondary schools. The federal government exercises very little control and contributes less than 5 per cent of the support of secondary schools. Opposition to federal control of education is traditional and strong, although, since 1917, the Smith-Hughes Act, the George-Deen Act, the George-Barden Act, and other bills have been passed for the support and partial control of vocational education. In 1958, the National Defense Education Act was passed for the support, and to some extent for the control, of instruction in science, mathematics, and foreign languages, and of guidance.

In the very great majority of other countries, while the support is largely local through local taxes and substantially through tuition, the control is to a very great extent national or provincial. The central office of education and the provincial officers of education in the provinces or subdivisions of the country exercise much control. This includes certification and the assignment of teachers, curriculum and the method of instruction to be followed, and the buildings and equipment to be employed. In each of these countries, a rather elaborate and thorough system of inspection is employed as insurance that the principles and regulations of the ministry of education will be followed.

**Degree of Democracy.** It is characteristic of American education that not only is the control vested in, and exercised by, local officials such as the boards of education and their appointees including superintendents, supervisors, and principals, but there are constant contacts between the local public and the schools. The public is frequently consulted by the school authorities with respect to plans for housing, curriculum change, and many other matters.

Furthermore, unlike situations in most other countries, parents and others of the community are invited and are welcome to visit and to inspect the schools and the teaching therein. In many schools, special days or evenings are provided, but parents are welcome at any time. In other countries there is nothing really like the Parent-Teachers' Association that exists in the United States.

Furthermore, individuals in the community are very often called upon to render special service such as assisting in sponsoring social activities, acting as teacher aides, supervising the playground and traffic, etc. In most communities there is or has been a citizens' advisory committee to study various problems of the schools in the community and to make recommendations to the board of education.

Also unlike situations in other countries, in secondary schools in the United States it is a very prevalent practice for teachers not only to permit but also to invite students in their classes to participate in the planning of the organization and details of learning activities for themselves individually and for the class as a whole.

In American secondary schools, students also play a part in management of extracurricular activities and in government for the school. Unlike the situation in other countries, students in American secondary schools hold office and, with the advice of sponsors, administer various types of clubs and other activities. Students in American schools also participate in what has come to be called "student government." Their responsibilities here are largely legislative and managerial, but this type of thing does not exist in secondary schools elsewhere.

Growing out of the past several decades has been the increased amount of teacher participation in the organization and management of secondary education. Committees of teachers are given opportunities to recommend and, indeed, in many communities, to select textbooks to be used in their classes. Increasingly over the years, teachers have been given the collective responsibility for planning the details of the courses of study in their schools, and individual teachers have been given much leeway in planning learning activities in their own classes.

In American schools, teachers also serve on various types of advisory and recommending committees having to do with administration of the schools, particularly in relation to such matters as teachers' salaries, tenure, load, and other matters of working conditions.

**Breadth of Objectives.** In American secondary schools, much less emphasis is placed upon written examinations that are administered by authorities from outside the schools. In other countries generally, and particularly in European countries, not only is admission to secondary schools conditioned on the passing of rather rigorous examinations at about the age of eleven or twelve, but graduation from the secondary school may be achieved only by the passing of examinations prepared by the ministry of education.

These conditions in themselves lead to emphasis upon the more or less temporary acquisition of large amounts of factual material. Taken together with other influences, the examination system results in a considerable emphasis upon intellectual achievements, particularly of the kind that are related to prescribed and favored subject matter.

In the United States, on the other hand, much more emphasis is placed upon other types of educational growth as being necessary for national, state, and local welfare, as well as for the happiness and well-being of the individual. Much more stress is placed, for example, upon development of democratic and humane ideals and attitudes and social and physical habits as well as intellectual skills, problem solving, desirable personality traits, and social adjustment.

It should be said that, particularly since World War II, progress is being made in most other countries, except those under totalitarian governments, in the direction of broadening objectives. For example, the new national aims for education in Norway include (1) the fullest possible development of the abilities and energies of each individual student, (2) the development of the personality of the student as an individual, (3) the development of the individual as a free human being. In England, the statement is made that intelligence needs to be directed by such qualities of character as goodness, kindness, and courage.

In 1962, an influential committee of business leaders in France recommended that French schools develop a more modern and flexible program with greater stress on practical applications of knowledge to today's realities. Similar action has taken place in recent years in several other European countries.

The actual practice of these aims in the schools of those countries is moving only slowly toward achievement. Indeed, in the United States, secondary education is still on the road toward practices that will give equal emphasis to the non-intellectual aims.

**Foreign Educators Perplexed.** Visitors from other countries often find it difficult to believe that the pattern and programs of our secondary schools are not under some sort of national formulation and direction. They are frequently somewhat incredulous when they are told about the great similarity of schools among sections of the United States with respect to educational programs, especially between districts in sections that have the economic ability to support education and districts of the same size in sections that do not, and that this similarity results from the great amount of communication between the teachers and school administrators in different school systems, through state and national associations in the subject fields, in administration, and of members of school boards.

Foreign visitors also frequently remark with amazement and admiration about the superior equipment in American secondary schools. This not only includes the more expensive, advanced types of laboratory and shop equipment, for example, in the field of electronics, but also such things as audio-visual projectors, provision for both closed- and open-circuit reception of TV, and rather expensive and modern equipment for teaching in business education.

## QUESTIONS, PROBLEMS, AND TOPICS FOR FURTHER STUDY

1. Write out notes for a presentation in class of the principal characteristics and fundamental principles of our American society at the present time.
2. In planning education in terms of the interest of the individual student and in terms of the interest of the nation, which is the more important, and how can conflicts be reconciled?
3. Do you think that schools emphasize relatively more than is wise in the interests of the individual or the interests of society? Give reasons for your position.
4. Be able to give a five-minute talk in class, on the subject "The Faith of the American People in the Public Schools."
5. Why do such a great majority of the American people believe in having a large majority of young people attend public rather than non-public schools?
6. Make a list of statements of the weaknesses and dangers in the American economy, and make suggestions as to what you think schools can do about these.
7. What problems does urbanization create, and what can the schools do with respect to those problems?
8. Discuss the population explosion and the problems it creates for us, and be able to give one suggestion for secondary education for each of those problems.
9. Discuss the challenge to secondary education found in recent and current changes in home living.
10. Discuss the challenge to secondary education found in recent and current changes in leisure.
11. Discuss the challenge to secondary education found in recent and current changes in mass communications.
12. Discuss the supplementary character of the school.
13. Do you believe that it is wise to have as much local control of our schools as exists in the United States?
14. What is meant by the "cooperative" approach to solution of school problems?
15. Explain in what ways objectives of the American secondary schools are broader than those of schools in other countries and why.

## SUPPLEMENTARY MATERIALS

### SELECTED READINGS

ANDERSON, VERNON E., and WILLIAM T. GRUHN. *Principles and Practices of Secondary Education* (2d ed.). New York: The Ronald Press Co., 1962.

Chapter 2, "History of the American Secondary School"; Chapter 3, "The Product of American Culture."

CONANT, JAMES BRYANT. *The Child, the Parent, and the State*. Cambridge, Mass.: Harvard University Press, 1959. Chapter 1, "The Child, the Parent, and the State."

COX, PHILIP W. L., and BLAINE E. MERCER. *Education in Democracy: The Social Foundations of Education*. New York: McGraw-Hill Book Co., Inc., 1961. Chapter 1, "The Dynamic Character of American Society"; Chapter 17, "Some Educational Responses to Social Change."

DOUGLASS, HARL R. *Secondary Education*. New York: The Ronald Press Co., 1952. Chapter 3, "Education and Society."

EDUCATIONAL POLICIES COMMISSION OF THE NATIONAL EDUCATION ASSOCIATION OF THE UNITED STATES. "The Contemporary Challenge to American Education." Washington, D.C.: The Association, 1958.

GIDEONSE, HARRY D. "European Education and American Self-evaluation," *Educational Record*, XXIX (July, 1958), 213–21.

LANGER, WILLIAM L. "The Role of the United States in the World," *The Bulletin of the N.A.S.S.P.*, No. 274 (May, 1962), 121–30.

McKEAN, ROBERT C. *Principles and Methods in Secondary Education*. Columbus, Ohio: Charles E. Merrill Books, Inc., 1962. Chapter 13, "Historical Antecedents."

PARKER, J. CECIL, T. BENTLEY EDWARDS, and WILLIAM H. STEGEMAN. *Curriculum in America*. New York: Thomas Y. Crowell Co., 1962. Chapter 16, "Comparative Education."

POUNDS, RALPH L., and ROBERT L. GARRETSON. *Principles of Modern Education*. New York: The Macmillan Co., 1962. Chapter 16, "Meeting the Challenge to Education in an Age of Crisis," pp. 432–41. (See also pp. 135–40.)

STILES, McCLEARY, and TURNBAUGH. *Secondary Education in the United States*. New York: Harcourt, Brace & World, Inc., 1962. Chapter 5, "Strengthening the Common Heritage."

TAYLOR, L. O., D. R. McMAHILL, and B. L. TAYLOR. *The American Secondary School*. New York: Appleton-Century-Crofts, Inc., 1960. Chapter 5, "The Teacher and Society."

THUT, I. N. *The Story of Education: Philosophical and Historical Foundations*. New York: McGraw-Hill Book Co., Inc., 1957. Chapter 6, "Plato"; Chapter 21, "Mental Discipline and the Authoritarian Background of Modern Education."

# 3

# The Educational Needs of Adolescents

Secondary education is essentially the education of adolescents. The period of adolescence is of unusual importance to educators and educational planners, since, in that period, very great physical, emotional, and social changes take place within a relatively short span of time.

Girls usually start to mature physically and physiologically at the age of eleven or twelve and are mature at the age of fifteen or sixteen. The corresponding period for boys is about a year and a half later. They start to mature at the age of thirteen or fourteen and are physically and physiologically mature at the age of sixteen or seventeen. Because of the differences in ages at which boys and girls start to mature and because they are concurrently exploring new areas of knowledge and activities of life, the extent and the importance of differences between students are greater at this time than previously.

## NATURE OF ADOLESCENCE

**A Period of Transition.** Adolescence is characteristically a period of transition. The word "adolescence," according to its derivation, was originally intended to mean "growing up" or "growing to maturity," and that, indeed, is the essential characteristic of the adolescent period. The boy now is becoming a man, and before he finishes secondary education he will be well on the road to physical manhood. Likewise, the girl is now becoming a woman and before graduation will have arrived at womanhood, though of course the young man and young woman will continue to grow and to change emotionally and socially for years after the high school period.

Boys and girls have been chafing at control by parents and other adults all through elementary school. Now, when physical and physiological changes take place in and on their bodies, making them conscious of the fact that they are now becoming adults, they strain harder at the leash and insist upon greater recognition and freedom. This creates a very important problem for parents and for teachers. It takes considerable knowledge of young people and careful study of each individual to know just how rapidly and in what areas the independence of the youngster may be safely conceded. Certainly, appropriate concessions must be made gradually all through the period of adolescence.

**Physical, Social, and Emotional Changes.** At the onset of puberty, most boys and girls change in the form of the body, the girls particularly, and there are periods in which for most of them there are spurts of growth, particularly in the case of boys.[1] In a great many cases, this results in creating a problem of motor coordination of the rapidly growing parts of the body and results in at least a temporary awkwardness, which, in turn, precipitates self-consciousness, embarrassment, and social and emotional problems.

With the physiological changes taking place in the body there are also shifts in the thought patterns of young people. There is increased consciousness of the existence of sex. This affects young people in a variety of ways, depending upon their natural dispositions, the experiences they have had, what they have read, the attitudes of adults and other young people around them, and any ideals and attitudes they may have picked up at church.

The great majority of girls at this period become quite concerned about their popularity with the boys. The majority of boys, however, are not so quick to feel the necessity for dating, though in recent years this difference has seemed to diminish greatly. At any rate, at this period two important developments take place: Both boys and girls tend to take more interest in things that concern their own sex and, therefore, to have a type of companionship with others of the same sex that did not exist before. (2) On the part of the great majority of normal boys and girls there develops an increased desire for social participation of various kinds including parties, dates, various types of group activities, telephone conversations, and note writing.

Adolescence is a period in which a great many conflicts in thinking and in emotions occur, some of which are very important, especially for

---

[1] Because of the variations among individuals, comparisons of *averages* appear to show that growth is gradual, and such comparisons are quite misleading.

those youngsters who apparently are unable to resolve them and, there-fore, develop at least in a mild form a type of emotional disturbance or mental illness. This has happened to a serious degree in so many young people recently that much more attention is being given to mental hygiene and to the possibility of the need for psychiatric treatment or advice for boys and girls; indeed, this may happen even before boys and girls reach secondary school, as a result of social experiences with other youngsters or with their parents.

## IMPORTANT PROBLEMS AND NEEDS OF ADOLESCENTS

**Sources of Information.** Over the years, a very greatly increased amount of knowledge about adolescence has been developed. This comes from a variety of sources.

We may better appreciate the needs of adolescents and understand them if we can recall the feelings, experiences, and development of our own youth. Originally the information concerning adolescence was gotten very largely from that source. Of course, there has always been the tendency for people to converse with others and to exchange information about their adolescent experiences and views about adolescence. From this source, of course, came largely the material that appeared in novels and other books about adolescence at a period prior to the past few decades. Because we have faulty memories and much imagination, data from this source must be reviewed with much skepticism.

In recent years, there have developed means of measuring various types of personality traits, including "projective" unstructured pictures and symbols, or situations which the individual describes and interprets as he sees them, and questionnaires and check lists, which were calcu-lated to bring out answers that when scored would give clues to person-ality characteristics.

However, more recently, there have been very careful objective studies of adolescence, including very important long-period studies of the growth of an individual, such as that carried out by Professor Lewis Herman, of Stanford University, in which he traced the histories of children through their periods of adolescence and into later life. These studies are most reliable and of great value.

Paper-and-pencil techniques have been employed to gather informa-tion about adolescents and their feelings, ideas, opinions, and social and other habits. These approaches employ not only questionnaires and check lists but also inventories, diaries, essays about oneself and one's experi-ences, and autobiographies.

Much information about adolescence has been gained by gathering observations about adolescent behavior as they were made either informally or in an experimental situation, by teachers, parents, counselors, ministers, social workers, and juvenile court judges and officers.

From all of these sources, along with experiences with adolescents on the part of some of the careful students of youth, there has developed a great amount of knowledge. There is sufficient knowledge today to enable us to have confidence in statements of the more important needs of adolescents, a brief survey of which follows.

**Developing Independence and Individuality.** As was mentioned earlier in this chapter, one of the important and in many cases distinctive problems of adolescents, parents, and teachers is the growing feeling of young people, which develops throughout childhood and definitely accelerates in adolescence, that one should be given more freedom to think for oneself and to do more as one pleases.

In the junior and senior high school, this problem is complicated by the fact that there is a great variation among parents as to the rate at which, and as to the degree to which, they have permitted youngsters to assume independence. In some cases, the youngsters have been completely dominated and have not been permitted to mature as they should, and, in others, the youngsters have been badly spoiled, have learned little discipline, and so have acquired independence and freedom too soon to form good practices in achievement. For this reason some variation in ways of dealing with different individuals must be adopted by teachers.

Nevertheless, in the main, there should be a policy of a gradual induction of adolescents into the realms of life in which they take on not only more freedom in thinking for themselves and determining their own course of action but also responsibility for that freedom and the actions growing out of it.

**Craving for Attractive Physical Appearance.** Constituting one of the most powerful influences upon personalities of adolescents are the experiences resulting from the recognition by themselves and by others of one or more unfortunate aspects of appearance. They are much concerned with great variations from the norm in height and weight. Tall girls worry much, often with good cause, as do "fatties" and flat-breasted and skinny-legged ones. Boys are affected, sometimes very greatly but usually less than girls, by shortness of stature, skinniness of arms, and obesity.

Both boys and girls worry much and, in many instances, develop unfortunate personalities and dispositions—withdrawal or aggressiveness particularly—as a result of homely features and figures. Even a temporary affliction such as acne takes its toll often in the form of excessive worry, shyness, and withdrawal.

Adolescents unfortunate in these respects need affection and counsel as to how their particular defect may be improved or how they may best learn to live with it.

**Desire for Peer Recognition.** Always, young people have attached much importance to the standing that they have had with other young people of the same approximate age. This phenomenon has become very much more pronounced in the past decade or two. This is, no doubt, attributable to a considerable degree to the fact that most young people no longer spend a great deal of time with their parents at work or leisure activities, with the consequent age stratification. Boys and girls tend to attach much more importance to their association with each other, to their acceptance by others, and to clannish ideas and ideals of their associates.

Acceptance by one's peers has become tremendously important, in many cases so impelling a goal as to lead to rejection of adult standards, to crime, to sex violations, to rejection of parents, or to suicide. A schism has developed between youngsters of a given age and people of other ages, particularly those of older groups who constitute a definite obstacle or threat to the freedom of the younger individuals. This has greatly complicated the education of adolescents.

Growing out of this also has been a very interesting duality and inconsistency: There has been a great revolt on the part of adolescents, and older people who behave as adolescents, against compulsion or conformity in standards, mores, and even laws imposed by adults; contrariwise, on the part of typical adolescents there is often an intense desire to conform to the ideals and practices of the particular gang to which they belong or to the acknowledged leaders of their group, and to a considerable extent to the young people of their age, nationally. This is particularly true with respect to various types of dress, cosmetics and hairdos, leisure interests (in music and dancing in particular), and social practices, particularly those that seem to defy the "stodgy" and "old fogey" ideas of older people.

In these respects, typical adolescents are personified sheep in spite of their desires to be "non-conformist" with respect to standards set up or imposed by older people or previous generations. They follow the thought and behavior of the bellwethers with respect to a great many things. But their loyalties are ephemeral, in a few months or in a few years they are stampeding after other idols in some other direction.

In planning, teachers and other educators must recognize this important phenomenon of social psychology and, while not necessarily conceding much to it, must learn to work with it or at any rate to learn how best to work against it otherwise than by ignoring it.

**The Desire To Be Able To Earn a Good Living.** Even though they stay in school longer, most boys and girls begin to think somewhat earlier nowadays about being able to earn enough money to satisfy their material wants, in many cases thinking it through to the needs of married life—particularly since there have been so many youthful marriages recently.

For the purpose of acquiring social status, as well as for other reasons, young people have in recent years been determined to start life with all of the conveniences and status symbols making up the material aspects of life, including, in particular, automobiles and house appliances (and new houses, no matter how small or poorly constructed). This stimulates adolescents to begin thinking seriously about being prepared for a type of vocation that will enable them to satisfy their material wants under this new philosophy of life. While some adolescents have greatly over-estimated the ease with which may be found employment providing adequate income to satisfy their desires, the great majority are quite serious in their desires to prepare themselves adequately vocationally. This motive may be employed to good advantage not only by teachers of vocational subjects but also by teachers of non-vocational subjects who are wise enough and have sufficient background to encourage students in academic subjects by pointing out the usefulness of academic achievement in attaining vocational goals.

**Need To Develop a Basic Philosophy and Set of Values.** With the changing and diverse sets of values on the part of adults—particularly those values which have to do with morality and social habits, with the declining influence of the religious institutions, and with the obviously limited morality in business and in government—young people are groping for something by which to steer. It is not easy for adults to guide them or to influence them greatly in this respect, because of the counter-influence of what they read in the newspapers, see in the movies and on television, and hear among their friends.

Because different individuals and different groups of individuals seem to have widely divergent sets of values, for many adolescents there is a very serious conflict, for example, between science and the apparently conflicting teachings of religion. There is also inconsistency between the standards of morality and decency that they see in the great majority of adults, on one hand, and the lack of morality and standards implied in the loose living of a great many people including, in many instances, their own parents, as well as the dishonesty described in the newspapers—in stories of crime and of dishonesty in the government, including the armed forces—and the relatively dishonest attitudes of many people toward the government, particularly at income-tax time.

Along with this, confusion has resulted from the conflicts between the widely divergent social, economic, and political views of the two large segments of the American citizenry—one believing that the government exists for the general welfare of all, and that this requires provision for a considerable degree of social security, for the care of the crippled, the physically and mentally ill, the poor, and the aged, and the other appearing to believe that social legislation might lead to communism, at any rate opposing big government spending.

There is distinct need for secondary school teachers as well as parents, ministers, and adults in general to provide opportunities through reading and discussions for young people to explore various possibilities with respect to the values of life. It is extremely important to the individual as well as to society that he or she wind up with a set of values—ideals and standards which will enable him to lead a happy, healthy life as a useful citizen. The school is not in a position to build its program for developing desirable moral ideals and behavior upon religion; indeed, it is not truly necessary that it be based upon religion. The values of life expressed by the Bible and also in Mohammedanism and Buddhism may be expressed without reference to any religion.

A large majority of young people come to school with a rather strong desire to take the side of decency, honesty, fairness, and so on, but these virtues tend to deteriorate and to be non-functional in the light of intense desires for status, recognition, and material possessions that prevail all about them, unless the former are strengthened by further thinking and attachment to emotions. This is becoming increasingly recognized by practically all the leading educators and sociologists in the United States.

A young person needs opportunities to think through with expert adult help what shall be his objectives in life, in other words, what he wants to get out of life and what kind of a life he wants to live. If, for example, he can arrive at the ideal that he wants to be able to provide the necessities and major comforts of life for himself and a family but that he is not using unscrupulous means to accumulate wealth or outstanding status, and if he feels that under any circumstances he wants to reach old age with the satisfaction of having done the right thing and having lived a useful life, the individual adolescent will have profited greatly from his educational experience.

**Finding Opportunities for Expression.** It is the nature of the ego of practically all individuals, unless changed by some unfortunate type of experience, to have a very keen and, indeed, a tremendously important desire to express themselves—orally or through creative writing, athletics, fine arts, music, ceramics, industrial arts, their dress and personal appearance, or socially, or otherwise.

Indeed, the normal individual has a very keen desire to express himself in at least several of these ways, and if these desires are thwarted there is great danger of emotional disturbance and mental illness—mild or serious. The presence of this need, so universal and so strong, points the way to the development of the program of study, to the selection of materials in the various subjects of study, to the selection of methods of teaching, to provision of opportunities for participation in extracurricular activities, and to the practice of affording individual students opportunities to express their ideas, ideals, and attitudes. This is particularly important in the cases of young people who are possessed of very great ability and propensity for "creativity." The importance of the identification of the creative child and adequate provision for him in the way of opportunities has been increasingly recognized in recent years and will be discussed later in this volume.

**Other Problems.** Many other types of problems that young people have are important, perhaps some of them as important as those discussed above, of which some are aspects or facets: Among those for which teachers and counselors should be prepared are the following problems and questions that come from actual cases:

1. Should I take up medicine because my folks want me to?
2. If sex is a normal thing, why don't people act like it was?
3. How can I get any social development when my parents won't let me have a movie date?
4. How much does a year's college cost?
5. How can I stop my mother from running around with men?
6. Is there any place for women in veterinary medicine?
7. How can I learn to talk to people?
8. Why do I daydream too much?
9. How can I learn to concentrate?
10. Why am I so nervous, and what can I do about it?
11. I can't get enough sleep and am so tired every day.
12. Why am I so shy in the presence of others of my own age?
13. Why don't I have more dates?
14. Is it fair for people to discriminate against me because of my race?
15. What should I do about military service?
16. My parents are poor and uneducated, and I am ashamed of them and my home. What should I do about that?
17. My boyfriend is likely to have to go into military service soon; should we be married now or wait until he returns, and should we enjoy life to the fullest now as he may be killed in war?
18. Should a Protestant girl enter a Catholic hospital for nurses' training?

19. Should a Jewish girl marry a non-Jewish boy?

20. Others dress better than I do. How can I earn money so that I can dress the way they do and can pay all of the expenses of the extracurricular activities?

21. Is it necessary to learn all of these dates and names of places? My uncle who is a very successful lawyer says that it isn't.

22. Should I study a foreign language in order to promote my understanding of people in other parts of the world when only a small part of the people of the world speak any one language except English?

23. My father says that I should try for one of the Ivy League schools, but my counselor says that I would find the going too tough and that I should go to a state college or a small church college.

24. Should I select my college on the basis of the religion of my parents?

25. I am absolutely sure that I could finish the three years of senior high school in two years and thus have a better chance of being able to finance a college education, but the high school principal won't let me. Is it true that bright, young people do not do well if they enter college at the age of sixteen or seventeen and they get into different kinds of trouble?

## COMMON VS. INDIVIDUAL EDUCATIONAL NEEDS OF ADOLESCENTS

**Important Needs.** There have been several useful statements of the more important common educational needs of young people. Perhaps one of the best and most widely known is that formulated by the Educational Policies Commission as "The Imperative Educational Needs of Youth":

1. All youth need to develop salable skills and those understandings and economic life. To this end, most youth need supervised work experience as well as education in the skills and knowledge of their occupations.

2. All youth need to develop and maintain good health and physical fitness.

3. All youth need to understand the rights and duties of the citizen of a democratic society, and to be diligent and competent in the performance of their obligations as members of the community and citizens of the state and nation.

4. All youth need to understand the significance of the family for the individual and society and the conditions conducive to successful family life.

5. All youth need to know how to purchase and use goods and services intelligently, understanding both the values received by the consumer and the economic consequences of their acts.

6. All youth need to understand the methods of science, the influence of science on human life, and the main scientific facts concerning the nature of the world and of man.

7. All youth need opportunities to develop their capacities to appreciate beauty, in literature, art, music, and nature.

8. All youth need to be able to use their leisure time well and to budget it wisely, balancing activities that yield satisfactions to the individual with those that are socially useful.

9. All youth need to develop respect for other persons, to grow in their insight into ethical values and principles, and to be able to live and work cooperatively with others.

10. All youth need to grow in ability to think rationally, to express their thoughts clearly, and to read and listen with understanding.[2]

The following excellent statement of the "Imperative Educational Needs of Junior High School Youth" was prepared by Helen Jewett Rogers:

In California a group of junior high school administrators modified this statement to fit the needs of junior high school boys and girls. The following statements are definitive of the needs of junior high school youth.

1. All junior high school youth need to explore their own aptitudes and to have experiences basic to occupational proficiency.

2. All junior high school youth need to develop and maintain abundant physical and mental health.

3. All junior high school youth need to be participating citizens of their school and community, with increasing orientation to adult citizenship.

4. All junior high school youth need experiences and understandings appropriate to their age and development, which are the foundation of home and family life.

5. All junior high school youth need to develop a sense of values of material things and of the rights of ownership.

6. All junior high school youth need to learn about the natural and physical environment and its effect on life, and the opportunities for using the scientific approach in the solution of problems.

7. All junior high school youth need the enriched living which comes from appreciation of and expression in the arts, and from experiencing the beauty and wonder of the world around them.

8. All junior high school youth need to have a variety of socially acceptable and personally satisfying leisure-time experiences which contribute either to their personal growth or to their development in wholesome group relationships, or to both.

9. All junior high school youth need experiences in group living which contribute to personality and character development; they need to develop a respect for other persons and their rights, and to grow in ethical insights.

10. All junior high school youth need to grow in their ability to observe, listen, read, think, speak, and write with purpose and appreciation.[3]

[2] Educational Policies Commission, *Education for All Youth*, pp. 225–226. Copyright 1944 by National Education Association and quoted with its permission.

[3] Helen Jewett Rogers, "The Emerging Curriculum of the Modern Junior High School," *Bulletin of the National Association of Secondary School Principals*, No. 170 (April, 1950), pp. 128–129.

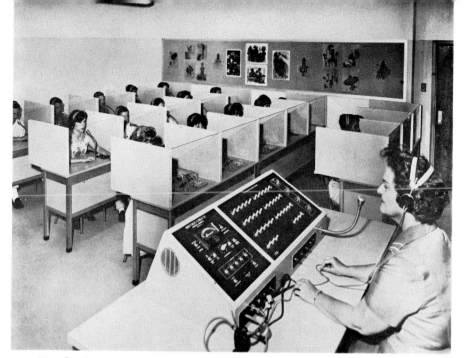

Teacher's station in a language laboratory of a Houston high school.

One type of language laboratory (San Diego City Schools photo).

Art class provides training and experience in a variety of mediums (Dwight D. Eisenhower High School, Blue Island, Ill.).

Art studio in a Norfolk, Virginia, high school.

It should be obvious that some needs are common or general needs in the sense that they are felt by all or practically all youngsters, while others are individual needs. These two types of needs merit some explanation and discussion:

It is a little difficult to differentiate between the common and the individual needs of students, since there may be a common need that embraces two or more contributory or subordinate needs that vary from individual to individual, for example, there is a need to develop vocational competence that is, in general, a common need, but some adolescents may choose to accomplish this need by choosing an agricultural curriculum, others by choosing a secretarial curriculum, and others by choosing a college-preparatory curriculum that will enable them to enter a college of engineering.

There are, however, some general common needs that apply to all individuals, toward the accomplishment of which fairly common procedures and materials may be employed, for example, there is the necessity for preparing to be an intelligent and effective citizen so that the advantages of living in a successful and well-organized country can be experienced. There are also the rather general needs for learning how to be an effective individual in the home, to get along with others, to manage finances, to raise children, etc. Even here, the needs may be somewhat different for those who will be fathers from what they will be for those who will be mothers and those who will not be married.

One may also look at the common needs from the point of view of the psychological outcomes of learning, for example, there are the following very important psychological educational needs in terms of psychological growth outcomes:

1. All adolescents should be trained in the disciplines, and techniques, and habits of careful, clear thinking including the ability to avoid being misled by advertising, political campaign material, or other forms of propaganda.

2. All adolescents need to develop skills in making decisions, checking them, verifying them, and modifying them as situations and conditions change.

3. All adolescents need to develop a thorough understanding of various types of social relationships including those between husband and wife, between parent and child, between grown son or daughter and an aged parent, between an individual and an organization, between an individual and his neighbors, between an individual and his fellow citizens in general, and between an individual and his fellow human beings in general.

4. All adolescents need to become acquainted with, to understand, and to appreciate more important elements in the American culture and in world culture in general.

5. All adolescents need to develop skills in communication, both written and oral, that will enable them to express themselves clearly, accurately, convincingly, and to be able to understand, evaluate, and appreciate quickly statements or writings of others.

6. All adolescents need to develop appropriate attitudes and habits of living, including particularly exercise, diet, and sleep, and of freedom from excessive worry, excessive daydreaming, or development of feelings of being persecuted, in order that they may live healthy lives mentally and physically and thereby be effective in their various activities.

7. All adolescents need to develop to a rather high degree a considerable number of interests such as interest in the welfare of their country, their state, and their community, interest in peace and the welfare of human beings in the world in general, an interest in several types of leisure activities, particularly one in each of the fields of reading, sports and physical activities, sedentary games, and television viewing of a satisfying and acceptable type, interest in conversation, and interest in the human beings about them.

All adolescents must develop skills in various types of social activities including meeting people, introducing people, talking on the telephone, and carrying on interesting and thoughtful conversations, etc.

Dr. Robert Havighurst, of the University of Chicago, lists the following "Ten Developmental tasks of Adolescence" that are very important from the viewpoint of the American middle class:

1. Achieving new and more mature relations with age-mates of both sexes.
2. Achieving a masculine or feminine social role.
3. Accepting one's physique and using the body effectively.
4. Achieving emotional independence of parents and other adults.
5. Achieving assurance of economic independence.
6. Selecting and preparing for an occupation.
7. Preparing for marriage and family life.
8. Developing intellectual skills and concepts necessary for civic competence.
9. Desiring and achieving socially responsible behavior.
10. Acquiring a set of values and an ethical system as a guide to behavior.[4]

It is clear that to give adolescents the education they need is not a simple thing to be accomplished readily by teachers who merely "know their subject matter."

[4] Robert J. Havighurst, *Human Development and Education* (New York: Longmans, Green & Co., Inc., 1953), p. 2.

Various suggestions as to how these common needs may be met at least in part will be found in other chapters of this volume, particularly those having to do with the curriculum, with the materials and subjects of instruction, with the methods of instruction, with guidance, and with extracurricular activities.

**The Degree and Types of Variation Among Adolescents and Their Needs.** Significant for the purposes of education, but of course in many other areas as well, are the very great and important differences among adolescents found in any secondary school and in secondary schools in general. While these differences have been very prominent in the junior high school for a great many years, it is only in the past decade or so that they have become of great importance in the senior high school. This is a result of the continued attendance in school through part of senior high school, if not through graduation, of young people of types which formerly dropped out of school much earlier.

Among the differences of most importance to education, and particularly to teachers and counselors, are the following:

1. Differences in the general academic ability—ability to learn, sometimes referred to as intelligence and usually measured by the I.Q. test
2. Differences in potentiality for growth and learning, such as aptitude in mathematics, in foreign language, or for creative work in art, music, and the industrial or ceramic arts
3. Differences in the type and conditions of the home from which the student comes—the culture, interests, and speech of the parents; the educational ambitions and plans of the parents for the student; and the character of the parents with respect to such things as industry, stick-to-itiveness, the respect for the rights of others, ideals of conduct generally, and social behavior
4. The interests of youngsters with respect to their aspirations and plans for the future. (These include such factors as what types of things they are more interested in doing, reading about, listening to, or watching. These also include relative interest in human beings and their activities, as well as vocational plans and plans for continued education.)

**The More Able and the Less Able Adolescents.** Among the most important differences, of course, along with interest and future planning are the differences in the ways in which the so-called bright adolescent and the so-called slow adolescent learn. These differences must be constantly kept in mind by teachers who have bright and slow students in their classes.

Following are listed the usual characteristics of the academically less able pupil:

1. He learns in shorter steps or units.
2. He needs more frequent checkups on his progress and more remedial work.
3. His vocabulary is more limited and less precise.
4. He needs to have many new words made very clear in meaning.
5. He does not see relative generalizations or meaning as readily.
6. He has less creative ability and less ability to plan for himself.
7. He is more interested in individuals and in practical topics.
8. He is slightly slower in acquiring mechanical and motor skills, particularly complicated ones.
9. In proportion to his dulness, he tires less quickly of mechanical routine tasks and he tires more quickly of difficult reading or abstract discussion.
10. He is quick to generalize crudely, is lacking in self-criticism, and is easily satisfied with superficial answers.
11. He is less envious.
12. He has had unhappy experiences with previous schoolwork and is hence more likely to be irritable in class, lacking in self-confidence, and more interested in non-school life.
13. He is more susceptible to the suggestions of other persons.
14. His difficulties in learning are cumulative.
15. He has a narrow range of interests.
16. He possesses a slow reaction time.
17. He tends to engage in overcompensating activities.
18. He is less able to see the end results of his actions. Remote, long-range goals are not impelling to him.
19. He fails to detect identical elements in different types of situations.
20. His attention span is short and must be reinforced by engaging appeal.
21. He especially needs evidence of his progress.

Following are characteristics of the typical bright student, which must be kept in mind when planning for him:

1. The bright student possesses greater energy and more curiosity.
2. He is usually more sociable and works better with others.
3. He is especially good in furnishing leadership in learning situations.
4. He is much more capable in dealing with abstractions and needs much less actual concrete learning material such as audio-visual aids, although they are very effective with him.
5. He requires much less repetition in drill work, although even with the brightest some drill work is necessary.

6. He perceives relationships much more clearly and quickly.
7. He usually prefers to work under his own planning and initiative and can do so more profitably.
8. He is much more interested in exploring new and advanced areas of learning, particularly book learning.
9. He becomes bored more quickly with simple routine tasks, particularly those the meaning of which he does not understand.
10. He learns mechanical processes much more quickly than the average pupil.
11. He dislikes tasks he does not understand and memorizing, by rote, although he is superior at it.
12. He has confidence in his own abilities and is much less sensitive to criticisms and suggestions.
13. He is very likely to appear lazy if given uninteresting things to do, and is likely to seek short cuts unless he possesses a rather wide range of worthy interests.

**Other Types of Variations.** There are also in secondary schools throughout the country at least a few young people who suffer from physical and health handicaps and speech defects and who require some special attention and guidance. Included among these handicapped children are those with definitely defective eyesight or hearing. Also, in most secondary schools, there are at least a few boys and girls who have very superior creative ability but who are not interested in most of their subjects and do not respond well to teaching in them. Furthermore, because of their frustration, these children with very superior abilities along some lines become "problem" adolescents with attitudes of hostility and negativism toward all aspects of the school situation except what may seem to be in the immediate area in which their creative talent lies.

With respect to sex, there is very little difference in the abilities of adolescents to do schoolwork. There is a much greater range of abilities within each sex. Nevertheless, there are differences in interests that must be taken into consideration in planning students' work, in guidance activities, and in management and discipline.

## QUESTIONS, PROBLEMS, AND TOPICS FOR FURTHER STUDY

1. Do you think that growth is gradual through the period of adolescence, or do you think it has a tendency to spurt?
2. What are the sources of information about adolescents? What do you think about the relative validity of these sources?
3. How serious do you think are the worries of adolescents about their physical appearance? Are they worse with boys or with girls?
4. What is meant by the statement "The adolescent craves emancipation?" And what, if anything, should be done about it in the schools?

5. Make a list in the order of their importance of the ten most pressing problems of the adolescent boy or girl.
6. What is meant by "peer recognition"? How strong do you think the desire for peer recognition is? Is it equally strong for all adolescents? Is it stronger with boys or with girls? Is it stronger with those of greater intelligence or with those of less? Is it stronger with those who come from homes of the upper economic level?
7. In what ways is the adolescent today principally a non-conformist and in what ways is he a conformist?
8. To what extent do you think young people worry about being able to earn a good living?
9. How do you account for the fact that some adolescents want to quit school and get married?
10. Write in what you think of as their order of importance the ten imperative needs of young people as set forth by the Educational Policies Commission in its publication *Education for All Youth*. Be able to add to them two important educational needs or problems.
11. What is your opinion of the importance of psychological educational needs such as those listed in the chapter?
12. What are the needs or objectives common to the three statements given in the chapter?
13. From the standpoint of the teacher, what do you think are the most important differences among young people? Do you think that there are many important differences between boys and girls?
14. What do you think ought to be done with the student who is highly creative and possesses great talent in one field but is not interested in, and will not study in, any other field?

## SUPPLEMENTARY MATERIALS

### Selected Readings

ALBERTY, HAROLD. *Reorganizing the High School Curriculum* (rev. ed.). New York: The Macmillan Co., 1953. Chapter 4, "The Characteristics of Adolescents and an Exploration of Adolescent Needs."

BARNES, MELVIN W. "The Nature and Nurture of Early Adolescents," *Teachers College Record*, LVII (May, 1956), 513–21.

BERNARD, JESSIE, et al. Teen Age Culture. *The Annals of the American Academy of Political Science*, November, 1961.

CHRISTENSEN, HAROLD I. "Adolescence—Madness, Mystery, or Milestone?" *The Education Digest*, XXVII (November, 1961), 29–31; *P.T.A. Magazine*, LVI (September, 1961), 46.

DOUGLASS, JOSEPH H. "The Extent and Characteristics of Juvenile Delinquency Among Negros [sic] in the United States," *Journal of Negro Education*, XVIII (Summer, 1959), 214–29.

FAUNCE, ROLAND C., and MORREL J. CLUTE. *Teaching and Learning in the Junior High School*. San Francisco: Wadsworth Publishing Co., Inc., 1961. Chapter 2, "Characteristics and Needs of the Early Adolescent."

GALLUP, GEORGE, and EVAN HILL. "Youth: The Cool Generation," *Saturday Evening Post*, CCXXXIV (December 23, 1961), 63–83.

GRAMBS, JEAN D., WILLIAM J. IVERSON, and FRANKLIN K. PATTERSON. *Modern Methods in Secondary Education.* New York: Holt, Rinehart & Winston, Inc., 1958. Chapter 3, "The Adolescent in the High School."

GREELY, ANDREW M. "Strangers in the House," *Catholic Youth in America.* London: Sheed & Ward, Ltd., 1961.

HANSEN, KENNETH H. *High School Teaching.* Englewood Cliffs, N.J.: Prentice-Hall, Inc., 1957. Chapter 5, "Making Schoolwork Meaningful."

HAVIGHURST, ROBERT J. "Early Marriage and the Schools," *The School Review,* LXIX (Spring, 1961), 36–48.

HORTON, ROBERT C. "Ten Important Obligations of Youth," *Phi Delta Kappan,* XLI (December, 1959), 100–101.

KELLEY, EARL C. *In Defense of Youth.* Englewood Cliffs, N.J.: Prentice-Hall, Inc., 1962. Pp. 44–90.

KLAUSMEIER, HERBERT J. *Teaching in the Secondary School.* New York: Harper & Row, 1958. Chapter 2, "Adolescents Today: Their Nature and Needs"; Chapter 3, "Learning with Meaning and Purpose."

PATTERSON, FRANKLIN. "The Adolescent Citizen and the Junior High School," *Bulletin of the N.A.S.S.P.,* No. 272 (May, 1962), 68–79.

ROMINE, STEPHEN A. *Building the High School Curriculum.* Chapter 5, "The Learner as a Basis for Curriculum Building."

ROTHNEY, JOHN W. M. *The High School Student: A Book of Cases.* New York: Holt, Rinehart & Winston, Inc., 1953.

SOUTHERN ASSOCIATION OF COLLEGES AND SECONDARY SCHOOLS. "The Growth and Development of Boys and Girls of Junior High School Age," *The Junior High,* July, 1960, 5–23.

## AUDIO-VISUAL MATERIALS

### Films

*Age of Turmoil.* McGraw-Hill. 20 minutes.
*Appointment with Youth.* McGraw-Hill Text-Film. 26 minutes.
*Emotional Maturity.* McGraw-Hill Text-Film. 20 minutes.
*Meaning of Adolescence.* McGraw-Hill. 16 minutes.
*Meeting the Needs of Adolescents.* McGraw-Hill. 19 minutes.
*Meeting the Needs of Adolescents.* McGraw-Hill Text-Film. 19 minutes.
*Physical Aspect of Puberty.* McGraw-Hill Text-Film. 19 minutes.
*Social-Sex Attitudes in Adolescence.* McGraw-Hill Text-Film. 22 minutes.
*The Changing Voice.* International Film Bureau, Inc. Educational Films. 45 minutes.

### Filmstrip

*Adolescent Development Series.* McGraw-Hill, 1953. 34 frames, silent, black and white.

# II

# NEW GOALS FOR
# SECONDARY
# EDUCATION

# 4

# Purposes and Services of American Secondary Schools

## OBJECTIVES OF EARLY SECONDARY SCHOOLS IN THE UNITED STATES

**The Latin Grammar School.** When our forefathers emigrated to New England, and later to other parts of the United States, the secondary schools that they set up were largely for the purposes of training young people in the beliefs of religious sects and of preparing the abler ones for colleges and the ministry. For example, "The Old Deluder, Satan, Act," of 1647, included the following:

It being one chief product of the old Deluder, Satan, to keep men from the knowledge of the Scriptures . . . it is therefore ordered, that every township in this jurisdiction, after the Lord hath increased your number to fifty householders, shall then forthwith appoint one within their town to teach all such children as usurp to him to write and to read, whose wages shall be paid either by the parents or masters of such children or by the inhabitants in general . . . provided those that send their children be not oppressed by paying much more than they can have them taught for in other towns; and it is further ordered, that where any towns shall increase to the number of one hundred families or householders they shall set up a grammar school [a secondary school] the master thereof being able to instruct youth so far as they shall be fitted for the university, provided that if any town neglect the performance hereof above one year that every such town shall pay five pounds to the next school til they perform this order.

As the Latin grammar school spread through the colonies, the purposes became somewhat broader, including also the purpose of preparing young people to become familiar with the intellectual culture of their time.

**The Academies.** The purposes and curriculum of the Latin grammar school were too narrow and impractical to suit a majority of the people, particularly those in sections of the country other than New England, and, beginning in the eighteenth century, schools called academies, with broad purposes, were established throughout the United States. The purposes of the academies included the preparation of young people for citizenship and certain types of vocations as well as for college. In the majority, an important purpose was indoctrination in a particular religious sect.

As is found throughout the history of education, there was rigorous opposition and considerable dragging of feet with respect to the academy programs that were intended to carry out these aims, so, in actual practice, the accomplishment of the objectives was not as great as had been originally planned.

A rather famous academy with a rather practical curriculum was established in Philadelphia at the suggestion of Benjamin Franklin. After several years of operation it was visited by Franklin, who was keenly disappointed, depressed, and angry at the dragging of feet and sabotage of the new idea by the classical conservatives. He exclaimed,

From the beginning, the contempt of your employees for the new, the English course has been allowed to damage it. They get you to give the Latin master a title but none to the English principal. To the Latin head you give two hundred pounds, to the English one-half as much money and twice as many boys. I flatter myself, gentlemen, from the board minutes it appears that the original plan has been departed from; that the patrons have been deceived and disappointed, that good masters have been driven out of the school and that the trustees have not kept faith.

It was obvious that the schoolmasters could not accept the purposes envisaged by Benjamin Franklin.

**Early High Schools.** It became apparent that the academies that were established were serving principally the aims of preparation for college and of religious indoctrination, and, beginning in the middle of the nineteenth century, the public high schools began to replace academies. The high schools addressed themselves to the broader purposes originally had in mind for the academies. Nevertheless, by reason of the efforts of the conservative educators, lack of funds, the small size of the schools, and the influence of colleges and of parents who hoped to send their sons and daughters to college, the "broadening" was actually very limited and took place only in a minority of the nineteenth-century high schools.

## MODERN CONCEPTS OF THE OBJECTIVES OF
## SECONDARY EDUCATION

**Transition to Broader Aims and Purposes.** Throughout the twentieth century there have been more vigorous and effective efforts to broaden the aims and curriculum of American secondary education. Prior to 1915, the statements of aims had been made largely in terms of subject matter to be taught and to be mastered, and the values to the students and to society were more or less afterthoughts, means of justification of teaching the subjects. Many national committees and hundreds of state and local committees set forth their views on the aims of education in terms of the coverage of subject matter and of various important items of subject matter to be mastered.

When parents, teachers, school administrators, and professors of education protested that the aims should be broader and should certainly include definite preparation for various activities of vocational, leisure-time, and other phases of life, the adherents to the classical "status quo" philosophy of aims and curriculum relied upon older concepts of learning.[1] Among these was what came to be called the doctrine of mental discipline and transfer of training, which held that training of the powers of the mind and character through the study of modern languages, college-preparatory mathematics, and chronological history resulted in the acquisition on the part of learners of determination, studiousness, powers of reasoning, powers of memory, and various other desirable powers. These claims were never proved and later were thoroughly discredited by psychologists.

It was also claimed that a classical-cultural curriculum should be maintained for *decorative* purposes. In other words, a student in secondary school should become acquainted with the cultural riches of civilizations so that he may enjoy a feeling of attainment and that he might carry on impressive conversations with others who possessed or wished to possess a knowledge of such things. The exhibition of the type of knowledge would serve as a status symbol.

**Opposition to the Broadening of Aims.** Unfortunately, professors of certain subjects in colleges and universities had vested interests and biased views on such matters, so college entrance requirements were set up and employed in terms of the supposed mastery of the preferred academic subjects,[2] until research in the 1920's and 1930's revealed that success in college was very little dependent on the pattern of subjects taken in high school.

[1] See table on p. 64.
[2] The actual pattern being usually determined by a vote by members of various subject departments.

A Comparison of the Latin Grammar School, the Academy, and the High School

|  | Latin Grammar School | Academy | Traditional H.S. | Modern H.S. |
|---|---|---|---|---|
| *Period of greatest influence* | 1635 until the Revolutionary War | 1751 until about 1875 | 1875 to 1925 | 1925 to present |
| *Type of students* | Boys—select few of superior intellect and upper economic level | Boys and girls—select few of superior intellect and economic status | Boys and girls of superior intellect and economic status | All youth through grade 10, and average or better through grade 12 |
| *Curricular offering* | Narrow—college preparation | Broad at first, then narrow | Broad but dominated by college-preparatory subjects and, in later years, vocational education | Broad and intended for all areas of living |
| *Articulation* | Parallel to elementary school | Generally built above the elementary school | Built above the elementary school | Built above the elementary school |
| *Locality* | Almost exclusively New England | Spread generally over the whole country | In cities at first, later in villages too; beginnings of transportation | In all communities with modern transportation |
| *Objectives* | Preparation for college, and the ministry | Religious influence; preparation for college and somewhat for life | Preparation for college and increasingly for life | Preparation for life including college |
| *Financial support* | Generally public | Generally endowed or private | Public; chiefly local at first | Local 50% to 75%; increasing state aid; 4% to 6% federal aid |
| *Control* | Generally public | Generally private | Public | Public |
| *Teachers* | Chiefly ministers | Chiefly males with some college education | Both sexes, with 3 or 4 years of college education | Both sexes with 5 years of college education |
| *No. of students* | Usually 20 to 50 | Usually 50 to 150 | Usually 75 to 300 | Usually 200 to 700 |

As a result of these types of opposition the actual functions of American high schools, as may be judged by the subjects taught, did not broaden greatly. Nevertheless, the purposes of broader education—preparation for citizenship, for home living, and for use of leisure time, as well as to make some contribution for vocation, gradually attained wider acceptance, and curriculums developed more in the direction of broader aims and purposes.

This broadening of aims and curriculum became very noticeable in the last quarter of the nineteenth century and the first years of the twentieth. Previously, in spite of the avowed aims and purposes of the high school, it had been attended largely by boys and girls of the upper classes, the majority of whom hoped, as it was also hoped by their parents, that they would go on to college. Accelerating rapidly after 1870, the proportion of students from middle-class homes attending and graduating from high schools increased substantially.

A direct descendant of nineteenth-century conservatism is the Great Books movement popularized by Robert Hutchins, Stringfellow Barr, Mortimer Adler, and the *Encyclopaedia Brittanica*. Most of the "great books" were written in a time of authoritarianism, before the time of democratic governments, the spread of communism, nuclear and space developments, cooperative labor unions, radio, television, national marketing, high-powered advertising, woman suffrage, and the emancipation of Negroes, and have very limited direct applicability to the conditions and problems of today.

**Recommendations for Change by Important Committees.** Recommending reforms in secondary education were several important national committees. Outstanding among them was the Committee of Ten, headed by President Charles W. Eliot of Harvard University, which studied the problems of aims and programs of secondary education and which published its famous report in 1893.

Although the Committee of Ten stated that secondary schools of the United States, taken as a whole, do not exist for the purpose of preparing boys and girls for college, the committee went on to say that

No differences should be made in the program for pupils who plan to enter college and those who go directly into adult life. Every subject which is taught at all in the secondary schools should be taught in the same way with the same extent to every pupil as long as he pursues it, no matter what the probable destination of the pupil may be or at what point his education may cease.

In preparation of the pupil for life or for college the committee spoke glowingly of the values of intellectual discipline, which they said would train "the powers of observation, memory, expression, and reasoning."

Prior to 1915, all national committees of any consequence on the aims and curriculum of secondary education were headed and dominated by college and university presidents and professors and had few high school teachers and school administrators as members. In 1912, the National Education Association appointed a committee made up largely of secondary school people which was to affect very greatly the course of secondary education, particularly after the first quarter of the twentieth century. This committee, The Commission on the Reorganization of Secondary Education, published in 1918 the first statement[3] of the objectives of secondary education, couched, *not in terms of mastery of certain types or parts of subject matter,* but *in terms of preparation for certain areas of life, in which subjects would be an important means to an end.*

In this epochal report, recommendations were made that secondary education should

1. Contribute whatever it may in the schools toward the development of sound physical and mental health
2. Develop mastery and command of the "three R's" and other fundamental processes
3. Develop in various types of activities qualities of personality and character that would enable the individual to be a worthy home member
4. Prepare as well as may be through secondary education for earning a living—vocational life
5. Through the acquisition of knowledge and attitudes, interests, and training, prepare the basis for citizenship in the nation, in the state, and in the local community
6. Develop such interests, knowledge, and attitudes as would result in the worthy use of leisure time such as would be satisfying to the individual and not in conflict with the standards of morality and good taste
7. Contribute to ethical character and ethical behavior in all types of situations

**Conflicts in Point of View.** The report of this committee had a very favorable reception by the great majority of the few parents who came to know of it, by the leaders in secondary education, and by the majority of teachers. Nevertheless, it did not become widely known, and it was a very startling document for conservatives who had always done their thinking about aims in terms of subject-matter mastery rather than in

[3] *Cardinal Principles of Secondary Education,* U.S. Office of Education Bulletin, 1918, No. 35.

terms of developing desirable student growth on a broad basis of the activities of life.

Although the first books opposing the Commission's findings were outstandingly successful commercially and second books by the same authors were produced very shortly thereafter, school people in general were not stampeded, and the general public reacted definitely in favor of supporting secondary education for the preparation of young people to meet the problems of life as they will find them and to carry responsibilities as they will be required to assume them.

There have been and still are important differences in points of view among authorities on education, the principal groups being

1. Those who believe in setting up objectives and doing most of their educational thinking in terms of subject matter and what it may contribute
2. The learner- or child-centered group, whose fundamental principle is that the general intellectual and social skills and habits and character of each individual should be developed with whatever subject-matter or other activities are needed and for whatever purposes these powers may be used—the complete and thorough realization of personality of the individual
3. The society-centered group, who have advocated the principle that the schools exist chiefly for national, state, and local needs, and that the welfare of the individual need not be considered except as it may contribute to the welfare of society. (One late development of this type of theory, which is quite different from the conception of its early founders, is the thesis that the school should have as its major purpose the education of young people against communism and for democracy and free enterprise.)
4. The very large number, perhaps the majority, of professors of education, school administrators, teachers, and parents, who seem to follow what may be termed eclectic philosophy of education, believing as they do (a) in the importance of subject matter as the means of stimulating and conditioning learning experiences and (b) in concentrating upon child growth and development of physical, social, and intellectual skills,[4] habits, interests, attitudes, and understanding, as well as the acquisition of factual subject matter for the purpose of preparing, as a primary responsibility, young people for the society in which they live—for its preservation and improvement, for the preservation and improvement of its ideals, and for finding success and happiness in it.

[4] Such as skills and habits in reading, problem solving, decision making, clear thinking, oral and written expression, getting on with others, leadership, and developing desirable ideals and socially acceptable behavior.

**Aims of General Education for All Students.** Following is a statement of the common needs and of the objectives of general education:

We need to help produce individuals who

1. Are skilled in communicating with others—which implies an ability to obtain another person's ideas through reading, listening, and seeing, and to express one's own thoughts effectively through speaking and writing
2. Are in possession of useful work habits, study skills, methods of thinking, and mathematical tools
3. Have a guiding set of democratic values which are used in making choices and judgments involving both personal and social affairs
4. Maintain good physical health through proper habits of rest, exercise, eating, and bodily routine, and the wise use of medical and dental care
5. Maintain a balanced emotional adjustment in both personal and social activities on a basis of understanding of human behavior
6. Enjoy living and working cooperatively with others
7. Are skilled in leisure-time activities that are personally satisfying and socially desirable
8. Are effective participants in a family group, understanding the major problems of family living, and have the skills and attitudes likely to lead to future worthy home membership
9. Actively and intelligently participate in the consideration and solution of local, state, national, and international problems involving the social, economic, political, and personal welfare
10. Utilize the scientific method wherever it is applicable, understand the basic discoveries of science and their influence on thought and ways of living, understand the basic maladjustments resulting from the discrepancies between scientific progress and existing social arrangements, and recognize the dangers in the control of science by any special interest group
11. Enjoy and appreciate beauty wherever it is found, be it in literature, music, art, or nature, and understand the arts as expressions of individuals and the culture
12. Have at least some understanding and skill in the use of the principal materials, processes, and appliances that characterize modern life
13. Are well oriented vocationally and are able to choose a satisfying and socially desirable occupation that will utilize fully their capabilities
14. Operate effectively as economic units, purchasing wisely and otherwise appropriately and intelligently handling economic affairs

## FUNCTIONS OF SECONDARY EDUCATION

The school operates in broad ways in order to achieve its objectives. Professor A. J. Inglis, of Harvard University, in 1918; Professor Thomas H. Briggs, of Teachers College, Columbia University, in 1933—both leaders in secondary education and former Latin teachers—have made widely accepted statements of the general functions of secondary education. Professor William T. Gruhn, of the University of Connecticut, outstanding leader in junior high school education in the United States in the past twenty years, made a statement of the special functions of the junior high school which has been widely quoted, widely discussed, and widely accepted. The functions set forth by these men are discussed in the immediately following pages.

**Development of "We-ness."** It is rather obvious that the United States, a melting pot, having drawn its citizens from all countries in the world either directly or through their ancestors, and with no simple religion to bind it together, must develop on the part of at least a great majority of its citizens a feeling of "we-ness" or "belongingness," in other words, a feeling that we are alike and that we belong together.

This function Professor Inglis and Professor Briggs called the "integrative" function. This means, briefly, that in the school the students acquire a common language, to some extent common interests (in reading, sports, and other areas), and common ideals that we have come to think of as American ideals and as representing an American way of life. It is because of the recognized importance of this function of secondary education that there has been very strong opposition to the setting up of rival secondary school systems as exist in many foreign countries. Many here hold that, since there is no common religion in the United States, it is extraordinarily important that the integrative function be effective.

**Development of Individual Variation.** It is not in conflict with the integrative function that the school operate not only to make people alike but also to make them different, that is, different in certain areas. Students need to be prepared for a great variety of occupations and a great variety of leisure and cultural interests. It has come to be very commonly accepted that, while we must have general education of the masses, special attention must be given to identifying youngsters who deviate from their fellows with respect to interest, qualities of various kinds, academic ability, and probable future vocational pursuits and to providing for them a variety of types of subjects and curriculums.

**Development of Systems of Values.** More recently, there has been a greater recognition of what seems to be a fact, namely, that secondary education should function in such a way that it stimulates and enables the young people to develop for themselves a system of values and a philosophy of life—something to cling to and to steer by. The importance of this function has been increasingly recognized as we have been having a diminution of the influence of religion, an alleged breakdown of respect on the part of young people for the older people, conflicts between communism and free enterprise and between totalitarianism and democracy, and a world that is not nearly as stable as previously and that is, therefore, much more confusing to the young people growing up in it.

To be sure, different people wish to emphasize different kinds of values. Some feel that the values stressed should be religious values; others, political values; others, psychological values; and, fortunately, many believe that the values should be broadly conceived and should not be based in any particular area or lead to a system of dogmatic indoctrination.

**Passing on the Cultural Heritage.** Although only lip service is given to it by many teachers and administrators, there has been, from the beginning of secondary education in this country, a belief that in the secondary schools we should be able *to pass on to the oncoming generations the cultural heritage of our people and the world—the cultural heritage of modern civilization.* This has been variously interpreted along such lines as (1) having young people become familiar with the older great books; (2) having young people become familiar with better art and music and the best fictional, philosophical, and historical literature; (3) having young people take on the ways of life and the mores of their elders; (4) having young people take on the political and religious beliefs of their elders.

It is probable that no one of these interpretations is sufficient and that the best statement of what cultural heritage should be passed on would include accumulated knowledge of various kinds, including, of course, modern additions, in various fields such as science, history, the social sciences, literature, art, and music, and would also definitely prescribe passing on to young people our approved ways of group and individual behavior, especially with respect to other human beings.

**Preparation for Adulthood.** Emphasized by Professor Briggs is the idea that schools should function so as to definitely prepare for adulthood. This involves the fundamental germ of the idea of education for life adjustment and, of course, comes to grips quickly with the matter of preparation of young people for marriage, home living, voting, rearing of children, and earning a living.

**Development of a Liberal Education.** Perhaps cross-cutting somewhat the previous function, it has often been stated that it is the function of education to provide a liberal education. A "liberal education" has been defined variously. Many believe that it means acquisition of general academic education; others, that it emphasizes almost exclusively classical education including the "great books"; and still others insist that a liberal education should encompass various aspects of life and culture and should result in the willingness and open-mindedness of young people to think about, and to become acquainted with, all sorts of ideas and cultural accretions.

**Preparation for Continued Learning.** It is certain that the senior high school today must function in preparation for college and continued learning. Secondary education must open doors for further discovery, as well as serving as an end in itself.

**Retention Function.** One of the functions of the secondary school is, by means of its program, of its curriculum adaptation, of participation in student activities, and of counseling, to keep on through the twelfth grade as large a proportion of educable students as it can and to come as near as possible to reducing the number of those leaving school before graduation to a minimum that includes only the most hopeless cases.

There are, nevertheless, some leading educators and many teachers who firmly believe that many adolescents of inferior learning capacity whose behavior is distracting and detrimental to the learning of others should withdraw from school, continuing their education, if at all, in adult-education classes after they have matured. It is quite possible that the major responsibility for salvaging the dropouts should be a community-wide responsibility.

**Special Functions of the Junior High School.** The classic statement of the functions of the junior high school formulated by Professor William T. Gruhn is as follows:

FUNCTION I:   Integration

To provide learning experiences in which pupils may use the skills, attitudes, interests, ideals, and understandings previously acquired in such a way that they will become coordinated and integrated into effective and wholesome pupil behavior.

To provide for all pupils a broad, general, and common education in the basic knowledges and skills which will lead to wholesome, well-integrated behavior, attitudes, interest, ideals, and understandings.

FUNCTION II:   Exploration

To lead pupils to discover and explore their specialized interest, aptitudes, and abilities as a basis for decisions regarding educational opportunities.

To lead pupils to discover and explore their specialized interests, aptitudes, and abilities as a basis for present and future vocational decisions.

To stimulate pupils and provide opportunities for them to develop a continually widening range of cultural, social, civic, avocational, and recreational interests.

FUNCTION III:   Guidance

To assist pupils to make intelligent decisions regarding present educational activities and opportunities and to prepare them to make future educational decisions.

To assist pupils to make intelligent decisions regarding present vocational opportunities and to prepare them to make future vocational decisions.

To assist pupils to make satisfactory mental, emotional, and social adjustments in their growth toward wholesome, well-adjusted personalities.

To stimulate and prepare pupils to participate as effectively as possible in learning activities, so that they may reach the maximum development of their personal powers and qualities.

FUNCTION IV:   Differentiation

To provide differentiated educational facilties and opportunities suited to the varying backgrounds, interests, aptitudes, abilities, personalities, and needs of pupils, in order that each pupil may realize most economically and completely the ultimate aims of education.

FUNCTION V:   Socialization

To provide increasingly for learning experiences designed to prepare pupils for effective and satisfying participation in the present complex social order.

To provide increasingly for learning experiences designed to prepare pupils to adjust themselves and contribute to future developments and changes in that social order.

FUNCTION VI:   Articulation

To provide a gradual transition from preadolescent education to an educational program suited to the needs and interests of adolescent boys and girls.[5]

With slightly varying emphasis, these are also important functions of the senior high school.

**Functions of the Non-public Schools.** Most of the functions of the non-public schools are those of public schools. It should, however, be mentioned that, in addition, many of the non-public schools are established for the purpose of giving those who attend them more religious training, especially in the particular denomination that supports the school.

A purpose and function of many is that of experimentation, even though this may not be the reason motivating the parents to send students to such schools.

Still another function of some non-public schools is to provide specialized vocational training with respect to repairing of automobiles or secretarial, clerical, or sales work.

Another service, by another type of non-public school, is the close supervision and guidance and the strict training given to problem young-

[5] William T. Gruhn and Harl R. Douglass, *The Modern Junior High School*, 2d ed. (New York: The Ronald Press Co., 1956), pp. 31–32.

sters who have become uncontrollable and have started on a career of juvenile delinquency.

Some non-public schools emphasize military training, which is thought to be, in most instances, useful for students planning to go into military curriculums.

A primary purpose of a type of non-public secondary schools is to prepare its students to pass college entrance examinations and to be accepted in college.

A considerable number of splendid non-public secondary schools have been established for the purpose of providing "quality" education. Although "quality" has been variously defined, and, indeed, has been adopted by a great many as a slogan for all sorts of proposals, a very large number of non-public schools not primarily college-preparatory or religious schools are offering what may be fairly designated as quality education. They are offering new curriculum materials, employing better staff, and are stressing guidance and counseling, small class size, and other quality features.

There are also many non-public secondary schools that exist for the purpose of providing education for exceptional youngsters. Many of these schools develop programs for adolescents of one or more of the following types: the emotionally disturbed, the physically crippled, the blind or hard of hearing, the very bright, or the mentally weak.

**Local Statements of Philosophy of Education.** Particularly in connection with the accreditation and evaluation of secondary schools, an emphasis has been placed upon the desirability of having each schoool develop for itself a statement of its philosophy of education, embodying the definite objectives it hopes to achieve and the functions it hopes to serve.

Illustrative of practice in the formulation of the basic philosophy of a secondary school is a statement prepared by the faculty of the Colorado Springs High School, which follows:

SAMPLE STATEMENT OF A SCHOOL'S EDUCATIONAL PHILOSOPHY

Colorado Springs High School stresses living of the abundant life. Our school must produce an informed and thinking citizenry—a citizenry that is appreciative of the heritage of the past and a citizenry that is well prepared to meet the practical demands of an ever changing society in an increasingly complex world.

We believe in the democratic way of life, and in passing on to each generation of students a desire to understand, to conserve, and to improve their social heritage. We strive to develop in them a realization of their responsibilities as well as of their rights and privileges as American citizens and citizens of the world.

We endeavor to provide all youth of secondary-school age in the community with the inspiration and environment best adapted to their wholesome growth and development. Our guiding principles concern the individual and society.

In accordance with the democratic ideal, we give prime importance to the dignity and worth of the individual. For this reason, we endeavor under the guidance of understanding teachers to offer each student training for emotional balance, physical fitness, worthy use of leisure time, and desirable human relationships. We endeavor to encourage mental alertness and independent thinking. We should assure a foundation for vocational efficiency and provide an integrated body of knowledge to meet individual needs.

## Specific Objectives

In order to achieve the aims expressed in our philosophy, our objectives should include intellectual development, emotional and physical maturity, desirable social behavior, occupational training, and spiritual growth.

I. Intellectual development; the student learns:
   (A) To seek the truth
   (B) To think clearly and logically
   (C) To develop effective study habits and to acquire fundamental skills and facts
   (D) To develop accuracy, thoroughness, promptness, and neatness
   (E) To communicate ideas effectively
   (F) To broaden interests
   (G) To appreciate culture and develop good taste
   (H) To utilize educational and cultural resources outside the school
   (I) To develop skill in applying facts and principles to new situations
   (J) To develop originality, initiative, and resourcefulness
   (K) To evaluate sources of information

II. Emotional and physical maturity; the student learns:
   (A) To develop a well-rounded personality
   (B) To improve mental and physical health
   (C) To develop a sense of belonging
   (D) To adapt to new situations

III. Desirable social behavior; the student learns:
   (A) As a person
      (1) To develop an ability to get along with others
      (2) To develop a spirit of cooperation and fair play
      (3) To make lasting friendships and gain the respect and admiration of others
      (4) To understand the ways and means of establishing successful family relationships
      (5) To develop right attitudes toward play and work: toward self-development; toward one's place in the world; toward the rights and the needs of others; toward the use and care of public property
      (6) To appreciate the importance of the dignity and worth of the individual

**Other Services Rendered by Schools.** Services which the schools render that may or may not be incidental to the principal purposes and functions but that are important characteristics of American secondary education, even to a much greater extent than in foreign schools, include the following:

1. *Food Service.* A very great majority of all types of secondary schools provide food in their cafeterias at cost, which is in most instances quite low because of the food supplied free at very low rates by the federal government.

2. *Health Service.* In addition to providing education for health, most secondary schools in the United States provide for health examinations including free or low-cost immunization against communicable diseases. In a fairly large and increasing number of schools, there are available the services of one or more school nurses, one or more dentists who perform services at very low cost for students whose parents are not financially able to pay usual fees, a psychologist, and, indeed, in recent years, a psychiatrist for a few cases of most obvious need.

3. *Transportation.* In the case of a large and increasing number of secondary schools, students are transported from home or near home to the schools. Furthermore, school buses are available for transportation to places in the community that afford desirable educational experiences.

4. *Financial Aid.* In a considerable and increasing number of schools, there is cooperation with the local service agencies, so financial and material aid may be given to students of indigent families. In a great many schools, work opportunities are provided, which enable secondary boys and girls to earn money to pay for their participation in extracurricular activities and for eating at the cafeteria.

5. *Safety.* Practically all the secondary schools today, even those in one-story buildings, have developed special programs for protection of students in case of fire, against accidents in the school, on the playground, and in interscholastic competition in sports.

6. *Records for Employers and College Admission Officials.* In most secondary schools today, rather elaborate records are kept of the students' achievements, participation in extracurricular activities, and certain qualities of personality, talent, and ability, which the school makes available in the interest of the student to college admission authorities and to the representatives of employing concerns.

7. *Guidance Service.* Increasingly, the American secondary schools are providing more and better guidance and counseling by better-trained counselors to assist young people in thinking about, if not deciding, their problems related to continuing their education, to selection and preparation for vocations, in finding their solution to the problem of military

service, overcoming health and physical defects and hazards, and in dealing with problems of personality development and social adjustment.

8. *Employment Service.* In increasing numbers, the schools are now providing facilities and services for students and former students in connection with assisting them in obtaining part-time or full-time positions, in considering change of position and occupation, and in retraining to obtain employment in a permanent position.

9. *Instructional Equipment and Aids.* The secondary schools are providing, to an increasing extent, rather expensive aids to, and materials for, learning. Among these are the school library, with its great variety of books and journals; audio-visual equipment including reception machines for radio and television programs; and, in some schools, closed-circuit television broadcasting, expensive science laboratories, materials, and equipment, shops for vocational and non-vocational industrial-arts training, studios and equipment for training in arts and crafts, instruments and rooms for training in band and orchestra, and various kinds of laboratories and equipment for home-economic education and for agricultural education.

10. *Services to the Nation.* Certain other types of services, which do not directly relate to the students but which are very important, include the following:

a. *Improving the Economics and Business Welfare of the Country.* It has been shown many, many times that, with increasing amounts of secondary education, public buying is stimulated and very greatly increased production of better-trained workers is definitely increased.

b. *Contribution to National Defense.* Schools have tended not only to condition their graduates in favor of the American ideals and the things they may be called upon to defend, but actually to improve the physical condition of the potential fighters. Furthermore, secondary schools have played a large part in the preparation of scientists who have contributed heavily to various types of military advances, particularly in the fields of atomic warfare and space weapons.

## QUESTIONS, PROBLEMS, AND TOPICS FOR FURTHER STUDY

1. Discuss the objectives of secondary education in the Greek and Roman times and in the Middle Ages.
2. How do you think the Renaissance and the Reformation affected the objectives of secondary education in Europe?
3. How do you account for the objectives of the Latin Grammar school being what they were?
4. What forces do you think contributed to broadening of the aims of American secondary education?

5. Do you believe that schools should prepare for all areas of education or that they should be content to concern themselves with the development of the intellectual powers and skills?
6. What are the four groups mentioned in the chapter that have different ideas about what aims of secondary education should be? What do you think about the positions of these four groups?
7. Which of the eight functions of secondary education listed in the chapter do you think are most important? List four in the order of their importance.
8. In what ways, if any, are the functions of the junior high school as stated by Gruhn and Douglass different from the functions of secondary education in general?
9. What do you consider to be the more important functions of non-public schools?
10. There are different types of non-public schools with different functions. Explain this statement in detail.

## SUPPLEMENTARY MATERIALS

### Selected Readings

Dewey, John. *Democracy and Education.* New York: The Macmillan Co., 1916. Chapter 4, "Education as Growth."

Douglass, Harl R. "Secondary Education." New York: The Ronald Press Co., 1952. Chapter 2, "Modern Basic Philosophy."

Gwynn, J. Minor. *Curriculum Principles and Social Trends.* New York: The Macmillan Co., 1960. Chapter 12, "The Changing Conception of the Aims and Functions of Secondary Education."

Hand, Harold C. "National Goals in Education." *The Bulletin of the N.A.S.S.P.,* May, 1962, 144–58.

Lee, Gordon C. *Education in Modern America.* New York: Holt, Rinehart & Winston, Inc., 1957. Part VII: Chapter 24, "The Scope of the Education Task."

Nelson, Clifford C. "The President's Commission on National Goals: Objectives and Methods." *The Bulletin of the N.A.S.S.P.,* May, 1962, 176–82.

Parker, J. Cecil, T. Bentley Edwards, and William H. Stegeman. *Curriculum in America.* New York: Thomas Y. Crowell Co., 1962. Chapter 2, "Philosophies and Aims of Education"; Chapter 3, "Aims: Schools and Survival"; Chapter 4, "Aims: Schools and Communication."

Rivlin, Harry S. *Teaching Adolescents.* Appleton-Century-Crofts, Inc., 1961. Chapter 14, "Contribution to the Adolescent's Personal and Social Adjustment."

### Audio-Visual Materials

#### *Films*

*Importance of Goals.* McGraw-Hill Text-Film. 19 minutes.
*Social Acceptability.* McGraw-Hill Text-Film. 20 minutes.

#### *Filmstrip*

*Your Educational Philosophy—Does It Matter?* Audio-Visual Materials Consultation Bureau, Wayne State University, Detroit. 40 frames, black and white.

## Recordings

*Personality Development in the Classroom,* #217. Louis P. Thorpe. Educational Growth Series. Educational Recording Services. Los Angeles. 36–44-minute discussion, 33⅓ rpm.

*The High School Curriculum for Life Adjustment,* #216. Harl R. Douglass. Educational Growth Series. Educational Recording Services. Los Angeles. 36–44-minute discussion, 33⅓ rpm.

# 5

# Education for Life Needs

## EDUCATION FOR CITIZENSHIP

**The Necessity for Education for Citizenship in American Democracy. Nature of Good Citizenship.** Good citizenship consists of behavior that does not violate laws of the community, state, and nation and that is in accordance with the accepted standards of good human relations; it requires willingness and ability to render service to community enterprises—all of this and more. The good citizen is willing and able to discharge with credit all the responsibilities of effective membership in the community, state, nation, and international groups that have for their objectives the maintenance and improvement of the welfare of all mankind.

Good citizenship entails cooperation with, and occasional leadership among, authorities and others at school, in the home, and in any group to which one belongs, including, for example, a business organization, a labor union, a service club, a woman's club, a church, and one's neighborhood.

**Unique Needs for Education for Citizenship in a Democracy.** In a totalitarian form of government, the important thing is that the citizen be prepared to obey the orders of some superior. In a democracy, however, education for citizenship is not only much different and much more important, but it involves much more. For example, it means the interest in, and ability to understand, the complicated economic and political issues and problems with which the society is confronted.

All of our presidents, indeed thousands of our leaders, have expressed their belief that adequate education of the future voters and the general public is essential. Some typical statements follow.

Promote then as an object of primary importance, institutions for the general diffusion of knowledge. In proportion as the structure of a government gives force to public opinion it is essential that public opinion should be enlightened.—GEORGE WASHINGTON

The members of society in every district must possess that knowledge necessary to qualify them to discharge with credit and effect these great duties of citizens on which free government rests.—JAMES MONROE

A popular government without popular information or the means of acquiring it is a prologue to a farce or a tragedy or perhaps both. Knowledge will forever govern ignorance; and the people which means to be their own governors must arm themselves with the power which knowledge gives.—JAMES MADISON

In the diffusion of education among the people rests the means and perpetuation of our free institutions.—DANIEL WEBSTER

Next in importance to freedom and justice is popular education, without which neither justice nor freedom can be permanently maintained.—JAMES A. GARFIELD

The theory of the state in furnishing more and better schools is that it fits us to perform better our duties as citizens.—GROVER CLEVELAND

**Increased Complexity and Seriousness of Problems Confronting American Democracy.** When our government was first formed, nearly two centuries ago, 90 per cent of our people lived on farms or in very small villages; all but a small portion of our food, goods, and materials were produced locally; the problems of our economic and political life and of our international relations were relatively simple. Since that time, they have grown steadily in complexity and importance at an increasing rate of acceleration. The great expansion and effectiveness of our public school system have helped to make it possible for our democracy to endure to be the oldest democratic government in continuous existence.

The problems it has been compelled to face have increased alarmingly in complexity and seriousness in this century, particularly in the last twenty years. Within the lifetime of many living Americans, the United States has participated in two very serious wars, and it is now dangerously threatened with a third one, which would probably result in almost complete destruction of our major cities and in the loss of the lives of a great majority of the inhabitants of the United States. In the past seventy years, there have been four serious economic depressions, one of which was so severe as to threaten the very existence of our economy and our way of life. In that period of time, we have seen the development of great and powerful business corporations, of powerful labor unions, and of the interdependence both of the United States and of all its people upon the rest of the world for their economic security and well-being.

**Types of Educational Growth Necessary for Good Citizenship. Information, Concepts, and Understanding.** To be an effective citizen and to understand our democracy, it is necessary for one to acquire a large amount of information and understanding. One must understand the nature of our government, its fundamental principles, and how it operates. One must understand the advantages and the dangers of a democratic society and form of government such as ours.

An effective citizen must know a great quantity of facts about our institutions and their problems, including, of course, our economic system with its free enterprise. He must have information about, and understand, a great many facets of our organized life.

**Ideals, Attitudes, and Interests.** The acquisition of information is necessary but is not enough. Education for good citizenship naturally includes the development of favorable ideals, attitudes, and interests. As the great English philosopher, statesman, and writer John Ruskin once said, "Education is not merely coming to know what one ought to know but to behave as one ought to behave." First of all, there is the necessity for developing a belief in democracy, democratic human relations, and a representative form of government. This involves the development of many ideals such as fairness; representation by those governed; teamwork for the general welfare; justice for all, regardless of color, creed, or social-economic status; equality of opportunity for education and for employment and economic progress; consideration of others and their general welfare; freedom from all imposed restrictions except those necessary for the protection of others and for the general welfare; obedience to, and respect for, the proper authorities; a willingness to abide by decisions of the voters or their representatives; a willingness to assume responsibilities along with privileges; and free speech and academic freedom.

Education for citizenship must emphasize the development of interests in the protection and improvement of the nation, its people, and its institutions; it must develop very favorable attitudes toward the features of democracy and freedom; it must develop interest and concern about the welfare of fellow citizens and the American people as a whole. Among other things, it must develop sufficient interest in all of these things, so that one will continue to read, study, and think about the problems that the country faces.

The Education Policies Commission has suggested the following as among the most important citizenship values that should be developed in young people: (1) wholesome personality, (2) moral responsibility, (3) a view of institutions as the servants of man, (4) acceptance of the principle of common consent, (5) devotion to truth, (6) respect for excellence, (7) moral equity, (8) belief in brotherhood, (9) acceptance of every man's right to the pursuit of happiness, (10) desire for spiritual enrichment.

That the high schools have not done a very good job of teaching the fundamental democratic ideals to their students is indicated by the results of a Purdue opinion poll which revealed the astounding facts that only 29 per cent of seniors believe that newspapers and magazines should be allowed to print anything they want to except military secrets; as many as 33 per cent believe that, in some cases, the police should be allowed to search a person or his home even though they do not have a warrant; 14 per cent believe that persons who refuse to testify against themselves should either be made to talk or severely punished; 25 per cent believe that the government should prohibit some people from making public speeches; 31 per cent believe that a foreigner should not be permitted to criticize our government; 28 per cent believe that people who have "wild" ideas should not have the right to vote; and 18 per cent believe that some racial or religious groups should be prevented from living in certain sections of a city.

**Habits and Skills.** To be an effective good citizen, one must develop skills in the performance of one's duties and in the achievement of one's social objectives, as well as habits of behavior as a good citizen. Indeed, the real test of good citizenship is the actual behavior of the individual and groups of individuals.

This means the development of appropriate intellectual habits and skills including, for example, skill in reading, in problem solving, in thinking, and in expression. It also involves social habits and skills including the habit of behaving in a way which is characteristic of the behavior of good citizens, for example, respecting the rights and feelings of others, skills in getting on with other people, and skills in social leadership. Good citizenship also involves physical habits and skills in the realm of actual behavior.

In this period of almost hysterical fear of communistic forms of economic life and of the totalitarian form of government, in a time characterized by a dangerous propensity for those who would appear well in the sight of others in order to gain political advantage or who would gain favor for any reason through false and exaggerated statements to attack unfairly individuals and organizations, it is easy to see why a rather wide variety of types of educational growth must be developed.

The good citizen has acquired a considerable amount of information about the problems the nation will face, he has developed skills in reading and thinking that will enable him to examine critically all that he reads and that he hears on radio or sees on television that would affect

Office practice in Southeast Miami (Florida) High School.

Class in computing machines—Springfield, Massachusetts.

Class in business machines (Pershing High School, Detroit).

Subgroup study of French (Mackenzie High School, Detroit).

his opinion on any controversial subject. Furthermore, he must have an interest in continued reading and study about these problems. Of critical importance is the development of the abilities that will enable him to make intelligent choices in the selection of those who will legislate for the benefit of the people of the community, of the state, and of the nation.

**Possible Contributions Through School Subjects. History and the Other Social Studies.** As was stated by Professor Edwin Carr, former president of the National Council of Teachers of the Social Studies, the potential contributions of the social studies to education for citizenship include the following:

1. The concept of democracy, like other concepts, becomes real as its elements are viewed in real situations in life about us and in the nation, and as compared to non-democracy in the United States and in other nations.

2. The social studies should provide students with an understanding of the main lines of development and operation of the principal American institutions.

3. The student of social studies should become aware, through study and through observation, that interdependence is the dominant feature of our society, whether society be regarded from a community, a national, or a world point of view.

4. Special attention should be paid to those factors of primary resources, world politics, and world topography that have operated to unify, to divide, or otherwise to affect the world and its peoples.

5. In fact, the student should appreciate the significance of cultural diffusion and the very real values obtained in cultural diversity.

6. The social-studies program should help students gain a clear concept of the full impact of science upon society.

7. The social studies should help students to develop a vital interest in community affairs by encouraging participation in community studies and surveys, by encouraging student-initiated programs for community betterment that grow out of the surveys and studies, and by utilization of the community to give meaning to social concepts.

The social studies must provide students with the opportunity to learn and to practice the numerous skills of intelligent citizenship. Through teaching and learning in the social studies, it is possible to develop on the part of the future adult citizen many of the accomplishments listed in the foregoing section of this chapter, particularly acquisition of (1) information of various types necessary for the citizen, (2) concepts and understanding of fundamental principles of human relationships, including the ideals of democracy such as those of free speech, honest government, equality of economic and political opportunity, etc., (3) favorable attitudes toward people of other nationalities, races, and religions and toward the fundamental characteristics of democratic living, and (4) interest in various aspects of community and group life—local, state, national, and international, involving interest in reading in a number of areas of current problems.

Two courses should be required of all students. The first is a year's course in American history that should have the tradition of liberty as its dominant theme. The second may be in government, problems of democracy, or civics—wherever a carefully structured unit can present the theory and practice of individual rights.

Courses with these approaches should be developed and required at the junior high school level to provide a basic groundwork and to reach the millions of students who drop out annually before the eleventh grade.

A positive presentation of the heritage, theory, and practice of American rights has always been implicit and fundamental in American education; however, this should be strengthened and made prerequisite to teaching about totalitarianism and its threat to freedom. A pertinent and timely comment by the editor of *Education USA*, a weekly bulletin of the National Education Association follows:

Teaching about the Bill of Rights, has tended to be descriptive and chronological, providing little analysis or opportunity to develop insight. As a new approach it suggests use of the case method, or problem-solving techniques, and of socio-drama to present material. Rights can be of interest and understood by students, when they see them as conflicts or issues which must be decided by an "umpire" or as problems to be solved.

Four major concepts should undergird teaching about the Bill of Rights. These are: respect for the dignity of the individual is of the essence in our society; ours is a government of laws, not men; the law, in the long run, reflects the ethics and morality of our society; and free men are responsible men.

While the classroom teacher . . . can immediately start to strengthen teaching in this area, many of the problems are so basic and widespread that meaningful improvement can come only through a nationally supported program.[1]

It is clear that instruction in geography in both the junior and senior high school, but particularly in the latter, must be greatly increased. It is exceedingly important that better provision be made for learning about people of other races, nationalities, religions, languages, types of government, and types of economic systems. It is particularly important that, with the very greatly increased necessity for people of the countries of Asia, Africa, and South America to feel favorably toward us and our

[1] "On Teaching the Bill of Rights," *Education USA* (December 13, 1962).

democracy and free enterprise, we know much more about them and understand them, as a means to developing good international and inter-people relations.

It has been becoming more definitely recognized in recent years that the subject matter in the field of history and the social studies needs certain very definite improvements in order to make a greater contribution to education for citizenship. For example, there is an increased recognition of the fact that courses in history should include much more material about the history, culture, and problems of people in parts of the world other than Europe and North America. In recent years, much more attention has been given in the schools to the study of the history and people of these parts of the world, which have always received relatively insufficient emphasis in secondary school courses in history and the social studies. In a considerable number of senior high schools, a semester or year course has been introduced in the field of social or cultural geography, which emphasizes study of peoples, cultures, governments, and more important problems in the light of modern developments and the current scene. In an increasing number of senior high schools, a semester course in comparative government is being offered in which there is study of democracies, limited monarchies, and dictatorships.

It would seem that every student from the seventh grade through the twelfth grade, except those of exceedingly limited academic ability, should be required to take a course in some subject of history or the social studies every semester that he is in school. Many believe that, instead of six years of work in the social studies in secondary schools, perhaps there should be eight or ten—both history and social studies being offered in most years.

There has been, in recent years, a most encouraging sign of widespread recognition of the need for much better provision for education in the field of economics. The National Education Association, The National Association of Secondary School Principals, and a number of other organizations including a number of lay business organizations have recommended that at least a year course in economics be taught in the senior high school. Indeed, a number of oustanding leaders and important educational and business organizations have recently gone on record as insisting upon offering, if not requiring, at least a semester of study of economics in every senior high school and a year of collegiate study of economics in the preparation of every teacher of the social studies.

In recent years, there has also been increased emphasis upon the desirability of having classroom discussion of various controversial topics and issues. Indeed, for a considerable number of schools, boards of education have adopted a stated policy upon which the teacher may rely as a guide in supervising the discussion of controversial issues in class. It is clear that young people must develop a high degree of skill in analysis and discussion of such issues and in the weighing of arguments for and against positions taken by writers and speakers.

**English.** In various aspects of the study of English in secondary schools, there is ample opportunity to contribute to education for citizenship. Democracy can succeed and continue to develop only when there exists a high degree of communication. Group discussions, participation in meetings, raising of questions, making of reports, reading and analysis of, and perception of fallacies in, newspapers, magazines, and radio and television broadcasts are phases of the behavior of good citizens.

In both written and oral work in English classes, the work of the students may well center around the problems of human relationship, of democracy, and of citizenship in a democracy. This type of approach has been used increasingly in the past several decades.

A great many books, articles, and plays contain much information and many ideas about human relationships and about citizenship in the family, neighborhood, and nation.

Many teachers of English choose much literature that is unusually well suited for education for citizenship, including, for example, such books as *The Grapes of Wrath, Hiroshima,* and many others. Furthermore, the English teacher at all times should be on the alert to identify and to give special attention to aspects of any of the literature studied that may be used to increase information and understanding about human relations; community, national, and international problems; or ideals, attitudes, interests, and intellectual skills appropriate for good citizenship.

**Science.** There are some very important learnings that should be developed in science classes because they contribute to education for better citizenship. Among these are the following:

1. There are no significant differences in the general native intelligence and in the potentialities for culture among the peoples of different racial and ethnic origins.
2. There are also equal possibilities for peoples of various races to become cooperative and generally quite civilized.
3. We need to understand the nature of biological and nuclear warfare, including the utilization of long-distance and fast-traveling means of attack and of defense against any country which might attack us.

Science is one of the fields in which there is excellent opportunity to develop habits and skills of methodology of clear and deliberate thinking.

**Business Education.** In business subjects, important contributions may be made to a better understanding of both the economic problems of the community, state, and nation and the place of business not only in community but also in national life. In view of the very inadequate offerings in the field of economics elsewhere, the contribution of business education is considerable.

Health and Physical Education. Contributions of health and physical education to good citizenship have recently become more widely recognized as increasingly important. In the first place, in matters of defense it is important that as high a percentage, not only of the young men serving in the armed forces, but of citizens in general, be in the best of health and enjoy maximum physical vigor. Furthermore, in health education—involving mental as well as physical health—the possibilities are great for reducing very materially the relative ineffectiveness of workers and parents, and also for greatly decreasing the incidence of mental and emotional ill health.

Just as it was said that the Battle of Waterloo was won on the playing fields of Eton, it has been clear that qualities of character, teamwork, cooperation, and leadership have been developing in various kinds of games and sports including interscholastic athletics, when these have been managed under desirable ethical and social standards.

Likewise, contributions to good citizenship may be made through the development of physical vigor, physical skills, and good health through participation in educational programs in the field of physical education.

Home Economics. In home-economics classes, very successful contributions may be made to education for citizenship. The nature of home-economics learning activities tends to emphasize cooperative work involving group problem-solving situations and techniques of working harmoniously with others on projects. Many of the learning experiences in home economics contribute to the development of satisfactory personal and social adjustments. Units in child development, family economics, and housing have much to offer the student in understanding of the problems and social-civic responsibilities of the family in the community.

Mathematics. The study of the pre-engineering type of mathematics in secondary schools—algebra, geometry, and trigonometry—makes little direct contribution to education for citizenship, but it does form a basis for types of scientific contributions and engineering efficiency that contribute to the well-being of the nation. In the field of arithmetic and general mathematics, the opportunities are much greater. Graphic, tabular, and percentage presentations reveal relative emphasis upon different governmental activities at various levels. Trends are revealed by comparing figures for various periods. The local community is studied directly; the others, through reports and reference material.

Money to pay for these activities is raised most commonly through taxes. Such criteria for a good tax as adjustment to ability to pay and economy in collection are backgrounds in the study of taxes and may be studied in classes in general mathematics. These should not be confined to textbook problems but should be personalized by asking, for example, "What taxes do you pay?" "How are they calculated?"

**Contributions of Fine Arts, Music, Arts and Crafts, and Recreational Education.** In these fields, there is ample opportunity to develop qualities of cooperation, fair play, and good citizenship; furthermore, being able to appreciate and to produce music and art results in the expenditure of leisure time in a way that is characteristic of a good citizen.

**Foreign Languages and Literature.** Development of the ability to speak one or more foreign languages contributes greatly to the possibility of developing better international understanding and international relationships. In order to achieve this, however, there must be development of ability to converse in the foreign language. This development is rarely achieved in two years of instruction. There have been, in recent years, tendencies to encourage more students to go on for a third and fourth year of study of a foreign language and to not offer much encouragement to the student who expects to take only one or two years.

In recent years, instruction in Russian and other foreign languages new to the high school curriculum has been established in many secondary schools in the country. As a result of new thinking about foreign languages, these are often begun either in elementary schools, with widely variant degrees of success, or in the seventh grade in junior high school.

**Mental Health and Sex Education.** In recent years, a very large and greatly increased number of most shocking and brutal crimes have been committed by individuals whose mental health has been impaired—persons who have temporarily or permanently lost the capacity to distinguish between right and wrong. It is also true that the person who is in the best of physical and mental health is less likely to become a burden upon the community or the state, either by his inability to support himself honestly or by reason of his need for institutional care.

A considerable part of misbehavior, bad citizenship, and immorality grows out of the lack of adequate training relative to matters of sex and of relationships between persons of different sexes. Whether the desirable information, attitudes, and ideals are developed incidentally to instruction in the more conventional subjects such as science and literature or in special classes in sex education, or, indeed, in connection with home-rooms and extracurricular activities, there are great possibilities, realized in considerable part by a small but increasing number of schools, of developing a wholesome attitude about sex. Desirable understanding and appreciation of the importance of sex and of dignified, wholesome relationships between those of different sexes include: attitudes and ideals relative to love and tenderness, and understanding and appreciation of the physical, moral, emotional, and social dangers of promiscuity or of violation of the conventions with respect to sex.

Whenever young people meet in groups and come under the influence of adults, there are a great many opportunities for developing habits and skills of cooperation; of respect for the rights, points of view, and feelings of others; and of getting on with others in group activities. Time and time again, ample opportunities present themselves for discussions that contribute to the development of good social ideals and moral standards.

It has been revealed in recent investigations of dropouts and juvenile delinquents that one of the contributing factors, at least to unsocial behavior and bad citizenship, has been unhappy experiences in school. Case records of young people who have gotten into difficulty with the law indicate that a rather high percentage of them first became involved in conflicts with the law at a time when they were unhappy in school, were receiving low marks and disapproval of teachers, and were usually humiliated, scolded, and punished by their parents. From their testimony, it would seem that there are altogether too many teachers who are far more interested in having youngsters "learn off" the material in their subjects and conform and submit to the domination of the well-meaning adult in the classroom than in the effects upon the lives of the students.

**In the Teaching of Any Subject.** Certain types of contributions that may be made to education for citizenship are possible products in any class taught by a teacher sufficiently interested and alert to capitalize on the opportunities that present themselves. Every teacher can give training in social cooperation, in group work, in developing habits of good citizenship, and in developing good attitudes toward students of varying ethnic, racial, and religious groups.

**Contributions of Extracurricular Activities. Clubs and Student Organizations.** The potential contributions of student clubs and organizations including athletic teams have been long recognized and in recent years have been more completely exploited. Indeed, many students of education insist that any program of education for citizenship is seriously incomplete unless it provides to a very great extent the opportunity for young people to develop social skills, habits, ideals, interests, and attitudes through participation in group enterprises other than those in the classroom. Furthermore, in recent years, most student organizations have been organized and managed in such a way as to make certain that a greater proportion of the potentialities for education are realized than formerly.

**Student Participation in Government and Management.** As is discussed elsewhere in this volume, the student council affords excellent opportunity to develop understanding and concepts of group management, in addition to the skills growing out of student participation. Secondary school principals have emphasized as the primary objectives of student councils:

1. The development of student responsibility, initiative, leadership, and school pride
2. The promotion of worthy citizenship training

**Guidance.** In recent years, concepts and practices in guidance have emerged from the rather provincial and narrow concept of guidance as consisting largely, if not completely, in helping young people make decisions relative to choice of an occupation and to their fundamental education problems. The development of better-trained counselors has resulted in better appreciation of the importance and responsibilities of counseling relative to problems of behavior, character, and ideals.

Furthermore, in various types of group guidance situations, in home-rooms, in core groups, and in other group situations, there are opportunities for young people to discuss the standards of good behavior, American ideals, and attitudes in regard to the rights of others, to contributing to the welfare of the group, to fairness and good sportsmanship, and to other such matters. As the leader of these discussions, the teacher may have excellent opportunity to influence the formation of ideals, attitudes, and interests, and consequently the present and future behavior, of students in the direction of good citizenship.

**Civic Work Experience.** In many communities, arrangements are made for secondary school students to participate along with adults in various types of community work projects—drives for funds; collections of old clothing, food, or furniture for the destitute; Red Cross services; planting of trees and shrubs.

It is generally believed that participation in such work not only serves a noble practical purpose but results in maturing civic interest and attitudes and a sense of social responsibility, as well as furnishing an understanding of adult community activities.

One of the most encouraging developments in connection with teaching citizenship and service is the tendency in recent years to give young people opportunities to render free service through such projects as the "Teenage Medic Program," in which high school students have assisted doctors, surgeons, and nurses.

## EDUCATION FOR LEISURE

**The Increased Need. A Challenging Trend.** Several challenging facts have caused educators to give much more attention to developing an effective program of education for leisure. One of these has been the greatly increased and increasing amount of time available for leisure. The average work week, which was 54 hours in 1910, has decreased steadily until by 1963 it had dropped to 38 hours. The indications in 1963 were that by 1970 it will have decreased to not more than 35.

**How Americans Spend Their Leisure Time.** A second major consideration is that, with the increased amount of leisure hours, there has been a greatly increased participation in viewing of television, automobile cruising, cocktail parties, and patronizing of night clubs, taverns, and dance halls. All of which are practices of dubious value to the individual or his society.

A third factor is the age-old belief on the part of many that "an idle mind is the devil's workshop," an old proverb which has proved to be possessed of more truth than was generally realized. More people concerned with American life, particularly sociologists, ministers, and educators, are beginning to realize that we cannot afford to default on the situation by failing to prepare people for pleasurable, acceptable, and useful expenditure of leisure time and by permitting them to drift into the types of leisure pursuits that are based more closely on egoistic and hedonistic appetites.

It is also becoming recognized that adolescence is a most important period for the development of permanent recreational interests and habits. At this period, sex maturation, with its accompanying urges and desires to participate fully in social life, impels adolescents to seek leisure activities of a social type. Along with that come decreased interdependence and association between adolescents and their parents and other adults, and other difficulties that impede in adolescents the acquisition of mature ideas and practices. There is convincing evidence[2] that our program of education to meet these developments for leisure has not been adequate. The incidence of crime by adolescents and very young adults and of mental illness among them has brought the matter tragically and forcefully to the attention of thinking people in general and of educators in particular. The fact that, much more than formerly, our leisure activities involve the consumption of alcoholic drinks is not encouraging.

One of the interesting developments in the field of leisure activities is the degree to which our leisure pursuits have become built upon, and

---

[2] FBI statistics revealing that arrests of teen-agers for drunken driving increased 65 per cent between 1955 and 1960 and are still increasing constitute only one of many such items.

intertwined with, efforts to gain and maintain status, attempts at social climbing, and business relations and activities.

Another questionable trend is the increased amount of leisure time involved in reading books and magazines or witnessing movies, plays, or television programs centered upon sex and violence. Not without unfortunate effects is the definite trend among adolescents and young adults toward spending leisure time in sedentary occupations rather than in occupations that involve physical exercise and exertion, especially out in the sun and fresh air.

**Additional Complications.** There is an increasing recognition of the unfortunate effects of the expenditure of leisure time almost entirely with peers of one's own age, while much less time is spent by parents and their children together, in recreational pursuits, with the development of the ties and affections almost certain to result from this association in leisure activities. Physicians and students of public health are almost unanimous in the belief that a great deal of ill health, both mental and physical, is attributable to participation in unwise leisure pursuits, particularly those involving the consumption of alcoholic liquors, excessive fatigue, narcotic drugs, or unfortunate diet.

Not only have the unfortunate effects of lack of adequate preparation for leisure become recognized, but the tremendous advantages of having developed appropriate leisure-time interests and activities, with their contributions to a much richer and happier life, are beginning to be more definitely understood and appreciated. The plight of the unfortunate individual who lacks satisfying leisure interests and activities, except of a primitive sort, is coming to be generally understood. For instance, physicians testify that a very large proportion of the patients who consult them because of worries and emotional difficulties are married women without sufficiently challenging interests and activities.

**Limited Success of Efforts.** In view of the vigorous, widespread efforts of teachers of literature, music, art, and other subjects to develop leisure tastes and leisure habits, there has been definite revamping of the procedures and practices intended to evaluate tastes. But difficulties have been encountered; for example, in spite of the efforts made to improve reading tastes, much of the material read by the typical adult is probably worse than none at all, consisting largely of cheap stories of sex and violence.

There is also a disappointment in the almost universal lack of really good taste in the field of music, particularly in connection with radio listening and best-selling records. Levels of taste in the field of art are also notoriously low among the general public.

Among the principles for classroom procedures that are finding greater acceptance among teachers in their efforts to improve taste are the following:

1. The development of taste and appreciation cannot be forced. Tastes and appreciation are long-term developments growing out of contacts and activities which are carried on under conditions of voluntary participation and relief from compulsion.

2. Materials must be adapted to the present status of tastes and interests and must not be presented prematurely. Much of the distaste for and indifference to the better things in English and American literature are directly attributable to the misguided enthusiasms of teachers who "pressed." Pressing in developing the tastes of people, young people especially, is as ineffective as "pressing" in golf, or "fighting one's cards" in bridge. One must let nature take its course under favorable conditions, realizing its course will leave much to be desired, at least for the present, in the cases of many pupils. Many persons have learned later in life to enjoy things they formerly despised when presented prematurely by teachers. The author of the discussion recalls clearly his negative reaction to Bryant's *Thanatopsis* when it was forced upon him by an "eager beaver" sixth grade teacher, who insisted upon memorization of the entire poem at a time when this pupil could understand but little of its real meaning. Later, with increased maturity and broader experience, the beauty of the inspiring thoughts became evident so that the poem became one of the writer's favorites—"So live that when thy summons comes to—"

3. Allowance and provision must be made for differences among individuals with respect to
   a) present status of taste or interest in any given field or activity
   b) rate of development of tastes and interests
   c) capacity for development of tastes and interests in each field.

4. It is usually conducive to the development of tastes to provide for and encourage subtly, but not too quickly, expression of reactions, either verbal or in some other form. It is natural for young people to want to "do something about" things that are beginning to interest them—to talk about them, to imitate others, to engage in appropriate physical activity, to play, to sing, and to dramatize, for example.

5. In directing the development of young people's tastes in music, literature, or art, it has proved wise not to overemphasize, particularly in the earlier stages, the forms of technical analysis. That must come gradually. At first, in literature, content is the thing; in music, it is pleasure in listening, playing, or singing; and not just looking for technical merit.[3]

**Possible Contributions Through Subject Field.** English. When one thinks of education for leisure, certain subjects come quickly to mind,

[3] Hubert H. Mills and Harl R. Douglass, *Teaching in High School* (2d ed.) (New York: The Ronald Press Co., 1957), pp. 116–17.

among them English and physical education. Among the contributions of English studies to education for leisure, the following are important and constitute an interesting challenge to teachers of English:

1. With the development of the mastery of oral and conversational skills, the individual finds it profitable and enjoyable to participate in a great many social leisure activities, and because of his poise and self-confidence he enjoys them much more.

2. With the development of interests and information and the practice of continuing to increase his information concerning new books, new plays, and better motion pictures and radio and television programs, not only does the individual enjoy his leisure time more in these areas, but he develops a background for discussing these things with others.

3. The individual who has developed an interest in certain types of good literature finds it exceedingly satisfying to sit down and spend a considerable amount of leisure time with good books and good magazines. Teachers of English are giving more and more attention in their classes to the reading of the better current books as they appear.

4. Letter writing constitutes an important type of leisure activity for a great many people, particularly those who have developed grammatical knowledge, skills, and habits.

5. Participation in dramatics develops interest and background which carry over into life in connection with appreciation of new plays as they appear, as do discussions of better actors and plays of previous years.

**History and Other Social Studies.** Today, one of the major reading interests and topics of conversation is related to national and international problems and current developments in political, economic, and business areas. Those who have developed a background of knowledge in these fields find it profitable as well as pleasurable to read rather widely in newspapers and in periodicals and current books on various aspects of public affairs. They may also participate with more poise and justifiable confidence in conversation about various events and problems in these areas.

**Science.** It is quite possible to develop on the part of both boys and girls an interest in science that will lead not only to increased pleasure in reading about scientific developments but also to the expenditure of a considerable amount of time on the part of many in hobbies such as those related to electricity and electronics, especially those concerned with radio and related devices, the raising and care of plants of various types, the operation and repair of engines and motors, and rocketry.

**Arts and Crafts.** The opportunities here for developing leisure-time interests and activities are legion. Almost any boy or girl can and should develop an interest in at least one such creative activity.

**Physical and Health Education.** The opportunities for teachers of physical education are so obvious as to need little discussion here. There has been a distinct improvement of the offerings for these purposes in secondary schools in recent years, including an increased emphasis upon such activities as swimming, skating, skiing, boating, camping, and other activities that do not require too much organization.

In spite of the alarm felt by many people at the development of "spectator-itis," a distinct contribution to education for leisure and for citizenship is made through developing interest in various types of sports in which one can be only a spectator, such as football, basketball, and baseball. The real evil lies, of course, in the spending of disproportionate time as a spectator while failing to participate in any type of physical sport.

## QUESTIONS, PROBLEMS, AND TOPICS FOR FURTHER STUDY

1. Do you think that, if, at the time of adopting the Constitution, our fore-fathers could have contemplated how complicated and important economic and other problems would become, they would have gone along with Alexander Hamilton, who believed that the people were not sufficiently intelligent or well enough informed to vote and that, therefore, democracy would not be practical?
2. In what respect do you believe that education to serve the nation is necessarily different in a free-enterprise democracy from that under totalitarianism?
3. List, in what you consider the order of their importance, the problems you believe to be the ten most important facing the American people today, and suggest what, if anything, schools could do to prepare future citizens to solve these problems.
4. Be prepared to give in class a five-minute talk on what teachers of your major subject could do to educate young people for citizenship, being sure to include more than you found in textbooks on that subject.
5. Be able to give in class, without the benefits of notes, two skills that the schools might develop as a means of education for citizenship, two ideals, two attitudes, two interests, two habits, and two fundamental understandings.
6. Be able to give in class a five-minute talk on education for development of moral and spiritual values, mentioning certain types of values toward the development of which you think the schools should contribute.
7. To what extent do you think the following is true: "You can't develop good citizenship through books and lessons; it must be done through democratic living."

8. List three kinds of extracurricular student activities that you think might well contribute materially to the development of good citizenship, and explain in what ways their contributions might be much greater than they are at present.

9. Be able to discuss in a five-minute talk the place that guidance plays in education for citizenship.

10. What do you think can be done in your subject to prepare young people for satisfactory and wholesome use of their leisure time?

11. Many people believe that television and the movies have very unwholesome effects upon young people, especially in connection with moral and criminal tendencies. What is your belief about that matter?

12. What are the arguments pro and con and what is your belief about the place of classical literature, classical art, and classical music in the high school curriculum?

13. What do you think the shools should do, if anything, in connection with (a) organization of social activities for young people during the school year and (b) offering of a variety of leisure activities during the summer vacation time?

## SUPPLEMENTARY MATERIALS

### Selected Readings

ADLER, IRVING. *What We Want of Our Schools.* New York: John Day Co., Inc., 1957. Chapter 6, "Moral Values and Juvenile Delinquency."

ALCORN, MARVIN D., and JAMES M. LINLEY. *Issues in Curriculum Development.* New York: Harcourt, Brace & World, Inc., 1959. Sister Mary Janet, "Moral and Spiritual Values," pp. 166–71.

CLINE, R. "Moral and Spiritual Values in Education," *Peabody Journal of Education,* XXXVII (March, 1960), 289–93.

CORMACK, MARGARET. "How Can Teachers Evaluate Growths in International Understanding," *Bulletin of the N.A.S.S.P.,* December, 1956, 228–47.

COX, PHILIP W. L., and BLAINE E. MERCER. *Education in Democracy: The Social Functions of Education.* New York: McGraw-Hill Book Co., Inc., 1961. Part VI: Chapter 19, "Education for Responsible Community Life."

DOUGLASS, HARL R. *Secondary Education.* New York: The Ronald Press Co., 1952. Chapter 9, "Education for Citizenship"; Chapter 10, "Education for Leisure."

GRINNELL, JOHN E. "Our Most Dangerous Neglect: A Program for Character Building," *The Education Digest,* XXV (April, 1960), 22–26.

LEE, GORDON C. Education in Modern America. New York: Holt, Rinehart & Winston, Inc., 1957. Part IV: Chapter 15, "Education and World Organization."

MILLER, RICHARD L. "An Approach to Teaching About Communism in Public Secondary Schools," *Phi Delta Kappan,* XLII (February, 1962), 189–93.

NATIONAL COUNCIL FOR THE SOCIAL STUDIES. Citizenship and a Free Society: Education for the Future (thirtieth yearbook). Washington, D.C.: National Education Association of the United States, 1960. Chapters 5, 7, 11, 13.

OUTDOOR RECREATION RESOURCES REVIEW COMMISSION. *Outdoor Recreation for America.* Washington, D.C.: Superintendent of Documents, 1962. A report to the President and to the Congress.

## Audio-Visual Materials

### Recordings

*Some National and International Educational Problems,* #238. Earl J. Mc-Grath. Educational Growth Series. Educational Recording Services. Los Angeles. 36–44-minute discussion, 33⅓ rpm.

*The Citizen Child: His Needs in a Free World,* #234. Mrs. John E. Hayes. Educational Growth Series. Educational Recording Services. Los Angeles. 36–44-minute discussion, 33⅓ rpm.

# 6

# Education for Life Needs (Continued)

## EDUCATION FOR MAKING A LIVING

**The Current Need for Education for Vocation.** Necessary Preparation for Work in School. Preparation for most vocations in the United States must be gotten largely on the job. This is particularly true in the manufacturing occupations where complicated machinery and assembly plants are employed. An increasing number of industries today provide what is frequently called "vestibule training," which is a short period of training given employees before they actually enter upon the work in which they have been employed by industry. Nevertheless, even for these occupations, much can be done in secondary schools in the way of preparing boys and girls to succeed in occupational life, to be more productive, to be more desirable employees, and to receive promotions and salary increases more certainly and rapidly.

**Trends in the Nature of Occupations.** The last few decades have seen very great, important, and wide-sweeping changes in the nature of occupations in the United States and the number of people employed in them. Notable developments have included the advancement of technology; the increased production per man in agriculture; the increased demand for various types of personal services such as those found in beauty parlors and barbershops; increases in the number of people employed in the installation and repair of radios and television sets and in other electronic occupations; increases in the number of people in various types of manufacture related to defense, in various kinds of food preparation and serving occupations, in driving of buses and trucks, and in research of various kinds, particularly economic, business, and scientific; and increases in the number employed as physicians, surgeons, psychiatrists, teachers, and school administrators, and in various aspects of the aeronautical industry. In many types of occupations, a greatly decreased number of people are employed, for example, in coal mines, on the railroads, and on farms. Moreover, a smaller percentage of workers in unskilled and semiskilled occupations are able to find employment.

These facts have changed our thinking about preparation for making a living and must be taken into consideration in our programs of education and counseling. Our programs must be thought through not only in terms of the present situation, but also, certainly to some extent, in the light of current trends.

**Need for Vocational Guidance and Counseling.** From the above, it follows quite logically that young people need very effective vocational counseling—counseling that will assist them in making good decisions, not only with respect to choosing the vocation they will follow, but also with respect to a possible changing of vocation if necessary or desirable, and with respect to preparation for employment and to getting employment.

A newly important area of vocational counseling is the counseling of girls. Many new occupations have opened up for women, and the number employed in some of them has increased very greatly. Another reason for the need for more and better counseling in the school is the fact that opportunities for Negro boys and girls to obtain employment have become greater in a considerable number of occupations. Certainly, these trends will continue for sometime; nevertheless, there remains responsibility for counseling girls in general and Negro boys relative to the limitations that will exist for some time in connection with employment.

**Vocational Education.** There are a variety of types of specialized preparation for vocational life, including vocational curriculums in secondary schools, vocational training in non-public vocational schools, training for vocation through adult-education programs of evening courses, and work-experience programs of several types.

**Vocational Curriculum in Comprehensive Secondary Schools.** In larger secondary schools may be found a variety of curriculums for particular occupations or groups of related occupations. In a considerable number of comprehensive schools in the United States, there are curriculums in training for agriculture, stenography and secretarial work, sales and general business, serving and catering occupations, cosmetic services, and a variety of trades such as printing, machine-shop work, plumbing, auto repair, mechanical drawing, and electrical or electronic work.

In practically all secondary schools, students following these curriculums may also take courses that will prepare them for home living, leisure, college, citizenship, and health. In an increasing number of secondary schools, students may take more subjects, this making it possible for them to take both a vocational curriculum and preparation for college.

Usually, vocational curriculums in comprehensive secondary schools do not begin until the eleventh grade, although some special preparatory courses may be taken earlier, such as typewriting and general courses in industrial arts. Vocational education as such has moved from the junior high school into the senior high school and, in an increasing number of communities, into the junior college.

**Beauty Shop Employees.** In the last three or four decades, the amount of business in beauty shops for women has increased eight- or tenfold, creating a large number of opportunities for employment. Formerly, these employees got their training in beautician schools or barber schools, but, in recent years, particularly with such a large majority of young people going on through senior high school, many hundreds of secondary schools have installed courses to prepare them for these occupations. Here again it is exceedingly difficult to duplicate in school the actual working situation.

**Work-Experience Programs.** In a large and increasing number of secondary schools in the United States are found opportunities for part-time jobs involving vocational training while attending senior high school. Some of these programs are subsidized by the federal and state governments and are known as the "diversified occupations program" or the "distributive education program."

The *diversified occupations* work-experience programs include the following major features:

1. The student spends two to four hours a day actively engaged in some type of occupation.
2. He attends school three to four hours a day and carries three full subjects or the equivalent.
3. The arrangement for his work activities is made by a representative of the school, usually having the title of "coordinator."
4. The arrangements for the work are agreed to by the student, the employer, the coordinator, and one or both parents.
5. The agreement calls for responsibility on the part of the employer for seeing that the youthful worker is instructed and given opportunities to learn an occupation.
6. The youthful worker is paid a wage that is the equivalent or almost the equivalent of that paid to similar workers who are not students.

7. The worker receives school credit for his work experience, usually one or one and a half year-credit units for the time he is at work, and usually not to exceed a total of four units.

8. The coordinator assumes serious responsibility for supervising the work of the pupil and his educational experiences, and he reserves the right and is charged with the responsibility of withdrawing the apprentice from his work (a) if he does not discharge his responsibility faithfully to his employer or (b) if the employer fails to provide reasonable opportunity for educational experiences or growth in the occupation in which the student is being trained.

The *distributive education* program is quite similar but is confined to the group of occupations referred to as "sales occupations." Students are trained to be clerks or salesmen or to work at occupations related to sales and distribution of goods or services and are given experience and on-the-job training under conditions very similar to those mentioned above for diversified occupations.

**Federal Aid for Vocational Education.** It is an interesting phenomenon in American public education that Congress has been uniquely generous in its appropriations for subsidizing vocational education. By a succession of acts beginning with the Smith-Hughes Act in 1917 and followed by the George-Deen Act in 1937 and the George-Barden Act in 1946, federal funds have been made available to states and schools to subsidize vocational education in order to improve its quality and the quality of the training of teachers of vocational education. Beginning with an annual appropriation of 1.7 million dollars for agriculture, industrial trades, and homemaking, the annual appropriation has been steadily increased to more than 90 million dollars and now also includes aid for distributive occupations, general shop, and guidance. Since 1918, the number of students in vocational classes has increased from 42,485 to approximately 3 million. The federal funds were distributed to the various states on the basis of approved courses and instructors in high schools within each state.

The operation of the plan is, briefly, as follows: Each state proposes a plan for distributing the money that it receives from the federal government, including the criteria and methods of procedure. When the state plan has been formulated and approved by the United States Office of Education, the State Department of Education may then receive requests from various secondary schools, outlining their plans, which must be in conformity with the general framework set up by the State Department of Education.

Federal support is also available for vocational counseling in secondary schools through this type of legislation as well as through the National

Defense Education Act (NDEA), passed originally in 1958. But the NDEA penalizes education for vocations, through its preference for mathematics, science, and foreign languages.

**Contribution of the Non-vocational Subjects and Activities.** Upon examination of the matter, it becomes quite clear that practically all subjects, and, indeed, the extracurricular student activities, make an important contribution to preparation for making a living.

English. Not only is it necessary in a large majority of occupations to be able to read printed and mimeographed material, but in many of them it is necessary to be able to write clearly and somewhat fluently. In practically all of them, the vocational effectiveness of the worker is improved by the development of the ability to express himself orally both precisely and fluently, and to understand clearly and precisely oral instruction. In many occupations advancement or even initial employment depends upon the ability to read to gather information from books, pamphlets, bulletins, and periodicals, as well as from mimeographed or typed materials.

Social Studies. Not only does the success of an individual in his vocational life depend upon the economic health of the country as a whole—which determines the amount of unemployment and, indeed, the wages paid and progress made—but the success of the individual as a worker may be enhanced by the knowledge, understanding, and attitude that he has gained in social studies in secondary school. This is true particularly of those who go into business occupations as owners or managers and of those who are to be self-employed as farmers, stock raisers, or fruit growers.

Workers who will become members of labor unions may profit much from the social studies. Labor unions have become a rather semi-official institution of American life, determining wages, hours, and, indeed, whether one may find employment in a given occupation. Along with this increase in power, there have developed abuses of power and various uneconomical, unsocial, and undemocratic practices by many union leaders. A study of labor organizations, their functions, organization, and improvement, in secondary schools is contributing and will contribute more to the improvement of this form of social organization, to the benefit of its members.

Science. Courses in secondary school science provide necessary preparation for medicine, dentistry, nursing, farming, engineering, and many other occupations including auto trades, automotive mechanics, airplane operation and repair, radio and television installation and repair, and various other aspects of electronics.

**Mathematics.** Mathematics, of course, is essential to those who are going on to college or to become engineers or scientists. Furthermore, mathematics in the junior high school grades plays a very important part in success in a wide range of vocations. The better mathematics teachers give much attention to the applications of arithmetic and algebra to the various types of vocations.

**Foreign Languages and Literature.** Greatly increased contacts of Americans with people of other countries, in connection with international relations and foreign trade, have increased the contribution of foreign languages to success in many vocations. The number of Americans employed abroad has increased more than tenfold as compared to 1940. A knowledge of the appropriate foreign language by these workers is very desirable.

**Business Education.** In addition to the vocational education courses, valuable contributions are made to preparation for vocational success by general business courses such as typewriting, general business, sales, and accounting and bookkeeping.

**Physical and Health Education.** It goes without saying that in most occupations the individual with the best physical health is likely to be more successful, to miss fewer days at work, and to possess the energy for planning and moving ahead. Furthermore, in recent years it has become increasingly recognized that good mental health including emotional adjustment plays a very large part in vocational success in all occupations and that poor mental health definitely accounts for the failure of a considerable percentage of people in occupational life.

**All Subjects.** No matter what the subject, there is opportunity for the student to learn and for the teacher to give training in habits of character that contribute greatly to vocational success. Employers increasingly attach more importance to reliability, ability to get along with others, alertness on the job, avoidance of excessive use of stimulants of various kinds, emotional control, willingness to cooperate as a member of the organization, interest in the industry, and, very important, maturity and a sense of responsibility. They often complain vigorously of the immaturity of the typical high school graduate and will avoid employing "dropouts."

**Extracurricular Activities.** What has been said concerning non-vocational subjects, with refernce to contributions to vocational success, may be said with respect to programs of student participation in extracurricular activities. Not only do these provide exploratory experiences of various kinds, but desirable character qualities are usually developed through participation in such activities.

A considerable amount of the information and experience needed by high school students in making intelligent vocational choices can be provided in extra-class situations. By his participation in activities such as those of an arts and crafts, music, photography, or radio club, the student can test his abilities in various fields of human endeavor. Interest in a vocation may be engendered by discussions in the school assembly and clubs. The programs of the homerooms can serve as a source of information in regard to (a) the requirements and opportunities in various occupations, (b) the abilities, knowledges, and skills required for success in different occupations, and (c) the social values of various occupations.

By engaging in individual and group projects sponsored by his school club, the student may acquire some of the habits and skills that are essential to success in any vocation, such as habits of accuracy, industry, and perseverance in a task, or social skills involved in working with others. For example, members of school clubs learn to work together not only in carrying out club projects but also in selecting their officers and in planning their club programs and social activities.

School clubs designed to serve students who have already made a vocational choice are found in many schools. The members of The Future Farmers of America Club not only study the personal satisfaction derived from farm life and the social significance of agriculture as a vocation but also consider many of the specific social and economic problems of farmers. The Future Teachers of America Club studies the significance of teaching as a profession as well as the education and personal qualities necessary for successful teaching. Business-club members not only consider the place of business enterprise in our society but also may conduct surveys of local business establishments to ascertain job opportunities and requirements.

## STRENGTHENING MASTERY OF THE FUNDAMENTALS AND PREPARING FOR CONTINUED LEARNING

**Contributing to Mastery of the Fundamentals.** *A New Attitude.* For many years there was an unfortunate and futile attempt to differentiate between elementary and secondary education on the basis of the assumption that elementary education was concerned very largely with the development of fundamental skills while secondary education built upon those skills rather than contributing to their development. This artificial, academic distinction has been pretty largely discarded.

In recent years, increased emphasis has been placed upon strengthening the proficiency of secondary school students in the so-called fundamentals. Originally, the secondary schools in this country were completely separate from the elementary schools and there was a feeling that elementary education and secondary education were two rather discrete areas of learning that did not need to overlap.

When the number of college graduates was relatively small and the typical elementary school teacher was a product of a two-year normal school, the secondary school teachers worked assiduously at developing and maintaining "status" and were somewhat contemptuous of whatever might be thought of as elementary education.

Education is a continuous process, and teachers in secondary schools must take up the educational growth of their students where it left off when those students left the elementary school. The importance of continuing to improve the fundamental skills begun in the elementary school has been increased by the fact that much larger numbers of students are entering secondary schools today with unsatisfactory mastery of fundamental skills. This is true not only of those entering junior high schools but also of those entering four-year and senior high schools.

It has become increasingly obvious that, to be effective in the world today as a citizen, as a worker, and in the use of his leisure time, an American must read well, think effectively, make accurate and reasonably swift computations, express himself in writing and orally with precision and effectiveness, and, indeed, write legibly and spell reasonably accurately. Recent investigations in Chicago, New York, and elsewhere show that unemploment and need for relief or charity are closely related to illiteracy.

**What Are the Fundamentals?** The word "fundamentals" and the expression "the three R's" have been used very loosely in discussions of education. The fundamentals, broadly conceived, include all of the following:

1. Mastery of the four fundamental operations with whole numbers, fractions, decimal fractions, and percentages and ability to solve problems involving their use; development of skill in evaluation of formulas; ability to interpret and to formulate statistics and to interpret and prepare graphs, charts, and diagrams expressing numerical fractions and relationships
2. Skills in reading, including rapid reading, reading for adequate comprehension, and critical reading; the ability to find reading materials needed in connection with an interest or problem one faces; penmanship, involving sufficient skill to be able to write rapidly and legibly; development of a rather large vocabulary for reading with precise understanding of word meanings
3. Ability to spell correctly in writing a very large proportion of the written vocabulary, and the habit and skill of consulting the dictionary when in doubt about spelling

4. Habits and skills involved in being able to understand the meaning of the speaking individual, and skills involved in being able to evaluate what one has heard and to detect errors of logic and false inferences (In recent years much more attention is being given to training for listening. With the increase in the importance of television and the radio, listening has come to occupy the place with reference to speaking that reading occupies with reference to writing.)

All along the line, but particularly in the seventh grade, it has seemed necessary to develop what may be thought of as remedial instruction, perhaps in the form of remedial sections of students in reading. This has been found necessary to ensure that students will be able to continue their studies in other fields effectively. In a number of schools, this remedial work involves more than reading, including as it does some of the English skills such as those in oral language and written composition. In some schools, too, special sections have been formed for students whose penmanship is far below satisfactory standard. Another notable recent development has been the increased effort being placed upon training in listening.

Not only as preparation for college and for other types of continued learning in and out of school, but also for purposes of citizenship and other objectives of education, more attention has been given to the improvement of vocabulary. This takes the form of increasing the size and scope of the vocabulary of students, especially in developing knowledge of the precise meanings of words, as a means to understanding what is read and heard, as well as for accurate and forceful oral and written expression. This is not only true in English classes; valuable contributions are made by the teachers of all subjects by means of concentration on the vocabulary of their particular subject field.

**Study Habits and Skills.**[1] Also receiving a greater amount of emphasis in secondary school classes is the emphasis upon development of study habits and skills. Analyses of the relative ineffectiveness of student learning, of the student of average and lower academic capacities and potentialities as well as of the bright student who is an underachiever, have revealed that the students' work in their classes may be definitely improved, not only through the development of reading skills, but also through the development of study habits and training in study skills. Often, this has taken the form of giving the students training in class as well as in home study in the types of study skills that are likely to be employed to greatest advantage in the particular subject, for example, in history, literature, mathematics, or science.

[1] See pages 246–247 for more detailed discussion of developing habits and skills.

**Computational and Problem-solving Skills.** In recent years, attention has been given to the fact that many youngsters arrive at the seventh grade, and, indeed, at the ninth grade, without having developed sufficient speed and accuracy in computational skills in arithmetic or mathematical types of problem solving to enable them to profit much from further instruction in mathematics. In many junior high schools, a special section has been formed for the laggards, and they have not been required to make futile attempts to master the regular arithmetic.

One of the greatest difficulties in arithmetic and in algebra has been the inability of boys and girls to perform satisfactorily in mathematical problem solving. Most attention is given in the remedial sections, and, indeed, to some extent in the heterogeneous sections, to the analysis of a problem as an approach to deciding upon procedure for its solution.

In an increasing number of schools in recent years, eleventh-grade students have been tested in skills in reading and computation, and those evidencing a very unsatisfactory mastery in these areas have been required to take a semester's or year's work in one or both of these fields and, in order to receive a diploma, to show on appropriate tests a growth in their ability in these fundamentals.

**Fundamental Interests.** What one does, what one reads, how one spends one's leisure time, with what group one is associated, one's success, one's vocation, and one's quality as a citizen are greatly dependent upon what interests one develops, particularly in adolescence. It has been increasingly recognized, too, that the nature and degree of a college student's interests play a prominent part in the marks he makes and in his continued college attendance.

**Fundamentals of Non-verbal Communication.** Spoken and written words do not constitute the only major means of communication between individuals. Pictures, diagrams, sketches, models, and many other kinds of non-verbal communication serve now as always as means of conveyance of ideas from human beings to other human beings. The most superficial comparison of current magazines and newspapers with those of a few decades ago will reveal the very greatly increased use of various kinds of non-verbal means of expression, particularly graphs, maps, diagrams, and sketches. This calls for education in the appropriate skills.

**Continuation of the Development of Other Types of Fundamentals.** Very prominent in education for citizenship, home living, leisure, health, and vocational success are certain other types of fundamental skills, attitudes, interests, habits, and ideals. Among them the following are very important:

1. Fundamental habits, skills, and understandings that enable one to associate better with, to participate along with, and to adjust to, other

human beings in the home, in the community, on the job, in leisure pursuits and wherever human relations and teamwork are involved require, of course, development of interests, skills, and habits in conversation and in social etiquette.

2. The great majority of interests of human beings have their origin in experiences in childhood or youth; although these may be changed in later life, they are relatively well fixed by the age of eighteen, especially those which are likely to be more prominent in determining one's vocation, leisure pursuits, and usefulness as a citizen.

Also influencing greatly one's success and happiness in this world—on the job, in the home, as a citizen—and, indeed, to an extent more great than was formerly realized, one's health, is the degree to which one has acquired the fundamental attitudes, habits, and skills for understanding and controlling oneself. Perhaps even more than the home, school may develop and train young people in self-discipline and control of emotional impulse so as to produce a desirable and effective balance of extroversion and introversion.

Other qualities of character the development of which has been begun at home and in the elementary school should receive attention as important educational objectives of secondary school teachers. These include such things as freedom from excessive selfishness and self-centeredness, interest in and regard for the common welfare, honesty, reliability, willingness to work, modesty, initiative, and the ability to exercise one's imagination and creativity.

Also among the important fundamentals already bgun in the elementary school and at home are the fundamental body skills. These are particularly important during the period of adolescence, when rapid growth results in awkwardness and precipitates the necessity for readjustment and the development of new body skills such as carriage; posture; eye, mind, and hand coordination; manipulation; and fundamental skills such as those involved in athletics, gymnasium work, dancing of various types, art, music, and shop work.

**Preparation for College and Other Continued Learning.** The College Admissions Squeeze. With more than one-third of all those who complete the sixth grade entering a university, college, or junior college and with the percentage likely to increase in the 1970's to between 40 per cent and 50 per cent, an increased importance must be attached to preparation of the secondary school student for college. By 1970, there will be 3 million students graduating each year from high school, and it is most likely that close to 2 million, twice the number in 1960, of those will continue their education. This great increase in applicants for college entrance will mean that the colleges and universities will be swamped and that the junior colleges will probably be taxed beyond their capacity to accommodate. Some if not the majority of universities, colleges, and junior colleges will operate on a trimester system enabling the student to graduate from college in two and two-thirds or at the most three years instead of four as at present. The shortage of employment opportunities in the summer and the prospect of inadequate college physical facilities and teaching staff make the possibility of the trimester system rather attractive.

This speedup will call for better preparation in high school. Under any circumstances, admission to the most selective colleges and universities will be even more greatly restricted and the standards for the students definitely increased as the quality of those selected becomes greater. Already in many colleges and universities the content and material standards in the first two years are being stepped up. As it now stands, more than one-half of the students now entering a college or university do not remain to receive a degree, the principal reason being their inability to meet satisfactory academic standards. All of this adds up to the desirability, indeed the necessity, of more effective preparing secondary school students for college.

**Preparation for College.** In the past, preparation for college has been limited to its effectiveness by the "lick and a promise" belief that, if the student studied certain subjects believed to have unusual college-preparatory values, this was about the best preparation for college that the high school could provide. Fortunately, this erroneous belief is disappearing. We now know that there are other and better ways of preparing for college.

Much of the preparation for college in the past, and, indeed, at present, has been really preparation to pass college-entrance-board examinations, which gives only meager assurance of success in college. The results of investigations have definitely shown that there is not a very high correlation between scores made on college-entrance-board examinations and grades made in college.

Investigations of the relative importance of the factors contributing to success in college (including those by the author of this volume, who gave a major part of his time for several years at the University of Minnesota to research in this area) revealed that *the degree of mastery of certain fundamental intellectual skills and habits and the breadth and precision of vocabulary* are very important in determining the grades made in many of the courses in colleges of arts and sciences, schools of nursing, and schools of business.[2] Indeed, for the majority of courses offered in departments outside of colleges of engineering, other than

[2] Good for high school seniors and juniors planning to go to college are *How To Study in College*, by Walter Pauk, 1962, and *Introduction to College Life*, by Norman Bell, Richard W. Burkhardt, and Victor B. Lawhead, both published by Houghton Mifflin Co., Boston.

courses in science, mastery of the skills in arithmetic is more important than mastery of those in algebra and, of course, far more important than mastery of those in geometry or trigonometry.

**Adult and Continuation Education.** With the greatly increased amount of time available for leisure—a result of the reduced work week, the reduced amount of time necessary to take care of household responsibilities, and the very greatly increased number of retired people—there has been a highly accelerated increase in enrolments in, and provisions for, adult education and continuation of education of high school graduates who do not go on to college, as well as dropouts who realize that they are poorly prepared for one or more areas of living.

With world conditions and problems changing at such an accelerated pace and with new knowledge developing at a similar pace, there is naturally a very greatly increased need for continuation of one's education. Indeed, this is true even after graduation from college, as doctors, dentists, lawyers, nurses, businessmen, and teachers have been learning.

Nothing has handicapped the American educational plan more than the tendency of American citizens to think of schooling as a kind of vaccination against ignorance, and to consider that a concentrated dose of it in youth makes one immune for a lifetime. Actually, the immunity lasts only a few years, and unless it is renewed by periodic inoculations in study and thinking, one falls victim to a chronic type of ignorance which is often more dangerous than the acute form, because the patient, incompetent to recognize the symptoms, doesn't know he has the disease. We meet such chronic sufferers from ignorance everywhere. They look all right on the outside. . . . But inside, their minds are suffering from atrophy. Instead of thinking through problems in the light of all available facts, they merely supply a pattern of opinions based on facts that went out of date along with their yellowing diplomas, and liberally garnished with prejudices that have accumulated in their minds like broken furniture in an attic.—ROBERT GORDON SPROUL

Preparation for adult education, like preparation for college, is perhaps best accomplished through the fundamentals referred to earlier in this chapter.

**Possible Contributions of School Subjects.** English. Among the subjects in which teachers may make the greatest contribution to the development of the fundamental skills and to preparation for college and other post-high school education is English.

The fundamentals in which the teachers of English may make the greatest contribution are spelling, reading (rapidly and critically),[3] penmanship, oral and written expression, outlining, vocabulary, and listening. It must be recognized, however, that the best results are obtained

---

[3] By 1962, three-fourths of urban secondary schools had added an advanced reading class.

when all teachers cooperate by encouraging and assisting students to employ good English in all of their oral and written work in class, and by assisting those whose skills are in the lower levels in diagnosis of their weaknesses and in development of interest in improving them.

English teachers also may make important contributions to various types of intellectual skills and understandings, to the social habits, skills, and understandings, to understanding of oneself, and to self-control. They may also play an important part in developing basic habits and attitudes of open-mindedness and cosmopolitanism.

**Social Studies.** Teachers of the social studies may contribute materially to the development of a number of fundamentals, especially critical reading, problem solving, good, clear, and logical thinking, intellectual and reading interests, and fundamental attitudes or ideals.

**Science.** Teachers of various science subjects have opportunities to develop, enrich, and make more precise the vocabulary in the field of science, developing fundamental concepts, habits, attitudes, and skills useful in the scientific approach to thinking and problem solving, which involves development of open-mindedness and habits of critically examining proposed solutions and of keeping the problem in mind until a satisfactory solution is found.

**Mathematics.** It is rather obvious that teachers of mathematics, particularly of general mathematics, may make very great contributions to the development of the fundamental operations and skills in problem solving. Furthermore, teachers of the pre-engineering sequence—algebra, geometry, and trigonometry—may make important contributions to the development of knowledge and skills that are very useful to college students in following curriculums in engineering, science, or mathematics.

**Foreign Languages.** Teachers of foreign languages may help to prepare students for graduate work in certain fields, especially science and mathematics. These fields are not as numerous as is often claimed.

**Physical, Health, and Recreation Education.** Teachers in these fields have challenging responsibilities, not only in the development of body skills, but also in the development of fundamental habits of living, including those related to diet, sleep, and exercise, which are much more important than teachers commonly realize. In various types of group work including competitive contests there are inviting opportunities to develop fundamental physical skills and habits of teamwork, emotional control, and good sportsmanship.

**Other Subjects.** In all subjects, there are, because of the necessary human relationships involved, ample opportunities of developing, particularly through group work, fundamental skills and attitudes of cooperation. Furthermore, every teacher has not only the opportunity but the responsibility for assisting youngsters to improve their vocabularies, study habits and skills, and English skills, particularly as their weakness in them becomes evident in their oral and written expression in class participation, examinations, and papers.

**Extracurricular Activities.** Sponsors of student organizations of various types may make valuable contributions to the development of fundamental skills of a variety of types including, particularly, oral-discussion, listening, and social skills, as well as habits of cooperation and participation in group activities, intellectual and other valuable interests, self-understanding, self-control, and fundamental character traits.

Increasingly, in recent years, counselors have had opportunities to stimulate students to take more interest in the development of many types of fundamental skills and fundamental social and character qualities. In analyses of reasons why a student does not do well in his classes, counselors and counselees have been able to identify weaknesses in one or more fundamentals and to develop plans for improvement. Likewise, counselors and counselees, in their efforts to solve the problems of misbehavior, have been able to put their finger on fundamental weaknesses of character, interest, and attitude that lie at the bottom of the disabilities and to think through programs that may lead to improvement.

## QUESTIONS, PROBLEMS, AND TOPICS FOR FURTHER STUDY

1. Professor Bestor, Admiral Rickover, and Dr. Hutchins believe that vocational education should be divorced from general secondary education and given to those unable to profit greatly by the higher type of secondary education. What do you think of that suggestion?
2. Carefully list the important values that may come from participation in work-experience programs, and be able to give a short talk on them in class.
3. Be able to discuss the "diversified occupations" and "distributive education" programs.
4. How does the United States differ from other countries in its provision for vocational education?
5. For how many different occupations should a senior high school of 1,000 students give specific vocational education?
6. What proportion of the workers in your community do you think are engaged in the occupations taught in the community's high schools?
7. What is your belief relative to how we should prepare young people for vocations, other than through vocational courses?
8. What do you think you could do, in teaching your major subject field, to prepare young people for success in vocations?
9. Specify some very new vocations for which you think preparation ought to be made in high schools today?
10. What do you think is the place of the junior high school in preparing for a vocation?

11. Be able to explain in class what is meant by fundamental body skills and what you believe relative to further development of fundamental body skills in secondary education.
12. What do you think are some of the most important fundamental character traits to the development of which all teachers should make some contribution?
13. What contribution do you think could be made by teachers of your major subject to developing strength in the fundamentals?
14. Be able to discuss in class, in a five- or six-minute talk, how you think a high school student should prepare himself for college.
15. What can be done by a teacher of your major field to prepare students for college?
16. What, if anything, do you think secondary schools should do in view of the increased need for, and trend toward adult education?

## SUPPLEMENTARY MATERIALS

### Selected Readings

ADLER, IRVING. *What We Want of Our Schools.* New York: John Day Co., Inc., 1957. Chapter 9, "The Three R's"; Chapter 10, "Secondary and Vocational Education."

BAUMAN, HENRY A., URSULA HOGAN, and CHARLES C. GREENE. *Reading Instruction in the Secondary School.* New York: Longmans, Green & Co., Inc., 1961.

DOUGLASS, HARL R. *Secondary Education.* New York: The Ronald Press Co., 1952. Chapter 10, "Education for Vocational Life"; Chapter 14, "Fundamental and Continued Learning."

GABRIELSON, GENE C. "A Special Teacher Can Teach Reading and Spelling," *The Bulletin of the N.A.S.S.P.*, December, 1962, 99–103.

HARRIS, RAYMOND P. *American Education.* New York: Random House, Inc., 1962. Chapter 9, "What Has Happened to the Fundamentals?"

HUNT, DEWITT. *Work Experience Education Programs in American Secondary Schools.* U.S. Office of Education, Bulletin 1957, No. 5. Washington, D.C.: Government Printing Office, 1957. Describes six types of work-experience programs and analyzes their operational procedures.

LEE, GORDON C. *Education in Modern America.* New York: Holt, Rinehart & Winston, Inc., 1957. Chapter 18, "Mass Media of Communication."

McLURE, WILLIAM P. "The Challenge of Vocational and Technical Education," *Phi Delta Kappan*, XLIII (February, 1962), 212–18.

NELSON, EDWIN L., et al. *Distributive Education: Curriculum Development in the High School Cooperative Program.* Washington, D.C.: U.S. Office of Education, 1960.

*Reading in the Secondary Schools.* Curriculum Research Report, Bureau of Curriculum Research. New York: Curriculum Center, Board of Education of the City of New York, 1961.

TAYLOR, L. O., D. R. McMAHILL, and BOB L. TAYLOR. *The American Secondary School.* New York: Appleton-Century-Crofts, Inc., 1960. Chapter 14, "The Improvement of Reading."

"Vocational Education in the Years Ahead," *The Education Digest*, XXVIII (March, 1963), 1–4.

Weiss, M. J. *Reading in the Secondary Schools.* New York: Odyssey Press, Inc., 1961.

"Well Educated To Do Nothing?" *The Education Digest,* XXVIII (March, 1963), 28–29.

### AUDIO-VISUAL MATERIALS

*Film*

*Teenagers Will Read.* McGraw-Hill Text Film. 26 minutes.

World geography at Lindsay Junior High School, St. Paul.

Helping with personal attractiveness in a Fresno, California, junior high school.

Machine-shop mathematics in a Peoria, Illinois, high school.

The Syracuse, New York, city band.

# 7

# Education for Life Needs (Continued)

## EDUCATION FOR PHYSICAL AND MENTAL HEALTH

**Effective Education for Physical and Mental Health and Safety.**
**Losses from Physical and Mental Illness.** Not only do current statistics reveal that the costs in lost time and money from physical illness run into several billion dollars a year, but the data also reveal that much of the physical illness is preventable. Comparable losses result from injuries, the preventable proportion of which is much greater.

Likewise, the annual financial costs of mental ill health run into billions of dollars, and a great deal of mental ill health is preventable or curable. Advances in mental hygiene and psychiatry in the past quarter-century constitute one of the outstanding scientific developments of all time. While it is fortunate that so much more is known about mental ill health than formerly, it is quite apparent that the number of people who suffer from some degree of mental ill health has been becoming progressively greater in recent decades. More than half of the beds in hospitals are occupied by patients with mental illness, in spite of the advances made in the treatment of mental ill health, which make possible treatment at home rather than at the hospital in an increasing number of incidences.

During World War II, between 8 million and 9 million, or approximately 40 per cent, of the American young men who were given physical examinations were found to be unfit for military service. Approximately 5 per cent of those drafted were rejected or soon released because mental illness made them poor military risks.

Recent statistics indicate rather clearly, although the figures themselves must be taken with a grain of salt, that young people in the United States cannot perform in physical-fitness tests nearly as well as can young people of European countries, particularly those of the U.S.S.R. Recognition of this discomforting fact by the Kennedy administration has resulted in improvement and extension of the program of physical and health education throughout the United States.

**Types of Contributory Growth Objectives.** Immediately, when one begins to think of how schools may make major contributions in the preparation of young people for important areas of life, there come to mind the types of growth that are necessary. For example, in efforts to prepare young people for mental and physical health, the following areas of growth are essential and should be encouraged in elementary and secondary schools:

1. *Information,* e.g., facts and principles of physiology, biology, mental hygiene, and other areas of science; and facts about first aid and traffic
2. *Understanding, principles, and general concepts* of the functioning of various parts, organs, and systems of the body; of personality and mind; and of germs as the causes of disease
3. *Habits,* e.g., development of habitual behavior in a great many situations—eating, care of the teeth, sleep, evacuation of waste from the body, and care in crossing streets, driving a car, handling a gun, and participating in water sports
4. *Skills,* e.g., bodily skills that may aid in health and safety, skills in reading that enable one to discover more about the care of one's body and mind, skills in games, skills in handling oneself in one's vocation so that possibility of injury is lessened, and skills in emergency measures
5. *Ideals* of a strong, healthy body, of a healthy and effective personality, and of good appearance
6. *Attitudes,* e.g., favorable attitudes toward matters of health; healthful mental and emotional attitudes toward other individuals; proper attitudes toward health and safety rules in home, work, leisure, and travel
7. *Interests* in health and in bodily soundness, in an attractive and healthy personality, in reading that yields information aiding in mental and physical health, and in activities that maintain health

**The Health Program.** A program for maintaining and improving health of young people and educating them in order to maintain and improve their health in later years must include at least the following:

1. *Healthful, Safe Environment for All Pupils.* This includes the control of communicable diseases, prevention of accidents, avoidance of

unhealthy and unsanitary conditions, and use of teaching methods that will secure the desired effects without causing worry or fear on the part of the pupils.

2. *Provision for Immediate Care for Emergency Health Conditions.* The school should be prepared to take immediate care of emergency health cases. Also, pupils should be taught to take care of emergency cases, detect symptoms of acute conditions, and give first aid in case of accidents.

3. *A Health Guidance Program.* This includes regular observation of students by teachers and health officers, periodic health examinations, and adequate health records. Not only do practically all secondary schools now provide for physical examinations at least once in the junior high school and once in the senior high school, but there has developed in most schools a much more effective program of obtaining the cooperation of the parents and the students in remedying defects and in improving the weak aspects of health. In a great many schools, professional dental and medical services are available, particularly for students who cannot afford badly needed dental and medical help; indeed, in recent years, a similar type of development has made it possible for a limited use of psychological and psychiatric service by students and the school.

4. *Capable Leadership in Developing and Carrying on a Cooperative Program of Health, Safety, and Physical Education by the School, the Home, and the Community.* The public-health agencies and law-enforcement agencies are directly involved in an adequate health program. The community recreational agencies also have a considerable contribution to make in a program of physical fitness.

There should be developed contact and cooperation among all the local public-health agencies, social agencies, and recreational organizations, for the purpose of coordinating all the resources and activities of the community, including those of the school, for the best possible program.

5. *Care that the Educational Activities of Students, Teachers, and Administrators Contribute to Healthy Personality Development Rather than Mental Ill Health.* This means, among other things, that, in the motivation of learning activities, teachers should stress constructive procedures and rely to a minimum degree upon fear and embarrassment, particularly in cases of students who are already working at or near to their probable capacity. This would apply to the making of assignments, to the administration and interpretation of tests, and to the giving of grades and reports to parents. It would require conferences with students about their work and problems.

6. *A Program of Recreation During the Summer Months, at Little or No Expense for Any Boys and Girls Who Wish To Participate.* The

expansion of summer programs of this sort by school and non-school agencies has been very great since World War II.

7. *A Physical Program Designed in Terms of the Capacities and Interests of All Students.* This means providing a program for both boys and girls, for senior high school students as well as for junior high school students. Such a program would include also a program of limited activities for several classes of boys and girls, such as those with less ability to participate in physical activities and those who are physically incapacitated from participating in normal activities, and a remedial program for those in need of specialized physical activities and exercise.

8. *Adequate Supervision of All Kinds of Competitive or Other Types of Strenuous Sports and Games.* The school should see that students who have weak hearts or other somewhat dangerous limitations do not participate unwisely, and it should provide adequate medical supervision for prompt action in case of injury, sudden illness, or other emergency. This would apply to all sorts of sports, including interscholastic athletics, intramural athletics, and ordinary gymnasium and outdoor play activities of a strenuous nature.

9. *Orientation of Every Teacher of Every Subject in Every Grade with Respect to the Objectives of Physical- and Mental-Health Education and with Respect to the Opportunities Available to Them in the Teaching of Their Subjects.*

10. *A Program of Safety Education that Would Include Training in the Driving of Automobiles and Would Involve the Orientation of All Teachers with Respect to the Possibilities for Education for Safety.* Education for safety is something to which every teacher may make a contribution, particularly instructors in various types of industrial arts and shop work, household arts, arithmetic and general mathematics, and science, as well as coaches and instructors in physical education.

11. *A Program Providing Wholesome Lunches for Students.* This involves a campaign to get all students to eat lunch in the school cafeteria and to see that the school lunches provide a balanced diet. This diet should offer some choice to meet the special needs of youngsters, particularly those who bring a note from home or from a doctor stating that certain foods should be avoided by reason of allergies. Such a program should require the elimination from the school building of dispensers of types of food and drink that would tend to interfere with good diet and good eating habits. It should also involve an attempt to reduce to a minimum, if not eliminate entirely, the eating of lunches at places off the school ground, and to reduce to a small minimum those bringing cold lunches from home. And it should provide opportunities for students of the least economic means to earn enough to pay for their school lunches.

**Possible Contributions Through School Subjects. English.** English is taught by an increasing number of teachers with emphasis upon the study of literature to increase understanding of oneself and in an attempt to reduce the tendency of learners to have unhygienic thinking about themselves and to misinterpret the acts and words of others. Literature can be chosen that may be so taught as to develop understanding of psychological problems, psychologically abnormal individuals, and such things as excessive introversion and daydreaming, unreasonable fears, sense of being unappreciated or persecuted, and the natural tendency for people to rationalize their own unsocial and psychologically unwise behavior.

Likewise, through the discussion of literature and other discussion in English classes, there may be developed normal understandings and attitudes in the area of social relationships between children and parents, between boys and girls, between an individual and his co-workers, and between an individual and his competitors.

Teachers trained in speech who have knowledge of mental hygiene may render a very valuable service to the field of mental health to young people who have speech defects, including stutterers and young people with cleft palates.

**Social Studies.** Maintaining mental and physical health is a matter, not only of individual responsibility and activities, but also, particularly in relation to communicable diseases, sources of food and water supply, and immunization, a matter of social responsibility, wisdom, and effort. Such problems are very natural items for study and discussion in classes in social studies.

Among other topics for such purposes are the following: provisions for adequate hospital and medical care, particularly for those who are unable to pay the normal costs; legislation to regulate the quality and labeling of foods and drugs; legislation for establishment of local, state, and national parks and other facilities for recreation and outdoor life; legislation leading to increased safety on highways, in factories, and in stores; and legislation and social action to prevent the spread of communicable diseases, particularly in slum areas. Young people should have the opportunity and, indeed, the responsibility for a careful study of the various health problems and such proposed solutions as medical, dental, and hospital insurance plans.

**Science.** All science subjects have potentialities for health education. In Junior high school science, much is being learned relative to prevention of infection, first aid, care of the vital organs, rest, recreation, diet, and communicable diseases. Opportunities in biology are prominent and

easy to identify, although some teachers still emphasize what they believe to be preparation for college, rather than preparation for living.

In recent years, there have taken place in biochemistry great developments that enable us to understand the proper care and various functions
of the human body.

Although not taught in many high schools, functional psychology is
very valuable in developing a background for mental hygiene and in
helping personality development. Here, too, is opportunity for young
people to understand the facts and basic principles of psychosomatic
medicine, about which the present generation of adults knows very little
and has many wrong impressions.

**Mathematics.** Possible contributions of algebra, geometry, and trigonometry to physical and mental health and safety are few. However, in
arithmetic and in general mathematics in the junior high schools and
in the general mathematics course offered for juniors and seniors of
many senior high schools, there are frequent opportunities to help students acquire information and understanding that contribute materially
to the possibilities of maintaining safety and health. Much material of
this type is presented through graphs, charts, tables, statistics, statistical
concepts, and formulas, as well as through percentages presented in either
numerical or graphic form. Many fields of health and safety are represented by such materials, including the areas of public health, accident
prevention, and driving safety.

**Home Economics.** Courses in home economics afford excellent opportunities for education in physical and mental health and safety. Learning
materials and activities in home economics may contribute directly to
the preservation of health. Healthful diet and nutrition, home nursing,
child care, household sanitation, first aid, psychological and emotional
problems of human relations, and home safety are among the relevant
topics frequently covered in such courses.

**Music, Art, and Industrial Arts.** Participation of students in the activities
involved in courses in music, art, and the industrial arts will contribute
to good mental health, not only at the time, but in future years, especially
to the extent that students acquire leisure interests and habits in these
areas. Diversion through participation in activities in these areas, as well
as in listening and admiring, has been noted to serve as a "tranquilizer"
for many tense young people. Either as spectators or as participants,
people find that their associations with music, art, industrial arts and,
indeed, to some extent, home economics and physical education afford
opportunities for relaxation that are helpful for both physical and mental
health.

Physical and Health Education. Most of the activities in courses in physical and health education contribute to the development of physical and mental health. Regular moderate exercise contributes definitely to the present and future health of all but a very few people. In physical- and health-education courses and activities, the individual tends to be most conscious of his body, its functions, and the need for caring for it and keeping it in good shape. The human physical organism, when in good condition, is able to resist fatigue and to recover quickly. It is also more likely to be free of infections of various kinds. Participation in physical- and health-education activities causes most students to become more conscious and appreciative of the need for good habits of sleep, rest, and diet.

Other Courses. In many junior high schools, a special course in first aid is given. Indeed, in several states it is required by state law.

In the very large majority of secondary schools of more than two hundred or three hundred students, thus being available to the great majority of secondary school students, are courses in automobile driving. In recent years, there has been a tendency to offer this course twice a year—once during the regular year and once during the summer. Because it seems to lead to reduced insurance rates as well as reduced accident rates, the course has become very popular. In most schools, no credit toward graduation is given. In a few schools, particularly junior high schools, similar courses have been offered in bicycle riding. In a small but increasing number of states, all senior and four-year high schools are required to offer a course in driver education.

Contribution of Sex Education. As a separate course in some schools and also as aspects of a number of subjects in practically all schools, instruction with respect to sex is now being given to the great majority of secondary school students. Sex education is opposed by some adults, both groups and individuals, most of whom do not understand its objectives, materials, or nature.

There is a need for reliable information about venereal disease. Sex education would be incomplete if it did not deal with this problem, its serious threat to health, and the ease with which it is contracted.[1]

**Contributions Through Extracurricular Learning Activities.** Athletics. Participation in sports contributes positively to improvement and maintenance of health in spite of the negative aspect of the current interscholastic athletic program. Participation in various kinds of sports under adequate supervision and with moderation not only contributes to health

---

[1] See "What Parents Must Know About Teen-agers and V.D.," by Dr. Leona Baumgartner, *McCalls*, January, 1963.

and physical vigor at the time but particularly in some sports such as tennis, golf, bowling, and hiking, throughout life as, indeed, the interest developed in competitive sports may make contributions to mental health.

It has come to be accepted as a medical fact that very intensive and vigorous participation in sports for a period of time followed by relative inactivity is dangerous to physical health. The solution perhaps is not so much in avoiding vigorous activities but in developing interests in sports and other physical activities which will make it possible and likely that individuals will taper off to a mild program in middle age to be followed the rest of their life.

**Other Activities.** The activities in many clubs make substantial contributions to physical and mental health and to safety education. Included among such clubs are organizations associated with physical education, arts and crafts, music, first aid, junior red cross, nursing, diet, safety patrol, and traffic.

Where homeroom programs are employed in developing a well-rounded program of education, it is very desirable to include discussion of topics related to first aid, sex education, safety guidance, health and hospital insurance, and the development of good health habits.

Almost any type of student organization that develops interest and provides for self-expression and physical contacts presents good possibilities for contributing to mental health and, indirectly, to physical health.

## EDUCATION FOR HOME LIVING

**The Need Today. Importance of Home Living.** The family in practically all societies, and especially in the American society, has been the basic and principal unit of social structure. It plays a very important part in our economic life, in health, and in education, and, indeed, it is a major factor in the happiness or unhappiness of the great majority of individuals. Psychiatrists, social workers, personnel workers, police authorities, and judges are rather unanimous in the judgment that, among the greatest causes of emotional disturbances and mental illness, ephemeral or permanent, real or imaginary, as well as being one of the important factors in crime and in physical illness, are conditions that exist and problems that develop in the home. Maladjustments in the home contribute heavily to labor turnover, absenteeism, alcoholism, periods of lowered efficiency, and serious physical injury resulting from machinery.

Those who have been in contact with delinquents testify that broken homes and other important problems of family life including working mothers, drinking parents, and emotionally unstable parents have been major factors in the great majority of incidences of crime and serious immorality on the part of children and adolescents, phenomena that have mushroomed alarmingly in the past few decades.

**Family Life and Health.** Family and home living constitutes the first line of defense against disease and injury, the major context in the treatment of injuries and the nursing of the ill, and the principal area in which to work to ensure maintenance of health through proper diet and rest. This has become increasingly true as hospital and medical costs have sky-rocketed in recent decades.

**Deterioration of the American Home.** In recent years, sociologists, ministers, and writers have predicted that, if certain present trends are not corrected, the American home and the family as a social unit are on the way to dissolution. While it may be attributed in part to the less unfavorable attitudes of people toward divorce and the increased opportunity for women to earn their own living, there has been a very marked increase in the number of divorces in recent years, particularly among young people below the age of twenty-five. There have also been great increases in the numbers of married people who have killed their mates, of young parents who neglect, abuse, or destroy their children, of teenagers who kill one or both parents, of suicides growing out of depressing marital relationships, and of incidences of unfaithfulness and adultery—all signs of the deterioration of human relations in the home.

**Increased Need for Consumer Education.** As compared to those of two or more generations ago, people today produce a relatively small proportion of their food in the home and do a relatively small proportion of the maintenance and repair of things about the home. Even in the preparation of food, only a fraction of the time and knowledge formerly needed is necessary for the modern family. A very great amount of food consumed in homes today has been prepared or "pre-prepared" before purchase. Very little of the clothing or furniture found in homes today has been made there.

Along with the increased responsibility for purchasing that confronts everyone today, there has developed a great amount of very seductive advertising to influence purchases. The talents of artists, musicians, and writers are employed to influence the buying decisions, wise and unwise, of consumers, particularly of the younger generation. While business concerns, doctors, and labor unions are powerfully represented by lobbies and influences in Washington and elsewhere, the consumer is, indeed, almost a forgotten man.

**Home and Leisure Activities.** There is a distinct challenge in the schools today to develop in young people interest in types of leisure pursuits that will tend to bind the family together and constitute pleasant and wholesome leisure activities in the home, along the lines of handicrafts; arts; music appreciation; singing; playing of instruments; discussions of current political, social, and economic affairs; care and repair of the home, home appliances, clothing, and automobiles; vegetable gardening; landscaping; reading of middle-grade and better books and periodicals, including fiction and semipopular treatises and discussions of economic, sociological, scientific, psychological, and philosophical topics and problems. To this end, teachers' of almost all subjects can and should make valuable contributions.

**Courses in Home Living.** The Senior Course. In a considerable number of secondary schools, there is now being given a semester or year course in family living, for eleventh- through twelfth-grade boys and girls. As it is ordinarily offered, it includes, among others, the following major topics: (1) understanding oneself, (2) child growth characteristics and needs, (3) the social functions of the family, (4) selecting a suitable mate, (5) factors that determine the degree of success or lack of success of marriage, (6) the responsibilities that come with married life, (7) planning and using a family income, (8) decorating and furnishing a home, (9) leisure and social activities within the home.

Other Courses. On page 125 is a typical outline of other courses, with major points of emphasis and clues to content.

**Education for Home Living Through Other Subjects.** Science. Since the health of the individual members of the family is one of the major factors in home living, instructors in science may make very valuable contributions in connection with nutrition, physiology, and hygiene. In science courses, too, much information may be given about drugs and their effects on the body and mind and about various types of diseases. Through science courses, also, much valuable information may be given that leads to greater safety in the home, particularly with reference to dust and gas explosion, spontaneous combustion, and asphyxiation.

Much can be and is done in most courses in the field of consumer education. For example, scientific facts can be communicated relative to water and food supply; the preparation and storage of food; treatment and disposal of sewage; the basic principles of physics involved with various kinds of machines including household appliances and the automobile, to air conditioning, refrigeration, radio and television, and other electric machines; and physics of heat and light as it is applied to heating equipment, electric lighting, electric and gas stoves, and so forth.

Through courses in psychology, much may be done in the way of education of the whole person. The functional type of course given in many high schools goes into the matters of good social relationships and mental, emotional, and social growth toward adjustment and social well-

SUGGESTED UNITS FOR EACH YEAR OF HOMEMAKING (by number of weeks)

| Grade | Family relations | Child guidance | Housing | Health | Management & consumer education | Food | Clothing |
|---|---|---|---|---|---|---|---|
| 7th | You and your friends, 3–4; fun for families and guests, 4 | Helping to care for younger children, 3 | Helping with the care of the house, 2–3 | | | Learning to cook, 8–10 | Learning to sew, 8–10 |
| 8th | You and your family, 2–3 | | Improving your home, 4 | When there is sickness in the home, 3–4 | Your family's money, 3 | | |
| 9th | Growing up happily, 2–3 | The child at play, 4–5 | The attractive bedroom, 3 | | Managing personal resources, 2–3 | Simple family meals, 9–10 | A pleasing appearance, 4; clothing for yourself |
| 10th | Getting along with your family and friends, 3–4 | Understanding and guiding the growing child, 3–4 | The livable home, 5–6 | Keeping the family well, 2–3 | The young consumer, 2–3 | The family's food, 9–10 | Being attractively dressed, 8–10 |
| 11th and 12th | Looking toward marriage, 3–4 | A child in the home, 4–6 | Planning for the home, 5–6 | Home care of the sick, 4–6 | | Food for fun, folks, and families, 8–10 | Special clothing problems, 8–9 |
| General for older boys and girls | Preparation for marriage, 4 | Living with children, 3–4 | A home to enjoy, 10–14 | | Wise spending for better living, 3–4 | Selection and preparation of food, 4–6 | Clothing for the family, 6–8 |

SOURCE: Berenice Malloy and Mary Laxton Buffum, *Education for Homemaking in the Secondary Schools of the United States* (Washington, D.C.: U.S. Department of Health, Education, and Welfare, 1958), Special Series No. 4, p. 9.

being, particularly among infants and children, and thus contributes to the efficiency of future parents in child rearing. The psychology of marriage relations also is usually treated in such courses.

**Arts and Crafts.** One of the major functions of arts and crafts of the non-vocational type is to provide training along certain lines that are very valuable for home membership. Among them the following may be listed: (1) acquaintanceship with, and skill in using, common tools, machines, and construction methods; (2) ability to make and to read drawings, charts, and graphs in planning construction work; (3) ability to judge quality and design in the products of industry; (4) knowledge and skills relating to care of a variety of types of things found in the home, such as ability in oiling a motor, sharpening a knife, repairing electrical circuits, and repairing furniture, and (5) a good sense of proportion in color harmony, interest in home furnishings of pleasing appearance, interest in, and taste for, an attractive home exterior, skills and taste for one or more arts and crafts activities, for example, woodworking, water color, painting, and metalworking.

**English.** Through study of literature led by an alert teacher with a good background in human behavior, much may be learned from characters in fiction, biography, and history, particularly with reference to the behavior, human relations, growth, and problems of the various age groups. As a result of study and discussion of personality traits of individuals, students in literature may grow in their understanding of those attributes of an attractive person that make one liked, respected, and easy to live with, as well as in their understanding of what makes an unpopular or ineffective person. All through junior and senior high school, boys and girls acquire from the study of literature and from related discussions a better understanding of themselves, their problems, and their behavior as home members, as well as a better understanding of their parents, brothers, and sisters, and of their behavior.

By participation in writing of themes and oral expression in class, students improve their ability to express themselves clearly, fluently, effectively, and attractively in words and thus increase their proficiency in communication with other members of the home. There is also opportunity to discuss such matters as politeness, courtesy, thoughtfulness, and diplomacy in conversation and discussion, particularly as they apply to home situations.

In English, there are opportunities to develop certain aspects of reading ability that contribute to home living, including the following: (1) the cultivation of reading interests as a means of pleasurable leisure pursuit and of enriching the background for frequent casual discussions of matters of interest to two or more members of the family and (2) the development of reading habits and skills that enable the student to acquire quickly and accurately the information and meaning from the printed page, having to do with problems in the home, that may be found, for example, in many magazine and newspaper articles and advertisements. The increased emphasis upon training in listening also definitely contributes to better home relationships and to development of the more admirable qualities on the part of people so trained.

**Social Studies.** Courses in social studies may make valuable contributions to preparation for home living that augment and reinforce educational experiences in other subjects. Because of the social studies, students are more able to grasp the concepts of (1) the family as the basic social institution, (2) the impact of various current trends and forces that tend to change the nature of the home, and (3) the nature of the more important disruptive influences and developments.

There is also an excellent opportunity in social studies classes for conveying information about ways in which society may attempt to control communicable disease, to increase safety from traffic and other accidents, to provide public recreation, to provide protection from impure and dangerous foods and medicine, and to provide highways, sewage disposal, pure water supply, fire protection, basic medical service, and many other requirements.

There is also ample opportunity in social studies classes for the discussion of current laws and proposed legislation relative to divorce, protection of children, education, sanitation, and building zoning, as well as opportunity for learning valuable things about the economic and business side of family living, for example, about social security, investments, insurance, borrowing, home ownership, allowances, savings, quality grade and weight of goods, budgeting, and sources of consumer information.

**Mathematics.** As is the case with respect to education for certain other areas of everyday life, the contributions of mathematics to education for home living are made largely through junior high school mathematics—arithmetic and general mathematics—and through the general mathematics course offered to juniors and seniors in secondary schools. Problem areas in which valuable contributions to education for home living may be made in mathematics courses include the following:

1. Problems related to planning the home, such as designing, landscaping, use of plans and scaled drawings, symmetry and proportion, and geometric design
2. Problems related to financing the home—calculation of interest; comparing cost of renting, buying, and selling; construction of budgets; bank transactions such as discounts and the like; cost of

consumer credit (instalment buying); rate of return on stocks, bonds, rentals, and loans; and plans for financial security through insurance, retirement allowances, medical and hospital services, and social security

3. Problems related to building a home, involving calculation of areas and volumes, board measure, use of formulas and graphs, formulating home operating expenses including cost of operating electric appliances, cost of fuels, computation of taxes of various kinds, and safety and accident prevention

4. Problems related to buying, including cost per ounce or pound of packages, economy-size buying, and adaptation of recipes to families of different sizes

5. Problems related to recreation, for example, planning the vacation trip and its cost, and costs of owning and operating an automobile

**Music.** In recent years, many children of secondary school age have been learning to sing and to play an instrument. This affords opportunities of family group music including duets, quartets, singing or playing with accompanists, etc. Perhaps of even greater value in the way of education for family living is the development of common interests in the appreciation of music which is so plentiful today in the forms of records, concerts, and television and radio programs.

**Business Subjects.** Valuable training for home living may be given in a number of business subjects including bookkeeping, typing, business arithmetic, business law, and, most important of all, the junior, or general, business course offered in many junior high schools.

**Physical and Health Education.** As was pointed out earlier in this volume, one of the principal contributions of home living is that connected with health, first aid, and home nursing. Through physical-health education, much may be learned about eating, sleeping, and other personal habits, but, to be really effective, this knowledge must be accompanied by the development of desirable everyday habits.

**Contributions Through Extracurricular Learning Activities.** Many of the clubs and student organizations in secondary schools may be so managed as to make valuable contributions to education for home living. Coming to mind first, of course, are future homemakers' and home-management clubs, but there are many others in which there are valuable opportunities.

In most schools where homerooms are provided, there are discussions of many topics that relate to home living, including dating, choosing a mate, marriage, "buymanship," thoughtfulness toward others, and personal appearance (involving matters of dress, cosmetics, coiffures, etc.).

In practically all clubs there is opportunity for the development of those attitudes, skills, and habits that have to do with cooperative group work.

Counseling. Increasingly, in recent years, counselors have been discovering that many of the problems about which young people need counseling and help are related to living in the home. Very serious for many youngsters are the problems growing out of the relationship to parents, discipline, standards and rules for young people of different ages, personal living habits, marital relations between their parents, relationships with older or younger brothers and sisters, and religion.

## QUESTIONS, PROBLEMS, AND TOPICS FOR FURTHER STUDY

1. How might the classroom teacher negatively influence the mental health of the students in his or her classes?
2. In what ways may a teacher of your subject of specialization contribute to education for good physical and mental health? (Add something to what is given in the chapter.) Which of these ways is most important?
3. Be able to give a four- or five-minute talk in class on the relationship between athletics and education for mental and physical health.
4. Select some student activity commonly sponsored in high school, and discuss it from the point of view of its possible contribution to mental and physical health.
5. What do you think are the main reasons for the increased number of people who suffer ill health?
6. Write a paper of some 800 to 1,200 words or give a six- to eight-minute talk on the mental health of the teacher, its importance, and how it may be maintained.
7. Do you believe that schools should provide free medical and dental service to students who are suffering health difficulties?
8. Be ready to give in class a seven- or eight-minute talk on what the school can do to educate students better as consumers.
9. There are people who argue that preparation for home living should be provided by the home and not by the school. What is your opinion, and why?
10. If you were planning a course on marriage and home living for seniors in high school, what would you emphasize in that course?
11. What phases of home living should be studied by boys in high school?
12. Do you believe that any course in home living should be required of all girls? If so, what should be the content of instruction, and at what age or grade level should it be offered?
13. What do you think a teacher of your subject of specialization can do in the way of contributing to education for home living?

## SUPPLEMENTARY MATERIALS

### Selected Readings

Bent, Rudyard K., and Henry H. Kronenberg. *Principles of Secondary Education* (4th ed.). New York: McGraw-Hill Book Co., Inc., 1961. Pp. 319–23.

FORKNER, HAMDEN L. "Educating for the Daily Business of Living," *NEA Journal*, XLII (December, 1953), 565–66.

MALLORY, BERENICE, and MARY LAXSON BUFFUM. *Education for Homemaking in the Secondary Schools of the United States*. Washington, D.C.: Office of Education, U.S. Department of Health, Education, and Welfare, 1955.

PARKER, J. CECIL, T. BENTLEY EDWARDS, and WILLIAM H. STEGEMAN. *Curriculum in America*. New York: Thomas Y. Crowell Co., 1962. Chapter 12, "Health and Physical Education."

SOUTHARD, WILLIAM M. "Mechanics for Homemakers," *The Education Digest*, XXVIII (September, 1962), 48–50.

# III

## TEACHING AND
## LEARNING MATERIALS

# 8

# The Materials for Learning Activities

With respect to the adaptation of the curriculum to the needs and conditions of the times, there has always been an important lag. In the first place, the high school curriculum in this country was patterned after that of European countries, and the process of adapting it to the needs of this country has been slow, though continuous and progressive. This has not only been true of the subjects offered in the high school and the requirements for graduation, it has been even more true with respect to the content of the subjects.

In the past few years, there have been very significant changes in the conditions and problems of life in the United States as well as abroad, particularly with respect to international relations and economic problems. The changes that have had important implications for education have been so profound and so rapid that the gap between the curriculum and the curriculum needs has increased and now challenges very seriously the attention of broad-minded and clear-thinking educators. As Alice said in *Alice in Wonderland,* "We have to run ever so fast to stay where we are."

## CURRICULUM TERMINOLOGY

**Terminology Confusion.** There was no standard terminology in writings and discussions on the curriculum of the schools. Different individuals used the same terms with different meanings and used different terms for the same concept. Naturally there was much confusion. Many writers and speakers use the word "curriculum" to mean all of the learning materials and experiences of the students, including the so-called extra-curricular activities, while many others continue to use the word "curriculum" to refer to the content of the subjects offered in the school. "Curriculum" has still a third meaning in that it is used quite regularly to mean a collection of subjects studied by a group of students with a particular objective in mind, for example, the agriculture curriculum, the auto mechanics curriculum, and the secretarial curriculum.

**Current Usage.** Before entering upon discussions of Learning materials, we need to specify what the various terms mean. Following are definitions of terms that seem to have widespread use among students of secondary education:

1. *Course of study:* detailed materials and activities planned to be employed for a given subject in a given field, such as the course of study for English II, for plane geometry, or for beginning physics

2. *Program of studies:* list of all the subjects offered by the school, arranged in the order of the years, e.g., for the seventh grade, the eighth grade, and the ninth grade in the junior high school

3. *Constants,* or *requireds:* terms used to designate the subjects required for graduation

4. *Electives:* courses not required; may include *free electives* and *limited electives* between which the student has a limited choice

5. *Unit of credit* (sometimes called *Carnegie unit*): the amount of credit given toward graduation for completing with a passing grade a subject for a year in a class that meets at least 200 minutes a week with outside preparation (e.g., one unit of credit is ordinarily given for a year of elementary algebra. In some schools semester units are employed—two semester units being equivalent to one unit)

6. *Core program:* integration of two or more subjects meeting in a larger block of time on the school program, with the learning materials and activities organized around problems of the students rather than in a logical subject-matter organization

7. *Unified,* or *large-block, program:* a plan in which two or more subjects are taught together in a long class period but are not integrated around problems (The most common of these is the combination and close correlation of English and the social studies.)

8. *General education,* or *common learnings:* learnings that are very desirable for all adolescents

9. *Fusion:* a combination of somewhat related school subjects, such as a fusion of literature and language or of English and the social studies

10. *Extracurriculum, cocurriculum, the third curriculum, student organizations,* and *extrasubject learning activities:* terms used to

refer to the organizations and activities of the students that are not regularly scheduled subjects for credit, including clubs, student council, and teams

11. *Student program:* the subjects that a student is carrying at a particular time, and the hours of the day and days of the week in which there are class meetings

12. *Subject:* a specific area of learning within a field, e.g., plane geometry in the field of mathematics, or economics or civics in the field of social studies.

13. *Broad fields:* a combination, usually a fusion, of two or more subjects closely related, such as English and speech, the various divisions of science in general science, or the social studies

14. *Curriculum prescription:* a subject that is not required of all students in the school but is required of all students in a given curriculum, e.g., typewriting in a secretarial curriculum

15. *Correlation plan:* teaching of two or more subjects at separate periods of the day but with simultaneous correlation between them, e.g., between the history and the literature of a certain period

16. *Experience curriculum:* a course of study that is organized as far as possible around the experiences and current problems of the students in the class

## TEXTBOOK MATERIALS

**Usefulness of Textbooks.** Secondary school teachers tend to rely heavily upon textbooks. Although in recent years the great majority of teachers have been employing a wealth of supplementary materials in addition to the textbook, the textbook continues to be the basis of most secondary school teaching and is marked by, among others, the following attributes:

1. It provides an outline that the teacher may, with appropriate modifications, employ in planning the work for the semester or the year.

2. It brings together in one volume an abundance of material that would require much effort on the part of the teacher or student to find otherwise.

3. It usually contains very useful aids such as pictures, charts, diagrams, questions, maps, problems, summaries, outlines, headings, exercises, and tables.

4. It permits the student to take home with him much of the material constituting the subject of study.

5. It serves as a permanent record for the teacher's reference in the course, particularly in connection with reviews.

6. It facilitates the making of assignments, although, to be sure, too many teachers make assignments too much in terms of the materials in the textbook rather than in terms of learning activities to be done in connection with them.
7. It relieves the teacher of responsibility for selecting and evaluating a great amount of materials for the course.
8. It provides a logical organization for use when the teacher is not able or does not have the time to plan a better organization of learning materials.

**Suggestions for Using Textbooks.** In using a textbook there are several important considerations that better teachers observe rather regularly. Among those are the following:

1. The textbook needs to be supplemented by explanations, discusions, collateral reading from the library and elsewhere, and other learning activities of a wide variety, particularly emphasizing the use and application of the textbook material.

2. The teacher should avoid the tendency to rely heavily upon recitation of textbook material as the major class activity of pupils.

3. Pupils need to be taught how to use the various aids including the Index, study questions, pictures, graphs, statistical tables, and headings.

4. Perhaps most important of all, the textbook needs to be supplemented with other materials and must be employed in such a way as to make a major contribution to the objectives of the course and of secondary education. It should be remembered that textbooks are written two or three years before their publication and, in some fields, in this age of knowledge explosion, quickly become out of date.

**Selection of Textbooks.** In recent years, teachers have come to play a larger part in the selection of textbooks, being permitted either to select textbooks for their own courses or to serve as members of committees to select textbooks for use in the courses taught by the teachers of the subject in the school or the school district. Since so much depends upon the textbook, most teachers naturally exercise great care in their selection. Among the important criteria to be kept in mind by teachers are the following:

1. The textbook should be examined in terms of its possible contribution to the educational outcomes of the course in which it is to be employed—its possibilities for assisting the student to acquire desired information, understandings, skills, habits, attitudes, interests, and ideals.

2. Textbooks under consideration should be examined very carefully to note the degree to which they contain most of the materials the teacher

would want to employ and the degree to which they are organized in a way that will contribute to understanding and retention by the students.

3. The textbook should be evaluated in terms of (a) accuracy of content, (b) relative emphasis and topics, (c) degree to which vocabulary is appropriate to students who will use it, (d) clearness and simplicity of sentence and paragraph structure and of introduction of new ideas, (e) attractiveness of style—interest-provoking qualities, (f) quality and number of learning aids such as pictures, diagrams, boldface headings, and italics, (g) quality and number of questions, exercises, and problems suggested for use in teaching and learning, (h) degree to which quality of the textbook has been brought up to date (this is particularly important in these years in the fields of science, history, and the social studies), (i) attractiveness of format, and (j) character of special provisions for bright and slow students.

## PROGRAMED MATERIALS

**Nature of Programed Materials.** In recent years, there has been a materially increased use of what have come to be called "programed materials." Programed materials, of course, are employed in connection with the so-called teaching machines, but they are also employed separately in the forms of "scrambled books" and other books resembling textbooks. The distinguishing and principal characteristics of a book of programed materials are the sequential nature of the materials and the use of devices to inform learners of the correctness of their response. It is claimed by some that programed materials facilitate provision for differences between students with respect to the speed with which they learn materials. The student may go on to the next item as soon as he has given indication of "knowing" one set of materials.

In all likelihood, programed materials will not be widely used at least for some time to come, for the following reasons: (1) Their use tends to emphasize the acquisition of facts to the neglect of other equally important educational outcomes. (2) This type of provision for individual differences is not the best, because it seems more desirable to offer bright students materials that differ from those assigned to slow students than merely to provide for differences in speed in going through a standard set of materials. (3) Most of the programed books are still in the experimental stage and are not as effective teaching tools as textbooks that have grown out of many years of study and experimentation. They need to be greatly improved. Following are questions that should be thought about in considering programed materials.

Criteria for Evaluating Programed Materials

1. What is the scope and sequence of programs which you have available for distribution at present and what other programs are you preparing?
2. What is the intended student population and what prerequisite courses (if any) are required for each of your programs?
3. Approximately how much time is required by the average student in a given grade to complete each different program?
4. Where will we find information about the qualifications of the authors of each of your programs?
5. Are the general aims and specific objectives of each program indicated in the unit or course description?
6. What is the reading ability level required for each program and how has this been determined?
7. How and where was each program tested?
8. Where in our geographical region have your programs been used and where in this vicinity are they being used at present?
9. Are your programs available in both "machine" and "programed text" formats?
10. What is the form of response required for each of your programs?
11. Are your programs designed to be used with separate answer sheets and are these supplied?
12. Is there a teacher's manual or guidebook for each program containing references, supplementary information, and suggestions for the use of other enrichment materials?
13. Do pre-tests, progress tests, and final tests accompany each program?
14. Are the tests provided diagnostic tests or achievement tests?
15. Are test-results norms tables available?
16. Which standardized tests may be used effectively with your programs?
17. Are your programs in mathematics and science based on "modern" mathematics and science concepts or are they traditional in nature?
18. Do you provide forms for recording student progress, achievement, and reactions?
19. What is the cost per frame and/or the cost per instructional hour for each of your programs?
20. And, finally, do you supply programs at discount prices for schools interested in pilot-study projects and research?[1]

**Programed-Material Terminology.** Following are definitions of terms being used in connection with programed instruction:

*Program:* A sequence of carefully constructed items leading the student to mastery of the subject with minimal error. Information is given to the student in small units to which he responds in some way—by completing a sentence, working a problem, or answering a question. Items are designed so that the student can make correct responses while progressing toward more and more complex material.

*Teaching Machine:* A device for presenting programs.

[1] From "Programmed Learning—20 Questions," by John R. Belton. *The Bulletin, N.A.S.S.P.,* Vol. 46, No. 278 (December, 1962), pp. 77–78.

*Frame or Item:* A self-contained question or statement in a program; it may or may not present new information. A frame may call for one or more responses. It may be more than one sentence long, its length being determined by the capacities of the students and the nature of the subject matter.

*Cue:* An aspect of a frame which helps (ideally forces) a student to answer the question correctly.

*Reinforcement:* Any stimulus which increases the probability that the immediately preceding response will occur again under similar circumstances. This is what is said to occur when the student sees the correct answer after he has made the appropriate response. Because it is reinforced, this correct response is more likely to occur in the future, i.e., it is "learned."[2]

## OTHER PRINTED MATERIALS

**Criteria for Selection.** Somewhat the same type of criteria is kept in mind by the expert teacher in selecting pamphlets, bulletins, newspapers, periodicals, and other printed materials for purposes of teaching, although biased materials are used by many teachers in connection with discussions of controversial issues and comparisons of different points of view.

Following is a statement of the criteria and procedures used in selecting printed materials other than textbooks in the Denver, Colorado, schools:

CRITERIA FOR THE SELECTION OF MATERIAL OTHER THAN TEXTBOOKS

(A) Authorship
    (1) The writer is competent to write in this field.
    (2) So far as can be ascertained, the writer supports the principles of American constitutional government.
(B) Material
    (1) No material expressing partisan, sectarian, sectional, or factional bias shall be used unless such bias is openly expressed and supported by objective data.
    (2) Material shall treat with respect all differing views presented to the students.
    (3) The conclusions presented in the material shall be supportable by evidence.
    (4) Material shall be in good taste and conform to generally accepted moral standards and spiritual values.

PROCEDURES FOR THE SELECTION OF MATERIAL OTHER THAN TEXTBOOKS

(A) Material other than textbooks must be evaluated in terms of the above criteria by the person or committee in the school ordering the material. Such evaluation may be by means of reading the material or through careful consideration of reliable sources of information, including reviews, books [sic] lists, and other aids.

[2] Published by The Center for Programed Instruction, Inc. See the April, 1961, issue of *Audio-visual Education,* for a much longer list of definitions of terms, including many new ones.

(B)   On orders for materials other than textbooks the signature of the person making or approving the order signifies that, according to his judgment and best knowledge at the time, the material meets the above criteria unless the statement of exception (see paragraph C below) accompanies the order.

(C)   If the material being ordered has special educational value and is to be used on a limited basis only, but does not meet the criteria in every respect, the following statement of exception must be completed and must accompany the order:

The material requested on the attached order does not meet the criteria for selection of material other than textbooks in the following respects:
. . . . . . . . . . . . . . . . . . . . . . . . . . . . . . . . . . . . . . . . . . . . . . . . . . . . . . . . . . . .

The material has special educational value, however, and will be used only on the following basis:
. . . . . . . . . . . . . . . . . . . . . . . . . . . . . . . . . . . . . . . . . . . . . . . . . . . . . . . . . . . .

The statement of exception must carry the signatures of the persons initiating and making the order and the signatures of the persons approving the order. This material shall be so marked as to indicate its limited area of usefulness.

(D)   Orders for material that does not meet the criteria in every respect must have the approval of the Director of Library Services and the Director of Instruction.

(E)   If for any reason questions are raised concerning such material, the Superintendent of Schools shall refer the questions raised to the reviewing committee herein provided for consideration and recommendation.

## AUDIO-VISUAL MATERIALS AND COMMUNITY RESOURCES

**Audio-Visual Materials.**[3] As was pointed out in Chapter 2, there has been a very great increase in the use of audio-visual materials in recent years. Among the types of visual aids employed by many teachers today are the following:

1. Projected pictures such as silent films, film strips, slides, and films with sound tracks may be available in the instructional-materials center of the local school or school system or may be rented or borrowed from a college or university in the state or from some commercial firm dealing in them. The overhead projector is used much more than formerly, especially with large groups. Better machines are now available for projection of opaque materials such as drawings and pictures in books and magazines; consequently, they are used increasingly.

2. Unprojected visual materials such as photographs; prints; paintings; pictures in newspapers, journals, and books; cartoons; charts; diagrams; graphs; maps; and posters are available.

[3] Discussion of procedures for use of audio-visual materials will be found in Chapter 13.

3. Televised materials and radio programs, via closed circuit and from outside, have become much more widely used than formerly. There are now several libraries of televised materials including video-taped courses. Information about these may be obtained by writing to the National Instructional Television Library, National Educational Television and Radio Center, New York, N.Y.; the Great Plains Regional Instructional Television Library, University of Nebraska, Lincoln, Neb.; or the Northeastern Instructional Television Library, Eastern Educational Network, Cambridge, Mass.

4. Objects, models, and specimens such as biological specimens, dioramas, working models, and exhibits in museums, as well as dramatizations, demonstrations, experiments and school excursions are types of visual aids that are employed to a great extent by superior teachers.

**Selecting Radio and TV Programs.** Not only should teachers of most subjects make at least some use of radio and television programs broadcast in their community, but they should be thoughtful in the selection of programs. Mills and Douglass have set up the following criteria for that purpose:

1. Are the purposes of the program in keeping with the objectives of the unit or course? In an English-language course of which correct pronunciation or good diction is one of the desired outcomes, the ability of the speaker or actors in these matters is important. If appreciation of drama or music is one of the outcomes sought, the nature of the production and the quality of the performance are essential criteria for selection.

2. Is the program relevant to the immediate learning activities of the class? If the class is in the initial stages of the study of a topic, the chief value of the program may be that of motivation. In the study stage of the topic on which students are assembling information, a radio program that presents factual material pertaining to the topic is desirable. In the culminating stages of the study of a topic, the radio program may serve as a climax to the students' activities.

3. Are the content and the manner of presentation such as will appeal to the interests of the class? The vocabulary and style of the presentation should be adapted to the abilities of the students. The character of the material should be such that it can be adapted for effective presentation on the radio. The presentation of the program should meet a high standard of excellence. The use of maps and supplementary reading materials and the study of unfamiliar words in the broadcast are effective methods of adapting the program to the abilities of the students.

4. Is the length of the program appropriate? The age and maturity of students are important considerations in making this decision. If the broadcast is too long, many of the important values of the program will

THE PERCENTAGES OF SECONDARY SCHOOLS USING OR EXPECTING TO USE
TO DIFFERENT EXTENTS CERTAIN TYPES OF AUDIO-VISUAL
AIDS

| Amount of Use | Films and Filmstrips | Language Laboratories | Tape Re-corders | Teaching Machines | TV Programs |
|---|---|---|---|---|---|
| 1955–1956 | | | | | |
| Much use | 24% | 0% | 6% | 0% | 1% |
| Some use | 72 | 6 | 70 | 5 | 17 |
| No use | 4 | 94 | 24 | 95 | 82 |
| 1960–1961 | | | | | |
| Much use | 58 | 9 | 33 | 1 | 3 |
| Some use | 41 | 26 | 63 | 12 | 48 |
| No use | 1 | 65 | 4 | 87 | 49 |
| 1965–1966 (est.) | | | | | |
| Much use | 75 | 40 | 60 | 10 | 21 |
| Some use | 24 | 43 | 39 | 55 | 65 |
| No use | 1 | 17 | 1 | 35 | 14 |

SOURCE: The National Education Association, *The Principals Look at the Schools,*
National Education Association Project on Instruction (April, 1962), p. 21.

be lost. The length of the program in relation to the length of the class
period also should be considered. In many instances, the optimum value
of a radio program can be attained only when it is followed by a discussion in which the students and the teacher participate.

5. Is the time of the broadcast suitable? Except in the case of a spot
program of considerable current significance, the radio programs selected
should not interrupt the daily schedule too seriously. However, the value
of the program, rather than its adjustment to a fixed schedule, should be
the determining factor. In this connection, schools encounter one of their
main difficulties in the use of commercial-station broadcasts. The recording of radio programs for rebroadcast at more appropriate times is one
solution to this problem. School-owned broadcasting stations can plan
their programs to fit the instructional schedule of the different classes and
schools; or they may repeat certain programs.

Teachers interested in using radio and television programs should
receive from the local broadcasters several weeks in advance, whenever
possible, a tentative schedule for the programs and should then plan the
use that may be made of them.

**Resources for Projected Materials.** Every reasonable large secondary
school is now equipped with at least one projection machine, and many
have a variety and several of each type. In most larger secondary schools,
there is a member of the staff who is in charge of audio-visual aids and

stands ready to assist the teacher in learning how to operate the machines and in becoming acquainted with materials available locally for his or her use.

A number of the commercial companies and the great majority of educational institutions preparing teachers have film-rental libraries from which films with or without sound tracks may be borrowed at very little cost, usually for no more than transportation expenses.

Not only do most visual materials provide for saving of time, since so much can be expressed so quickly, but usually they are of more interest to students than printed materials. Experimentation has repeatedly shown that, when appropriate visual materials are presented with the better instructional techniques, not only is the understanding more thorough, but the material is retained longer.

In most secondary schools today, there are special rooms for the pre-viewing of various films, so that the teacher can decide whether he wishes to use it and can plan the preparation of the learners for viewing of the film. In an increasing number of schools, there is a curriculum-materials center in which audio-visual materials, as well as a great variety of printed materials, are catalogued and available.

**Community Resources for Learning Materials.** In recent years, there has been a greatly increased use of community resources for the purpose of education. In the community, it is usually possible to find good mate-rials for use in connection with teaching and learning, materials that give more reality and provide more interest on the part of the learners. Furthermore, this affords an opportunity to learn the uses and applica-tions of the subject matter in various activities of life. In recent years, school buses have been made more and more available for conveying students on trips in the community for observations in connection with their classes. Beginning teachers may learn from other teachers who have been longer in the community the most appropriate places for learning excursions. In many schools, a record of community resources, usually indexed by subject, has been built up and made available to teachers. Typical visits that have been used with success by teachers are listed below under the fields to which they are appropriate.

1. *Art:* dwellings; commercial and public buildings and landscap-ing; exhibitions; meritorious pictures and pieces of sculpture in private homes and public buildings; local scenery
2. *Business subjects:* local places of business, including banks, trans-portation offices, and telephone and telegraph offices—for viewing of records and for other activities
3. *English:* movies; offices of local publications; public addresses of various types; public library; radio stations

4. *Science:* farms, greenhouses, nurseries, floral life, and animal life; industries employing scientific principles; industrial plants where principles of chemistry, physics, or bacteriology are employed; local water supply; community health centers; dairies

5. *Foreign languages:* homes of inhabitants of the community who speak the pertinent language

6. *History and social studies:* buildings or other points of historic interest; museums; files of newspapers; public offices and agencies, such as courts, city councils, and school-board meetings; penal or correctional institutions; public meetings and addresses on political or economic subjects; substandard housing sites; welfare agencies, chambers of commerce, and other community organizations; labor unions; hospitals and homes for the aged and handicapped; centers of supervision of local health laws

7. *Home economics:* grocery, dry-goods, clothing and household-appliance stores; homes; hotels and restaurants; nursery schools; local markets

8. *Industrial arts:* shops, factories, or other places where the arts studied are being practiced and where processes and conditions of work may be observed

9. *Mathematics:* various places in which may be seen geometric designs; sites of various situations on which measurements and problems involving computation may be based; where prices of goods may be found; places where instalment-buying and small-loan figures may be found.

10. *Music:* performances by professional or amateur musicians

Somewhat the same techniques must be employed with field trips and excursions as with the use of film. The teacher should

1. Be familiar with the place to which the class will go
2. Think through its possibilities as educational material
3. Plan a procedure for the trip, including what the teacher might do to be sure the student gets the most effective educational experience from the excursion
4. Plan a follow-up including explanations and discussion and a checkup on what the students learned

Students are often expected to do a certain amount of preliminary discussion and related reading before making the trip.

**Lectures and Discussions.** Analyses of the use and discussion of the techniques of the lecture and the management of discussion groups are given in Chapter 13 of this volume.

**Human Resources in the Community.** For many subjects, there are in most communities individuals who may be utilized as excellent sources of learning experiences for students. These may be brought into the class to talk, or committees of students may interview them and report back to class. In any instance, both the students and the individual in the community must be given some information and coaching by the instructor.

## THE EDUCATIONAL FUNCTION OF LEARNING MATERIALS

**Relation to Educational Objectives.** While there are still many teachers who believe that certain bodies of subject matter should be taught to young people for whatever educational results may be achieved by so doing, there have been over the years an increasing number who think of curriculum or learning materials as means to an end—the objectives of the subject field and of secondary education in general.

According to the latter and more modern and more widely held view, the materials in the courses of study should be selected, organized, and taught in the way that will result in the greatest contribution to the important types of growth that, in turn, are developed, so that the learners may function well in life as members of the home, in making a living, in their leisure, in connection with maintenance of mental and physical health, as effective citizens, and in continuing to learn.

To select and plan the teaching of learning materials in this fashion is a very complicated but necessary task of the teacher who wishes to be a truly superior educator. The more advanced and more modern teachers regard teaching as a highly developed art and not as a trade.

**Subject-Matter and Learning Needs.** Selection and organization of learning materials as well as of the methods of instruction should be carried on in the light of the educational and growth needs of the students. The more immediate and pressing the need seems to the student, the easier it is for the instructor to motivate learning activities. Nevertheless, it is possible to cause adolescents to see the importance of future needs and the desirability of preparing to be able to meet those needs by acquiring information, understanding, skills, habits, attitudes, ideals, interests, and tastes that may be developed by participating in learning of a given subject. Other things being equal, the more frequently the student will have need of these educational acquisitions, the more worthwhile he is likely to find the study of the subject.

**Guide for Teachers.** In the majority of secondary schools today, there are available to teachers of various subjects courses of study that have been developed as curriculum guides for teachers. While, in general, a teacher is expected to plan the work for the course according to the fundamental outline set forth in the course of study, it is not intended to be followed slavishly. Indeed, it is expected that the teacher will exercise considerable initiative in working where he or she thinks that the learning and instruction situation may be improved. In many schools there are available to teachers resource units (described later in this chapter) that contain suggested materials and methods.

**Avoiding Pitfalls and Fallacies.** In constructing courses of study and in planning methods of instruction, superior teachers avoid certain pitfalls and avoid building upon certain discredited, fallacious doctrines or assumptions that trap less able instructors. Stated briefly, some of the most common of these are as follows:

1. *The Part-Whole Fallacy.* Quite frequently, the whole of a very large amount of subject matter is included because of the recognized value of a portion of it.

2. *The Contribution-to-Civilization Fallacy.* It does not follow that subject matter that has contributed materially to the development of civilization constitutes for that reason effective instructional materials. For the purposes of education, content must be judged on the basis of its usefulness in producing desired changes in students, rather than in terms of its historical significance.

3. *The Failure To Distinguish Between Certain and Contingent Values.* The value of some subject matter for educational purposes is limited because of the possibility that, within the probable lifetime of the student, the subject matter will become obsolete, no longer true, or inapplicable to changed conditions, or that the needs of individuals or of society will change in such a manner that the value of the subject matter will as a consequence be materially lessened. Other subject matter is of such nature that such possibilities are remote.

4. *The Selected-Student Fallacy.* Materials being considered for courses of study should be evaluated in terms of the needs, interests, and capacities of all the students, with whom they will be used. One must avoid the fallacy of thinking in terms of the bright student to the exclusion of the less capable, or in terms of the student who will remain for further schooling and the student who will go to college to the exclusion of the student whose stay in school is near its end.

5. *The Tendency To Overemphasize Propaedeutic Values.* It is natural for teachers to think of education in terms of preparing for the next stage of schooling. As a consequence, there is the danger of evaluating instruction and instructional materials on the basis of their contribution to more advanced studies. The fact of students' leaving school before graduation, as well as the lack of wisdom in minimizing the intrinsic and direct values of the subject matter, condemns this misplacement of emphasis.

6. *The Confusion of Production and Consumption Values.* Many teachers seem bent upon making their students composers of music,

Dance interpretation in a Detroit high school.

Life insurance, physical and health development, and preparation for
leisure fun (Pershing High School, Detroit).

First aid class in a Yonkers, New York, high school.

artists, writers, or specialized producers. There should be courses adapted to this important goal, but, for the general group of students, there are, for every exceptional student destined to be a producer, at least a score of individuals destined to be consumers, and the capacity of the more numerous for acquiring training for consumption should not be sacrificed.

7. *The Failure To Recognize the Limitations Imposed by Time and the Relative Immaturity of the Students.* The ambitious teacher who is an adult and a specialist in his field finds it difficult to be satisfied with the limited progress that a cross-section of immature adolescents may be expected to make in a few short years, even under most favorable conditions. Teachers who fail to recognize limitations attempt impossible amounts of facts and skills and impossible levels of learning, with the results not only that student interest is deadened but that the achievements of all but the most gifted are much less gratifying than they should be.

8. *The Misinterpretations (Honest or Not) of What Is Known About Transfer of Learning from One Field or Application to Others.* One of the arguments used in support of placing materials in the curriculum, and to an even greater extent in support of retaining materials already there (particularly those for which other values have seemed to diminish, if indeed they ever existed to any great degree), has been the theory that training received in a specific situation would transfer in material amounts to other specific situations. For example, it was believed that reasoning abilities and powers, skills, and techniques developed through the study of mathematics are available for use in connection with problems in business, in politics, and in various other areas; it has often been claimed that development of habits and powers of observation in science would transfer to a great many non-scientific areas of life. Space is not available here to go into details of the experiments on this subject. It must suffice to state here the more important general conclusions, which are as follows:

a. Transfer of training really does take place.

b. Training received in one field does not transfer in its entirety to other fields, and commonly it transfers only in small proportions.

c. The amount of training that may be transferred from one field to another depends upon certain factors including the following: (1) the similarity of the field in which the training was received to the field to which it is to be transferred, particularly similarity of content, similarity of vocabulary, and similarity of procedure; (2) the degree of general intelligence of the learner who is to engineer the transfer; (3) the degree to which the ideal of transfer has been generated in the form of some general principle, attitude, or ideal and the extent to which the possibilities of application in other fields are thought of at the time that the learning to be transferred takes place.

d. Not only is there much lost in transfer, but occasionally there is such a thing as negative transfer or interference with future learning by reason of previous learning.

## PARTICIPANTS IN THE SELECTION AND ORGANIZATION OF LEARNING MATERIALS

**Federal and State Authorities.** With few exceptions, the federal government has exercised little direct influence on secondary education in the United States. Where subsidies have been given, as in the case of federal assistance for vocational aid under the Smith-Hughes Act, the George-Deen Act, and their replacements, some supervision in a general way is exercised in order to ensure good courses of study effectively taught. The federal government has influenced courses of study in science, mathematics, and foreign languages under the National Defense Education Act, first passed in 1959. With these exceptions, the federal government leaves the matter of instructional materials to the states and local communities.

While all state legislatures have legal authority in connection with the curriculum of the public schools, they have exercised that authority sparingly. In a considerable number of states, one or more of the following subjects are required by law to be taught: state history and government, civics and citizenship, health and physical education, American history and the Constitution, and, more recently, driver education. In a few states, there have been laws relative to the offering of instruction in safety, on the effects of alcohol, and in connection with certain types of days such as Arbor Day and the birthdays of famous men. Altogether, however, the influence of the state legislatures is not great.

The state departments of education have exercised a somewhat greater influence on the curriculum. In many states, the state education department has been empowered to set up standards with reference to the offerings and the requirements for graduation. There has been much opposition to this, and, in recent years, state education departments have tended to exercise less and less authority, being content to issue suggestive courses of study and to extend and improve their facilities and quality of advisory service. Developed by the state department of education, there are available to teachers in most states courses of study that are, with few exceptions, intended for advisory and optional use.

In a number of states, there is a statewide textbook commission that selects books to be used in the secondary schools. A majority of states do not follow this procedure, and, in most of those that do, three to five books are selected from which teachers may exercise an option. The exercise of such power by state authorities is generally opposed by educators who believe that different teachers and different schools in different localities of the state may best use different textbooks—those suited to the needs of the particular class, teacher, or school. In some states, teachers in larger districts are not required to use textbooks adopted for the state.

There have been, for some years, discussions of proposals for a national curriculum to be formulated by a national committee of educators and scholars. Opposition to the idea has been rather general, and probably the nearest approach will be the recommendations of national committees in various fields such as mathematics, the social sciences, and biology.

**Accrediting Agencies.** The large majority of our states are in areas for which there is a regional association of colleges and secondary schools, those exist largely for the purposes of evaluating the schools and preparing lists of accredited schools. This is described in detail in Chapter 19. The direct and indirect influences of accrediting associations upon the details of the curriculum are not great, and, in general, they are useful.

**The Local Board of Education.** In most states, practically all of the authority for determining what shall be taught in the schools is delegated to the board of education of the local school district. Ordinarily, this board of education does not participate in determining curriculum details but leaves that to the professionals—the teachers and the administrators. Boards of education, in general, reserve the right to pass upon what subjects shall be offered and what subjects shall be required for graduation, as well as to examine the content of subjects and the methods of teaching when protest or objection is raised by individuals in the community, or upon request by organizations to have the course of study changed to meet their particular needs.

Local boards of education rely largely upon the administrators and supervisors in their schools, and these rely largely upon the teachers for the selection and organization of learning materials. They exercise leadership particularly in connection with stimulating the teachers to study problems of course-of-study organization and improvement and to make recommendations. They also are of assistance to teachers in connection with the obtaining of materials that are needed by them and in providing the time for them to be able to approach their responsibilities carefully and deliberately.

**Consultants.** In recent years, there has been a very substantial increase in the use of professional consultants. These are often specialists from a college or university in some particular field of the curriculum, such as

English or mathematics, but they are also frequently specialists in the curriculum in general or are especially informed in new developments or in some special aspect of the curriculum, such as the core and unified studies. Consultants and consultation service are also obtained from other school systems and state departments of education.

**Lay Pressure Groups.** Not to be overlooked, and certainly in most instances to be vigorously opposed, are non-educational organizations that attempt to influence what is taught in the schools. Among the types of those are the following:

1. *So-called Patriotic Societies.* Most of these organizations are interested in seeing that the schools teach loyalty according to their particular concept of loyalty and in seeing that teachers do not teach or lend encouragement to what are alleged by the organization to be communistic or un-American doctrines and ideas.

2. *Financial, Industrial, and Commercial Organizations.* These organizations are constantly quite active in exerting influence to have the contents of courses be such as would meet their approval and be favorable to their financial interests. Of this general type are local groups of professional men and businessmen and individual business concerns, such as banks, dairies, bar associations, medical associations, factories, religious groups, and parent-teacher associations.

3. *Labor Organizations.* Labor groups have not been very active in attempts to influence the content of subjects taught in schools, although there is some evidence that they have become more active in the future. They have been active in getting compulsory-attendance laws passed and enforced, in favoring free textbooks, and in having labor problems given some consideration in high school classes.

With the development of a better type of school-board member; of security for teachers, especially by means of legalized tenure, and of increasing confidence of teachers in their own professional background and ability to work constructively on their own rather than under pressure, the influence of various types of extra-official agencies and organizations has not been great. Indeed, the work of most of them, particularly those who have been at all successful, has been in cooperation with the teachers and school authorities.

**The Teacher and the Learning Materials.** The teacher is the major determinant of what is actually taught and what is studied by the students. He participates not only in the selection of textbooks and the development of courses of study but also in working on all the details of using the textbooks, of following the courses of study, and, in general, of determining what is actually taught and how.

In addition to the responsibility of the teachers for the selection, organization, and presentation of materials to the students in his or her classes, increasingly in recent years they have participated as members of committees in a considerable number of matters affecting the curriculum of the whole school, such as determining what subjects shall be offered, the grade level at which they should be offered, the textbooks to be adopted, the development of courses of study or guidelines, and the development of resource units. They also influence the learning experiences of young people in schools by sponsorship and assistance in managing various types of student clubs and through services in counseling.

In order that teachers may have time to discharge these responsibilities effectively, they are employed, in an increasing number of districts, for ten or more months including one or more weeks in which school is not in session. During this time they are required to work on the problems of the school, principally those related to curriculum improvement and methods of teaching. In addition, the practice is becoming much more common of reducing temporarily the load of some teachers who will carry on leadership activities and spend much time at work on problems of curriculum improvement. Frequently, these teachers serve for the time as coordinators, assisting and giving leadership to other teachers in creative work and developing ideas and materials to be presented to the other teachers for consideration, review, criticism, suggestion, and approval.

**Other Agencies Affecting the Curriculum.** In addition to the official agencies mentioned in the foregoing pages, there are professional organizations and agencies that influence or at least attempt to influence what is taught in the schools. Among those may be mentioned the following: (1) committees of state and national professional organizations, such as the national committees now at work on preparation of new materials for instruction in secondary school courses in mathematics and science; (2) The Commission of the National Council of the Teachers of English; (3) committees of the National Council of the Social Studies, including a very important committee on the improvement of economic education; (4) The National Council of Teachers of Mathematics; (5) the American Mathematics Association; (6) The Department of Home Economics; (7) The Association for Supervision and Curriculum Development; (8) The Department of Audio-visual Instruction; (9) The National Association of Secondary School Principals; (10) the Music Educators National Conference; (11) The American Association of Health, Physical Education, and Recreation; (12) The National Science Teachers Association; (13) The Vocational Education Association; (14) The

Speech Association of America; (15) The United Business Association; (16) the American Industrial Arts Association, Inc.; (17) the Department of Foreign Languages; (18) the National Art Education Association; and (19) the National Business Education Association.

Institutions of higher education also influence the curriculum of secondary schools through their entrance requirements and through the influence of instructors in education and in subject-matter fields.

Much influence is wielded by those who construct standard tests and various types of national examinations such as the National College Entrance Examinations and the National Merit Scholarship Examinations, both of which place particular emphasis upon certain types of teaching objectives. In recent years there has been widespread opposition to the increased emphasis upon subject-matter testing by national agencies.

## QUESTIONS, PROBLEMS, AND TOPICS FOR FURTHER STUDY

1. What are the limitations or weaknesses of relying almost entirely upon the textbook for the course of study?
2. What kind of printed materials other than textbooks could you use to advantage in teaching your field of specialization?
3. To what extent would you rely upon audio-visual education in teaching your subject?
4. In teaching your subject, do you believe that you would make any use of community resources and, if so, of what type of community resources?
5. Be able to give in class, in your own words, a definition of each of the curriculum terms found in this chapter. Ask your instructor for further definition of any that are not perfectly clear to you.
6. Be able to explain the function of learning materials in the educational process.
7. Do you believe that the federal government should play a greater or a smaller part in deciding what is taught in the schools? The state legislature? The state department of education?
8. With what phases of the determination of what should be taught in the schools should the local board of education concern itself?
9. Be able to give in class a seven- or eight-minute talk on the lay pressure groups and their influence on the curriculum, being sure to mention to what extent they are useful or harmful.
10. Do you believe that the statement "The teacher is by far the most important influence in determining what is taught," is an overstatement?
11. To what extent do you think the average teacher keeps in mind the objectives of secondary education? The objectives of the particular subject taught?

## SUPPLEMENTARY MATERIALS

### Selected Readings

Alcorn, Marvin D., and James M. Linley. *Issues in Curriculum Development*. New York: Harcourt, Brace & World, Inc., 1959. Chapter 7, "Programs for Meeting Common Needs of Learning."

ALPREN, MORTON. "What Curriculum Developments Are Finding Their Way into Practice?" *Bulletin of the N.A.S.S.P.*, March, 1962, 13–18.

BENT, RUDYARD K., and HENRY H. KRONENBERG. *Principles of Secondary Education* (4th ed.). New York: McGraw-Hill Book Co., Inc., 1961. Chapter 12, "Trends in Curriculum Planning"; Chapter 13, "The Curriculum: General Education"; Chapter 14, "The Curriculum: General Education"; Chapter 15, "The Curriculum—Special Interests: Academic."

FAUNCE, ROLAND C., and MORREL J. CLUTE. *Teaching and Learning in the Junior High School.* San Francisco: Wadsworth Publishing Co., Inc., 1961. Chapter 4, "The Curriculum: General Education"; Chapter 5, "The Curriculum: Exploratory Experiences."

FRENCH, WILLIAM M. *Education for All.* New York: Odyssey Press, Inc., 1955. Chapter 2, "Curriculum: The Present Controversy."

FRYMIER, JACK R. "Our Schools: Which Way NOW?" *The Clearing House,* XXXIII (January, 1959), 283–86.

GWYNN, J. MINOR. *Curriculum Principles and Social Trends.* New York: The Macmillan Co., 1960. Chapter 13, "Trends in Curriculum Development in the Secondary School."

HANDLIN, OSCAR. "Live Students and Dead Education." *Atlantic Monthly,* CCVIII (September, 1961), 29–34.

HANSEN, KENNETH H. *High School Teaching.* Englewood Cliffs, N.J.: Prentice-Hall, Inc., 1957. Chapter 3, "What Do Our High Schools Teach?"

LEONARD, J. PAUL. *Developing the Secondary School Curriculum* (rev. ed.) New York: Holt, Rinehart & Winston, Inc., 1953. Especially Chapter 13, "General Education for All Youth."

RINKER, FLOYD, WALTER AUFFENBER, GALEN JONES, and JOHN E. DOBBIN. "New Developments in Secondary-School Program and Services," *Bulletin of the N.A.S.S.P.,* XLV (April, 1961), 189–95.

SHANNON, J. R. "Tough Courses," *The Clearing House,* XXXIII (January, 1959), 259–62.

AUDIO-VISUAL MATERIALS

*Films*

*Broader Concepts of Curriculum.* McGraw-Hill Text-Film. 21 minutes.

*Field Trip.* Norfolk County Schools, Virginia Department of Education. 10 minutes.

*Film Research and Learning.* International Film Bureau Inc. Educational Films Mag. 14 minutes.

*How To Make and Use a Diorama.* McGraw-Hill Text-Film. 20 minutes.

*How To Make Handmade Lantern Slides.* Indiana University. 22 minutes.

# 9

# Selection and Organization of Learning Materials

## COURSE-OF-STUDY CONSTRUCTION

**Types of Planning.** In determining what materials of instruction shall be employed in any subject in the secondary school, there are three principal phases of activity and responsibility: (1) the planning for the entire year, most of which must be done before school begins, indeed in the cases of experienced teachers, much of it during the previous year; (2) the planning in connection with the various units of instruction and learning that make up the semester and the year; and (3) the planning for each day's class meeting.

In every stage of planning, certain important fundamental objectives, factors, and principles must be kept in mind. Among the most important are the objectives of secondary education: education for citizenship, education for home living, education for leisure and a culturally enriched life, education for earning a living, education for physical and mental health, and preparation for continued learning. Furthermore, in connection with each of these, those engaged in determining what shall be taught must think of what information; what understanding; what intellectual, physical, and social skills; what intellectual, physical, and social habits; what interests; what ideals; and what attitudes contributing to education for the important areas of life may be developed by use of the unit of subject matter being employed. Each curriculum planner will naturally concentrate upon what information, skills, habits, etc., may be developed by use of materials in the field of his particular subject specialization, for example, English, social studies, physical education, or music.

**Types of Approaches to Selecting Materials for Learning and Instruction.** One useful approach to the problem is the *survey method*. For example, investigators have employed newspapers and magazines as means of determining what are the things about which information should be taught and what skills in reading and understanding should be taught. This applies not only to such fields as the social studies but also to mathematics, the sciences, and other courses. Sometimes this survey method is employed in respect to part of a subject, for example, what graphs and diagrams need to be introduced so that the general reader may understand the content of widely read publications.

Another approach is that of *job analysis*. This is used particularly in the field of vocational education. The investigator in the field makes a careful examination of the activities of the people working in the particular vocation, in his effort to discover what information, skills, habits and so forth are needed for successful employment in that particular vocation. This type of approach is also used in other fields, to discover, for example, the activities of homemakers today, or the issues on which voters are called upon to make decisions.

Still another approach is the one referred to as the method of *expert opinion*. An individual or a committee acquainted with the field, having given considerable study to the problems of objectives, curriculum materials, and instructional methods in the subject, issues a publication indicating what material should be included.

All along, naturally, there must be kept in mind the interests and capabilities of students in the class for which the material will be used, including, of course, the vocabulary difficulty. The task of determining what are the best materials for instruction in any given year of any particular subject is, indeed, a very complicated one, and no teacher or group of teachers will do a perfect job; nevertheless, sincere effort must be put forth in order that a truly effective curriculum may be developed.

Furthermore, as conditions of life are constantly changing and as new knowledge in various fields and new knowledge about education become available, improvement of course-of-study instruction is seen as a continuous process.

**Adaptation to Individuals.**[1] While, to be sure, courses-of-study materials must be selected with a view to the mass of students, there must definitely be kept in mind the capabilities and needs of those with less than average and those with superior capacities for learning.

The problem of the determination of what materials shall be used for students in sections for the less able and sections for the more able is a much more difficult one. It is fairly easy to do this for the abler students

[1] This problem is discussed more fully in Chapter 15.

in the junior and senior years, as they may use courses of study employed in colleges for their freshmen. This, nevertheless, does not constitute a very superior curriculum, as most college courses of study leave much to be desired.

Within heterogeneous classes, much differentiation in course-of-study materials is called for. This means not only some planning for the entire year but also very definite planning from day to day.

**Planning for the Year.** Most teachers today, particularly beginning teachers, do considerable thinking and planning about the course-of-study materials they will use during the coming school year. Most beginning teachers get copies of textbooks and courses of study, if they exist, for the subjects that they will teach. Among other things, these teachers will plan an apportionment of the materials through the year and set up a tentative time schedule to which they will adhere fairly closely.

The best teaching can be done if the teacher makes a survey of the library and the audio-visual aids available in the school system and lays plans and perhaps makes appointments for the obtaining of films, slides, and projectors.

During the year, there will be committees of teachers, especially those teaching the same subject, charged with the responsibility of planning the selection and organization of materials for the following year. From time to time, too, groups of teachers will have the responsibility of setting up criteria for the consideration and adoption of textbooks and will make recommendations to their superior officers for textbooks to be purchased and employed.

## THE UNIT PLAN OF ORGANIZATION

**Nature and Types of Units.** The great majority of high school teachers today break up a year's work into subdivisions that are frequently referred to as large units. They may include only a few days, or they may include a longer period.

*The large-unit plan emphasizes total patterns of learning rather than isolated bits of knowledge presented in a series of daily assign-study-recite topics.* In addition to being comprehensive in scope, the learning materials and activities of a unit must be organized in such a manner as to have *unity,* or *wholeness.* This essential unity may be achieved by a logical arrangement of subject matter either around a significant topic, theme, or generalization or around the student's interest, a recognized need, or a significant social problem. Despite the lingering influence of the stimulus-response theory of learning and the practical difficulty presented by the existing organization of the high school that is built around the traditional daily recitation, the unit plan has been given great impetus in recent years, as a consequence of the spread of the Gestalt psychological theory and the endeavors of teachers to organize the learning experiences of students in harmony with some of the modern concepts of learning.

Units are frequently classified as *subject-matter units,* in which the materials are organized according to the logic of the subject matter involved, and as *experience-type units,* in which the learning experiences are "bound together" by some central theme of interest to the pupil or by some significant social problem. This distinction is misleading in that, in both types of units, subject matter is employed, although it is used differently. In the experience-type unit, the learner's interest is the point of departure in the learning activities, thus providing a psychological organization of the learning materials, in contrast to the logical organization of the subject-matter unit.

Many teachers do not attempt to include all of a course in units. This permits more intensive study of the units and greater mastery of the materials covered. Some fill in around the units, while others omit materials that do not fit into any units. The latter is often referred to as the "block and gap" approach. When it is used, care must be taken to see that materials of much value for future instruction and learning are not omitted.

The more important differences in types of teaching units are shown in the table on page 158.

**The Project as a Learning Unit.** A learning project may be a course-of-study unit, or it may grow out of a unit. The project plan was first used in the teaching of agriculture and home economics. Teachers of these courses, realizing the need for extending the scope of their subjects beyond the textbook and the meager laboratory equipment and materials, assigned supplementary exercises for students to do on their farms and in their homes. The work on these projects was carried on in a natural physical environment. The student saw in the project the challenge of a real task, which gave unity to the activity. With limited supervision, the student makes his own work plans, marshals his energies, and evaluates his own efforts in achieving his goal, namely, the construction of a material product. Today, group projects are employed by many teachers.

## CORE ORGANIZATION

**Units in the Core.** The core plan is employed in many junior high schools and in some senior high schools. Around problems and centers of interest, materials from two or more subjects are more or less integrated for study and teaching. The following are other characteristics of

COMPARISON OF UNIT TEACHING TECHNIQUES

I. Procedures for Introducing or Initiating the Unit

| Teacher-Control Approach: (Teacher determines unit.) | Student-Choice Approach: (Students determine unit.) | Teacher-initiated Cooperative Approach: (Teacher determines unit.) |
|---|---|---|
| 1. Introduction: Teacher gives overview of unit-orients and motivates students.<br>2. Getting work under way: Teacher may make assignments, give directions for beginning work, or give out guide sheets, differentiated assignments, outlines, or workbooks. | 1. Introduction: Teacher suggests different units.<br>2. Discussion of units by teacher and students.<br>3. Choice of unit by students.<br>4. Making plan of work by teacher and students. | 1. Introduction: Teacher gives overview of unit —orients and motivates students.<br>2. Making plan of work by teacher and students. |

II. Procedures for Developing the Unit

| | |
|---|---|
| (Guide sheets usually furnished and provision made for individual differences.)<br>Learning Experiences<br>  a. Directed study<br>  b. Discussions, forms of<br>  c. Practice<br>  d. Lecture-demonstration<br>  e. Developmental work<br>  f. Review—summarization<br>  g. Organized drill | Nature of work depends upon plan worked out cooperatively by teacher and students. These procedures lend themselves to the use of problems and projects. The work may be done individually or by groups. |

the core type of organization: (1) It is taught in a large block of time including two or more periods. (2) It emphasizes the experiences from social and personal problem areas of the student or of life in general. (3) It cuts across subject boundaries and draws upon content from any source needed to solve the problem. (4) The problem-solving approach is employed in the study and discussion. (5) Cooperative planning by the students and teachers is involved in setting up research activities.

**Pros and Cons of the Use of Core Units.** Among the advantages claimed for the core program are the following:

1. The core provides an opportunity for a teacher to get to know his pupils well.

2. The core, as defined by its characteristics, is compatible with what we know about how people learn.
3. The core can serve as a focus for the student for his whole program, wherein experiences in and out of school may be related to the problems studied.
4. The core provides an opportunity for study of social and personal problems of concern to young people.
5. The core provides an opportunity for field trips and other learning experiences that need a longer block of time.
6. The core includes activities and functions often assigned to special periods in the schedule, such as homerooms, social affairs, clubs, and other extracurricular activities.
7. The core provides a situation in which more functional learning of the basic skills as well as social skills can be planned.

The principal disadvantages that seem to apply to the core are

1. The public can find a convenient point of criticism in an unfamiliar or new type of curriculum organization and approach.
2. It is more difficult to teach core classes than the conventional class with a preplanned sequence.
3. Few teachers are prepared to teach the core.
4. More materials are needed in a core class.
5. The core program takes more staff time in planning together.

## LARGE-UNIT PROCEDURE

**Unified Studies Organization.** Junior high schools in the Shawnee-Mission High School District, Merriam, Kansas, have a unified studies program that embraces language arts, social studies, and science at the seventh- and eight-grade levels, and language arts and social studies in grade nine.[2] Resource units, prepared over a period of years by groups of teachers, are available for the required and optional units. Each unit contains a statement of the significance of the unit, specific objectives, outline of content, activities (introductory, developmental, and culminating), sources of information, and suggestions for evaluation.

**Principles of Procedures for Successful Cooperative Planning Units.** The following are useful suggestions for the cooperative planning of units of instruction:

(1) Guide the group during the planning period to develop plans which are so definite and so clear that all know what to do and how to do it.

2 Ralph E. Chalender, "A Unified Studies Approach," *Educational Leadership*, Vol. 18, No. 3 (December, 1960), pp. 161–164.

UNIFIED STUDIES SCOPE AND SEQUENCE, SHAWNEE-MISSION DISTRICT, MERRIAM, KANSAS

| Seventh Grade Required | Eighth Grade Required | Ninth Grade Required |
|---|---|---|
| We Are the Junior High School | Looking Ahead | Looking Ahead |
| Let's Improve Our Communication With Others | Let's Improve our Communication with Others | Let's Improve our Communication with Others |
| How Do We Find Our Way Around the World? | How Did the United States Become a Nation? | Careers |
| We Live in Many Communities | Westward Expansion and Civil War | Interdependence in a Shrinking World |
| Living in Harmony with Myself and Others | How Do We Govern Ourselves in a Democracy? | The United Nations |
| What Is Science? | How Did the United States Become the Greatest Producer of Goods in the World? | One or more of the following: |
| How do Plants and Animals Grow? | Conservation of Natural Resources | Africa, China, Russia, South America, Western Europe |

(2) Anticipate difficulties in carrying out plans as made and be ready to call a group conference when difficulty occurs and before discouragement and work stoppage can result in disorder.

(3) Guide during the planning period so that sufficient work is outlined to keep all individuals and groups busy over a reasonably long period of time. Planning will keep the sequence going so that lack of work does not cause disorder.

(4) Call for replanning conferences if work develops unevenly. Workers may be reassigned and activities redistributed.

(5) Keep in touch with the various activities by moving from group to group in the class, by participating, by asking questions, and by making suggestions thus exercising both guidance and control.

(6) Foresee certain common occasions for disorder and forestall them by developing with the students regular routines

    (a) For having all materials, tools, and supplies ready before need for them arises;

    (b) For distributing materials, tools, supplies, books, and papers quickly and in an orderly manner;

    (c) For using reference materials, particularly when many students wish to consult an inadequate number of references;

    (d) For holding conferences with individuals who need help;

    (e) For using as helpers any individuals who may for any reason be unoccupied for a time.

(7) Introduce new activities to small groups directly concerned, so that tryout will be made without the confusion which might result from misunderstandings within a large group and from too many persons trying a new process without sufficient guidance.

(8) Constantly give direct and indirect training in the conventions and routine of group work; taking turns, not interrupting, turning to some other aspect of the work instead of standing around waiting for tools or materials in use elsewhere, signing in and out for tools and materials, etc.

(9) Assist students to develop plans for their own activities: budgeting time, scheduling group conferences, announcing times for individual conferences, etc.

(10) Constantly develop directly or indirectly, the understanding that freedom carries responsibility, and that self-control and cooperation are advantageous to the students themselves and not merely something required by the school.[3]

**Resource Units.** In many schools, there are developed what are called *resource units*, usually prepared by a selected committee of teachers working under the supervision and with the help of a department head or a subject supervisor. These are not units to be followed specifically by teachers but are, rather, advisory in nature. The resource unit is usually planned by a committee of teachers for the benefit of all teachers teaching the subject in which the unit belongs. The resource unit is made up of the following:

1. A statement of the nature of the unit and the learning outcomes (information, skills, habits, interests, etc.)
2. An outline of the subject matter involved in the research unit
3. Problems, questions, and content relating to the various parts of the subject-matter outline
4. Suggested activities of the learner and resources available to them
5. Suggestions for culminating activities at the close of the unit and for other means of evaluation

Among the advantages of a large unit are the following:

1. As compared to the daily recitation unit, it provides flexibility, making it possible to have more or to have less study, discussion, or other activity on any given date, for example, an entire day may be spent in getting started on the unit and several days in the study of it, without a great deal of discussion or recitation.

2. It is possible to have more extensive and better teacher-pupil planning, and, therefore, a large unit stimulates and provides for more pupil initiative.

3. It provides for better integration and interrelationships of the materials over a period of several days or even several weeks.

4. It provides for closer pupil-teacher relationship, particularly during the time spent in study in class.

[3] By permission, from *The Guidance of Learning Activities,* by William H. Burton, (New York: Appleton-Century-Crofts, Inc., 1952), pp. 447–448.

## DAILY PLANNING

There must also necessarily be planning of instructional materials day by day. During each class meeting, the effective instructor will go over the possible materials, with a view to selecting for emphasis those most likely to result in desirable learner growth; the effective teacher will also make plans for procedures in class in connection with the materials and the students' use of them. Naturally, careful attention should be given to the planning of explanation, lecture, and the use of audiovisual materials or field trips.

**Written Lesson Plans.** Most teachers, at least for the first few years of teaching a course, make for each day a plan on something of the following order: Down one half of a page or large card is an outline of the materials that are likely to be touched upon in one way or another, including notes for lectures and explanations, and opposite these items, on the right-hand side of the page, are notes relative to procedures— questions to ask, explanations to make, visual aids to employ, and things for the students to do. Many teachers keep these plans in a loose-leaf notebook and save them, modifying and improving them each year.

In planning, more effective teachers attempt to keep constantly in mind the objectives of the particular lesson or unit, of the course, and of secondary education in general. This is very complex and difficult for the beginning teacher. Nevertheless, much time and effort should be expended along this line. It is very unfortunate that the beginning teacher has to teach as many courses as the experienced teacher. This means that the beginning teacher must either spend much more time each week in planning or be satisfied with less effective leadership of learning. Teachers who are on their way up improve and perfect their planning from year to year. Many, however, discover that they can "get by" and seem to give satisfaction the first year and are content to rest on their oars, which really means, of course, losing ground.

## ORGANIZATION OF THE SUBJECT PROGRAM

**Required and Elective Subjects.** In the early secondary schools, the offerings were not great, and, consequently, there were few electives. Furthermore, since it was believed that the favored subjects—foreign languages, mathematics, science, and history—trained general powers of the intellect and that there was much transfer of training, it was very common to say that what is taught does not matter, since one subject is as good as another for mind-training objectives (provided, of course, it was one of the favored subjects).

In the latter part of the nineteenth century, however, schools became larger; there were students entering secondary school who did not wish to take a great majority of their work in foreign languages or in the academic subjects; and there was a demand for an opportunity for students to choose at least some of their subjects. At this time, an outstanding and well-known educator, President Charles W. Elliot of Harvard College, rationalized the situation at Harvard, where a great many new subjects had been added, far more than a student could complete even in ten or twelve years of study, by setting up and advocating generally the elective system.

Principals and superintendents who were very anxious to permit students to take subjects according to their interests and academic ability were eager to follow this example, and, by 1910, the elective system was rampant in American secondary schools. Under pressure from students and parents and also teachers of some subjects who wished to build up enrolments in their classes, the number of required subjects diminished and the number of electives increased.

In recent years, it has become obvious that many high school graduates have blind spots in very important areas such as mathematics, history and the social studies, and science. This situation has been very vigorously attacked by a great many educators who have been inclined to think of the needs of the American nation—of the necessity for seeing that graduates have sufficient background in academic subjects to be good citizens, understanding the scientific-political-economic world in which they live, form good habits of home living, and utilize leisure in ways that involve academic knowledge and academic skills.

More study of history, the social studies, mathematics, and natural science is being required for graduation from four-year and senior high schools. A rather typical requirement in schools today is four years of English, three years of history or social studies, two years of science, and two years of mathematics of some sort, all after the eighth grade.

**Recent Trends.** Alexander's survey of secondary school trends revealed the following:

1. Offerings in foreign languages have markedly expanded. Small high schools have added one or more languages; larger high schools have added the third and fourth years of one or more.

2. Sixty-three per cent of the principals interviewed believed "too little" emphasis was placed upon science five years before, 55 per cent, on mathematics. Only 17 per cent believed this situation still existed in science; only 16 per cent, in mathematics.

3. Fifty-two per cent of the principals reported that some subjects (principally science, mathematics, and foreign languages) had been shifted downward during the preceding five years.

4. Sixty-three per cent of the principals said that grouping by ability or achievement had increased in their schools. The same percentage expected further increases during the next five years.

5. Thirty-one per cent of the principals expected to have team teaching ("a plan whereby two or more teachers are jointly responsible for the instruction of a group of pupils") in 1965–1966, although only 12 per cent (in contrast to 5 per cent a year before) reported having it at the time.

6. Forty-nine per cent described as "none" their use of TV programs in 1960–1961 (2 per cent, "much use"; and 48 per cent, "some use"), as compared with 82 per cent for "none" in 1955–1956 (1 per cent, "much"; and 17 per cent, "some"), and only 14 per cent anticipated "none" in 1965–1966 (21 per cent, "much"; and 65 per cent "some").

7. Sixty-eight per cent of the respondents believed their schools expected more from pupils at the time than five years before.[4]

In each of these curriculums, there were four kinds of subjects: (1) the constants—required of all students for graduation; (2) the curriculum prescriptions—required only in their particular curriculum; (3) the limited electives, for example, the choice between household arts and industrial arts or between algebra and general mathematics; and (4) the free electives.

One of the curriculums offered by most schools is the "general" curriculum. In it, there is usually a rather small number of required subjects and great freedom is accorded the student in choosing. This type of curriculum has been severely criticized because it permits the student to gather a sort of hodgepodge of subjects that he likes, or thinks he would like. There has been, in recent years, a substantial increase in the proportion of required subjects.

In schools that are large enough to offer a section in each of the academic subjects for those of less academic interest and ability and another section for those of superior academic talent, the requirement for graduation of a considerable number of academic electives is a very practical and desirable provision. Dr. James B. Conant, in his well-known national study, *The American High School Today*, advocated that, after the eighth grade, students should take four years of English, at least two years of science, at least two years of mathematics, three years of

[4] William M. Alexander, "Assessing Curriculum Proposals," *Teachers College Board*, Vol. 63, No. 4 (January, 1962), pp. 287–288.

history and the social studies, and several years of a foreign language. He would make some exceptions to these in the case of the student of very limited capacity for progress in academic subjects.

With the development of a greater amount and an improved quality of guidance and counseling, there has been a trend toward using the multiple-curriculum organization, but only for advisory purposes. Indeed, some larger schools have returned to the single curriculum with constants and electives, leaving the choice of subjects to the student, conditioned upon the approval of his counselor and one of his parents.

**Junior High School Curriculum Organization.** In most junior high schools, two types of curriculum organization are still employed: (1) the single constant with few electives, in grades seven and eight, and (2) the multiple curriculum, in grade nine. In recent years, more junior high schools have been employing the single-constant-with-electives curriculum in all three grades.

In junior high schools, the number of electives in grades seven and eight is not great, usually no more than a choice between home economics and industrial arts, the former usually taken by girls and the latter by boys, and a choice of music or art in the eighth grade with both music and art offered as electives in the ninth grade. The subjects offered in each of the three grades in a very large majority of junior high schools are English, social studies, science, mathematics, home economics, industrial arts, music, art, physical education, and a foreign language.

**Senior High School Curriculum Organization.** In practically all senior high schools there are offered college-preparatory and general curriculums and at least one curriculum in business, usually in secretarial work. In about two-thirds of the schools there are industrial arts and home-making curriculums, and in one-third of the schools there is an agriculture curriculum. The industrial arts offered include a number of diversified types such as automobile mechanics and other vocational trades.

The college-preparatory curriculum usually includes English in every year, two years of science after the ninth grade, frequently algebra and geometry, two years of history and social studies after the eighth grade, and frequently two years of a foreign language. There are, however, in many and an increasing number of schools more than one variety of college-preparatory program, for example, (1) a mathematics-science-pre-engineering college-preparatory program that emphasizes preparation in mathematics and science and (2) a humanities college-preparatory program that emphasizes history, English, and foreign languages.

# CURRICULUM SCHEDULING AND ENROLMENTS

**Length and Number of Periods.** All but a few schools follow a definite schedule of classes meeting and being dismissed at certain designated times through the day. More than two-thirds of junior high schools now have seven periods in their daily schedule; approximately one in four still has a six-period day; and less than one in ten, eight or nine periods.

In senior high schools and four-year high schools, the schedule usually consists of six longer periods, although there has been in recent years a definite trend toward the seven-period schedule with a longer school day. In the six-year secondary schools, the most common plan by far is the seven-period schedule.

In recent decades, there has been a rather universal shift toward the longer period, usually from fifty-two to fifty-five minutes net, not including passing of classes. In schools operating on the eight-period day, the class periods are usually forty to forty-two minutes in length. In some schools, one period thirty to forty minutes in length is given over to homeroom, assemblies, or clubs. There are also, in many schools, two or three lunch periods of approximately twenty-five to thirty minutes each, and classes are dovetailed in around them.

**Student Enrolments.** For several decades, until recently, it was a rather standard practice to require the students to carry four subjects meeting daily, with outside preparation or with double periods, in addition to one, two, or three other subjects meeting fewer times with less preparation. There has since about 1945 been a trend toward permitting bright students in many schools, and the average student as well in some schools, to carry five such "solids." The number of year units earned after the eighth grade varies a great deal from student to student and from school to school. In many and an increasing number of schools, the typical student graduates with twenty or more units of credit earned after the eighth grade. The number of units taken by students has been increasing. A small but increasing number of students complete as many as twenty-four units in the four years.

# QUESTIONS, PROBLEMS, AND TOPICS FOR FURTHER STUDY

1. To what subjects would the job-analysis method be most applicable? The survey method?
2. To what extent do you believe that the student should participate in the cooperative planning of units of instruction in your field?
3. What kinds of help in course-of-study construction can be obtained from outside the local community?
4. How would you use the large-unit method in your major subject? How would you use the core?

5. Do you believe in the use of a written daily lesson plan?
6. How would you use a resource unit?
7. What do you think should be the courses required for graduation from high school, after the ninth grade? In junior high school? In high school?
8. Do you believe that many students should take five "solids"? Why or why not?
9. To what extent could you use TV in your major subject?
10. What electives do you believe should be in the junior high school?
11. How long do you believe the school year should be? Why?
12. Do you believe in long or short class periods? Why?
13. How many periods in the daily schedule would you favor? Why?
14. From time to time, there have been people who have advocated breaking away from organization of learning materials into subjects and merely studying the problems of life, using materials from as many subjects as may apply to each problem. What do you think of that idea? How do you account for the fact that the number of subjects offered in the high school has increased in recent years? Would you add any other subjects?

## SUPPLEMENTARY MATERIALS

### Selected Readings

ALBERTY, HAROLD B., and ELSIE J. ALBERTY. *Reorganizing the High School Curriculum* (3d ed.). New York: The Macmillan Co., 1962. Chapter 5, "The Roles of Direct Experience and Organized Subjects in the Curriculum"; Chapter 6, "Curriculum Designs for General Education," pp. 199–233; Chapter 7, "Curriculum Designs for Specialized Education"; Chapter 12, "Resource Unit Development: Principles, Procedures and Illustrations."

DOUGLASS, HARL R. *Trends and Issues in Secondary Education.* Washington, D.C.: The Center for Applied Research in Education, Inc., 1962. Chapter 3, "Curriculum Offerings, Organization and Administration."

DOUGLASS, HARL R. (ed.). *The High School Curriculum* (2d ed.). New York: The Ronald Press Co., 1956. Chapter 14, "The Core Curriculum"; Chapter 15, "Large Units as Basis for Course Organization"; Chapter 20, "Organization and Administration of the Curriculum."

GREEN, J. J. "Some Ideas About the Secondary School Curriculum," *National Catholic Education Association Bulletin*, LII (February, 1956), 18–26.

GRUHN, WILLIAM T., and HARL R. DOUGLASS. *The Modern Junior High School* (2d ed.). New York: The Ronald Press Co., 1956. Chapter 4, "Curriculum Trends and Organization"; Chapter 5, "The Core Curriculum."

GWYNN, J. MINOR. *Curriculum Principles and Social Trends.* New York: The Macmillan Co., 1960. Chapters 6, 7, 9, 15.

HARPER, PAIGE S., DALE PARNELL, EUGENE E. OLIVER, CLYDE M. GOTT, JOHN W. SIMMONS, and MATTHEW F. NOALL. "The Daily Schedule: Shorter Periods, Longer Periods, Variable Periods, OR WHAT?" *The Bulletin, N.A.S.S.P.*, No. 263 (April, 1961), 12–17, 110–15.

LEONARD, J. PAUL. *Developing the Secondary School Curriculum* (rev. ed.). New York: Holt, Rinehart & Winston, Inc., 1953. Chapter 14, "Developing Core Courses"; Chapter 15, "Organizing and Using Units of Work"; Chapter 16, "Developing Resource Units"; Chapter 17, "Developing Classroom Units."

McKEAN, ROBERT C. *Principles and Methods in Secondary Education.* Columbus, Ohio: Charles E. Merrill Books, Inc., 1962. Chapter 3, "Practice in Selecting and Organizing Content"; Chapter 6, "Selecting and Using Instructional Materials."

MILLS, HUBERT H., and HARL R. DOUGLASS. *Teaching in High School* (2d ed.). New York: The Ronald Press Co., 1957. Chapter 14, "Teaching Instructional Units"; and Chapter 16, "The Core Curriculum."

POUNDS, RALPH L., and ROBERT L. GARRETSON. *Principles of Modern Education.* New York: The Macmillan Co., 1962. Chapter 9, "Selecting and Organizing the Materials of Instruction"; Chapter 11, "Organizing the Total Curriculum of the School."

RISK, THOMAS M. *Principles and Practices of Teaching in Secondary Schools.* New York: American Book Co., 1958. Unit II, "The Organization of Courses of Instruction and Units."

RIVLIN, HARRY N. *Teaching Adolescents in Secondary Schools.* New York: Appleton-Century-Crofts, Inc., 1961. Chapter 4, "Teaching a Unit," pp. 36–55.

ROMINE, STEPHEN A. *Building the High School Curriculum.* New York: The Ronald Press Co., 1954. Chapter 8, "Selecting and Organizing Curricular Materials and Experiences"; Chapter 11, "Building and Using Units and Courses of Study."

WATKINS, RALPH K. *Techniques of Secondary School Teaching.* New York: The Ronald Press Co., 1958. Unit III, "How Can the Teacher Organize for Learning?": Chapter 5, Logical Organizations in Learning.

WRIGHT, GRACE S. "Requirements for High School Graduation in States and Large Cities," Bulletin 1961, No. 12. Washington, D.C.: U.S. Office of Education, 1961.

## AUDIO-VISUAL MATERIALS

### Film

*Characteristics of a Core Program.* Teachers College, Bureau of Publications, Columbia University, New York. 20 minutes.

### Filmstrip

*Core Curriculum Class in Action.* Wayne University, 1949. 50 frames, silent with captions, black and white.

### Recording

*Developing a Core Program in the High School,* #227. Harold Alberty. Educational Growth Series. Educational Recording Services. Los Angeles. 36–44-minute discussion, 33⅓ rpm.

# 10

# The Subject Fields of Study

## HISTORICAL BACKGROUND

**Development of the Subject Fields.** In education of adolescents in primitive societies, there was very little attempt to organize curriculum materials in logical subject-matter divisions. The organization was a psychological one, from the point of view of present and future needs of the learners.

Later, when secondary schools were provided in the early centuries B.C. for the children of the upper classes in the various countries around the Mediterranean, the instructional materials came to be organized on the basis of subjects. To do that was perfectly natural, since the manuscripts used in instruction were specialized according to subject field. In Greek, Egyptian, and Phoenician schools, subject divisions apparently appeared as far back as 1000 or 1200 B.C. Subject organization became rather definite also in the Roman schools by the time of the birth of Christ. By A.D. 300, the Roman curriculum had become fairly definitely fixed and consisted of what came to be called "the seven liberal arts," which included grammar, rhetoric, dialectic, arithmetic, geometry, astronomy, and music. The grammar was Latin and Greek grammar; the rhetoric was what we would call today "English composition"; dialectic was a combination of logic and public speaking, emphasizing debate; astronomy had to do largely with matters of religion and superstition, although it included some related science. Music was studied only theoretically and psychologically. Arithmetic and geometry were primitive forms of their present equivalents.

In addition to these, in both Roman and later Greek schools science became part of the curriculum under the name of natural philosophy, which was rather all embracing, including both physical and biological science.

**Expansion of the American Secondary School Curriculum.** When the academies and first high schools were established in America, there was really significant expansion of the curriculum as compared to that of the Latin grammar schools; yet it was not until the twentieth century that non-academic subjects began to find their way into the typical American high school. Between 1890 and 1920, there were added in the majority of high schools courses in home economics, typewriting, general science, speech, social studies, shorthand, bookkeeping, agriculture, various skilled trades, crafts, music, art, and other electives. In the first quarter of the twentieth century, Spanish was added to the offerings of many secondary schools, but German was dropped by many during World War I. Since 1955, an increasing number of schools have been offering Russian.

**Trends in Enrolment.** Naturally, with the expansion of the curriculum, the percentage of high school students enrolled in any one subject declined, although, as a result of the very great increase of students attending secondary schools, the number of students enrolled increased in practically every subject. Nevertheless, the number of students enrolled in some subjects has diminished; among those subjects are physical geography (which has been replaced by general science), botany, English history, ancient history, and German.

Subjects in which the greatest increase in enrolments has occurred, in recent years, are general mathematics, algebra and geometry, economics, physics, chemistry, history of non-Western civilization, world cultures, Russian, Chinese, Spanish, music, health and physical education, distributive education, diversified occupations, speech, journalism, shorthand, typing, and various types of shop work, especially in electronics and auto repair.

## AGRICULTURE

**Rise and Decline.** Immediately following the Smith-Hughes Act of 1917, which provided state and federal aid for schools offering courses in agriculture with instructors of approved preparation, there was a great increase in the number of schools offering courses in agriculture and an even greater increase in the number of students enrolled.

In the last quarter-century, there has been a great decline in the proportion of the population living and working on farms. Furthermore, farming has become much more specialized. Agricultural specialists such as wheat growers, corn growers, cotton growers, sheep raisers, cattle raisers, and poultry specialists are replacing general farmers. The percentage of gainfully employed workers who are in agriculture and allied occupations has been decreasing for more than 100 years. In 1960, only one out of ten of all employed people in the United States were in agriculture, as compared to one out of four in 1930 and one out of two in 1900.

Automation and increased use of machines—particularly in cotton, wheat, and corn—have decreased the number of workers needed in those occupations to less than 10 per cent of those formerly employed. In spite of the fact that there is rather generous state and federal aid for approved vocational courses in agriculture, the number of schools offering the course has slowly decreased, although the number of students has remained fairly constant.

**Objectives of Vocational Agriculture.** The objectives of vocational education in agriculture are to develop in students the abilities to

1. Choose among agricultural occupations
2. Start and advance in farming
3. Produce farm commodities efficiently
4. Market farm commodities effectively
5. Conserve soil and other natural resources
6. Perform mechanical activities of the farm
7. Improve farm living
8. Cooperate effectively in agricultural affairs
9. Become good farmer citizens

In general it is desired that they be given a basic background for developing abilities to

1. Provide and maintain appropriate farm machinery and power equipment
2. Produce high-quality products efficiently
3. Market agricultural products economically
4. Conserve and improve the soil
5. Engage in cooperative buying and selling activities
6. Keep, analyze, and use farm records
7. Work with other farm and rural people in projects for the improvement of agriculture and community life
8. Effect programs that have a desirable bearing an agriculture
9. Plan and obtain desirable legislation
10. Provide an FFA (Future Farmers of America) chapter leadership training school
11. Hold local, state, and national FFA public-speaking contests
12. Hold parliamentary procedure contests
13. Prepare and put on radio and TV programs
14. Have FFA members participate in state and national FFA conventions.

**Courses in Vocational Agriculture.** Courses in vocational agriculture vary a great deal from state to state and, indeed, from school to school. The type of instruction offered will depend upon the type of agricultural occupations available in the state. However, a considerable number of secondary schools offer training as follows: one year of animal husbandry, including poultry; one year of crop production, including horticulture; one year of farm management; and a year of advanced farm mechanics. The instructors prefer that the courses be taken in the order given above, the animal husbandry, of course, being taken largely by ninth graders; but, in general, the courses are open to students of any grade.

**Organization of Vocational Agricultural Courses.** Vocational courses in agriculture, as usually given, consist of four-year units of work, one for each of the grades nine through twelve. Classes ordinarily meet five times a week for a double period, although sometimes periods may be omitted in lieu of work done on a project in agriculture at home. Sometimes two of the units may be carried in one year by a student who starts the program after the ninth grade. Each year unit consists of the following divisions of work:

1. Group, individual, individual on-farm
2. Agricultural mechanics, or farm shop work
3. Supervised farm practice (production and improvement projects and supplementary farm training jobs)
4. FFA activities

In each year, the student has several major units, usually involving a project at home. These units may be of a recurring type, that is, certain parts of them are taught each year through the four years.

**Variations in Subjects Taught.** The vocational agricultural courses taught in high school differ from state to state, depending upon the effects of farming or related activities prevalent in that state. For example, in most southern states there would be units in tobacco production, in cotton production, in citrus fruit production, and probably in production of some tropical fruits including dates, olives, and figs. In northern states, none of these would be offered.

In at least a few states, units are offered in each of the following: poultry production, swine production, dairy production, sheep production, turkey production, farm horse and mule management, potato production, corn production, sugar beet production, wheat production, barley, oats, and rye production, field bean production, sorghum production, commercial truck and fruit crops, special truck and flower crops for seed, meadow hay production, production of alfalfa and other legumes, home vegetable production, range and pasture management, soil and water conservation, windbreaks, shelterbelts, tree planting and home beautification, bee keeping, farm management and record keeping, marketing, cooperation and cooperative organizations, farm credit, farm law, taxation and insurance, national farm organizations and federal farm agencies, and farm safety.

Each year, a student will spend approximately three months in farm mechanics in the shop. Also, each year, he will spend three or four weeks on the 4-H Club and their work and their activities. There will be some laboratory work in the school, but a great deal of laboratory work is on supervised projects at home or elsewhere out of school. The time of the year for various units depends upon the season according to the nature of the unit.[1]

There are many occupations related to agriculture and for which agricultural education is necessary as a basis, including the following:

*Agricultural business:* buying farm products; selling feeds, seeds, fertilizers, dairy products, and farm machinery; managing farmers' cooperatives

*Agricultural industry:* food preservation and processing; manufacture of farm implements and supplies; preparation of fertilizers

*Agricultural professions:* veterinary medicine; agricultural education; agricultural extension; agricultural journalism; agricultural banking; government service in the United States and other countries

*Agricultural services:* repairing farm machinery; constructing and repairing farm buildings; assisting farmers in record-keeping and income-tax reporting; spraying farm crops[2]

Most of the youngsters interested in agriculture in some form or another, even to a small degree, belong to a 4-H (Heart, Home, Head, and Hand) Club. The objectives and activities of the 4-H Club are broader than vocational agriculture, including emphasis upon character education and education for home living.

**Related Courses.** The education of future farmers should include courses in other fields, for example, science, general mathematics, economics, and general business. There is a trend toward better general education of the future farmer in the fields of English, history, science, and mathematics. Much of the training needed can be and is acquired on the job. Compared to several decades ago, the average farm today is much better

[1] Much of this material has been taken or adapted from "Vocational Agriculture: A Guide for Course Construction," prepared originally by Dr. G. A. Schmidt of the Colorado A & M College and published in 1961 by the State Board for Vocational Education, State Office Building, Denver.

[2] From *Facts You Should Know about Agricultural Education in the Public Schools,* p. 5. The original draft was prepared by H. M. Hamlin, Professor of Agricultural Education, University of Illinois, Urbana. 1961.

informed; he uses much better methods and can pass them on to young people working with him.

**General Agriculture.** A small but slowly increasing number of schools offer a course in general agriculture, which, though it serves somewhat as an exploratory course for those who include agriculture among their vocational possibilities, is actually for the general education of students not intending to be farmers.

## ARTS AND CRAFTS

Until after the beginning of the twentieth century, a great many secondary schools offered neither fine arts nor crafts as subjects, although in grades seven and eight in the elementary schools instruction of a simple and restricted nature was usually given. Because of the expense involved, it was principally in drawing and in painting with water color; indeed, textbook companies published "drawing books." In many schools, the drawing period was spent in an attempt to reproduce on paper or in a drawing book some fruits or flowers or some other object placed toward the front of the room where it would presumably be easily seen by all of the students.

In the last quarter of the nineteenth century, industrial arts began to be offered in many schools, particularly woodworking, which was called "manual training" because one of the avowed objectives was to train the hands and to develop eye-mind-hand coordination. This seemed to make it non-vocational and "respectable." This practice continued when junior high schools were formed.

In many academies in the nineteenth century, and later in the four-year high schools and senior high schools, courses in arts were introduced, but most frequently the instructors had very limited repertoires and the young people got their training in only one or two phases of art. More recently, instructors with broader training have become available, and, as the schools have grown larger, two or more instructors could be employed with somewhat different training. Consequently, the great majority of high school students today can get training in five, six, or even more fields of arts and crafts, including ceramics, painting, and drawing. Indeed, a number of youngsters used this opportunity for the purpose of exploring their talents and interests. Arts and crafts are usually offered for credit, frequently for one-half the usual credit for a full period five times a week.

The principal objectives of arts and crafts are for recreational purposes, although some students have the talents to follow a particular craft as a profession. These courses also contribute to preparation for home living, mental hygiene, and preparation for leisure and recreational activities.

## BUSINESS

Courses in business are offered both for preparation for vocation and as general education. The vocational courses lead to many different occupations, but the two principal fields are secretarial work and sales.

**General-Education Business Courses.** Far more students are enrolled in typewriting than in any other business course. An increasing number of students have been learning to type not only as a part of their general business training but also for personal use and as a part of their preparation for college and, indeed, for the latter years of secondary education. Typing is ordinarily offered in each grade above the eighth grade, but the large majority of the students are in either the ninth or the tenth grade. First-year typing is usually offered five times a week, with one or two practice periods a week in schools with the longer period and five double periods a week in schools having the shorter period.

Many secondary schools offer a course in general business education. It goes by a number of names such as "junior business training," "general business," "introduction to business," and "everyday business." It is usually offered as a ninth-grade or tenth-grade course meeting five times a week with outside preparation.

Other courses offered for the purpose of general business education as well as to provide a basis for vocational business education are economic geography, business letter writing, personal salesmanship, and commercial law. These courses are usually offered in the larger high schools.

**Vocational Business Education.** With the increased number of students completing high school, there has been an increase in students, particularly girls, enrolling for vocational business-education courses. The majority of them take what is called the stenographic or secretarial curriculum, which involves courses in typewriting and shorthand that are taken usually in the eleventh grade, and a general secretarial course involving advanced training in typewriting, shorthand, and a considerable number of other secretarial duties. Because of an increased demand for male secretaries for lower-rung jobs in business and industry, there has been a slight increase in the number of boys taking secretarial training. Those following the secretarial curriculum are also required to take work in English, general mathematics, and social studies.

In recent decades, there has been a very great increase in the use of all kinds of machines in business. Many of these machines are very expensive, and the great majority of schools are unable to purchase them. This is particularly true of the computer machines. Nevertheless, practically all of the larger schools have purchased a variety of machines and provide training in the use of them for both secretaries and those following the accounting curriculum. The machines most commonly found for training in secondary schools are typewriters, calculating machines, duplicating machines, dictating and transcribing machines, and bookkeeping machines. In an increasing number of schools a course is offered in "business machines."

**The General Clerical Curriculum.** A great many senior high schools offer to a rapidly increasing number of boys and girls a curriculum for those who wish to prepare themselves to do clerical work in business but do not wish to be secretaries. The business courses in this curriculum include typewriting, filing, simple adding machine operation, business use of telephone, and non-specialized clerical work such as classifying, sorting, checking names and numbers for accuracy, filling in forms by hand, collating, stapling, and other similar duties. Some of those following this curriculum also take a course in sales. Most graduates of this course go into positions as mail clerks, file clerks, switchboard operators, reception clerks, shipping clerks, multigraph operators, record clerks, verification clerks, transcribing machine operators, typists, and the like. Some go into business on their own.

**Bookkeeping or Accounting Courses.** The first course to be introduced in secondary schools in the United States was one in "accounts." Now called bookkeeping, it is usually offered as a one-year course in the eleventh grade but is open to twelfth graders. Some schools offer a second-year course in "bookkeeping," which is really in elementary accounting. A great many of those taking the first-year course in bookkeeping take it for personal and general reasons rather than as vocational education, wishing to be prepared to do the bookkeeping related to small business, farms, clubs, lodges, churches, and home and family affairs.

**Distributive Education.** Vocational training in salesmanship is usually offered under the title "distributive education." Federal and state subsidies may be obtained by schools that offer distributive courses along the lines prescribed by the state and federal authorities. The vocational segment of the course consists of two parts: (1) a course in psychology and techniques of salesmanship and (2) actual experiences in the local community, the student usually spending fifteen to twenty hours on the job, under the supervision of the coordinator of the distributive-education program. This type of work experience, which is broader than salesmanship, is described elsewhere in this volume.

**Enrolments in Business Courses.** About half of the enrolments in business courses in secondary schools are in first-year typing. This is because so many students take it for personal use. Other courses that enrol large numbers of students are general business, second-year typing, first-year bookkeeping, first-year shorthand, business work experience, office machines, office practice, business mathematics, and business English.

Several subjects have enrolments that are smaller but have increased greatly in recent years. Among these are courses in record keeping, business law, stenographic office practice, retail merchandising, advanced general business, and consumer economics.

## ENGLISH

Instruction in English includes a number of divisions such as language and grammar, oral speech and oral composition, written composition, English literature, American literature, dramatics, and journalism. A year course in English is required in all but a very few schools in grades seven through eleven and, in the majority of schools, in grade twelve also.

**Junior High School English.** Before the advent of junior high schools, usually there were two English subjects offered daily in grades seven and eight—one in the language arts including spelling, language and grammar, speech, and composition, and the other in American and English literature. When the change was made to the one longer period, the relative amount of time and emphasis given English was greatly reduced. It is thought by many that this is rather unfortunate and has resulted in mediocre quality of achievement of high school students in spelling, language, and grammar.

In the senior high school, language, grammar, composition, and speech arts, on the one hand, and literature, on the other, are taught separately by some teachers and are integrated by others. Required in practically all schools in grades ten and eleven for many years, English is now being required in practically all schools through grade twelve.

**Language and Grammar.** During the 1930's and 1940's, there was a very material swing away from the teaching of grammar, in view of the fact that it had been shown that many students seemed to learn the rules and facts of grammar without experiencing a corresponding improvement in their ability to use written and spoken language. When teachers accepted this trend and gave very little attention to the teaching of formal grammar, the results obtained seemed to be even worse.

Increased importance is being attached to the abilities to speak and to write fluently, particularly the former. These abilities give social status, and the corresponding inabilities contribute to loss of social status.

Furthermore, the lack of ability to speak correctly and fluently, and to a lesser extent to write fluently, with legible penmanship, diminished the possibility of vocational success in many occupations. It has become obvious that not only scholastic success in college but also effectiveness in written and oral communications—reading, listening to the radio, watching television, conversing, etc.—depends upon the possession of a fairly large vocabulary with precise rather than fuzzy and inaccurate meanings.

**Reading.** With the greater recognition of the tremendous importance of the ability to read well—to read some things with good comprehension and retention; to read other things rapidly, getting the general gist; and to read still other things critically, developing skills and habits of analysis, especially for evaluation of political and sales materials—much more attention has been given to the degree to which young people in the schools are learning to read well. Sensational commercial publications such as "Why Johnny Can't Read," "Educational Wastelands," and "Quackery in the Schools," while for a time misleading many as to the true situation existing in the public schools, served a purpose in directing attention to the need for improvement in the teaching of reading. With the development of the radio and television, many young children have erroneously conceived the idea that it is not very important to be able to read, so that many arrive at the seventh grade with very inferior reading ability and habits.

In an increasing number of schools, sections have been organized for poor readers in the seventh grade, to provide special instruction in reading in order not only that the students may read well, in general, but also that they may read well enough to succeed in the subjects of instruction that require ability to read, particularly science, mathematics, history, the social studies, and literature. Even in senior high school and in college, groups of young people of limited reading ability are gathered together for special instruction.

**Written Composition.** In recent years, there has been an increased emphasis upon the importance of developing skills in written composition. This has grown out of the discovery that a great many young people have not developed a very satisfactory level of such skill and fluency, and also out of an increased appreciation of the importance of being able to write well.

English teachers have been notoriously overloaded and, for that reason, have required what is thought by a great many careful students of the matter to be too small an amount of written work, and have spent too little time in reading what students write and in diagnosing weaknesses and giving remedial instruction. In recent years, there has developed a

Safety education at Granby High School, Norfolk, Virginia.

Driver education at Mumford High School, Detroit.

Driver training with simulators—Atlanta.

Science at Roosevelt Junior High School, Peoria, Illinois.

very pronounced trend toward reducing the load of the English teacher—in some schools to four classes daily, in other schools to five classes of twenty to twenty-five students, and in still other schools, in which the size of class is not decreased, by providing assistants who do much of the reading and marking of student themes and who furnish the teacher with data relative to the weaknesses both of the individuals in the class and of the group, as a basis for planning special remedial instruction.

**Literature.** A great deal of controversy has gone on for a quarter of a century regarding what should be the objectives and the materials for literature instruction in secondary schools. A generation or so ago, the bulk of what was studied was classical literature. Teachers prided themselves on being able to teach these classics, and it was considered very respectable to emphasize such items as Scott's "Lady of the Lake," Burke's "Speech on Conciliation," the poetry of Shelley and Keats, the *Pickwick Papers,* and the Sir Roger de Coverley papers. In recent years there has been a pronounced tendency to the teaching of current and what might be called middle-brow or upper-middle-brow levels of literature of the type of John Hersey's "Hiroshima," "Cheaper by the Dozen," "Mama's Bank Account," and other similar books.

Literature has been taught less and less for the purpose of developing powers for literary criticism of the writing of literature, or to provide status value by enabling the student to discuss authors and works not generally known to the less well educated, and more and more for such very important and practical purposes as the following: (1) to develop habits and tastes of the general public for reading of what might be called middle-grade literature of quality; (2) to develop an understanding of one's self and of other human beings in their various relationships, including the psychology of human relationships in the home, in business, in politics, and at leisure; and (3) to develop an understanding of sociological, political, and economic problems and problems of international relations.

**Speech.** For the past several decades, an increased amount of attention has been given to speech education in addition to those provided in the usual English classes. But, unfortunately, a great many teachers of English have majored and minored too narrowly to be able to teach well all phases of English including speech.

Most youngsters need to have some training in speech, to develop the ability to express themselves orally somewhat fluently, precisely, and correctly, without too much embarrassment. In both junior and senior high schools, there are some youngsters who need special remedial training in speech by reason of inability to enunciate clearly, because of unusual embarrassment and nervous tension not only in talking to a group but in ordinary conversation, or by reason of some speech defect such as stammering, lisping, or indistinct speech resulting from a cleft palate. Special sections in speech are now formed in most schools and are taught by teachers with special training in speech.

**Other Areas.** English teachers, like most other teachers in secondary schools, are beginning to give a little more incidental attention to diagnosis of, and remedial work with, individual students in spelling and penmanship.

**Current Trends.** There are certain important trends in the materials and methods of teaching English in secondary schools that are worthy of mention even though they may not as yet be characteristic of the majority of secondary schools:

1. English instruction is being more and more integrated into idea-centered units that involve a number of the aspects of English, including reading, oral discussion, language, literature, and speech.

2. Language and grammar are taught, especially in senior high schools, more and more in connection with the oral speech and written composition of the students, and a great emphasis is made upon providing for practice that will tend to improve the habits and skills of correct speech and writing.

3. There is a greater degree of integration of the various aspects of the language arts, as opposed to separate teaching, for example, discussions and written compositions are related to the literature being read.

4. There is more individualized instruction based upon an inventory of reading interests and a diagnosis of speech weaknesses.

5. More attention is being given to the teaching of English, particularly of literature, in a way that will give the student a better understanding of the psychology of himself, of other people, and of human relationships. This may be done not only in the study of literature but also in connection with all discussions and written compositions.

## FOREIGN LANGUAGES

Foreign languages constitute a field in which there have been not only a great deal of criticism and suggestions for changes but also a very great change in practices and a great demand for increased enrolments. In 1963, 30 per cent of all high school students were enrolled in some class in foreign language, as compared with 24 per cent in 1958. In the order of number of students, Spanish was first, with Latin and French close behind. Although far behind, German enrolled 65 per cent more students than in 1958. Enrolments in Russian more than tripled between 1958 and 1963, while in Italian there were fewer students—only 20,000. Enrolments in Latin have also increased slightly in recent years. Though a few schools have recently added two years of some foreign language to their requirements for graduation, the number having this requirement is still small.

**Foreign Languages in the Junior High School.** Until recently, many teachers and others believed that a study of Latin in the junior high school constituted a most useful basis not only for study of modern foreign languages but also for understanding of English grammar and language. Research investigations showed, however, that no materially greater contributions were made to these objectives by the study of Latin than by the study of some other foreign language.

In a rather large and increasing number of junior high schools, foreign language is taught in the seventh grade for beginners and for those who have studied it in the elementary school. In practically all junior high schools, at least one language is offered in the eighth and ninth grades. These classes are usually taught by a large and increasing number of teachers who have had much training in a foreign language and who are, in many instances, quite facile in the speaking of the language. Many teachers emphasize conversational facility, although to a great extent instruction is still largely in translation and syntax.

**Foreign Languages in the Senior High School.** In many senior high schools, third-, fourth-, and fifth-year courses in a foreign language, and, indeed, in some a sixth year, have been added. This is a result of the growing conviction that the superficial study of a foreign language for two years results in a very inadequate and superficial mastery of the language and that real results are obtained only after the language has been studied at least three or four years.

Because of the greater interest in foreign language, in many schools more modern foreign languages are offered, and in an increasing number Russian and Chinese are offered. In some schools, one foreign language is being dropped in order to increase enrolments in the others sufficiently to ensure third- and fourth-year classes large enough to warrant the offering of advanced work.

Enrolments in foreign languages have probably been increased somewhat by the spread of the rather fuzzy idea that, by studying the grammar including the various irregular verbs of a foreign language, we may better appreciate the peoples of other countries. The facts that there are hundreds of foreign languages in this world and that each of more than twenty of them is spoken by at least 50 million people brings to mind to many the limitations of the study of one foreign language as a means of understanding the peoples of the world.

**Important Trends.** There has been a definite trend in foreign languages to study of the customs, economic conditions, and government of the people speaking the language. The desire of instructors to make rapid progress in the grammar, translation, and speaking of the language has been a deterrent to the trend to utilize the time in the study of language in an attempt to achieve one of the avowedly important objectives, namely, a better understanding of the people of other cultures.

In recent years, there has been a very pronounced increase in the use of various sorts of audio-visual and technological aids in instruction in foreign languages. Most prominent among those has been the tape recorder, by means of which the student may hear the language spoken correctly, may hear his own pronunciation and enunciation, and may make comparisons. In an increasing number of schools, there have been established language laboratories in which for each student there is a station equipped with a recording device and other audio equipment centrally controlled by the teacher, usually from an elevated platform at the front of the room.

There is also an increased use of recordings and various types of visual materials, the later being used principally, of course, for the study of the geography and the people of the country or countries in which the language is spoken.

The more clear-thinking and culture-minded instructors in Latin have been attempting to have more students of Latin understand better our indebtedness to Greek and Roman culture, and they have often described factors bringing about the decay and passing of the Roman Empire as comparable to certain developments and characteristics of recent life in the United States and western European countries.

## HISTORY AND THE SOCIAL STUDIES

**Objectives.** Obviously, the principal objective of instruction in history and the social studies is education for intelligent patriotism and citizenship. There are, however, other objectives, since the study of history and the social studies makes contributions to other areas and problems of living.

History and the social studies make some contribution to home living by increasing understanding of the family and problems confronted in matters of consumer efficiency. History and social studies also contribute to preparation for success in business fields, in the professions, or in labor.

Reading is a major diversion of the American public. Through the study of history and the social studies, interests are developed that are followed by most high school graduates in the form of reading of current journals and books on historical and social subjects, especially paperbacks. The number of books published in these fields and the number of copies sold have increased greatly in recent years.

**Offerings, Requirements, and Enrolments.** More than those in any other field, the offerings in the field of history and the social studies vary from school to school and have been undergoing slow but constant change for several decades. A typical offering includes geography in the seventh grade, United States' history in the eighth grade, social studies (usually emphasizing civics) in the ninth grade, history of the world in the tenth grade, United States' history and government in grade eleven, and social studies of some sort in the twelfth grade (usually involving social problems or economics).

In recent years, there has been a definite increase in the number of schools offering economics for a semester or for a year. There has also been an increase in the number of schools offering courses on the history and culture of countries other than Europe and the United States. There are still many schools offering a course in history of the local state. In a few states, "patriotic" politicians in the legislature have passed laws requiring that history of the state be offered in schools, and in a small number of states it is required of students. It has, however, been dropped by many schools, and enrolments are usually small when it is offered as an elective. Courses in ancient and medieval history are practically disappearing from the secondary schools, these periods of history being taught rather sketchily in the course in world history.

Since 1960, there has been an increase in the proportion of students taking history and the social studies. Indeed, an increased number of schools are requiring for graduation more units in these subjects. It seems that the number enrolled in the social studies will continue to increase as it becomes increasingly recognized that the safety of our people calls for a citizenry much better educated in matters of international relations and national economics than are citizens today.

The offering of United States' history in the junior high school and a very similar course in the senior high school has long been criticized. Some schools are reducing the course at one or the other level to a semester in length, and in many schools articulation has been brought about and duplication reduced by deciding upon different emphases at the different levels. For example, it has been pointed out by Dr. Edgar B. Wesley, an eminent authority on the teaching of history and the social studies, that, in the junior high school, the course might well center around the theme "The Building of the Nation," with approximately two-thirds of the time devoted to the period between 1776 and 1876. He suggests that, in the senior high school, the course should be organized around the theme "A Democratic Nation in a World Setting," with at least one-half of the time devoted to the period since 1865.

Special courses in current events have all but disappeared from American secondary schools; in their place has developed the custom of having discussions of current events in practically all courses in history and the social studies. In some schools, one day a week is given over in one or more courses to discussion of current events in certain predetermined areas that are thought to be of unusual interest and unusual importance at the time.

**Scope and Sequence.** There is no single best scope or sequence for organizing the required social studies in grades seven through twelve. A committee appointed to study the problem, by the National Association of Secondary-School Principals, suggests these possible approaches to scope and sequence organization:

### Illustration One

| | |
|---|---|
| Grades 7 and 8 | American history to 1870; local, state, Federal government, and United States geography. |
| Grades 9 and 10 | World geography and world history, both courses organized according to culture areas. |
| Grades 11 and 12 | United States history (since 1870, with a brief overview of the history prior to 1870), and much attention [to] modern economic, governmental and international problems. |

### Illustration Two

| | |
|---|---|
| Grades 7 and 8 (first semester) | Broad field, geographic centered, socioeconomic units on key and representative regions and nations of the world. |
| Grade 8 (2nd semester) | The citizen and his local, state, and national government (functions, relationships, structures, and agencies featured). |
| Grade 9 (1st semester) | Introduction to the understanding of peoples and their institutions (major anthropological and sociological concepts). |
| Grades 9 and 10 (2nd semester) | History of selected eras, peoples, and nations of the world with full attention to contemporary aspects and problems. |
| Grade 11 | United States history and government (with important economic units). |
| Grade 12 | Contemporary problems that challenge the citizen (limited to 6 to 10 live issues—political, economic, and social, local to international in scope). |

### Illustration Three

| | |
|---|---|
| Grade 7 | World Vistas—history of the peoples of Eurasia and Africa. |
| Grade 8 | History of the United States to 1876. |

| Grade 9 | A. History of a state. |
| | B. American government and citizenship—national, state, and local. |
| Grade 10 | History of the United States since 1876. |
| Grade 11 | World cultures—Western and non-Western. |
| Grade 12 | Contemporary problems at home and abroad. |

Whatever scope and sequence is followed in a local school must be logically developed to avoid unnecessary repetitions . . . The mobility of population suggests more attention to a nationally accepted definition of scope and sequence.[3]

**A Course on Communism?** Since the late 1950's, there has been much talk and some action in favor of offering a course on communism, or at least a unit on communism in some course in the social studies. To many this seems a doubtful procedure, since the teacher of a unit on communism would be almost certain to be under terrific pressures by emotionally excited grandstanding pseudopatriots and anti-Communists who would insist that anything but a misleading, inaccurate indoctrination against communism is a definite indication of a lack of true patriotism on the part of the teacher. Most probably a high-presure anticommunism course would lead to indifference or antagonism on the part of adolescents.

**Important Trends.** Increasingly, teachers of history and the social studies are employing a problems approach, much use of discussions, greater use of visual material, much use of supplementary readings, and greater use of community resources. In recent years, there has been increased emphasis upon the importance of the development of understanding and of attitudes, particularly those inherent in the fundamental philosophy of the American way of life. Tests and evaluative techniques of various types have been developed and are increasingly used in an attempt to discover what the effects of the instruction and learner activities have been.

## QUESTIONS, PROBLEMS, AND TOPICS FOR FURTHER STUDY

1. Do you believe that every student should have some experience in exploring his interests and talent in the several arts and crafts? If so, for what reason?
2. Do you believe that every student should take a general business-education course? Give reasons for your answer.
3. Do you believe that insufficient stress is placed on grammar in the schools? Be able to support your position firmly.

[3] Delmas J. Miller *et al.*, "Social Studies in the Comprehensive," *Bulletin of the N.A.S.S.P.*, No. 266 (September, 1961), p. 6.

4. Do you believe that students should be given more training in written composition? What are the reasons for your position?
5. What kind or kinds of literature do you believe should be taught in the junior high school? In the senior high school?
6. To what extent do you think attention should be given to speech in the secondary school?
7. Do you believe that all students should be encouraged to take Latin as a basis for improvement of their English and as a basis for modern-language courses?
8. Which foreign language do you think most students should take? Why?
9. It has been recently stressed that students should take more than two years of a foreign language. What are the arguments for and against that position?
10. What contribution do you think the study of a foreign language makes to better international understanding? What foreign language or languages would you recommend for that purpose?
11. Write down what you think should be the changes in what is taught in the social studies in the junior high school and in the senior high school.

## SUPPLEMENTARY MATERIALS

### Selected Readings

ABRAMOWITZ, JACK. "Implications of the Conant Report for the Social Studies," *The High School Journal,* XLVI(8), 259–67.

BAHR, GLADYS. "The Contribution of Secondary School Basic Business Education to General Education," *National Business Education Quarterly,* XXX (December, 1961), 62–77.

BECKER, JAMES M. "Education for Participation in World Affairs," *Bulletin of the N.A.S.S.P.,* XLIV (September, 1960), 143–50.

BENT, RUDYARD K, and HENRY H. KRONENBERG. *Principles of Secondary Education* (4th ed.). New York: McGraw-Hill Book Co., Inc., 1961. Pp. 349–54, 425.

BUSINESS EDUCATION FORUM. "The Changing Business Program in High School," *The Education Digest,* XXVI (April, 1961), 47–50.

CARDOZIER, V. R. "Redesigning Agricultural Education Programs for the Public Schools," *Bulletin of the N.A.S.S.P.,* No. 270 (March, 1962), 173–83.

COMMITTEE FOR CURRICULUM PLANNING AND DEVELOPMENT. "English Language Arts in the Comprehensive Secondary School," *Bulletin of the N.A.S.S.P.,* XLIV (October, 1960), 45–48.

EVANS, WILLIAM H. "Composition, Reading and the Conant Report," *The High School Journal,* XLVI(8), 268–78.

FRASER, DOROTHY M. *Current Curriculum Studies in Academic Subjects.* Washington, D.C.: National Education Association of the United States, 1962. Chapter 4, "English Language Arts, pp. 43–51; Chapter 5, "Modern Foreign Languages," pp. 54–71; Chapter 6, "Social Studies," pp. 72–85.

GROSS, RICHARD E., and DWIGHT W. ALLEN. "Time for a National Effort to Develop the Social Studies Curriculum," *Phi Delta Kappan,* XLIV (May, 1963), 360–66.

HARTSHORN, MERRILL R. "Current Critical Issue in Secondary Education—Social Studies in the Comprehensive Secondary School," *Bulletin of the N.A.S.S.P.,* No. 263 (April, 1961), 312–26.

HATFIELD, W. W., and ELIZABETH BOESHORE. "Advances and Trends in the Teaching of English," *Issues in Curriculum Development*. New York: Harcourt, Brace & World, Inc., 1959, pp. 127–36.

HAUGH, OSCAR M. "Developing a Course of Study in English in the Small High School," *University of Kansas Bulletin of Education* XVII (May, 1963), 127–32.

KAI-YU HSU, SHAU WING CHAN, THEODORE CHEN, GEORGE STREM, HENRY YANG, RICHARD M. CLOWES, FRANK B. LINDSAY, and EVERETT V. O'ROURKE. "Chinese Language Instruction in California Public Schools," *California Schools*, XXXIII (September, 1962), 341.

KEEZER, DEXTER M. "The Importance of Economic Education in the Secondary School," *Bulletin of the N.A.S.S.P.*, No. 272 (May, 1962), 223–32.

KOSTBADE, J. T., and J. M. BALL. "Geography and Education for Citizenship," *Bulletin of the N.A.S.S.P.*, No. 253 (February, 1960), 159–65.

KRUG, EDWARD A. *The Secondary School Curriculum*. New York: Harper & Row, 1960. Chapter 9, "English," pp. 233–56; Chapter 10, "Foreign Language"; Chapter 12, "Social Studies," pp. 297–319; Chapter 14, "Fine Arts."

LABRANT, LOU. "High School English Today: A Brief Overview," *Bulletin of the N.A.S.S.P.*, No. 279 (April, 1963), 52–61.

LALLY, ANN M. Art Education in the Secondary Schools," *Bulletin of the N.A.S.S.P.*, No. 262 (March, 1961). Chapter 2, "The Curriculum," pp. 10–29; Chapter 3, "Scheduling Art in the Secondary School," pp. 30–31.

McLENDON, JONATHAN. *Teaching the Social Studies: What Research says to the Teacher Series No. 20*. Washington, D.C.: National Education Association of the United States, 1960.

MARLAND, S. P., JR. "Placing Sex Education in the Curriculum," *Phi Delta Kappan*, XLIII (December, 1961), pp. 132–35.

MAXWELL, GERALD W. "Are You Up to Date in Basic Business Content?" *Business Education Forum*, XVI (October, 1961), 232–35.

MORELOCK, CHARLES F. "Journalism Teaching in Kansas High Schools," *University of Kansas Bulletin of Education*, XVII (May, 1963), 121–26.

MUSSELMAN, VERNON A. "The Business Curriculum," *National Business Education Quarterly*, XVI (May, 1958), 29–34.

NATIONAL SOCIETY FOR THE STUDY OF EDUCATION. *Development in and Through Reading* (Sixtieth Yearbook, Part I). University of Chicago Press, 1961, Chapters 17 and 18 (reading programs in junior and senior high schools).

OLSON, MILTON C., and EUGENE L. SEVEARINGER. "Business and Economic Education," *NEA Journal*, LI (April, 1962), 43–44.

PARKER, J. CECIL, T. BENTLEY EDWARDS, and WILLIAM H. STEGEMAN. *Curriculum in America*. New York: Thomas Y. Crowell Co., 1962. Chapter 11, "The Fine Arts."

RAPPAPORT, DAVID. "Does 'Modern Math' Ignore Learning Theory?" *Phi Delta Kappan*, XLIV (June, 1963), 445–47.

"Recommendation for Economic Education in the Schools," *The Education Digest*, XXVII (April, 1962), 46–49.

TAYLOR, L. O., DAN D. McMAHILL, and B. L. TAYLOR. *The American Secondary School*. New York: Appleton-Century-Crofts, Inc., 1960. Chapter 14, "The Improvement of Reading."

WAGNER, LEWIS E. "Process in Closing the Materials Gap in Economic Education," *Bulletin of the N.A.S.S.P.*, No. 270 (March, 1962), 100–112.

# The Subject Fields of Study (Continued)

## HOME ECONOMICS OR HOUSEHOLD ARTS

Courses in home economics or household arts are offered at all levels of secondary education and in all types of public secondary schools including junior high schools, senior high schools, four-year high schools, and six-year high schools. With the rapidly diminishing number of small high schools—those with less than 200 students—the number of schools with not enough students to offer a course in home economics has become very small. In most school systems, home-economics courses are offered in every grade from the seventh through the twelfth. (See pages 124–125, for a suggested course arrangement for grades seven through twelve.)

Homemaking education for youth and adults as a part of the public school program now serves, at some time during the secondary school years, approximately one-fourth of the total high school population. Approximately half of the girls and about 1 per cent of the boys enrolled in high school take some home economics. Some states require that a three-year program in home economics be offered—one year at the seventh- or eighth-grade level, one year at the ninth-grade level, and one year in senior high school.

Home economics is placed in the school program in several ways: as a special subject, in a core curriculum, and in connection with other subjects. In the secondary school program, it is found most often in the seventh and eighth grades as a special subject for girls, although there is a trend toward making it a part of the core program for all pupils. Some schools still require foods and clothing for one-half or one full year; but increasing numbers are offering homemaking for the full year, each year consisting of a series of units with experiences designed to give the pupil an understanding and appreciation of his own personal development at the early adolescent level and a realization of his own role as a member of the home and family group.

In the senior high school curriculum, because the student is more interested than previously in looking at the family objectively, is nearer to the establishment of his own home and vocation, and is developing special interests, a more specialized program can be given with more intensive units.

In the senior high school, home economics is offered in one, two, or three years, depending on the enrolment, facilities, and availability of teachers, usually as an elective, more often only for girls, although more courses in social and family living are being made available for both boys and girls. Courses or units in health and home nursing, child development and guidance, consumer buying, housing, and related arts also are becoming more available in the senior high schools.

**New Shifts in Objectives and Emphasis.** In the past few decades, there has been much change with respect to the objectives, content, and methods of teaching home-economis courses for general education. This is the result of changes in American homes.

In very few American homes today are foods canned or preserved; breads, rolls, and pies made; or clothing constructed. As a matter of fact, cooking, as such, has become a lost art in many American homes, since in the grocery stores and supermarkets all but a few of the kinds of food served in the home are sold prepared and ready to go on the table or require but a little heating, perhaps browning. Each package carries full and explicit directions for completing preparation of the food.

Clothing can be purchased approximately as cheaply as the cloth required to make the clothing oneself, and the responsibilities in the home with respect to clothing have diminished to jobs of repair and some types of cleaning. As a matter of fact, with the advent of coin-operated washing and dry-cleaning machines, very little cleaning is done in any but lowest-economic-level communities.

With these and other changes taking place, home-economics courses are stressing more and more, and giving more time and attention to, such things as

1. Home selection and decoration
2. A good diet, selection of food, planning and organization of meals, good food habits
3. Tastes in grooming and dressing that enable students to have a good appearance involving the selection of clothing, styles, how

to adapt clothing purchases to the type of individual, lasting qualities of various types of goods, and ease with which they may be cleaned and pressed

4. Child care and child rearing, involving the psychology of child growth and development, matters of discipline and training, first-aid activities in the home, diagnosis and treatment of simple diseases, particularly those by which children are affected, and family nursing

5. Problems of family finance, including purchasing, budget making, insurance, investments, taxes, pensions, and borrowing at reasonable rates of interest

6. Repair and operation of appliances, including knowledge and skills in the operation and simple repair of such things as vacuum cleaners, disposers, washing machines, dishwashers, and electrical circuits, as well as replacement of blown fuses, reading of meters, simple painting and staining, and fixing of leaking faucets and clogged drains

Throughout the country, hundreds of thousands of homes are built each year for newly married people. It has been observed that the majority of these homes are poorly built and will soon deteriorate. The inferior materials and workmanship are in most instances not readily observable, and the prospective purchaser should learn how to discover what is out of sight. Tastes may profitably be developed with respect to the shape and color of the exterior of the house and its placement on the lot. Some taste in landscaping of lawn, shubbery, and trees is also useful.

More attention is being given to the development of taste for interior furnishing and decorating, involving walls, floors, furniture, drapes, etc. It is clear that the trend in home-economics education is definitely away from great emphasis upon the cooking of foods, or the production of clothing, and in the direction of consumer education and personal relationships.

There appears to be greater need for learning how to get along together in the home and community. This implies an understanding of one's own behavior, other people's bahavior, and the desired behavior of people in happy family living. Experiences in social living are vital to young people to help them in boy-girl relationships and in planning for the establishment of happy families.

Some courses offer opportunities for boys and girls to discuss the social and economic problems of homemaking and family living. An investigation of the interests of eleventh- and twelfth-grade boys and girls, listed by high school teachers, gives clues for content: boy-girl relations, clothing and personal grooming, everyday problems of the teen-ager, housing problems of concern to high school boys and girls, learning to understand children, living together in the family, looking toward marriage, personal and family finances, personality and character development, healthful living, and looking ahead to a vocation.

**Senior Course in Home Living.** In a great many secondary schools, there is offered in the eleventh or twelfth grade a semester's or a year's course in home living, open to both boys and girls, although in some schools there are separate sections for each sex. In this course, some of the content of general home-economics education is offered at a somewhat advanced and condensed level, but the unique contribution of such a course is instruction about relationships between the members of the home, including such matters as the courtship and selection of a mate, the causes of marital unhappiness and divorce, ideals, personality characteristics, and elements of character. This instruction makes for successful family life, understanding in rearing of children, skill in handling home finances, and healthful living.

In the early 1960's, one in every four new marriages ended in divorce. The current divorce rate is seven times what it was 100 years ago. The juvenile delinquency rate has nearly tripled in 20 years. The illegitimacy rate has tripled since 1938. More than 200,000 emotionally disturbed persons are admitted to state and local hospitals annually. All these problems in human relationships, and many others, either cause or can be traced to difficulties in family life.

**Vocational Household Arts.** In recent years, the people of the United States have been eating a much larger percentage of their meals out of the home. As a matter of fact, various estimates put that ratio at between two and three times as many out-of-home meals as compared to the number in 1950. Naturally, the number of positions in the preparation and serving of food in commercial establishments has correspondingly increased. There is a much greater demand for cooks and assistant cooks and for managers of restaurants and cafeterias. Preparation for such vocations is potentially one of the major fields of home economics in senior high schools. Other areas in which courses are offered and preparation made include commercial laundry work; home nursing; garment making, fitting, and alteration; and interior decoration.

In school districts in which diversified occupation programs are operated, there is opportunity to get on-the-job training in a number of fields—in restaurants, cleaning and pressing establishments, hotels, child nurseries, and stores selling home furnishings. The nature of the particular activities in a number of these vocational activities is such that they cannot be easily offered in school and can be gotten better on the job, particularly because it is difficult to provide a realistic situation in school.

## MATHEMATICS

At least five types of mathematics are offered in secondary schools in the United States: (1) general mathematics, (2) the pre-engineering sequence, (3) vocational mathematics, (4) the "new" mathematics, and (5) remedial arithmetic.

**General-Mathematics Courses.** General mathematics begins in earnest in the seventh grade, where, while much of the material is arithmetic, there is also some algebra in the form of formulas and equations to be solved and concepts to be learned of the fundamental axioms such as "Equals added to equals gives equals." Also beginning in the seventh grade is the study of the geometry of lines, figures, and solids, though ordinarily no proofs are required.

General mathematics of this type is required in the seventh and eighth grades in practically all schools, although special sections of remedial arithmetic are offered in a fairly large and increasing number of junior high schools in the seventh grade and in a great many in the eighth grade.

In the ninth grade, general mathematics, if not actually required, is strongly urged upon all those not taking algebra. General mathematics in the senior high school has had an up and down career. In the 1940's, the number of schools offering a course in general mathematics in the eleventh and twelfth grades increased, and in the 1950's, the trend tapered off and seemed to subside; now, in the 1960's, it has started up again.

**The Engineering and Science Sequence.** Inherited from the academies and early college-preparatory high schools, there is offered in most secondary schools today a sequence that is very serviceable for those planning to enter schools or colleges of engineering or to major in mathematics or in physical science in a liberal arts college. Algebra is usually offered in the ninth grade, and approximately one-half of the ninth-graders in the United States today are taking algebra.

In the tenth grade, the offering is usually plane geometry, although, in a considerable and increasing number of schools, plane and solid geometry are combined in the tenth grade. The skepticism of psychologists, educators, and people in general relative to the superior qualities of geometry for training the mind has increased, and the revaltively minor value of it in engineering has contributed to this trend.

In the eleventh grade, the typical offering is second-year algebra or, more often, trigonometry and third-semester algebra. A considerable number of schools still offer algebra and solid geometry in the eleventh grade and advanced algebra and trigonometry in the twelfth grade.

**The "New" Mathematics.** In recent years, particularly since the commotion created by Sputnik and with the increased availability of foundation funds, there has been very much activity in attempts to improve the curriculum and instruction in secondary school mathematics. Some four or five national commissions and committees have been appointed and subsidized to work on the problem. Just what the ultimate effects on instruction in mathematics will be is still problematical. The reports and materials already made available to teachers and the general public involve a new vocabulary—many of the words and terms being for the same concepts and operations—and more integrated materials of instruction. It still remains to be proved that many but the very superior and interested students can study the new mathematics materials to advantage, and teachers generally are very much confused by the new and strange vocabulary and arrangement of materials. Some of the new materials are, nevertheless, being incorporated in courses in the majority of secondary schools.

**Mathematics for the Superior Student.** Without question, however, there will be some effect—minor or greater—on the organization and content of mathematics in the curriculum after the eighth grade for students of superior mathematical ability.

In some junior high schools, teachers have proudly demonstrated that they are able to teach first-year algebra to superior eighth-grade students. Under some circumstances this is a dubious practice, since many of these students enrolled in such a course do not plan to go on to become engineering, science, or mathematics majors, and, thus, they have much need of the eighth-grade mathematics for which the algebra is often substituted. At any rate, it is rather clear that in an increasing number of schools there will be a mathematics sequence of courses that will carry many students through some introduction to analytical geometry and calculus in the twelfth grade.

A plan that has much merit provides for teaching in the ninth grade what usually is taught in the first three semesters of algebra in high school, in the tenth grade plane and solid geometry, in the eleventh grade college algebra and trigonometry, and in the twelfth grade analytical geometry and elementary calculus. Where this sequence has been followed with superior students, results have been gratifying.

Studies of the mathematical needs of college students have indicated that, while for those entering colleges and schools of engineering or in some departments in the liberal arts college the algebra-geometry sequence is indispensable, a majority of college and university students will have greater need for the mastery of arithmetical computations, problem solving, and the use of formulas—all of these with speed and accuracy.

**Vocational Mathematics Courses.** Though not materially increasing in number, many large senior high schools offer specialized courses in mathematics for those taking an agricultural, business-education, or shop curriculum. It has been pointed out that the general mathematics courses are very suitable for these specialized groups, and in many schools, particularly those with less than 1,000 students, general mathematics is substituted for the vocational mathematics course.

**Remedial Mathematics Courses.** It has been becoming increasingly noticeable and distressing that many students get into the seventh grade without having mastered enough of the fundamental arithmetic to have very much chance of doing successful work with the ordinary seventh-grade materials and instruction in mathematics. In a rather large and increasing number of schools, special sections are provided for those who have not done well on the tests given at the end of the sixth grade or at the beginning of the seventh grade. A review of the fundamental operations with whole numbers, common fractions, and decimal fractions and of their application to various areas in life constitutes the bulk of the work in the seventh grade for these students. In the eighth grade, decimal fractions and percentage and their applications constitute the bulk of the work for these students, while in the eighth grade emphasis is on decimal fractions, although there is a considerable amount of material in very elementary non-theorem geometry.

## MUSIC

Music education in the early part of this century was very largely confined to informal group singing. Later, bands, orchestras, and choral groups began to be formed in more and more secondary schools, until, by 1950, practically all secondary schools had organizations of each of these types. Offered first as non-credit student activities, they later became incorporated into the curriculum, and today the typical secondary school offers courses in all three of these areas for credit in the regular program.

The teaching of different types of music has for several decades been moving to occupy a more important place in the secondary school curriculum. With the recognition of broader objectives and with the adaptation of materials and methods of instruction to these broader objectives, there has been increased recognition of the value of the study of music.

**Objectives of Music Education.** The following are the objectives envisaged by leading thinkers about music education:

1. The more enjoyable and higher level of constructive expenditure leisure time—greater enjoyment and enrichment of life

2. Appreciation of an important phase of culture, not only that of music but also that of the emotions and the social and psychological background expressed by outstanding music
3. Knowledge and appreciation of great contributions of outstanding contributors to various kinds of music
4. Opportunity to make a contribution that, even if relatively minor, is important for mental and, indeed, physical health
5. Opportunity for personal achievement and self-expression
6. Experiences in cooperation that nurture and develop those qualities of personality and character that make for cooperative living and group participation in life activities
7. For many students, the opportunity to explore their interests and talents with reference to the choice of a musical occupation and for the beginning training and background for some who will follow such a vocation.
8. A unifying influence on American home life, through development of common interests, and consequent common associations, in musical activities in the home
9. Community experience in music, which will enable many to find a greater satisfaction in life.

Learning materials and activities should be, and, indeed, to a great and increasing extent are, provided in the secondary school curriculum for imparting various levels of mastery and achievement in music. Of course, most people can develop only a consumer's interest—the background for enjoying music produced by others.

A slightly higher level is attained by an increased number, as producers of vocal or instrumental music in choral groups, orchestras, bands, quartets, duets, or, indeed, as soloists. Especially in the case of those learning to play an instrument, there is a necessity for learning the basic technical background of music, such as the reading of notes.

The majority of secondary school students cannot hope to reach the third level, which means the production of vocal or instrumental music of a sufficient quality for participation in vocational public performances such as concerts and recitals. Likewise, a few, but a precious few, may be well started on the activities having to do with the composition or at least arrangement of music or with the leadership of instrumental or choral groups.

There are great individual differences among students in their capacities and interests in music. Some may become soloists, while some may participate in choirs, others in quartets, and still others as assistants to the instructors, as leaders of ensembles.

All types of music are now begun in the junior high school, although prominent at that level is the course in general music that emphasizes appreciation.

**Place of Music in the Curriculum.** Recently, educators have been inclined to emphasize subjects of cultural value to society. Judged by this criterion, music holds an undisputed high position. An awareness of the rich world of music is a heritage which every child is entitled to share. An appreciation of music will endow students with a longlong joy that will enrich their lives.

Music may also be included in the curriculum because of its socializing power. The child learns cooperation and teamwork when he plays in an instrumental group or sings in a chorus. It is pleasurable and democratic to contribute the individual personality to the benefit of the group. Every child should have the opportunity to play an instrument or to sing, even though he is not particularly talented. Music is included in the curriculum because it fulfils the criterion of providing for a fuller life and worthy recreational activities. People do not have to be accomplished musicians to enjoy listening to music and participation in music activities.

Definite goals for teaching and for studying music ought to be agreed upon by the teacher, the students, the administration, and probably the community. Guideposts are necessary in order that effort and thought can be effectively channeled. Though specialization has in the past received much emphasis and the ability to perform well and to win contests has been the objective of many musical activities, the principal objective of music education in the public schools should be appreciation and enjoyment, whether the child acquires these by actively participating in a musical activity or by listening. Good music education is for the deeper and wider appreciation of music, which, in turn, will bring pleasure to the child both while he is in school and in his adult life.

**Recent Developments.** No subject field has grown more in recent decades in the secondary school curriculum than has music. Not only have enrolments increased, but more types of instruction in music are offered and the quality of performance is obviously much better than a few decades ago.

General music continues to be taught in most school systems, usually in the junior high school, sometimes in the senior high school, and sometimes in both. As taught in the schools, general music does not always include the same things, but it commonly includes the basic simple theories of music, including ideas of pitch and scale notation, timing, rhythm, etc., as well as something about the types of music and the development of an understanding and, if possible, an appreciation of the various types.

Vocal music has been taught in some fashion or other in most secondary schools, since the establishment of the academy in the early part of the nineteenth century. It has, however, matured into a more advanced type of music including such things as *a cappella* and other various types of choirs, large groups, small groups, quartets, duets, solos, etc. This has all grown out of the very simple instruction in music in the elementary school classrooms and assemblies, accompanied by very superficial instruction and practice in singing.

At about the beginning of the present century, there began to be formed various types of instrumental groups—bands, orchestras, etc.; this practice began with young people who had had private music lessons performing for the benefit of the other students in chapel, in assemblies, and in what was called "literary" societies.

Instrumental music has in recent years been begun in many schools, even in the elementary schools. In practically every 6-3-3 school system today, instrumental music is begun in the first year of the junior high school. In fact, junior high schools of some size quite frequently now have at least two bands, an advanced band and a beginning band, and, indeed, many have three bands, either one for each grade or one for each of three different levels of performance, while a few have four bands, one for each grade and one made up of the most advanced pupils that is usually chosen for public performances.

While band directors struggled along by themselves until recently, in the past decade or two there has grown a practice of providing them with assistants, either an assistant band director, a lay aide, or student aides, thus enabling them to give some individual instruction and, in some schools, quite a bit of instruction to groups smaller than an entire band, for example, to groups playing wind instruments, stringed instruments, or percussion instruments.

Having originated as an extracurricular activity, frequently with practice limited to after school, not providing credit toward graduation, the band has now become a regular subject to which school time is allotted, and participation in it may result in the acquisition of several year units of credit toward graduation.

In the past quarter of a century girls have been enrolled in bands in increasing numbers, bands originally having been made up only of boys.

Along with the bands, orchestras of various sizes have been developed, including, particularly in the past few years, orchestras for stage appearances and for dancing.

Instrumental Ensemble. Educationally speaking, a good instrumental ensemble is good, not because it is able to play a superior type of music, but because it is good for the students who are in it. In certain large high schools in underprivileged areas of large cities, the concert band and the dance band have proved to be extremely effective morale builders. They give youngsters of the potential-dropout type a sense of belonging, of personal worth, and of team spirit that is highly valuable. Such organizations, properly conducted, are recognized as potent stabilizing influences in these difficult schools. Again, the marching band, with its formations and pageantry, has proved to be a cultural influence of no mean significance in many high schools, particularly in the South.

On the other hand, when one is dealing with the young people of a middle-class or upper-middle-class community, the undeniable musical limitations of the band take on educational significance. Such young people, relatively sophisticated and "civilized," will respond to musical opportunities very different from those suitable to underprivileged boys and girls. In such social and human settings, there may be excellent reasons for stressing the orchestra in preference to the band.

Small-group instrumental ensembles offer certain distinctive advantages. They make for informality, flexibility, and wide diffusion of music throughout the school. It is quite possible to organize a great amount of student leadership and student teaching in connection with such groups. As a matter of fact, in some schools a surprisingly large number of small instrumental ensembles are successfully maintained almost entirely by student initiative and activity, with only general encouragement and direction by the members of the music staff.

**Trends in Junior High School Music.** During the junior high school years, the child is keenly desirous of successful experiences and of winning the approval of his associates. During this adolescent period, the child is able to acquire skills easily if motivated and guided properly.

There has been a substantial increase in the number of choral and instrumental groups. In the past, the more talented junior high school students were permitted to perform in senior high school instrumental groups or choruses. The present trend is to have separate organizations as a part of the junior high school curriculum. As a result of this development, music publishers are printing specific vocal and instrumental music for this age group.

General music classes are being provided for junior high school students who show little musical talent. For those pupils who demonstrate marked interest in music, music theory and harmony are being offered by some schools.

**Other Trends.** The music activities in high schools have undergone a radical change from the classical to the popular, in an effort to please the public. The concert band has moved from the school to the athletic field, where marching skills and intricate formations can be displayed to advantage. In some instances, the philharmonic orchestra has changed its repertoire from "musician's music" to popular music. The chorus, too, has been influenced by this trend toward giving the public what they like to hear. The motivation behind this trend emerged from the idea that it was useless to educate the public in music; it appeared to be far easier to entertain them. For this reason, many high school music teachers are chosen on the basis of their showmanship rather than their musician-ship. This practice, when overdone, has led to unfortunate results, the musical growth of the child being forgotten in an effort to make public performances that would contribute public-relations benefits to the school.

Other important trends in high school music are as follows:

1. The emotional strain of music contests and their unhealthy educational results have been recognized. Music festivals, in which students hear other groups or individuals perform and receive the benefit of criticism without being pigeonholed into, say, a first or second rating, have become a definite trend in high schools.

2. More interest is being taken in combining choruses and instrumental groups for programs and activity experiences.

3. Greater emphasis is being placed upon group instruction in vocal and instrumental classes than upon individual instruction.

4. The public-relations value of music has been recognized and used to good advantage, although, in some cases, music groups have been exploited for this purpose.

5. The general trend is toward the participation of every child in a musical activity, whether band, orchestra, or chorus.

6. A growing trend is to begin actual playing and singing rather early in the study of music, to reduce to a minimum the amount of preliminary formal preparation for playing and singing, and to correlate theoretical and technical music instruction with playing and singing, having the former grow out of needs developed in the latter.

7. There is an increasing trend toward avoidance of excessive early concentration upon difficult classical music. It is becoming accepted that (a) musical procedures that do not have a sensible reason for being should not be employed; (b) though drill is needed, to be sure, in order to learn musical skills, drill should never be divorced from the main purpose of public school music; and (c) the teacher should emphasize that study of musical techniques is for the broader purpose of musical and expressive self-realization. Probably the major trend in high school music is toward capitalizing on the public-relations value of music. In some cases, this altogether worthy purpose has been allowed priority over the real educative values of music.

8. There is a trend toward providing opportunities to study the history and literature of music, along with development of skills in performance.

**General Music.** General music is offered in a large and increasing number of senior high schools. In many schools, it is a part of the core or homeroom programs. Today, general music is studied for credit and occupies a place in the schedule just as other subjects do. In many schools, small-group instruction in instruments is given.

There is no doubt that a properly organized course in general music can feature certain very important aspects of the art of music that are almost certain to be ignored, or at best slighted, in a program that consists of nothing but specialized performing organizations. A general course provides a very good opportunity for dealing with the social backgrounds and cultural ramifications of music and for revealing much of the traditions, the personalities, and the immense variety and scope of the art. This would suggest a general music course of one definite type, but it would not be the only pattern that could be rewardingly set up. There is, in fact, no standard plan for the general music course. The title has no standardized meaning. The point is to create a learning-teaching situation designed to realize certain contemplated aims better, more surely, and more universally than would otherwise be possible.

In recent years, more emphasis has been placed upon the all-school or large chorus, the specialized choir, the glee club, and such less formal vocal organizations as quartets.

The large chorus is certainly, in most situations, an exceedingly effective educational agency. Much excellent, interesting, and inspiring music is available for it. It offers genuine musical opportunities and challenges to many young people whose musical competence is limited. When properly managed, it is an effective socializing agency, it can be an effective link between the school and the community, and last, but perhaps not least, it is comparatively inexpensive.

The same, assuredly, is true of the *a cappella* choir. Fine choral singing by highly selected groups is having a remarkable voyage nowadays. But the decision whether to support and promote such an organization should not be made on a basis of fashion. In some situations, there are many students who will gain a great deal from the serious challenge which the best type of choral singing involves and who will lose something of real value if such an opportunity is not available.

The glee club, as ordinarily understood, is a more informal, free-and-easy type of musical organization than the chorus or the choir, and the same is usually true of vocal quartets. The educational potentialities of such organizations depend largely upon their freedom and informality. They are also effective socializing influences.

## PHYSICAL, HEALTH, SAFETY, AND DRIVER EDUCATION

**Physical Education in the Schools.** In the early secondary schools in this country, no provision was made for physical education except in the boarding schools for boys, where the students were taught games and sports as a part of the leisure education of young gentlemen.

In the 1890's and the first decade of this century, physical education was introduced in many elementary schools and spread into a considerable number of secondary schools. There were, however, few specially trained teachers, and, indeed, until the twentieth century, very few secondary school buildings included a gymnasium. Gradually, interscholastic athletics and classes in physical education were established in more schools, and the teachers colleges began to train teachers for physical education.

Then came World War I, when a rather large percentage of the draftees, especially those from southern states, where few schools were then providing physical education and health services, were found to be so deficient in matters of health and physique that they were rejected as poor military risks. When the statistics of this situation became available in the early 1920's, many secondary schools established for the first time courses in physical education, and a considerable number of state legislatures required that physical education be offered, a few legislatures insisted that it be required of all boys, and a few states required it of all students, both boys and girls.

Likewise, in this period, the practice spread throughout the country of requiring of all students every two or three years a physical examination, somewhat superficial, to be sure, but, nevertheless, of such a nature as to reveal many weaknesses that called for remedial treatment. After 1925, the field of remedial physical education developed and teachers were prepared for it. Instead of being excused, boys and girls who were not able to participate in regular exercises in the larger schools were classified for special types of physical education that would take into consideration their individual condition and, in many instances, improve it.

**Athletics.** Under the stimulus of the development of intercollegiate athletics, secondary schools throughout the country began early in this century to develop programs of interscholastic athletics, until, by 1925, practically all secondary schools had teams in one or more sports and usually three or four. Most schools also had some type of competitive sports for girls. In recent decades, competitive sports for girls have not been kept up in many schools, although, in the past few years, there has been a reactivation in that area in many schools (probably stimulated by the ease with which the Russian women have in recent years defeated American women in sports and physical contests in the Olympic Games).

A rather large number of injuries in competitive sports aroused people generally to the need for careful supervision and frequent physical examinations of young people participating in the sports. As a result of this growing concern, most schools now have insurance programs that would reimburse the injured for medical and hospital expenses. All along, there has been a great deal of criticism of the excesses of interscholastic athletics, especially with respect to overemphasis upon winning and dishonest or unethical practices of recruitment and certification of eligible players.

There has also been the criticism that training in athletics was given to the few who needed it least. For this reason, intramural programs have developed throughout the country, until the majority of secondary schools of more than 300 students have intramural programs for boys and many of them for girls. The intramural program, however, does not receive the attention, the supervision, and the coaching that goes to the varsity team.

After World War II, we were flooded with more distressing statistics relative to the magnitude of the percentage who were rejected for service in the armed forces for physical defects and for weaknesses in mental and physical health. The prospects of having a good physical-education program and an interest in a strong, disciplined, and trained body were given a big boost after President Kennedy took office in 1961. An outstanding war hero just entering upon middle age, he was quite athletic in his activities and interests, still participating in touch football and other vigorous sports after becoming president.

At approximately the same time, Americans were confronted with the facts that, in comparisons of achievements in physical feats and vigor, boys in the United States were behind those in most European countries, notably Russia. Attention of Americans generally was called to the fact that a great majority of young people of the United States take very little regular exercise, do not participate in any sort of physical sports, have grown rather "soft and flabby," insist upon riding even short distances in automobiles, and become quickly exhausted in square dancing or in dancing the "twist."[1]

From a survey undertaken in the public schools of Springfield, Missouri, the President's Council on Youth Fitness concluded that students who maintain a high level of physical fitness tended, on the average, to have the best grades, the fewest absences, the heaviest load of extracurricular activities, and the most healthy attitudes as judged by their teachers.

---

[1] Their elders have begun to ride power-lawn-mowing machines and to ride around golf courses in little carts.

**Offerings and Requirements Today.** While the situation changes from year to year, physical education (usually physical and health education) is required for boys in every year in the great majority of junior high schools, and usually also for girls. Of senior high schools, the percentage requiring physical education for both boys and girls in every year is relatively small but growing significantly each year. A majority of them require at least one if not two or three years for all boys.

There is no standard practice with reference to the number of times that classes in physical education meet a week. When schools shifted to the longer period of approximately fifty-five minutes and to the six-period day, physical education was usually scheduled for two or three periods a week, in spite of the complaint of the instructors in physical education that physical exercise, to be really effective, should be a daily matter. In a considerable number of schools, the classes meet three times a week, and in the minority, although in an increasing number, four or five times a week, especially when physical and health education are combined, as is being done in an increasing number of schools.

**Objectives.** Physical education has been taught in recent years not merely for the development of big muscles or strength but also for other important objectives such as (1) development of general physical tone, vigor, and health; (2) development of the smaller muscles, together with mind-body coordination for more skillful use of all parts of the body; (3) development of interests and skills that may contribute materially to the enjoyment of leisure in the home and away. (Much more attention is being given now to golf, tennis, and other sports which can be continued after school days are ended.) In addition, valuable contributions are made to the development of such intangibles as teamwork and sportsmanship.

**Health Education.** Until the last quarter-century, health education did not occupy an important place in the secondary school curriculum, even though health education in the form of physiology and hygiene was offered in the great majority of elementary schools. With the spread of general science in the junior high schools, instruction in physiology and hygiene became a part of that subject matter. There is a recent though small trend toward reversing the tendency, particularly since so much of what was offered as general science in the junior high school will have been taught to many students before they will have entered junior high school.

Few senior high schools offered instruction in health education, until the instructors in physical education began to incorporate health education into their courses. Although statistics are not at present available, it is probably true that, in the great majority of high schools, particularly those of more than 300 students, health education is offered as a part of a program of combined physical and health education.

**Safety Education.** A course in safety education for a semester or the equivalent is offered in the seventh or eighth grade in many elementary and junior high schools. A number of states require that it be offered, and in three states there are legal provisions that it be required of all students, although in many schools in these states it is a unit in a course rather than a full semester course in itself. For many years safety education has been given incidentally in courses in general science, general mathematics, or social studies.

**Driver Education.** Having gotten under way in an impressive fashion in the 1950's, Americans have become two-car and even, in some instances, three- or four-car families. This means that, in many instances, at least one younger member of the family drives a car. Statistics show that a disproportionate number of car accidents involving serious injuries and deaths have been collisions in which at least one car was driven by a teen-ager or someone in the early twenties. Not only has the number of accidents increased, but the percentage of accidents that involve young people has been so very great that insurance rates for cars driven by teen-agers without driver training have more than doubled. Because of these developments, there has for a period of more than twenty years been a movement to instal courses in driver education in every senior high school.

Insurance rates are definitely lower where the young driver has had a course in driver training, and the statistics and testimony of traffic officers and judges indicate that the possibility of serious accident is much less for those who have had such a course. As a result, driver training for young people is very generally indorsed.

Local automobile dealers all over the United States furnish, at very low cost, dual-controlled driver-training cars. A great many high school instructors have qualified to give instruction in driver education and, with the present trend, it seems that by 1970 practically all senior high schools will be offering such a course and that the very great majority of boys and girls will have taken it before graduation. The course is most often offered without credit. More recently, there has been a tendency to offer the course during summer vacations as well as in the regular academic year.

## SCIENCE

**Junior High School Science.** In the last decade or so, there have been many far-reaching changes in the content and organization of science courses in the elementary and secondary schools. Because of the greatly increased interest in space exploration and the highly sped-up efforts to surpass the Russians in scientific achievements, science has received a great deal of attention, whereas twenty years ago seventh-grade science consisted very largely of various types of courses in nature study and elementary physiology, hygiene, and health. Much more science is now being taught in elementary school grades from three to six. Most elementary school teachers have been improving their knowledge in the area, and a considerable number of publishers have brought out new textbooks for instruction in those grades. As a result of the increased amount of knowledge of science previously learned, a considerable amount of adaptation of junior high school courses is being or has been made. With the crowded program in grades seven, eight, and nine, it is quite likely that there will be an increase in the already large number of schools that give only the equivalent of one semester of science in each of grades seven and eight.

Junior high school science teachers have been, as one instructor put it, "between a rock and a hard place" with youngsters coming into junior high school with a considerable amount of knowledge in science. The typical junior high school course in general science that prevailed prior to 1960 duplicates much of what is now being taught in grades five and six. A logical consequence of this development has been reduction of the amount of time given to science in junior high school. Another alternative is to bring down into the junior high school some of the science taught in the senior high school. In some junior high schools, biology is now being offered in the ninth grade, although the study of biology is relatively not very popular among students today, because of their great interest in various aspects of physics, chemistry, and astronomy. The practice in the ninth grade is quite varied, and the future is hard to predict: Some schools still offer a full year of general science, some a half-year of general science, some none at all, and some a unit of biology. A small, but an increasing number offer a course in general physical science, covering the most elementary aspects of space science, earth science, meteorology, nuclear physics, and astronomy.

In general, the science courses offered in the seventh and eighth grades are required, and, in an increasing number of schools, science is also required in the ninth grade.

The nature and objectives of junior high school science courses are not vocational, except insofar as they might give some basic preparation for college and for vocations. The objectives are, rather, to contribute to better use of leisure time and to enrichment of life by means of understanding the scientific aspects of what is going on around us—space explorations, military preparedness, advances in technology and industry, etc.—and to promote better health, better preparation for college, and more intelligent citizenship.

**Senior High School Science.** Here too are considerable confusion and variety of practice. Among the new offerings in the senior high school are physics and chemistry courses to which only abler students are admitted. These courses are of several types:

1. A so-called college-placement course similar to the beginning course ordinarily offered in colleges and universities, but unfortunately, in many cases, patterned after college courses that are not up to date and that have been or are being revised
2. A combined advanced course in physical science, including physics and chemistry, particularly physical chemistry, as this material is applied to rocketry, space exploration, etc.
3. A so-called seminar in science, in which individual students and groups of students read widely along the lines of modern scientific developments and bring into class reports about which there is discussion
4. In a few schools, an elective course in astronomy and related meteorology and atmospheric science

In the past few decades, much less attention has been given to what used to be called physical geography—materials related to earth science, meteorology, etc.—than in the past.

**Current Trends in Instruction.** Even more in science than in most fields, changes have been occurring in recent years relative to the detailed learning materials and methods. Among these changes are the following:

1. In the junior high school, there have been increased amounts of group experimentation and demonstration by students in the class period.
2. In the senior high school, there has been an increased amount of individual or small-group laboratory work.
3. There has been a continuation of the trend toward having the laboratory work more closely integrated with textbook discussion.
4. An increased amount of homework has been assigned in science.
5. There has been a greatly increased use of audio-visual materials, particularly the overhead projector and microfilms.
6. There has been an increased use of the lecture method, particularly very carefully prepared illustrated lectures to large groups of students of more than one class section.

While there is a tendency to give great emphasis to those aspects of science relating to space exploration, rockets, etc., commonsense has begun to assert itself, and other areas of science that are so valuable in connection with health, the home, local industry, agriculture, and so on are being restored to their important places in the science curriculum.

There is also a trend, particularly in the last few years, toward return to emphasis upon training in methods of scientific procedure in thinking, as opposed to the emphasis upon facts that has characterized science instruction for several decades.

**Science Fairs and Science Camps.** Many schools have developed in recent years what is called a "science fair." The science fair, which ordinarily takes place in the spring, is not only an educational opportunity, it also provides much expert motivation of youngsters through their study of various scientific matters in order to prepare exhibits for the fair. One of the most successful annual science fairs has been conducted by the Oakland, California, public schools, from whom information may be obtained.

Many other schools, both elementary and secondary, have inaugurated a "natural science camp." This is conducted in the summer. Natural science camps are organized and operated by the local recreation department in cooperation with the local school system, although they may receive state aid. These camps usually last two or three weeks and charge a fee that provides for food, shelter, field trips, and camp equipment, in addition to instruction and supervision by carefully selected instructors. A good example is that conducted by the Berkeley, California, school district in cooperation with the Berkeley Recreation and Parks Department, from either of whom information can be obtained.

## TRADE AND INDUSTRIAL-ARTS EDUCATION

**Beginnings.** Toward the latter part of the nineteenth century, in more and more secondary schools, there were established courses in various types of industrial arts and crafts, including courses definitely intended for vocational education. Vocational shop courses were very expensive as compared to academic courses, and the quality of the equipment, instructors, and methods of instruction in industrial arts and vocational courses were at first very inferior.

Various groups of people in the United States, including the National Association of Manufacturers, urged that the work in these areas be extended and improved. In 1917, Congress appropriated $1,660,000 (since increased to more than $20,000,000) for vocational courses in trades and industries, home economics, business, and agriculture. These funds may not be used for general-education courses in these fields.

**Objectives and Place of Industrial Arts.** Industrial-arts courses are of two types: vocational and non-vocational, or general. General-education courses are offered in order to provide general industrial experience of common value to high school students, to provide exploratory activities with a view to leading students to discover their aptitudes and to learn about activities in various fields of industrial arts, to develop an apppreciation of design and quality in the products of industrial arts, and to offer the basic training for students who would elect to follow a vocational curriculum in trades and industries.

In spite of the opposition of those interested only in intellectual education, more and more schools are installing courses in industrial arts and other fields of vocational education, and, since 1950, enrolments have been increasing materially each year. Since many students of below-average academic ability and interest who might formerly have dropped out at the age of sixteen are attracted to these courses, enrolments in these areas are certain to remain high.

Already a variety of "trades and industry" courses have expanded, particularly in the fields related to electronics. With the development of new occupations and automation, and with the spread of secondary education into new fields of vocational preparation, this area of education is becoming increasingly important.

Specific preparation for vocation is no longer found in junior high schools but is found almost entirely in the upper two years of senior high schools and in junior colleges.

**Types of Vocational Industrial-Arts Programs.** Vocational industrial-arts programs in the secondary schools may be of various types—indeed, many single schools offer more than one type.

In the all-day vocational program, the student devotes approximately three consecutive clock hours to practical work on a useful and productive basis and is given instruction, sometimes in special classes, in related technical subjects. There has been an increasing trend to substitute general-education courses for some of the work in related technical subjects.

**Work Experience as Vocational Education.** The diversified-occupations program and the distributive-education program are good examples of cooperative-work-experience vocational programs. Both may be approved for state and federal subsidies.

In the cooperative-work-experience program, usually offered as a course in "diversified occupations," with state and federal aid, the following types of occupations are commonly included among those in which students may get training:

1. Occupations in the field of the selling of goods and services
2. Clerical occupation
3. Restaurant and other food-preparation and -handling positions

4. Various building and automobiles trades
5. Other trades and occupations in industrial fields
6. Various types of positions as aides to nurses, dentists, embalmers, and printers

The distributive-education program includes training for a great variety of occupations related to the sale and distribution of goods.

Diversified-occupations or distributive-education courses are usually open to eleventh- and twelfth-graders only. The students generally work between fifteen and twenty hours a week and receive one full academic unit of credit. They usually carry three courses at school. Paid for their work at slightly less than the local going rate, they are visited and inspected by a coordinator from the school several times a month. There are definite agreements between the employer, the student, and the school, including

1. Agreement of the student to give honest, conscientious service and to be regular and prompt in showing up for work
2. Agreement of the employer to teach the student about the occupation

**Approaches to Vocational-Education Instruction.** Most secondary schools offer for at least two or three types of occupations vocational courses involving two subjects in each of the eleventh and twelfth grades, which students carry in addition to their general-education courses and in which no work experience outside of school is included. Many smaller schools offer a general industrial-education program in which a number of related occupations are taught in a single curriculum, for example, a single course in auto mechanics might include auto body painting, body and fender repair, wheel alignment, and other allied phases of automobile repair. Continuation or part-time programs are offered in many schools for students who are graduates or dropouts and who wish to continue their education along the line of their occupation or to get general education.

Machines are replacing unskilled labor; fewer people are involved in agriculture each year; workers are more mobile; many more people are engaged in personal services, for example, as beauticians; and industries have been shifted and are shifting from one section of the country to the other, for instance, the textile mills are shifting from New England to the South. These and other recent developments create problems of adjustment of vocational education to the needs of American life.

Among other things, administrators of secondary schools must make a careful study and prediction of the availability of employment positions in the community for those who complete any particular vocational curriculum. The mobility of the American people, however, tends to decrease the importance of this consideration and creates certain other problems that administrators must solve.

**Industrial Arts as General Education.** Industrial-arts education, which is now generally accepted as a part of general education, has the following objectives:

1. *Developing the skills necessary to plan and construct useful projects with common hand tools, simple machines, and construction materials in a workmanlike manner.* Men and women who can efficiently build needed items for their homes have an additional source of joy of living and at the same time can give a touch of individuality which adds charm to home living.

2. *Providing experiences with tools and machines typical of modern industry so that the students can explore and test their interests and abilities in industrial work.* Industrial arts gives boys and girls a chance to test their interest and ability in working with tools and materials typical of modern industry. It gives them valuable information about the industrial world so that they may choose their life vocation more effectively. If a student selects an industrial vocation, the training in industrial arts will serve as a background for future vocational training.

3. *Developing a skill in reading and making drawings, charts, and graphs.* Training in industrial arts gives boys and girls skill in reading drawings, charts, and graphs and in making drawings to express their ideas and for planning construction work. The ability to read working drawings is more important for most people than skill in making them.

4. *Developing the ability to recognize quality and good design in manufactured products.* Skill in choosing manufactured products that have good design, durability, and fine workmanship is constantly becoming more important. As technological developments continue, people tend to buy more and more manufactured products.

5. *Developing the skills necessary to maintain and service the commonly used products of industry.* Everyone today is surrounded in his home and community by ingenious mechanical and electric devices that add efficiency to living but require adjustment, lubrication, cleaning, and replacement of parts. Plumbing fixtures and washing machines, air-conditioning units, water heaters, sewing machines, television sets, and other such appliances are typical examples.

6. *Providing a concrete medium for learning in mathematics, science, language, arts, and social science.* Some of the educational work in the past has proved ineffective because the instruction was presented in a purely verbal setting. Industrial-arts education provides an opportunity

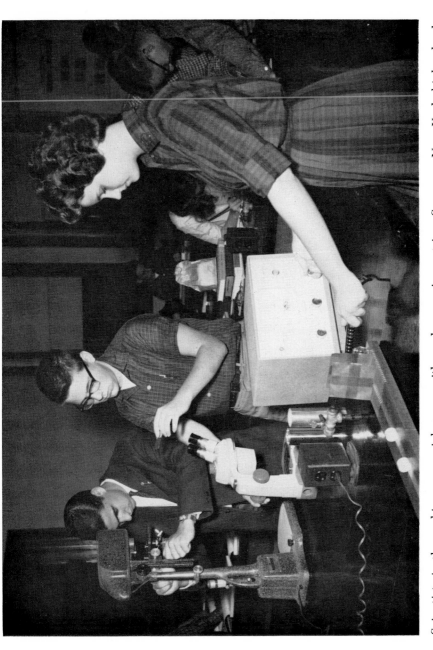

Scientists in the making: a special group with modern equipment in a Syracuse, New York, high school.

The four-station laboratory unit provides a splendid opportunity for small-group instruction and work (Dwight D. Eisenhower High School, Blue Island, Ill.).

Wave testing of an amplifier in an electronics class (Westchester County Publishers, Inc.).

to learn by experimentation, construction, and observation of real construction activities.

7. *Developing an interest in handicraft as a valuable medium for creative expression in leisure hours.* People need interesting and wholesome leisure-time activities. Industrial-arts-education courses give boys and girls an opportunity to learn leather tooling, plastic craft, weaving, carving, cabinetmaking, metalworking, etc., for this purpose.

8. *Developing social understanding and ability to work with others, as a leader or as a cooperative member of the group.* Industrial-arts-education classes provide many opportunities to foster habits of social efficiency, which are highly important to success in living and working with others.

## QUESTIONS, PROBLEMS, AND TOPICS FOR FURTHER STUDY

1. Do you believe that home-economics courses should include training in grooming and in dress?
2. Do you believe that students in high school should be given training in psychology and child rearing?
3. Be able to give in class the reasons why many people believe that high school students should be given much more training in home finance.
4. How many types of mathematics do you think should be offered in the high school? Be able to explain your position.
5. Do you believe that all students should study algebra?
6. Should music be a required course in a secondary school?
7. What do you believe should be done about teaching appreciation of good music in high school?
8. Do you believe that physical education should be required of all students every year? If so, what kind of physical education?
9. What do you think ought to be done to improve interscholastic athletics in schools?
10. Do you believe that young people are too "soft and flabby" for their own welfare and for national defense? If so, what is the cause?
11. Do you believe that health education should be taught as a separate course, in connection with physical education, or in connection with science?
12. What is your opinion of the effectiveness of driver education?
13. With the great developments of science in recent years, do you believe that all students should study science every year in school, and, if so, indicate what subject or field should be taught in each grade.
14. Do you believe that science for the less able students should be different from that for the abler students? Be prepared to support your answer.
15. In what science courses do you believe laboratory work should be required?
16. Do you think that high schools should offer courses for barbers and beauty shop workers?
17. Do you believe that there should be special federal aid for vocational education and not for English, the social studies, or other non-vocational courses?

18. Some people say that every student going through high school should be taught to earn a living. How do you think that could be carried out? Is it practical?
19. In what fields do you think vocational education should be given, other than those covered in some high schools today?
20. What are the most important things that the high school can do in preparing young people to succeed in a job?

## SUPPLEMENTARY MATERIALS

### SELECTED READINGS

ABOURN, ELLSWORTH, et al. "Education in Science," School Life, XLV (October, 1962), 2–36.

BENT, RUDYARD K., and HENRY H. KRONENBERG. Principles of Secondary Education (4th ed.). New York: McGraw-Hill Book Co., Inc., 1961. Pp. 312–15, 357–58 (music in the curriculum); 315–19, 374–76, 412 (industrial arts).

BINGHAM, ELDRED N. "Science—Its Significance in the Secondary-School Program," Bulletin of the N.A.S.S.P., March, 1962, 190–97.

BROWN, R. D., and HARLOW BERQUIST. "Instrumental Program in a Junior High School," Bulletin of the N.A.S.S.P., November, 1956, 96–99.

DOUGLASS, HARL R. Trends and Issues in Secondary Education. Washington, D.C.: The Center for Applied Research in Education, Inc., 1962. Chapter 4, "Content of Subjects Offered."

DOUGLASS, HARL R. Modern Administration of Secondary Schools (2d ed.). Boston: Ginn & Co., 1963. Chapter 19, "Physical and Health Education and Athletics," pp. 441–69.

FEHR, HOWARD F. "High School Mathematics for the Second Half of the 20th Century," Bulletin of the N.A.S.S.P., No. 239 (April, 1958), 318–24.

FEHR, HOWARD F., and McLANE SAUNDERS. "Teaching Modern Mathematics," The Educational Digest, XXIX (January, 1963), 41–43.

FISCHLER, ABRAHAM S. "Modern Junior High School Science: A Recommended Sequence of Courses," Bulletin of the N.A.S.S.P., No. 269 (February, 1962), 226–27.

FRASER, DOROTHY M. Current Curriculum Studies in Academic Subjects. Washington, D.C.: National Education Association of the United States, 1962. Chapter 3, "Mathematics," pp. 27–42.

HALE, HELEN E. "Quality Science for the Junior High School," Bulletin of the N.A.S.S.P., December, 1960, 36–40.

JOHNSON, PHILIP G. "Changing Directions in Science," School Life, XL (October, 1962), 27–30. Summarized in The Education Digest, XXVIII (February, 1963), 48–50.

KINSELLA, J. J. "Some Reflections on the General Mathematics Situation," School Science and Mathematics, LIV (June, 1954), 431–38.

KRUG, E. A. Secondary School Curriculum. New York: Harper & Row, 1960. Chapter 15, "Industrial Arts"; Chapter 17, "Music"; Chapter 19, "Home Economics."

McKIBBEN, MARGARET J. "New Developments in Secondary-School Science," The Education Digest, XXVI (March, 1961), 34–38.

MARLAND, S. P., JR. "Placing Sex Education in the Curriculum, Phi Delta Kappan, XLIII (December, 1961), 132–35.

MAYOR, JOHN, R., and JOHN A. BROWN. "New Mathematics in the Junior High Schools," *Educational Leadership*, XVIII (December, 1960), 165–69.

MOISE, EDWIN. "The New Mathematics Programs," *The Education Digest*, XXVIII (September, 1962), 28–32.

MORELOCK, CHARLES F. "Journalism Teaching in Kansas High Schools," *University of Kansas Bulletin of Education*, XVII (May, 1963), 121–26.

MOULY, GEORGE J. *Psychology for Effective Teaching*. New York: Holt, Rinehart & Winston, Inc., 1960. Chapter 2, "The Determinants of Behavior," pp. 22–60; Chapter 8, "General Natures of Learning."

NATIONAL SCIENCE TEACHERS ASSOCIATION. *Planning for Excellence in High School Science*. Washington, D.C.: The Association, 1961.

OTTO, ARLEEN C. *New Designs in Homemaking Programs in Junior High Schools*. New York: Teachers College, Bureau of Publications, Columbia University, 1958.

PARKER, J. CECIL, BENTLEY T. EDWARDS, and WILLIAM H. STEGEMAN. *Curriculum in America*. New York: Thomas Y. Crowell Co., 1962. Chapter 7, "Factors That Influence the Teaching of Science"; Chapter 8, "Science in the Schools."

PASTER, JULIUS. "Historical Backgrounds and Pupil Activities in the Teaching of Industrial Arts in the Public Junior High Schools of New York City," *Bulletin of the N.A.S.S.P.*, No. 269 (February, 1962), 159–61.

RAPPAPORT, DAVID. "Does Modern Math Ignore Learning Theory?" *Phi Delta Kappan*, XLIV (June, 1963), 445–47.

ROMINE, STEPHEN A. *Building the High School Curriculum*. New York: The Ronald Press Co., 1954. Chapter 6, "The Nature of Learning as a Basis for Curriculum Building," pp. 133–49.

SNADER, DANIEL W. "Secondary School Mathematics in Transition," *School Life*, XLII (March, 1960), 9–13.

VAN TIL, WILLIAM, GORDON F. VARS, and JOHN H. LOUNSBURY. *Modern Education for the Junior High School Years*. Indianapolis: The Bobbs-Merrill Co., Inc., 1961. Chapter 14, "Science and Mathematics."

VENABLE, TOM C. *Patterns in Secondary School Curriculum*. New York: Harper & Row, 1958. Chapter 19.

VERNIER, ELMON L., *et al.* "Health, Physical Education and Recreation in the Secondary School," *Bulletin of the N.A.S.S.P.*, No. 257 (May, 1960), 1–196.

WARE, HERBERT W. "About That New Mathematics Program . . . ," *Bulletin of the N.A.S.S.P.*, No. 275 (December, 1962), 83–89.

# IV

## STIMULATING AND
## GUIDING LEARNING

VI

# 12

# Teacher Leadership in Learning Activities

## THE ROLE AND RESPONSIBILITY OF THE TEACHER

Teaching by the better modern teachers is a complicated cooperative procedure involving the participation of students, parents, and other people in the community; it requires the assistance and direction of heads of departments, principals, and supervisors, and to some extent it is dependent upon textbooks. Nevertheless, the teacher occupies the key position and has the greatest influence on, and responsibility for, the learning of the students in his classes.

**The Fields of Responsibility.** From the beginning, the teacher has great responsibilities. In addition to participating in the selection of textbooks and supplementary learning materials, the teacher plans the outline of the work for the year and the semester, plans the unit in each semester's work, and plans for each day the activities of the students and his own as well.

One of the most important responsibilities of the teacher has to do with obtaining the cooperation of the pupils. Indeed, it is at this point that the poorer or more unfortunate teachers fail and the better or more fortunate teachers are successful, and it is with respect to this factor that the success of the students as learners and the teacher as leader depends most greatly.

While it is desirable for the students to participate in planning their own learning activities, without any question the teacher must take much responsibility and do much planning in connection with what might be thought of as "assignments"—in other words, the decisions as to what the learners should do as learning activities for the day or for the unit.

**Other Subject-teaching Responsibilities.** The instructor's responsibility only begins with the assignment. He should work with the students in their learning activities, particularly those taking place in the class period, giving help and suggestions and also indicating special projects for the abler and more creative students, as the situation may seem to warrant.

Then, of course, there is the responsibility of the instructor of checking to see to what extent the students have progressed as was hoped when the assignment was planned—by evaluating oral recitation or discussion, papers handed in, test and examination papers, projects completed, and other culminating activities.

**Extrasubject Responsibilities.**[1] The more valuable teachers today also render high-grade service as director, coach, supervisor, or sponsor of at least one extracurricular learning activity—a club, a team, the student council, or some other non-subject learning organization. The instructor has the responsibility of seeing that pupil participation in these activities results in valuable educational growth and that they are so planned and conducted as to make the major potential contributions of that particular activity.

The modern instructor takes seriously the responsibility for counseling the individual pupils in his classes. This includes, among other things, refraining from giving advice in situations in which he is not competent, particularly if the situation calls for some other member of the school staff who is more specialized in the area in which the problem or question lies.

The instructor also has a definite responsibility for adapting the instruction to the needs and conditions of the local community, utilizing community resources. He also does his or her part in keeping the community informed about the work of the school and in developing good will for the school, its program, and its staff.

## GETTING OFF TO A GOOD START

**Learning About the School and the Community.** A new teacher should obtain from the principal of the secondary school in which he or she is to teach both information concerning textbooks and course-of-study guides, if the latter are available for the field. As early as possible, he should also gain information from the principal about the student body and the types of homes from which his students will come, including

[1] Discussed more fully in Chapters 17 and 18.

materials the principal may have forwarded from the local chamber of commerce.

All of this is very desirable, even if the teacher is to attend a workshop or preschool session before school opens in the fall. Not only will a new teacher be able to participate more intelligently in such activities, but he will have formulated a number of questions and gotten in mind a number of points about which information would be useful.

The new teacher should also obtain from the principal a copy of the student handbook and a copy of the teachers' handbook, if there is one, which usually includes the rules and regulations for faculty and students of the school. The new teacher should also obtain as much information as he can from the principal and student-activity sponsors concerning any extracurricular activity that he will be called upon to sponsor or to assist with. The teacher should, as early as possible, preferably in the spring or summer, visit the school and inspect its library, with a view to ascertaining what will be available and with a view to suggesting purchases that may be made in time for the opening of school in the fall.

Before school opens in the autumn, the new teacher should obtain information about such matters as how absences and tardinesses are reported, recorded, and cleared; the standards and rules for pupil conduct; the amount of homework expected; the procedure for requisitioning equipment and supplies; what is expected of teachers in the way of public relations; the hours they are expected to be in the building; the nature of the marking system; the facilities for duplicating materials; the provision of textbooks, workbooks, and supplies for students; whether it is customary to call students by their first or last name; and the nature of the relationships to the head of the department, the principal, the assistant principal, the supervisors, and the superintendent of schools.

The teacher also should acquire information about the community that would include such things as the economic and cultural status of the community or the large groups in the community, the community attitudes toward such social practices as drinking alcoholic beverages and smoking, the important community religious cleavages or factional differences, and the community resources available for field trips and excursions useful for teaching the teacher's particular subject.

**A Good Beginning.** Very important in establishing good human relations with students and ensuring cooperative behavior is getting off to a good start, especially for young teachers or teachers in a new school. Successful teachers make the following recommendations:

1. Be prepared with as much knowledge of your students as possible.
2. Have the first week's work planned very carefully, but be ready to deviate from the plan as the need may arise.

3. Make definite assignments involving a reasonable amount of work.

4. Check on the previous day's assignment every day of the first week or two.

5. Do not attempt anything spectacular or radical during the first few days.

6. Do not be too severe or too cordial and informal—be natural.

7. Make careful preparation in advance:

   a. To see that chalk and erasers are available if needed
   b. To see that any visual or auditory equipment or materials to be used are available and in working order
   c. To ascertain if textbooks, workbooks, or other similar needed materials will be immediately available
   d. To provide for work to keep pupils busy, especially if textbooks, workbooks, paper, or other equipment is lacking

8. Comment only to a minimum extent about yourself, your standards of discipline, etc. Keep all discussion on the work at hand.

9. Avoid any unusual tenseness or self-consciousness. Do your best to feel at ease and confident.

10. Call students by their names as soon as possible. New teachers and teachers in large schools should prepare in advance for each class, using a piece of cardboard or paper no smaller than 8½″ × 11″ for a seating chart, perhaps in the form of intersecting lines forming rectangles for as many rows and as many seats as there are in each row. In these rectangles may be written the names of the students according to where they sit. Naturally, the teacher should become independent of the chart as soon as possible. Correct pronunciation of all names should be learned at the outset. If there is any doubt, ask the pupil to pronounce it first.

11. Make a special effort to come to know, in the first few days or weeks, *the student leaders,* to call them by name, and unostentatiously to establish cordial relations with them.

12. If textbooks or supplies are to be distributed, know where and when they may be obtained, what records should be kept, and how the students are to make payments or deposits for them.

13. Plan each day's class with a view to having the subject matter and procedure well in mind, including the assignments.

14. See that the work of the first week is not dull, though it is not wise to attempt to make the work far more interesting than the work of later weeks will be.

15. Ascertain how well prepared the students are for the work ahead. This may be done by means of a formal placement test, board work, written assignments, carefully planned class discussion, or a combination of these. Ordinarily, time should be taken to review only those things in which a considerable number of students are weak and which are

prerequisite to good work in the class. A few individuals may be asked to do a little extra remedial work.

16. Consult older teachers or the principal on any and all perplexing problems. Do not permit a situation to get out of hand, and do not work at a disadvantage.

17. In matters of discipline, act with confidence and restraint. Petty infractions should be overlooked the first day or two, but disturbing conduct must be dealt with in a firm way indicative of self-confidence.

18. Handle promptly all reports called for by superior officers. Promptness is unusually important at the opening of the year.

19. Be familiar with general school regulations in order to cooperate with authorities to see that regulations are observed from the start.

20. Show a sense of humor and a basically human disposition. (This can be overdone, just as severity is so often overdone the first week.)

## OBTAINING COOPERATION OF THE PUPILS

It is unusually important in secondary schools in the United States that the instructor be skilful in obtaining the cooperation of the pupils so that they will participate regularly and wholeheartedly in the learning activities necessary for their maximum potential growth in the subject. In other leading countries, the secondary school students have more academic interest and are more highly motivated by their desire to stay in secondary school and go on to college—an ambition which can be realized only by a minority, since the schools are more selective in other countries.

Some enthusiastic teachers who are well versed in their subject go into the classroom under the unfortunate illusion that the students will appreciate their scholarship and be willing to extend themselves in order to acquire some of the wisdom accumulated by the instructor in his college classes. These teachers do not realize the necessity for special attention to the problems of motivation, of obtaining pupils' interest. As a result, many of these beginners are disillusioned and become dissatisfied with teaching and bitter toward the adolescents of today and the administrators of the school, who, it seems to them, do not work at the job of frightening the students into more effort at learning.

**Stimulating Interest and Effort.** As was pointed out by John Dewey a half-century ago, as well as by many others since, the effort that one puts forth and, therefore, the achievement that one obtains in learning activities and, indeed, in most areas of activity in life are related to the degree of interest that one has in accomplishing certain objectives and in participating in the activities necessary for the attainment of those objectives. Not only is the amount of time spent in efforts of learning dependent upon the goal and the nature of interest, but the effectiveness of the learning activity is very definitely conditioned by the nature and the degree of interest.

While there are various means of stimulating and motivating student learning activities, it has been observed for many decades that the most wholesome and effective type of interest and motivation is that which grows out of pleasurable experiences in participating in learning activities and in being in contact with learning materials that seem to have obvious value as preparation for life needs.

**Types of Incentives to Learning Activities.** Incentives not related to interest in the subject may be apparently effective, at least temporarily, in motivating student learning activities, but, in the long run, they are to be used only when a subject-interest approach does not seem to be effective. For example, forcing or persuading young people to do arithmetic exercises, to practice typing, to practice on the piano, or to study a history textbook may be effective temporarily and at a low level of attention, but in the long run this does not develop a permanent interest; indeed, it may cause the students actually to dislike the subject and to avoid further study of it in later life.

**Natural vs. Forced Attention.** It should be noted that the educational growth resulting from study or other learning activities is definitely in proportion to the degree of attention given. For that reason, motivation and interest are very important. Attention, however, may be of two types: (1) natural or spontaneous attention such as that given to things that are especially interesting, strange, or in some way important to the learner or (2) forced attention that is the result of the willpower of the individual in applying himself to learning activities. While, of course, forced attention must be employed, it should be recognized that it does not contribute nearly as greatly to educational growth as does spontaneous and natural attention, and, therefore, the efforts of the better teacher are concentrated upon developing motivation and interest of the types that will result in natural rather than forced attention.

**Direct and Indirect Interests.** Some learning activities are in themselves pleasurable; the pupils enjoy performing them. With knowledge and study of what interests adolescents, the instructor may be able to so plan that more of the learning activities will be of this type than otherwise. But, for a great proportion of the subjects in the high school curriculum, the degree of enjoyment experienced by the average student in learning activities is not great enough to compete successfully with the bids to engaged his time and attention in outside activities that are really more fun. There is, therefore, often the necessity for employing incentives that develop an indirect interest.

**Positive and Negative Needs as Motivation.** Indirect interest and generic needs may be characteristically positive or negative. In instances where the student participates in learning activities with a view to avoiding censure, low grades, or some other type of punishment, negative types of need and motivation are experienced. In general, human beings are more easily and more greatly motivated by positive needs, that is, needs that involve obtaining something desirable.

**Generic and Specific Needs as Motivation.** Interest in a large proportion of learning activities needs to be stimulated by instilling in the pupil a feeling that he has a need for the growth likely to result from his participation. The need may be generic, that is, a type of need to which a great many learning activities even in different subjects might contribute, such as making a certain average, getting ready for college, or satisfying the teacher or one's parents.

The need, on the other hand, may be quite specific and, being so, may develop a higher type of interest. A specific need involves a feeling on the part of a pupil that he needs to develop in a particular type of growth that will result from studying the subject matter and participating in related learning activities; such types of growth might be represented by improvement of his speech, acquisition of skill in typewriting, or acquisition of knowledge about national economic and political problems.

One of the reasons given by many dropouts and other students for their failure to work up to their capacities is a feeling on their part that the particular learning was not very useful. It has been reported by many teachers that the quality of student learning activities is greatly improved by tying the subject matter to its application in the life of the student in the community about him or, for that matter, to the current events and problems of the day as they are read about in the newspapers and heard about over the radio and television.

**Motivation and Need.** Next to the pleasure of participation in learning activities, the best type of learning motivation is a stimulus that comes from a feeling of the need to acquire the knowledge, skills, understandings, and other types of educational growth that apparently will result from such participation. Needs may be general or specific. Desire to perform learning activities to meet a general need, for instance, to acquire an education, to be well informed, or to make good grades, is not a very impelling type of motivation.

On the other hand, when a student feels that it is necessary to acquire certain specific skills, habits, information, understandings, attitudes, interests, ideals, or appreciations in order to accomplish some specific objective that he has at the time, for example, to be able to get on well with his parents, to get ready to enter college, to repair television sets, to repair a car, or to perform in public, the situation is favorable for effective application to learning activities.

Of course, the closer the need is from the point of time, the more effective it is. With young people, a need that is years, or even months or weeks, ahead is not an impelling invitation to work. If the need is for tomorrow, the next day, or the following week, it is much more effective as motivation.

When a pupil feels that he ought to try to learn because he needs to learn or improve in order to obtain or achieve something that he wishes, such as a good grade or an opportunity to enter college, to be able to get a good job, to satisfy his curiosity, to win a contest, or to "shine" at home or with his friends, he is "motivated." He studies or practices to attain an objective to satisfy a need or desire that he feels. The need may be one that all his classmates sense—a common need—or it may be a need or desire that only he or he and a few others sense—an individual need.

Arousing and adapting to the needs, abilities, and potentialities of the individual high school student is too complicated a matter to be treated thoroughly in this book. Indeed, at this point we can go no further, but we refer the reader to Chapter 15.

**Choosing Incentives for Learning Activities.** In deciding what type of incentive to employ, the more successful teachers give consideration to three important criteria:

1. The universality of appeal: the proportion of the pupils involved who will be motivated to learning activities by the incentive
2. The power of appeal: the degree of interest developed in the learning activity by means of the incentive
3. The concomitant educational outcomes, which are very important to better teachers and include the nature and amount of the educational effects of the use of the particular incentive upon (a) the pupil's attitude toward the subject and interest in it, (b) his attitude toward the teacher and the school in general, (c) his attitude toward himself and his capacities, including confidence in himself, and (d) the development of social and ethical characteristics rather than unsocial and unethical characteristics likely to grow out of an excessive or wrong use of competition.

It has been observed that the fear of failure has considerable power of appeal for a small number of students. It has unfortunate educational effects, however, and develops unfortunate attitudes toward the subject, the teacher, and the school, in particular, and toward education, in general. Mediocre teachers may employ threats and appeals to indirect interests and negative needs to such an extent that the attitude and interest of the youngster toward the particular subject are not good and act in future years as blocks to continued learning in that field. Many parents have asserted that they would have preferred that their child had not had the subject at all rather than to have paid for what little he learned the price of the destruction of his interest in that area.

In the long run, the teacher will gain by "leaning over backward" in his effort to be honest with students in motivating interest. Claiming grossly exaggerated values for the study of a subject is not only unethical, it is likely to undermine the confidence of students in the teacher and in his subject.

**Purposeful Learning Activities.** Students are much more easily interested in "purposeful learning," which, in this sense, means participating in learning activities that have, in addition to the learning goals, the purpose of producing something worthwhile or of rendering worthwhile services to the school, the community, and other people.

## IMPORTANT FACTORS IN LEARNING

In directing learning activities of students, the teacher must operate according to the laws and principles of learning and must keep in mind the more important factors which facilitate or prevent learning.

**Pupil Activity, Recitation, and Review.** All learning is the result of physical, mental, or emotional activities and experiences of the learner: seeing, hearing, smelling, feeling, or thinking. All types of learning—acquisition of information, understanding, skills, habits, attitudes, interests, and ideals—develop as a result of experience, or what happens within the learner as a result of his activity and contact with his environment.

It is difficult but, nevertheless, necessary for the teacher to realize and to keep constantly in mind, therefore, that the activity of the teacher is important only insofar as it stimulates effective student learning activities. Unfortunately, there is an additional challenge in that the same learning experience does not happen to all individuals studying the same materials or performing the same learning activities.

**The Factor of Satisfaction or Annoyance.** Whether or not one tends to remember a fact or to repeat an act depends upon the degree to which it has given one satisfaction or an unpleasant experience. This is often referred to as "the law of effect" in learning.

This effect factor operates in a rather complicated fashion. For example, we tend to remember the most unpleasant experiences although they may not be repeated, for example, a very humiliating or physically painful experience.

It has been observed that things learned when the learner is in a pleasant frame of mind tend to be remembered, while those things learned under duress and compulsion when the learner is not in a pleasant frame of mind tend to be forgotten. It has also been shown that knowledge of the results of one's attempts at learning tends to reinforce learning and to improve it if the results have been favorable.

**The Factor of Association.** It has long been commented upon by psychologists that certain laws or principles of association apparently govern learning of all kinds—facts, habits, skills, ideals, attitudes, tastes, and interests. When one fact, thing, person, or idea has been in our consciousness at the same time as has another, and especially if the two are consciously associated, each of these tends to be recalled when the other is in mind. This is particularly true of sequences. When one has experienced several facts in close succession in time, they tend to be associated one with another so that, when one comes back to mind, the rest of the sequence of ideas tends to be recalled. The same factor is operative in the development of skills and of habits; in fact, very frequently the sequence is so well established in our neural system that, once it is started the rest of it may be repeated even with very little or no conscious effort on the part of the individual. Frequently, a person is heard to say, "I never see this place but I think..."

This principle has very important implications for students. Among them is the fact that whatever one desires to retain should be associated with other ideas so that, when any one of those is brought to mind, the fact in question tends to be recalled.

Another important implication of the factor of association is that, if the school subject matter is taught and learned in connection with its application in life, it tends to more easily recalled, to have more meaning, and to be available for use when the situations to which it may be applied arise. Failure in this is one explanation of the fact that, very frequently, an individual who possesses a great store of facts seems not to function well in life—he does not happen to think of the right thing to do even though he may have the factual knowledge that would help him.

**The Factor of Apperceptive Background, or "Mind Set."** It is well known that how one interprets an experience depends very much upon one's previous experiences. How any particular individual will respond to what he reads, hears, or sees is conditioned to a great extent by his previous related experiences. Books of schoolboy howlers or boners have been written, containing thousands of examples of this phenomenon, for example, the student who wrote "The corset crated cross-eyed bear" instead of "The consecrated cross I bear." Her previous experience and "apperceptive mass" had more to do with corsets, apparently, than with the word "consecrated."

The "mind set" also conditions learning for particular situations. For example, what might be interesting in one situation might not be so in another, depending upon what the mind set of the pupil is at the time. Quite frequently, interruptions are unwelcome, even though they might be welcome under other circumstances, because they conflict with the present mind set. It has been an observation of many teachers that, frequently, when they have gotten their students started on a study of some particular topic and an interruption occurs, such as an announcement over the public-address system, which may be somewhat irritating and which destroys the mind set, after the interruption has ceased it is necessary to build up a similar mind set to continue the learning activities effectively. It has often been noticed that, when one is listening for a telephone call, one may hop up to answer the telephone even though it is the doorbell that is ringing.

Growing out of the factor or principle of apperception, or mind set, three applications to teaching are important:

1. New learning activities should be begun in such a manner as to utilize previous mind sets, previous experience, and the stock of understandings.
2. Time and care should usually be devoted to setting the stage by discussions, reviews, or explanations to prepare the learner.
3. The probable effect of any learning materials, methods, or activities upon the pupil must be thought of in terms of what he already knows or does not know and of his interests, abilities, concepts, and tastes.

Throughout the history of education, many writers have formulated principles of teaching based upon this factor, such as the following: from the simple to the complex, from the concrete to the abstract, from the near to the remote, from the psychological to the logical.

**The Factor of Readiness.** A facet of the factor of apperception and, indeed, of the interest and effect is the factor of readiness. The degree to which the pupil may profit from learning experiences depends upon the degree to which he is ready to undertake the learning activity. In planning learning activities, it is very desirable to think of the background that the learners have for them, including such matters as preparatory experiences in the subject field in question, the vocabulary of the pupils, their reading ability, the probable degree of their interest in the activities contemplated, and their belief or disbelief that the results of their learning will be worthwhile to them. It is impractical to attempt to force too fast the development of understandings, interests, skills, and especially tastes, interests, ideals, and appreciations. To do so is likely to result in unfavorable attitudes toward learning materials, learning activities, the teacher, the school, and adult leadership in general.

**The Factor of Attention and Vividness.** Learning experiences conducted under conditions of lack of interest or when the pupil is not attentive and alert result in a low degree of learning, if any at all, or unfortunate learning, as exemplified by inaccurate performance of skills. In addition to the factor of motivation, the characteristics of the learning materials have much to do with the factor of attention and vividness. For example, use of various types of audio-visual aids, effective personality on the part of the teacher, and elimination of distractions tend to result in vividness. Study with TV on is relatively ineffective.

**Transfer of Training.** Much faith is placed by many teachers in the transfer of training from subject-matter situations to life-application situations. But, in most cases, the amount of transfer is less than imagined. The degree of carry-over, or transfer, is known to depend upon the following factors:

1. The degree to which there is identity or similarity between the situation in which the study or training is conducted and the field or situation to which the transfer is made with respect to (a) content: ideas, facts, principles, concepts, vocabulary, and (b) procedure of study or of action
2. The general intelligence or imagination of the pupil, which will enable him to recognize that the things learned apply to various new situations
3. The extent to which, in the learning situation, a general idea is held before the pupil, for example, the ideal of neatness, or the extent to which transfer possibilities are emphasized, such as the possibilities of transfer of ideas of grammar or vocabulary from the study of French to English grammar or vocabulary

## PLANNING PROGRAMS OF LEARNING ACTIVITIES

Whether assignments are made by the instructor or worked out cooperatively by the students and the instructor, the instructor must see to it that the students have a definite idea as to what their responsibilities are and at least sufficient background to get well under way in their learning activities for the day or for the unit. The instructor must check carefully to see that there is definite understanding about this on the part of the pupil. Superior instructors in secondary schools manage this phase of the planning so as to distribute the learning activities of the students fairly evenly from day to day and to avoid the unfortunate situation of having the great amount of learning activities to be done for one particular day and very little for another.

Many of the better teachers have students cooperate in planning learning activities. Many teachers have the plans for a unit mimeographed and distributed to the members of the class so that there will be no misunderstanding and so that they may have it at hand for reference and thereby avoid the misunderstanding that comes from their forgetting or from their failing to take adequate notes about the assignment.

The assignment or plan must meet such criteria as the following:

1. Were the learning activities definitely contributory to the acquisition of information, understanding, skills, habits, attitudes, ideals, and interests that are important for the objectives of secondary education?
2. Did the assignment give adequate consideration to the differences in abilities and past experiences of the individual pupils?
3. Were initiative, originality, and creativity challenged?
4. Did the assignment place undue emphasis upon the acquisition of facts, particularly relatively unimportant facts, as compared to their contributions to such things as intellectual skills, broad understanding, ideals, attitudes, and interests?

**Home Study.** Careful attention should be given to the amount of independent study to be done during the school day under the various types of organizations of learning activities that have been stimulated by the movements toward team teaching and toward the idea of dividing the student's time between being taught in large classes and participating in smaller groups and in independent study. There is a great need for careful planning for independent study in the school as well as outside the school.

Certain types of activities are particularly well suited to out-of-school learning. A committee of which Norman Cousins, Editor of *The Saturday Review*, was the chairman suggested the following:

1. Participating in community activities—public forums, town meetings, church and social programs, Community Chest drives, concerts, lectures, etc.
2. Sharing in the life of the family—taking part, in terms of age-level interests and abilities, in the common activities, duties, and pleasures of the home
3. Taking part in extracurricular school activities—developing attitudes of school participation as well as those of leadership
4. Becoming citizens of the world of the arts—learning how to derive lasting satisfaction from great books, music, painting, and sculpture

5. Listening to, discussing, and reporting on desirable or important radio or TV programs or motion pictures, with the emphasis on alert discrimination and appreciation, rather than passive reception

6. Pursuing interesting and worthwhile hobbies, which often enlarge personal and social horizons

With the increased emphasis upon training in independent study, preparation for college, and a greater number of study periods in the school day, "homework" should consist more of the type that may be done at school and that, in some subjects, calls for use of the library.

**Current Important Trends in Instructional Procedure.** In recent years, there have been many observable trends in instructional procedures. Among the most important of these are those involving provision for the following:

1. More independent study on the part of the student
2. More out-of-class study at home, in study halls, or elsewhere—and of a type that cannot be done by others
3. A much greater use of audio-visual materials
4. A greater use of problem-solving procedure
5. More discussion of controversial issues
6. A greater use of the suggestions of students in planning learning materials and learning procedures for themselves
7. A greater use of various kinds of teaching machines, particularly tape recorders
8. A greater use of individual and group projects and other types of immediately purposeful learning activities
9. Less emphasis upon competition as motivation, and greater emphasis upon interests growing out of the feeling that the knowledge, skills, habits, ideals, attitudes, etc., likely to result from study are worthwhile because the learning activities are in themselves interesting
10. More attention and alertness to development of ideals and moral attitudes
11. Much more attention to development of intellectual skills as compared to memorization
12. More alertness to opportunities to develop democratic and social relations among all the students in the class and in the school
13. More attention to teaching procedures that will develop abilities to succeed in college or in further independent study
14. More use of blackboards and bulletin boards

**Authoritative vs. Developmental Methods.** On the basis of use, distinct advantages are claimed for both the authoritative and the developmental methods of teaching. The purported values of each method are summarized below.

Advantages of authoritative method:

1. Time is economically used.
2. Subject matter is presented in a logical manner.
3. Less ability and ingenuity on the part of the teacher are required.
4. Definite, formal presentation is preferred by many students.
5. Students are given a body of tangible subject matter.
6. Mastery of material presented by authoritative methods can be ascertained by accepted instruments of measurement.
7. The nature and difficulty of the material may justify the direct, authoritative method instead of more time-consuming methods.
8. Retention is facilitated by reference to textbooks or notes on the lecture.

Advantages of developmental method:

1. There may be highly important concomitant outcomes such as (a) pupil initiative, (b) independent habits of study, (c) techniques of problem solving useful in meeting problems outside of school.
2. Independent activity required of the pupil satisfies conditions of effective learning.
3. Retention can be reinforced by the pupils repeating the developmental process.
4. More complete response of the pupil in the initial learning makes it more permanent, thereby reducing need for excessive drill and repetition.
5. The reality and vividness of the pupil's experience in reaching a conclusion or solving a problem for himself contribute to greater understanding.
6. The activities involved in developmental methods make a greater appeal to active, energetic adolescents than do those involved in the methods that foster passivity.
7. This method presents greater opportunity for the teacher to observe and diagnose the individual pupil's methods of study, personal qualities, and needs.

## HELPING STUDENTS TO DEVELOP STUDY HABITS AND SKILLS

Increasingly, teachers are giving attention to training students in the matter of study habits and skills. This is becoming increasingly important as assignments involve more home study and study in the library and study halls.

Mills and Douglass make a number of practical suggestions for improving the study habits and skills of students.[2] According to them, the teacher should attempt to make an accurate appraisal of the difficulty encountered by pupils. To do this, he or she should look at such things as the scores of each individual on tests of silent reading; achievement tests; analyses of oral and written work; and informal tests of skills in the use of the textbook, the dictionary, and other reference material. In addition, the teacher is helped by observation of each student's study procedure in the class period; asking the student to make a description of his study habits and schedule; data concerning home conditions for study; information relative to the student's work or other outside activities; an inventory of the student's interests including reading interests; and information from the student relative to his ability to concentrate, his feeling of fatigue, his hours of sleep, and the regularity of his meals.

Among the study abilities that ought to be developed are the following:

1. Power to concentrate
2. Independence in study
3. Accuracy and speed in locating study materials
4. Competence in evaluating materials
5. Ability to organize materials
6. Skill in outlining and summarizing study materials
7. Ability to read with comprehension and speed
8. Efficiency in use of library materials and audio-visual aids to learning
9. Facility in taking notes on reading and lectures
10. Ability to relate new learnings to previous knowledge

To acquire these abilities, students should be encouraged to develop the following study habits:

1. Studying at definite time and place
2. Arranging physical environment favorable for study
3. Keeping study materials in order
4. Keeping a study plan
5. Keeping complete notes on readings, discussions, and lectures
6. Studying assignment soon after it is made
7. Looking up unfamiliar words
8. Reflecting upon reading
9. Memorizing significant concepts, facts, and generalizations
10. Reviewing main points of previous lesson
11. Reviewing lesson before class
12. Supplementary information from one text by use of library reading materials and audio-visual aids

---

[2] The discussion is based on Chapter 9 of "Directing Study Activities," in *Teaching in High School* (2d ed.), The Ronald Press Co., 1957.

13. Underscoring key words and making marginal notations in text-book
14. Staying at learning tasks until they are completed

The teacher should become familiar with one or more of the following: *Teaching Study Habits and Skills* by Ralph C. Preston, published by Rinehart in 1959; *A Practical Guide to Effective Study* by Charles L. Gunthorp, published by the Exposition Press, Inc., of New York City, in 1957; *Learning To Learn* by Donald E. R. Smith and others, published by Harcourt, Brace & World, Inc., of New York City, in 1961; and *Learning and the Teacher*, issued by the John Dewey Society in Washington, D.C. in 1959. Students may well be encouraged to read *Study Your Way Through School*, published by the Science Research Associates of Chicago.[3]

**Teaching Reading Skills.** Teachers of all academic subjects should provide training for developing reading skills. Following are suggestions that have proved successful and have been recommended by successful teachers:

1. Have the pupil make a brief, rapid survey of the chapter, ascertain its general theme, and obtain an over-all view of the material.
2. This general overview may be followed by a general reading of the material, sentence by sentence, to get the exact meaning of each sentence, graph, and table.
3. The student may then review and reread the main ideas in the chapter, with a view to learning the principal points.
4. This should be followed by making a summary of the gist of each paragraph.

It has been found that the rates of reading of a great many people can be very materially increased. Some teachers find it desirable to give students training in class in rapid reading, suggesting to them that they make their eyes pass more quickly across the line and that they try to grasp small groups of words rather than each individual word.

One of the more important needs for improvement of reading is to train students to look up the meaning of any word the exact meaning of which is not clear to them. Indeed, some students in senior high school and many in junior high school may profit by reading with a dictionary at hand.

[3] Proved very useful to students are such tests of study skills as the Spitzer Study Skills Test and the Stanford Advanced Study Skills Test, the former being expressly adapted to grades nine through twelve and the latter to junior high school grades, published by Harcourt, Brace & World, Inc., of New York City, and the "BOCES Study Skills Checklist," published by the Board of Cooperative Educational Services of Bedford Hills, New York.

A great and increasing number of teachers, particularly in the fields of English, social studies, and science, are giving their students training in the use of the library, taking their students into the library occasionally for a period, particularly at the beginning of the semester, and explaining to them how the library may be best utilized for the study of their subject.

**Remedial Reading.** A steadily increasing number, though still a small proportion, of students coming into junior and senior high school read so poorly that special classes are formed for them as the means of improving not only their reading speed and comprehension but also their chances of succeeding in classes involving reading.

**Study Habits. Supervising Study in the Class Period.** Particularly where the long period can the large unit are employed, the class period provides an opportunity for the teacher to work in the classroom with individual students or with small groups of students. Until recent years, there was a tendency for many teachers to have most of the study done during the class period rather than in study halls or at home. In view of the shift in educational thinking toward higher standards and the development of habits of, and skills in, independent study on the part of the students, this practice is being drastically modified. Nevertheless, where the longer periods are employed, provision is made by most teachers for some study in class. For this reason, it is desirable, in many instances, to have in the classroom some materials for study.

With the shifts toward the seven-period day and toward the four-period-a-week class instead of the six-period day and the five-period-a-week class, there is greater opportunity for students to work in the study hall, in the library, or in the laboratory. Indeed, there has been a growing feeling that students in senior high school should spend more time in the library, particularly if they are planning to go on to college.

During the class periods, many teachers break up the class into small groups for group study or for group projects, and the teacher moves from group to group as he or she is needed. Indeed, in some schools where ability grouping by classes is not employed, the teacher divides the class into four or five ability groups including one of least ability and one of greatest ability. The grouping is always somewhat flexible, and students are shifted from group to group. In some instances, various groups prepare different parts of the work at hand and present it as their part of the whole in group discussions or culminating activities.

**Small Groups or Subgroups.** A considerable number of teachers have found it effective to employ small groups and subdivisions of the class for work on projects in the community. To be sure, many teachers set up committees at the beginning of the semester and appoint others as need develops.[4]

[4] See Chapter 14, for more detailed discussion.

## AUTHORITARIAN VS. DEMOCRATIC METHODS

**Authoritarian Methods in Other Countries.** In the secondary schools of all countries other than the United States, including those of the U.S.S.R. and its satellite countries, authoritarianism characterizes the principles and procedures. Since the schools are quite selective in other countries, and only a small minority graduate from a secondary school, there is a great struggle on the part of students to do well so that they may complete secondary school and be admitted to a college or university. This makes the problem of interest level quite different from that in the United States. In many other countries there prevails the idea of "take it or leave it."

In other countries, the lecture method and the textbook assignment followed by recitation and oral and written quizzes constitute a very large part of the instructional and learning procedures. The students participate very little cooperative planning concerning either the learning materials or the learning activities.

**Practice in the American Secondary School.** In the United States democratic and developmental methods are employed to a much greater extent than in other countries, although here also authoritarian methods are employed to some extent by all teachers and to a great extent by some. Developmental methods require more skill, industry, and patience on the part of the teacher, as well as more understanding of the nature of young people and greater amounts of imagination and creative planning. It has been noted not only by Americans but also by visitors from abroad that young Americans seem to have more initiative and imagination than do young people of other countries of a corresponding age. This is usually attributed to the types of experiences they have had in the American elementary and secondary schools.

## QUESTIONS, PROBLEMS, AND TOPICS FOR FURTHER STUDY

1. Be able to give in class a seven- or eight-minute talk on what the beginning teacher should do prior to the opening of school in the fall.
2. From the suggestions made for getting off to a good start in school, pick out the eight or ten that you think are the most important and be able to explain them fully.
3. It has been said by some people that people do best those things in which they are most interested. Is that always true?
4. Be able to discuss in class the relationship between interest and attention.
5. Be able to give a short talk in class on immediate vs. deferred needs, positive vs. negative needs, and generic vs. specific needs as motivation.
6. Make an outline for a five-minute talk on "Criteria of a Good Assignment."
7. Give some examples of the operation of the factor of association.

8. In what way do you think that you, as a teacher, might employ the factor of mind set, or apperceptive background?
9. Do you believe that some of the growth that develops in your subject might transfer to other subjects or to life in general? Explain your position fully.
10. Which of the current important trends listed in this chapter do you think are the most important or the most sound?

## SUPPLEMENTARY MATERIALS

### SELECTED READINGS

ALBERTY, HAROLD B., and ELSIE J. ALBERTY. *Reorganizing the High School Curriculum* (3d ed.). New York: The Macmillan Co., 1962. Chapter 10, "Teachers and Principals at Work."

ANDERSON, VERNON E., and WILLIAM T. GRUHN. *Principles and Practices of Secondary Education* (2d. ed.). New York: The Ronald Press Co., 1962. Chapter 8, "Instructional Practices and Relationships."

BARD, HARRY. *Homework: A Guide for Secondary School Teachers.* New York: Holt, Rinehart & Winston, Inc., 1962.

DOUGLASS, HARL R. *Trends and Issues in Secondary Education.* Washington, D.C.: The Center for Applied Research in Education, Inc., 1962. Chapter 2, "Basic Theory and Philosophy."

FAUNCE, ROLAND C., and MORREL J. CLUTE. *Teaching and Learning in the Junior High School.* San Francisco: Wadsworth Publishing Co., Inc., 1961. Chapter 3, "The Learning Process."

GRAMBS, JEAN D., WILLIAM J. IVERSON, and FRANKLIN K. PATTERSON. *Modern Methods in Secondary Education.* New York: Holt, Rinehart & Winston, Inc., 1958. Chapter 6, "How To Plan for Learning and Teaching."

HOFFMAN, EARL G. "Good Classroom Climate: The Teacher's Function," *The Bulletin of the N.A.S.S.P.,* December, 1962, 5–11.

KLAUSMEIER, HERBERT J. *Teaching in the Secondary School.* New York: Harper & Row, 1958. Chapter 3, "Learning with Purpose"; Chapter 4, "Democratic Living in the School."

MCKEAN, ROBERT C. *Principles and Methods in Secondary Education.* Columbus, Ohio: Charles E. Merrill Books, Inc., 1962. Chapter 5, "Planning Classroom Experiences."

MILLS, HUBERT H., and HARL R. DOUGLASS. *Teaching in High School* (2d ed.). New York: The Ronald Press Co., 1957. Chapter 1, "Emergence of the Modern Concept of Teaching"; Chapter 6, "Basic Principles of Learning and Motivation."

MOULY, GEORGE J. *Psychology for Effective Teaching.* New York: Holt, Rinehart & Winston, Inc., 1960. Chapter 9, "Guiding the Learning Process," pp. 243–66; Chapter 10, "Motivation," pp. 267–91.

RIVLIN, HARRY N. *Teaching Adolescents in Secondary Schools.* New York: Appleton-Century-Crofts, Inc., 1961. Chapter 3, "The Desire To Learn: Motivating and Leading."

WATKINS, RALPH K. *Techniques of Secondary School Teaching.* New York: The Ronald Press Co., 1958. Chapter 10, "Motivation."

AUDIO-VISUAL MATERIALS

*Films*

*Broader Concept of Method: Part I—Developing Pupil Interest.* McGraw-Hill. 13 minutes.
*Motivating the Class.* McGraw-Hill. 19 minutes.
*We Plan Together.* Teachers College, Columbia University. 20 minutes.

# 13

# Developing Important Types of Pupil Growth

In directing learning activities of students, the teacher must operate according to the laws and principles of learning and must keep in mind the more important factors that facilitate or prevent learning.

All learning is the result of some physical, mental, or emotional activity that goes on in the pupil—seeing, hearing, smelling, feeling, thinking, or some motor activity. All types of growth—acquisition of information, understanding, skills, habits, attitudes, interests, and ideals—develop as the result of some experience in his mind or body, as the result of physical, mental, or emotional activity growing out of contact with his environment. It is difficult but, nevertheless, necessary for the teacher to realize and to keep constantly in mind that *what really counts is not the activity of the teacher but the activities and the experiences of the pupils.* Unfortunately, different individuals have different experiences when studying the same materials or performing the same learning activities, this necessitates knowing the pupils as individuals and making appropriate adaptations.

Some things can be learned as the result of one experience, but others require repetition in order to be learned, and, indeed, in some there must be drill or practice that involves repeating the activity many times before the desired level of mastery is obtained.

It is unfortunate from some standpoints of education that what is learned tends to be forgotten, sometimes very quickly, unless it is "over-learned." This applies particularly to the acquisition of factual information that does not seem to the pupil to be of great importance. Such facts are easily learned, easily tested, and easily and quickly forgotten, as has been proved by Tyler[1] and others. That this happens makes it necessary for the teacher to provide for review from time to time to bring back into mind the facts once learned or to provide practice from time to time to keep the skill from deteriorating too much. Acquired skills tend to remain with us longer than acquired information.

## HELPING STUDENTS TO ACQUIRE INFORMATION AND UNDERSTANDING

The most effective and most commonly used approaches to imparting information and understanding involve

1. Learning from textbooks or other reference books
2. Learning from lectures
3. Learning from audio-visual aids
4. Learning from class recitations or discussions
5. Learning from observation

Learning from the use of textbooks or other reference books is discussed elsewhere in this volume.

**Imparting Facts and Understanding by Telling.** While in college and university classes lecturing is used very frequently as a means of instruction, particularly in lower-division classes of considerable size, it has not been looked upon with favor at the secondary school level. It is used rather frequently by many teachers for short periods of telling, particularly in connection with making explanations and giving brief supplementation to a textbook or introducing or giving a preview of a new chapter, topic, or unit.

In recent years, particularly in secondary schools in which team teaching is employed, there has been an increased use of telling to large groups. It is presumed that, in these situations, *a superior lecturer will make the presentation, will have a reduced teaching load so that he may make very careful preparation, and will use audio-visual aids.* Even in situations where team teaching is not involved, there has been slightly increased use of carefully prepared lectures to classes, particularly groups of two or three sections of the same subject.

Certain advantages may come from telling. The most important of these are the following:

1. The lecture may be adapted better than a textbook to the abilities, interests, previous knowledge, and needs to the pupils in the class.

[1] Ralph W. Tyler, "What High School Pupils Forget," *Education Research Bulletin,* No. 9 (November 19, 1930), pp. 490–492.

2. In some instances, there may be economy in that students may be saved time consumed in looking up materials, particularly where there are not enough copies of the materials for the entire class.
3. Through telling one can put life and meaning into the words in a more attractive and appealing way than is possible through cold print.
4. It is possible for the students to raise questions during and at the close of the lecture in a way that is not possible when they are reading.
5. When done correctly, telling serves as an example of good oral English expression and tends to counteract the tendency of adolescents to employ careless, incorrect speech.
6. In telling, the teacher may, by use of inflection, relative emphasis, and pauses, bring out more fully the meaning of the words.

**Dangers and Limitations.** Nevertheless, the use of the lectures has dangers and serious limitations. Among the more important ones are these:

1. Unless the lecturer chooses his materials, particularly his beginning, wisely, he will not find it easy to keep the attention of the students. Many lecturers have learned that the use of audio-visual materials and the use of occasional questions to the students during the lecture minimize this danger.
2. The pupil is likely to sink into a low level of attention, since he is not particularly active. Here, again, the opportunity to ask questions and the insistence of the lecturer that the students take notes and be prepared to react to the lecture lessen this danger.
3. Many high school teachers are not good lecturers; they have not had enough practice under conditions of very careful planning to have developed a very satisfactory degree of skill. On the other hand, because of their personality, or as a result of practice or both, some high school teachers are excellent lecturers. Among the weaknesses of many high school teachers is the tendency to talk too long, too much or too fast about some points in the lecture.

Without any question, a telling requires very careful planning, not only in content but also in expression and supplementary aids. Furthermore, the lecturer must be so thoroughly familiar with the content that he is not tied to his notes and can use his personality to the maximum advantage while lecturing.

**Planning and Telling.** Very careful planning, involving the following elements, should be employed for telling:

1. Carefully considering the time to be devoted to telling
2. Familiarizing oneself with the materials and how they will be presented

3. Anticipating important questions that students are likely to ask and how they should be answered
4. Thinking through the material to be told, with a view to including applications, examples, and illustrations
5. Thinking of occasions where telling may be profitably interrupted for stimulating questions to come from the class
6. Testing in advance any experiments, films, or apparatus to be used
7. Making and becoming familiar with easily read notes that will ensure sequence and prevent forgetting
8. Planning a few interesting or amusing expressions or examples to present to the class
9. Making certain that all charts, diagrams, chemicals, apparatus, etc., that are going to be used are at hand and can be displayed effectively

**Good Lecture Procedure.** The following are procedures found to be effective in telling:

1. Begin by arousing some curiosity or developing a problem-solving attitude by means of a question or problem.

2. Give the hearers some idea of the principal things to be gained from the telling.

3. Adapt the pace to the ability of the class to follow.

4. Provide for pauses in which the students may reflect on what has been presented.

5. Adapt the pace of speaking to the difficulty of the material being presented and the ability of the class to take notes, avoiding rapid talking and employing the same pace throughout. Check up occasionally on the hearers by a question or exercise to see if there is adequate understanding.

6. Talk to the hearers in an informal way, as you might talk to a group outside of the classroom; avoid "lecturing."

7. Enunciate clearly and carefully with your face toward the class.

8. Be relaxed, to avoid self-consciousness and stage fright.

9. Avoid lengthy unplanned digressions.

10. Hold the pupils responsible for the content of the talks just as you would assigned textbook material. At the end of the class, give a short oral or written test, for the purposes of both testing and diagnosis; this may be followed by supplementary telling.

11. Employ, wherever possible, visual materials such as graphs, charts and diagrams, still pictures and slides, motion pictures, objects, specimens, and models; use the blackboard. It is also desirable to employ verbal illustrations and examples of the more important points, utilizing, when possible, ancedotes and stories.

12. Depending upon the degree to which the pupils are skilled in note taking, some preliminary training and instruction should be given to hearers about the taking of notes, which, of course, should be brief and not necessarily in the words of the lecturer.

**Using Films and Slides in Telling.** In recent years, use of films and slides for telling and explaining has greatly increased. Good procedure in the use of films or slides includes the following steps:

1. The teacher should preview the film or set of slides, for the purpose of becoming familiar with its content and organization.
2. The teacher should prepare a brief list of the main features emphasized in the lesson.
3. The pupils should be given an assignment that includes

    a. Reading materials giving information in brief story form in regard to the general nature of the film or set of slides
    b. If a sound film is used, a list of the unfamiliar words, to study in order to understand the sound track
    c. A list of questions pertaining to the main points of information included in the film or set of slides
    d. A list of suggested things for which to look

4. The showing should be followed by a class discussion of the main points presented.
5. Individual pupils should read and give reports to the class on special problems suggested.
6. Usually, if a film is used, it should be shown again, with stops at any time to deal with questions raised by the class.
7. A test should be given, based upon the film or slides, related reading, and class discussions.
8. There should be a final follow-up to correct any misunderstandings and to implement important points and outcomes.

In the use of any type of audio-visual material, or a field trip requiring more than a few minutes, there is definitely a need for certain techniques that the best teachers use regularly, including (1) careful preparation of the students with respect to that for which they are to watch and (2) a follow-up that emphasizes the more important things and provides for discussion, explanation, and checking up on what the student got from the materials.

**Problem-solving Procedures.** In the acquisition of knowledge, problem-solving procedures not only are usually effective in situations to which they can be applied, they also develop habits and skills in reasoning that are in themselves very important incidental outcomes. Two types of problem solving employed in school as well as in everyday thinking are (1) the development of a generalization from individual cases and

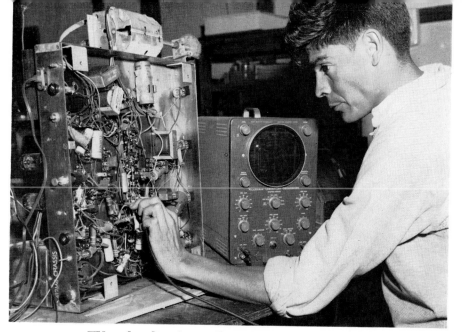

TV and radio class—Albuquerque, New Mexico.

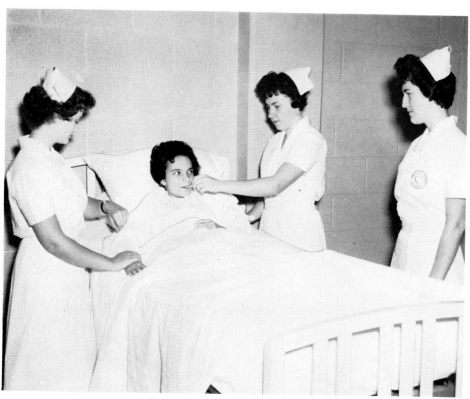

Preparing for nursing in high school—Syracuse, New York.

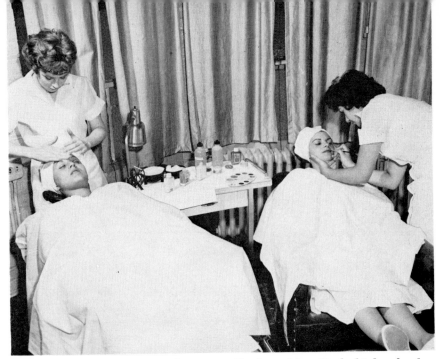

Teaching massage and makeup in a Yonkers, New York, high school.

Metal shop at Granby High School, Norfolk, Virginia.

(2) the solution of a specific problem by reasoning from one or more generalizations that are already known and one or more facts that are already known.

An example of the first, or *inductive*, type of procedure may be seen in the development of the rule for the squaring of the binomial in algebra. The object of the teaching and pupil study is to develop a generalization to enable one to write out an expression that is the square of a sum or the difference of two quantities, for example, the square of $X + Y$, $2a + 3b$, $4 + 5$, or $X - 1$. Students are asked to multiply the binomial by itself, let us say, $X + Y$ by $X + Y$, obtaining of course $X^2 + 2XY + Y^2$, then to multiply several other binomials that are sums, such as $2a + 3b$, $X + 1$, or $4 + 5$, and also some which are the difference between two quantities, such as $X - Y$, $A - 2B$, or $6 - 4$.

Upon looking at the products obtained by multiplying a binomial by itself, some students will observe that the resulting project is always a square of the first quantity in the binomial plus or minus twice the product of the first and second term plus the square of the second term. The sign of the cross-product term in the middle is also observed to be the same as the sign between the two terms in the binomial being squared. Having developed the generalization in this fashion, the students not only understand it better but retain it longer.

This inductive procedure may be employed in a multitude of situations in all subjects. In some subjects, many cases should be necessary to arrive at a general conclusion, and, in others, only one case. As an example of the latter type, it is not necessary to dissect a great many frogs or even two frogs to arrive at certain generalizations on the structure of a frog. However, it is very desirable, in many cases, to draw a generalization from several examples. For example, in attempting to discover whether a Republican president had in recent decades been more conservative or more progressive than Democratic presidents, one must not confine the matter to one or even two presidents. Furthermore, in many cases, one does not come up with a hard and fixed conclusion which will apply to all cases in the future. Many generalizations arrived at are expressed in terms of probability, that is, they might indicate that, since in the past all or at least a great majority of the cases have been of a particular type, it is rather probable that in the future other such cases will be of that type.

Even more common is what is known as the *deductive* approach to problem solving. In this type of problem solving, one wishes to come to some conclusion relative to a specific situation. For example, is the word "dec*ei*ve" or "dec*ie*ve"? In solving this problem, one may reason thus: In spelling "e" comes before "i" except after "c." In this particular case the letters "e" and "i" follow "c," therefore the "e" should come before the "i." In "relief," on the other hand, "i" should come before "e" because the two letters follow not a "c" but an "l." In other words, a specific problem may be solved by discovering or calling to mind a generalization that applies and that is called a *major premise*. One also must show how the generalization applies to the special case, that is, one must establish the *minor premise*. The major premise in the instance of the spelling of words where the two letters "e" and "i" follow a "c" is that "e" should come before "i," while in all other words the "i" precedes the "e"; the minor premise is that the two letters as used in the word "deceive" follow a "c"; the conclusion is derived from the major premise and the minor premise.

In recent years, greatly increased use has been made of problem solving. Students are more easily interested in this procedure for the acquisition of facts, and, as was indicated above, it is an effective means for developing understanding and permanent retention.

**Helping Students To Acquire Concepts and Understanding.** One of the most important types of educational outcomes is the acquisition of general concepts. These range all the way from understanding of the meaning of commonly used words to more complicated and abstract concepts such as (1) the meaning of democracy; (2) the nature of communism; (3) animal and human physical evolution; (4) the concept of the unified personality, or of the unity of mind and body; (5) the concepts of nuclear fision and atomic energy; (6) the concept of the evolution of our language and its words; (7) the concept of infinity—infinite space, infinite heat, etc.; (8) the concepts of parents' love for their children and of the family; (9) the concept of the expanding universe; (10) the concept of infinitesimally small bits of matter; and (11) the concept of conversion of matter to energy.

One of the characteristics of the change in our educational theory and practice in the last half-century has been a shift from the learning and recitation of poorly understood facts toward the development of understanding of the facts and processes learned. It has been discovered in psychological laboratories as well as in classrooms that the retention of educational growth, particularly of learned facts, but also of attitudes, ideals, skills, and habits, depends upon intellectual understanding of materials, facts, principles, and processes. Indeed, it seems that the short and the sure way home is probably a roundabout way of making certain that youngsters understand at least the principal things that they are attempting to learn and those things upon which what they will be learning later will be logically based. One of the characteristic differences between an ineffective teacher and a true educator is the relative emphasis they place upon understanding as a factor in teaching and learning.

One of the tests of understanding is the ability to apply what is learned to new situations. In fact, in the field of tests and measurements, techniques have been developed for the purpose of measuring the ability to apply, and they are tending to replace tests that merely measure recall of facts.

**Helping Students To Remember.** In attempts to ensure retention of information, the following principles have been found to be effective:

1. The material to be learned should first be well understood by the pupil, and he should get a good overview of the whole of it in the form of a summary.
2. If there is some natural sequence of organization, attention should be called to that as a type of association which will facilitate learning and promote retention.
3. Discussion of uses and application will also assist in learning and in retention.
4. If there is much to be learned, the first few repetitions should involve only part of the material, which may be joined with the rest in later stages of the learning effort.
5. All along, the leader should be thinking of ways to maintain interest and to prevent discouragement.

**Purposes and Types of Reviews.** Information, skills, habits, ideals, attitudes, interests, and appreciations, once developed, may tend to disappear. This is particularly true of information, which, according to careful studies, tends to disappear very materially in a few weeks and very substantially in a few months. It is, therefore, necessary to provide for reinforcement and, to some extent, relearning, particularly in the case of information that is desired to be a permanent acquisition. In this case, a number of reviews at different times is desirable.

The review ought to differ from the experiences first employed to acquire the information. The more prominent purposes of review are the following: (1) to help the pupil to perceive the relationships among the various items and elements of a unit or body of subject matter; (2) to emphasize the important concepts in a day's lessons, in a unit, or in a semester's work; (3) to provide a basis for diagnosis of a pupil's forgetting or of deterioration of a skill and to rebuild where rebuilding is most necessary; (4) to set up an apperceptive background and basis for the approach of new units; and (5) to furnish additional evidence of the degree of the pupil's achievement.

Among the types of review employing approaches somewhat different from those used in the original study of the material, the following are recommended by successful teachers: (1) selective recall, in which the student is asked to recall in sequence or in relationships more important ideas in a unit or a semester's work; (2) comparison, in which the pupil is required to make comparisons between facts learned on different days; (3) cause and effect, in which the student is asked to establish a connection and relationship between one fact or principle that he learned earlier and one that he learned later, on the basis of cause and effect relationships; (4) summary, in which the pupil is asked to summarize the sequence of more important items in a large unit or semester's work; (5) analysis, in which the student is asked to analyze a number of items of subject matter presented on different days.

Some teachers employ review quizzes; some employ some form of socialized reviews such as the panel discussion in which questions are asked of a selected panel of students by their classmates. Under any circumstances, a review should be selective, involve reorganization of the learnings, and locate the weaknesses of the learning.

## HELPING STUDENTS TO ACQUIRE HABITS AND SKILLS

In spite of the belief that some seem to hold that drill is not modern or necessary, it is rather evident that practice and drill often are necessary, particularly with reference to the development of skills and habits of either the intellectual or the motor type. This is especially true in the teaching of typewriting, foreign languages, sports, and the use of machines. In addition, there are general mental skills that ought to be improved, such as the ability to think through the problem solving, in reading, in formulating answers, and in speech in general.

Likewise, there are very desirable habits that ought to be cultivated and that can be developed only by practice and repetition, such as habits of speech, habits of neatness in the laboratory and shop and elsewhere, and various types of social habits.

**Practice and Drill Procedures.** Certain procedures are found to be very useful in drill and practice for the development of skills and the formation of habits. Among the more important, the following may be mentioned:

1. The pupil should be led (a) to believe that the habit or the skill is worthwhile and (b) to acquire a desire to acquire it.
2. The pupil should have clearly in mind exactly what the elements or movements in the skill or habit are, as a means of perceiving the right pattern and avoid practicing mistakes.
3. Where possible, the skill should be demonstrated by someone who is adept in it.

4. Habits and skills should be developed in situations as nearly as possible like those in which they will be used.
5. The instructor should determine the degree of skill that is desired and avoid excessive drill.
6. Speed should always be subordinated to accuracy in the early stages. It is much more important that the pupil repeat the act accurately at first; he can be helped to develop speed after accuracy has been achieved.
7. Care should be taken to notice at the first appearance errors or omissions that should be corrected, if this is possible. Individual diagnosis and drill must be provided according to the needs of the particular pupil.
8. Learning situations should not be complicated at first, but they may be developed to involve more complex skills as learning proceeds.
9. Practice should be continued a bit after the stage of desired proficiency as a guaranty against forgetting or deterioration, and provision must be made from time to time for review.

The instructor should bear in mind that, to most youngsters, drill and practice are usually distasteful, particularly if they are not well motivated or fail to develop some direct interest in the actual drill or practice procedure. It is also important to keep in mind that, if the individual student sees no value in acquiring the skill or memorizing the facts or is unsuccessful in meeting the standards set by the teacher, there may be unfortunate concomitant growth effects—development of distaste for the practice and a lack of confidence in the teacher.

Physical skills, once acquired, tend to remain rather permanently, particularly if there is occasional practice, for example, the skill one develops in playing tennis, riding a bicycle, or operating a machine tends to stay with one much longer than does memory of historical dates, names, and places, or of grammatical rules.

## HELPING STUDENTS TO ACQUIRE VALUES, IDEALS, ATTITUDES, TASTES, AND INTERESTS

**Values, Ideals, and Attitudes.** Perhaps the principal reason why teachers do not make as great a contribution toward the development of ideals and attitudes as the importance of these things would call for is the fact that any particular ideal or attitude is not developed in one day's work or a unit. Ideals and attitudes grow over periods of time, and contributions must be made by a great many teachers of different subjects in different grades. Following are important ideals to the development of which teachers can contribute: honesty, reliability, fairness, desire to be of service to others, correct and accurate speech, good fellowship, good health and physical vigor, and cooperation. Likewise, the contributions of many teachers in a variety of subjects and grades are necessary for the development of important attitudes such as tolerance toward individuals of other races, nationalities, and religions, open-mindedness, and a dislike for waste, physical violence, cruelty, hypocrisy, and dishonesty.

The ideas and attitudes essential to good American citizenship, toward which all teachers should make contributions, involve, of course, individual freedoms, acquiescence to majority rule, protection of the rights of minorities, and interest in state and national social and political questions.

All school departments and all subject-matter areas are responsible for developing value scales and structure. A few examples may point up possibilities in some areas.

1. Assemblies
   a. Patriotic
   b. Inspirational
   c. Devotional
   d. Deliberative (on youth problems)
2. Student-council activities
   a. Leadership for behavior codes
   b. Sponsoring of courtesy and "respect for others" campaign
   c. Setting a high moral tone for the school
   d. Service projects
3. Guidance
   a. Emphasis on self-discipline and assuming personal responsibility
   b. The ethics of personal growth
4. Social studies
   a. Emphasis on the American heritage
   b. Ideas of brotherhood, justice
   c. Culture comparison
   d. Stress on family relationships
   e. Study of right decisions at crucial moments
   f. Respect for religion
   g. The necessity for faith
5. Health education and physical education
   a. Sex education
   b. The ethics of sportsmanship
   c. The ideal of physical and mental fitness
6. Science
   a. Developing a sense of awe and wonder at our universe
   b. Reverence for life
   c. Belief in truth
   d. Logic

7. English
   a. Through literature, developing a concern for meeting problems created by life's needs
   b. Character delineation in drama, biography, the novel
   c. Literature of national ideas
   d. Interpretation of life
   e. Developing aesthetic appreciation

In developing values, ideals, and attitudes, there must not be too much pressure or persuasion, otherwise hypocrisy and negative reactions are developed instead of the desirable outcomes. Much more effective is having the students read biography or fiction about individuals who possessed or practiced desired attitudes and ideals, and having group discussions.

**Tastes, Appreciations, and Interests.** Many leaders in educational thought have said that one of the major characteristics of an educated person is the possession of educated tastes and interests. Among the tastes and interests that should be developed in secondary schools the following may be mentioned: interest in reading good literature, in new developments in science, in social thinking and economics, in people of other countries and their ways of life, in problems of taxation, in problems of labor and employment, and taste and appreciation for good literature, art, and music.

**Principles of Developing Tastes, Appreciations, Ideals, and Interests.** The efforts of many teachers to develop desirable tastes, ideals, and attitudes have been conspicuously unsuccessful. It is not difficult to identify the most probable causes of these failures. Stated in terms of positive principles of procedure calculated to yield a great degree of success in developing growth in ideals, attitudes, interests, and tastes, especially in the fields of art, music, and literature, they may be summarized as follows:

1. The development of ideals, tastes, attitudes, and interests cannot be forced. They are long-term developments growing out of contacts, experiences, and activities that are carried on under conditions of voluntary participation without compulsion.

2. Materials for developing tastes, ideals, interests, and attitudes must not be presented prematurely. Much of the distaste for, or at least indifference to, the "better" things is directly attributable to the misguided enthusiasm of teachers who "pressed." "Pressing" in developing this type of growth in young people is as ineffective as "pressing" in golf, or "fighting one's cards" in bridge. One must let nature take its course under favorable conditions, realizing its course will leave much to be desired,

at least for the present, in the case of many pupils. Many persons have learned late in life to enjoy things they disliked when presented prematurely by teachers.

3. Allowance and provision must be made for differences among individuals with respect to

a. Present status of tastes, ideals, attitudes, or interest in any given field or activity
b. Rate of development
c. Capacity for development

4. It is usually conducive to the development of this type of growth to provide for and encourage subtly, but not too quickly or aggressively, expression of reactions, either verbal or in some other form. It is natural for young people to want to "do something about" things that are beginning to interest them—to talk about them, to imitate others, to engage in appropriate physical activity. For example, to play, to sing, or to dramatize.

5. In directing the development of young people's tastes in music, literature, or art, it has proved wise not to overemphasize technical analysis, particularly in the earlier stages. That must come gradually. In literature, content is the first thing to emphasize; in music, it is pleasure in listening, playing, or singing, and not just looking for technical merit.

## MENTAL HYGIENE AND CONCOMITANT GROWTH OUTCOMES

As a result of the pupil's experiences in school, he develops ideas, attitudes, interests, ideals, and habits and skills that were not intended and that have no relationship to the learning materials and methods in terms of growth. These types of incidental outcomes, which differ greatly from one pupil to another, are in many instances very important. The clearheaded, farseeing teacher will be alert to the possibilities of developing such types of growth and will attempt to set up learning activities and to employ learning materials that will not contribute to undesirable types of growth—attitudes, ideals, etc.—but that will have valuable incidental growth outcomes.

Not only is a pupil's degree of interest or dislike or distaste for a particular subject influenced by his experiences in studying it, but, quite frequently, the pupil develops attitudes—toward the subject field, the school, the teacher, adult authority, learning in general, himself, his parents, or his classmates—that are very unfortunate and, in some instances, tragic.

**Mental Hygiene.** In recent years, much has been learned about mental hygiene and mental health. Furthermore, much more importance is now being attached to mental hygiene and mental health, because it has been becoming obvious that an increasing number of young people are not developing mental and emotional health and sturdiness. A considerable proportion of their failure to do as well in school as they can and a considerable amount of juvenile delinquency are definitely traceable in many students to an alarming amount of emotional and personality difficulties.

There has been, in recent years, a tendency for school administrators to urge teachers to learn more about mental hygiene and the development of personality both for their own sake and so that they may avoid practices in their teaching, particularly with reference to motivation of students in learning, that are thought to be bad mental hygiene. This has particularly to do with pressures for grades, scolding and punishment of young people, and the like. Teachers who have not taken a course in, or read a book on, mental hygiene or personality development should lose no time in filling that important gap in their professional knowledge.

**Social and Emotional Development.** In spite of the energetic efforts of those opposing any emphasis upon the education of aspects of the human being except his intellect, educators, parents, doctors, and students of human relations in general insist that not only the home but also the school has a very important responsibility for providing an environment that will enable boys and girls to develop social attitudes and habits and to participate in activities that promote normal emotional reactions marked by balance and control.

Of course, many teachers have realized the importance of these types of outcomes and have attempted to avoid situations that would present negative or unfortunate influence upon social or emotional development. Evidence of this is the lessened emphasis upon punishment and marks given in school and the increased opportunity given to young people to participate in extracurricular activities and in planning their own learning activities in classes.

Furthermore, an increasing number of teachers and to an increasing extent are planning activities in and out of class that will contribute to good social and emotional development. This is evidenced by provision for the formation of groups of youngsters for various types of learning activities. The problem is particularly important for youngsters who are compelled to attend school either by law or by inability to get positions and, therefore, are living in an environment that is distasteful to them. This group of youngsters comprises an alarming proportion of dropouts, juvenile delinquents, and emotionally disturbed young people. They do not always come from homes of lower levels of culture and are not always students of inferior intelligence. Most parents prefer very much that their children be in the classroom with a teacher, who makes a positive rather than a negative contribution to their social and emotional development.

Working together in classes in a sort of democratic living is very valuable experience in overcoming, at least in some measure, the provincialism and biases that many children get in their homes with respect to people who are somewhat different from them in economic status, religion, color, or ethnic origin. People who differ from one another in some of the above respects tend not only to be unappreciative but suspicious and actually hostile to people of other groups unless they have had experience with them.

## QUESTIONS, PROBLEMS, AND TOPICS FOR FURTHER STUDY

1. In your major subject, when and how often are you likely to use drill and review teaching?
2. What is your opinion of the use of the lecture in teaching junior high school students? In teaching senior high school students?
3. If the lecture is used in either junior or senior high school, what are the most important suggestions of which you can think? What mistakes would you try to avoid?
4. In your major subject, is there much opportunity to use films or slides? For what particular purposes would you be most willing to use them?
5. In your major subject, what are the most important suggestions you can make for drill work?
6. Be able to explain in class what is meant by each of the chapter's suggestions on how to facilitate remembering, giving an example when you can.
7. Can you think of any ways in which you could train students in your field for better study habits and better skills?
8. How important is the training of students in critical reading? Does it have any place in the teaching of your major subject?
9. Offer six or seven good suggestions for study by students of your major subject.
10. In your major subject, are there opportunities to develop ideals and attitudes? Be specific, giving some examples of the ideals and attitudes and how you might contribute toward their development.
11. In your major subject, are there opportunities to develop tastes and interests? Be specific, giving some examples of the tastes and interests and how you might contribute toward their development.
12. What do you think is the major reason why efforts to promote art, music, and literature appreciation on the part of young people are often ineffective.

## SUPPLEMENTARY MATERIALS

### SELECTED READINGS

DALE, EDGAR. "Teaching Critical Thinking," *The Education Digest*, XXIV (May, 1959), 29–31.
DOUGLASS, HARL R. *Modern Administration of Secondary Schools*. Boston: Ginn & Co., 1963, pp. 167–97. Chapter 9, "Improving Student Learning."

FAUNCE, ROLAND C., and MORREL J. CLUTE. "The Learning Process," *Teaching and Learning in the Junior High School.* San Francisco: Wadsworth Publishing Co., Inc., 1961, pp. 51–70.

GORDON, JULIA W. "Values in the Classroom," *The National Elementary School Principal,* LIII (November, 1962), 30–34.

KLAUSMEIER, HERBERT J. *Teaching in the Secondary School.* New York: Harper & Row, 1958. Chapter 3, "Learning with Meaning and Purpose."

*Mental Health in Modern Education* (fifty-fourth yearbook, National Society for the Study of Education), Part II. University of Chicago Press, 1955.

MILLS, HUBERT H., and HARL R. DOUGLASS. *Teaching in High School* (2d ed.). New York: The Ronald Press Co., 1957. Chapter 7, "Different Kinds of Growth."

MOULY, GEORGE J. *Psychology for Effective Teaching.* New York: Holt, Rinehart & Winston, Inc., 1960. Chapter 3, "Growth and Development," pp. 61–87; Chapter 4, "Physical and Motor Development," pp. 88–106; Chapter 5, "Emotional Development," pp. 107–42; Chapter 6, "Social Development," pp. 143–84; Chapter 7, "Intellectual Development," pp. 185–224; Chapter 12, "The Higher Mental Processes," pp. 317–41; Chapter 13, "Attitudes," pp. 342–64; Chapter 16, "Personal and Social Adjustment," pp. 426–52.

RISK, THOMAS M. *Principles and Practices of Teaching in Secondary Schools.* New York: American Book Co., 1958. Chapter 4, "The Learning Outcomes"; Chapter 5, "Emotionalized Learning Products."

RIVLIN, HARRY N. *Teaching Adolescents in Secondary Schools.* New York: Appleton-Century-Crofts, Inc., 1961. Chapter 14, "Contributions to Adolescents' Personal and Social Development."

WATKINS, RALPH K. *Techniques of Secondary School Teaching.* New York: The Ronald Press Co., 1958. Chapter 6, "Drill Experiences in Learning"; Chapter 7, "Acquisition and Understanding of Ideas"; Chapter 9, "Appreciation Building."

"What Can We Do To Help Boys and Girls Develop a Sense of Values?" in *Improvement in Secondary Education Through Group Studies* (seventeenth yearbook, Pennsylvania Branch N.A.S.S.P.), pp. 60–66.

## AUDIO-VISUAL MATERIALS

### Films

*Chalkboard Utilization.* McGraw-Hill Text-Film. 15 minutes.

*How To Use a Classroom Film.* McGraw-Hill Text-Film. 18 minutes.

*Promoting Pupil Adjustment.* McGraw-Hill Text-Film. 20 minutes.

*The Feltboard in Teaching.* College of Education, Wayne University. 10 minutes.

*Using the Classroom Film.* Encyclopedia Brittanica. 22 minutes.

*Using the Classroom Film.* Laboratory School, University of Chicago. 22 minutes.

*Using Visual Aids in Training.* Castle Films. 14 minutes.

*Visual Aids to Instruction.* United World Films, Inc., U.S. Army. 10 minutes.

# 14

# Group Procedures in the Classroom

## THE RECITATION AND SUPERVISED STUDY PROCEDURES

**The Passing of the Recitation.** For a great many decades, the class period was usually employed almost entirely within what may be termed the recitation and assignment procedure. Daily, in each class, an assignment was made to the students indicating what should be studied, what should be handed in, and what should be learned. On the following day, the teacher would request the students to close their books, and he would spend a large part of the hour in an oral quiz to discover the degree to which the students had done the assignment, making explanations where they seemed most necessary, many teachers recording in a classbook a grade for each student's recitation. Toward the end of the period, the teacher would introduce the assignment for the following day, making such explanations as he deemed necessary (or for which time remained). Often, during the latter part of this, the bell was ringing and students were starting to leave the classroom.

This assignment-recitation procedure came under heavy fire as more came to be known about learning. Obviously, it was wasteful, attention of many students was casual or non-existent at almost any given moment, and it promoted an unfriendly teacher-pupil relationship and contributed to misbehavior. Alternative methods were tried and found not only to be more pleasant and preferred by the students but to result in the development of growth outcomes of a type little or less fully developed in the older approach.

In the 1930's and 1940's, there was such a great swing away from recitation that many teachers were ashamed to admit that they employed it at all. Nevertheless, most teachers including many of the best ones found a place for some oral quizzing to check on the need for further explanation and stimulation.

**The Laboratory, or Supervised Study, Procedure.** In place of part of the recitation, there came to be employed what was first known as the supervised study procedure and later on as the laboratory procedure and the group discussion procedure.

Where the laboratory, or supervised study, procedure was employed, there were usually two concomitant developments: (1) a longer class period of about fifty-five minutes and (2) a large unit in which there might be an assignment to, or at least an undertaking of responsibility by, the students; some teaching; considerable study that might involve a number of class periods and would probably be interspersed with some explanation and individual help by the teacher; and finally some culminating activities that would bring the unit to a close with some sort of a logical conclusion and evaluation of student progress.

## TYPES OF GROUP PROCEDURES

In guiding group learning activities, particularly in schools with longer periods and larger course-of-study units, more and more teachers have for a considerable number of years been employing and recommending the use of group discussions as the means of providing good learning experiences for their students. These discussions are of various types including (1) a discussion of the material being studied; (2) planning of the new unit of work, including projects and other learning activities and evaluation, and (3) culminating activities. In a considerable number of subjects, particularly literature, history, the social studies, and, to some extent, the sciences, teachers have been discovering that discussions by the students that are more than mere recitation or rehashing of the items studied provide effective learning experiences.

In recent years, there has grown the practice of spending more time in discussion of controversial issues as a means of orienting individuals to the issues in the world in which they will live and as a means of developing skill in analysis of issues and of arguments on various sides of issues.

**Democratic Living in School.** When a class of some twenty to thirty individuals constitutes a social group that should to some extent live together, plan together, and work together, there are excellent opportunities for developing skill in working with other people, in leadership, and in diminishing excessive shyness that characterizes some boys and girls. It is difficult for some teachers to get in the swing of a cooperative living situation. They seem too strongly tempted by domination, which tends to encourage conflicts. Some of the types of evidence of domina- . tion and resulting conflict are the following:

1. Teacher arbitrarily prescribes some activity: "Don't do it that way. I'll tell you what to do."
2. Teacher answers "No" when pupil asks if he can do something.
3. Teacher tells a child to go to another part of the room.
4. Teacher postpones something without giving any reason or setting a future date: "We can't do that now."
5. Teacher uses disapproval, blame, shame, obstruction, or interruption to secure different behavior from a pupil.
6. Teacher uses warning, threats, conditional promises: "If you can't do what you're supposed to do, you'll have to go out in the hall."
7. Teacher calls to attention: "Jimmy, face this way, won't you?"
8. Teacher deprives children of specific materials, activities, rights, or privileges, including corporal punishment, sending a pupil out of the room, keeping him after school, and sending him to the principal's office.[1]

**Characteristics of Cooperative Group Procedure.** Among the types of integration and cooperation are the following:

(1) Teacher helps student to define, redefine, or progress with the problem. The problem must have been stated and accepted by the pupil.
(2) Teacher agrees with, approves of, or accepts the student's contribution. This is a response to spontaneous or self-initiated behavior; approval of the pupil's selection is given when several answers or new answers are possible.
(3) Teacher extends invitation to go ahead in response to the pupil's wish, suggestion, or expression of need.
(4) Teacher asks questions regarding the student's expressed interest or activity.
(5) Teacher comments on such interest or activity.
(6) Teacher accepts the responsibility for action by a child that is inconvenient, unjust, or unfair to another child; he also admits his own ignorance or incapacity.[2]

**Class Group Organization.** The teacher has the responsibility of developing some type of class organization, whether it be merely the old-fashioned routine of familiarizing the students with attendance requirements and other ground rules or a more modern, cooperative

[1] Herbert J. Klausmeier, *Teaching in the Secondary School* (New York: Harper & Row, 1958), p. 99.
[2] *Ibid.*, p. 100.

class organization with seating arranged for discussion, a selection of class officers, and the appointment from time to time of class committees.

In the classes of many of the more experiment-minded teachers, not only are student officers elected, but committees are appointed of the following types:

1. A steering committee, which is an advisory committee, to plan procedures and to make suggestions to the teacher
2. A materials committee, which may make suggestions with respect to what is in the library or else may be employed in the study of a unit, the attack of a problem, or the completion of a project
3. A human-resources committee, which has as its responsibility primarily the identification and recommendation to the teacher of individuals in the community who may be used as resources either through the avenue of interviewing or by being present in a class to answer questions or to present material to the class
4. A classroom committee, which has to do with the more physical aspects of the classroom, such as general appearance, lighting, ventilation, bulletin boards, getting projection machines, etc., and with developing suggestions for better housekeeping by the students
5. A social committee, which may occasionally recommend and plan some out-of-class activity such as a picnic or an excursion.

Usually, where this type of procedure is employed in junior high schools, the teacher appoints these committees and the membership is rotated to give different pupils a chance to participate. In the senior high school, it is a fairly common practice for the committees to be selected by the president of the group. Where elections are held, teachers should exercise caution that not too much actual class time is wasted.

Beginning teachers should be very careful about what they assign for committees of students to do. The responsibilities of the students should be in harmony with their maturity, the time available, and their interests. Likewise, beginning teachers need to work with their class, particularly during the latter's first experiences and to assist the students in keeping the problem before them, avoiding digressions, and making progress. This, however, must not go so far as to constitute an Indian-giving type of domination—giving the student responsibility and then discharging the responsibility for the student. In some instances, the chairman of the committees should be selected by the instructor, particularly with youngsters who are not accustomed to committee work and where the responsibility is in an area in which one of the students in a committee has an unusually good background of experience and familiarity. Perhaps in the majority of cases members of the committee should select their own chairman.

**Students as Presiding Officers.** Some teachers have the class president or other officer preside at times in class discussion. Other teachers are very critical of this procedure, especially at the junior high school level, insisting that much time may be wasted and claiming that, at any rate, the expertness of the teacher is not fully utilized. In any event, when a student presides, there is some necessity for coaching him outside of class time and a definite necessity for insistence upon serious and effective procedure being followed.

**Sociodrama, Forum Discussion, and Panel Discussion.** A variety of special discussion methods are employed in secondary schools. Among them is the sociodrama method, in which some of the students take parts in the presentation to the class through dramatization of the ideas under study. This ordinarily includes planning by the class and out-of-class preparation by the students taking part in the sociodrama. In employing sociodrama, there are procedures which have been shown to be more successful than others, and these are set forth by Klausmeier as follows:

1. Select a situation that the class understands well. Generally, such situations arise in informal discussions of the topic being studied.
2. Allow sufficient time in setting up the situation so that the setting and the roles are understood by the class.
3. Emphasize the fact that the student is playing a role not portraying his own feelings and attitudes; he is not supposed to act as he really feels about the situation.
4. Attempt to get students to volunteer for all the roles; in case none do, select students who you know are not shy or easily upset.
5. Prepare the audience for observing. An effective technique is to say simply: "Notice how John and Mary play their roles. If you would do differently, you will have a chance after they finish. Treat Mary and John as you want them to treat you when you play the role."
6. Stop a student when he steps out of the role or cannot carry on. Some students volunteer as an attempt to overcome their feelings of insecurity with braggadocio but become inadequate and sometimes helpless in the situation.
7. Get other students to play the roles after the first group has finished.
8. Expect students to be considerably nervous when playing a role for the first time.
9. Summarize role-playing presentations in a short class discussion when this is feasible.[3]

The forum discussion method usually involves having four or five students present brief prepared statements of the different points of view on a topic, or summaries of different parts or aspects of it, after which the members of the class interrogate them. The panel discussion method

[3] Herbert J. Klausmeier, *Teaching in the Secondary School* (New York: Harper & Row, 1958), pp. 272–273.

is quite similar, although in some instances the panel makes no original presentation but the entire period is taken up by discussion. In organizing a panel discussion, use the following procedure:

1. Have the topic discussed sufficiently by the whole class to make sure that the students understand it clearly and are interested in getting and presenting information relevant to it.
2. Help the students to organize a panel group and to select a chairman to guide the panel in securing information.
3. Help the chairman and panel members to allot responsibility for securing information and devising graphic aids and demonstrations for its presentation.
4. Aid the class in devising forms for recording information.
5. Help the students to develop a conversational style in panel meetings.
6. Assist the chairman and students in drawing up a presentation plan based on each member's specific responsibility for an area of information.
7. Help the chairman to plan his presentation, including in it a clear statement of the topic and brief introductory remarks about it.

**Avoiding Waste of Classroom Time.** Teachers always find that the amount of time available for class meetings is too small and that they are not able to get more than a fraction of the things done that they would like to do. Many teachers are able to get much more done than others, as they operate more effectively and have less waste of their own and their pupils' time in the classroom. Among the suggestions offered by those who carefully study this problem are the following:

1. Careful planning should be made for every group meeting, and some of it should be reduced to the form of notes. A routine should be planned that can be followed from day to day without explanation, particularly with respect to such matters as checking attendance, distributing supplies, turning in papers, etc. In connection with the collection of papers from students, it saves time to collect them by rows, having each student place his paper on top of those that come to him and then pass them all forward to those at the end of the rows, who will, in turn, pass them on to the teacher, so that the papers will be in a definite order every time. This order may correspond with the entry of names in the classbook, in which case further time can be saved.

2. Student aides may be used for a variety of activities, thus saving the teacher time and improving the quality of the learning. They may help in the use of audio-visual aids in routine collection and distribution, in acquiring references, and in assisting the less able students.

3. Many teachers find that they can use to splendid advantage lay aides living in the community, although it is remarkable how much difference there is among the abilities of teachers to employ aides effectively.

4. Much confusion and waste of time can be avoided if students are asked to occupy the same seats every day and the seating plan is organized in some sort of chance fashion so that close friends do not sit next to each other.

5. It is well to develop a careful system for record keeping, simple and involving not too much time spent on recording, but nevertheless kept religiously, and to avoid keeping records that are not required by the administration and are not used to good advantage by the teacher.

6. The teacher should be somewhat reluctant to act as a collector or announcer for various causes. Indeed, he should not act in this capacity unless the individual organization has made a request to the principal and has secured his approval.

7. Administrative officers today are providing an increased amount of clerical service for mimeographing, recording, etc., and teachers should plan carefully to delegate to the office clerical work of this type rather than to do it themselves.

8. Many people have discovered that it is not necessary to require students to hand in written work in as large amounts as they had previously, and less importance should be attached to such written work. Students may, upon occasion, assist in checking each other's work for mistakes.

9. It has been observed that there are great differences among teachers with respect to their conciseness in discussions; some are inclined to be very discourteous and aggressive, while some are inclined to enjoy relating little details and digressions that have little to contribute to the matter at hand. There are also important differences with respect to the clearness with which they express themselves. Perhaps it may be said that better teachers speak clearly and at an appropriate pace, probably rather slowly.

10. Many people have discovered that time may be saved by beginning the class on time and insisting in a friendly but firm way on getting the cooperation of the "tardies." It has been observed that the teacher who hesitates to begin on time and to put pressure on the "tardies" finds that they come later and become more numerous.

11. A wasteful procedure is that of leaving things that are important to say, for example, the assignment or suggestions or completing the assignment or terminal work of the unit or project, until just before the bell rings, when the students are not in a receptive mood—indeed, in a good many cases, on their feet and ready to go.

12. Another waste of time lies in the failure to assist committees to plan appropriately their joint activities and responsibilities and those of all members of the committees.

13. It seems that some teachers learn much more quickly than others to make very quick and accurate decisions with respect to activities of the pupils along lines of making maximum contribution to educational growth and keeping at a minimum activities of some students that are distracting to the rest of the class and that diminish the returns from their educational activities.

While teachers should cooperate with their administration in connection with the non-teaching chores that they are asked to do, it is quite legitimate for teachers to urge that they, individually and collectively, be relieved of excessive non-teaching assignments and activities such as supervision of study halls, of student conduct in the halls between classes, and of the lunchroom.

**Student Participation.** As abilities and desirable attitudes are developed through guided activities, informed instructors seek the fullest possible participation of students in every learning situation. Their rule of thumb is: Do nothing a student is capable of doing. To increase student participation in a lesson, instructors can adapt the following procedure to the capabilities and needs of each student and class:

1. Encourage student-instructor planning, execution, and evaluation of the lesson.
2. Lead students to suggest possible avenues of approach to and applications of the subject matter.
3. Keep the entire group in the picture, even when working with individuals.
4. Make the group a circle not a triangle. (Do not dominate, judge, or "steal the show," nor permit a student to do so.)
5. Vary activities (dramatization, panel discussions, audio-visual aids, oral reports, blackboard work, student lectures, committee work, guests).
6. Stimulate socialization, critical listening, and inter-criticism by referring one student's question or reply to another student for comment or additional information, for example, "What's your reaction to that, George?" Then, have the respondent ask another why he agrees or disagrees.
7. Don't exploit "star" pupils or volunteers; the diffident need encouragement and are often more profound. Involve all in a creative, cooperative, and courteous enterprise to learn.
8. Student errors in fact or in oral or written English should be corrected unobtrusively (merely supplying the correction, without stopping the recitation), unless the mistake is typical enough to require concentrated drill.
9. Cultivate an audience situation by changing your position; e.g. moving to or toward the rear of the room; by insisting on audibility; by using hand signals to get speakers to stand, face the class, and speak up; by discouraging chorus answers; and by insisting on group courtesy to a student, chairman, or

speaker. (At the end of the period, the instructor and not the bell should adjourn the class.)

10. Students' questions, animated responses, evident enjoyment, rapt attention, and an unwillingness to leave the room at the end of the lesson usually indicate that the instructor has inculcated self-direction—the first step in self-improvement.[4]

**Student Management in Group Discussions.** To get discussions started, the teacher must phrase thought-provoking questions related to the topic or problem under investigation. To assure student progress in discussion techniques, the teacher must help students appraise the relevance and importance of contributions, the adequacy of expression, and the quality of respect shown to ideas expressed by others. An informal class discussion should draw from the students conformance to these general guides for carrying on intelligent discussion:

1. Secure acknowledgment from the chairman or teacher before speaking.
2. Make statements related to the problem.
3. Be courteous and respect the rights of others.
4. Phrase questions carefully and clearly.
5. Speak clearly so that everyone hears.
6. Listen attentively to the speakers.
7. Contribute your share but avoid monopolizing the discussion.
8. Defend your statements and ideas when supported with facts but avoid arguing.
9. Enter a discussion expecting to learn from your classmates.
10. Recognize that most of the major problems of living together are solved by groups of people who try to work them out together.
11. Take written notes of points with which you disagree or which are new.
12. Take responsibility for summarizing a discussion when you feel it will help get the whole group thinking more clearly.[5]

**Small Groups or Subgroups.** The committee method involves the appointment of subgroups to work on various aspects of a topic or unit and to present them to the class for discussion and evaluation, or to work on a project related to some aspect of the topic. The "buzz session" method, sometimes called the "Phillips 66" method, involves breaking up the class into subgroups of approximately six students each to discuss the different aspects of the problem or topic and then having one member of each subgroup present its conclusions and findings to the entire group for evaluation and discussion.

**Teaching Small Classes.** Many teachers divide classes into subgroups, each to work somewhat separately from the others for a time, maybe

---

[4] From Richard L. Loughlin, "On Student Participation," *The Bulletin*, N.A.S.S.P., Vol. 46, No. 278 (December, 1962), pp. 35–36.

[5] Herbert J. Klausmeier, *Teaching in the Secondary School* (New York: Harper & Row, 1958), p. 260.

part of a class hour for several consecutive days. Indeed, some teachers employ small groups to some extent almost every day. The small groups may work on separate projects related to the unit, each individual in the small group being assigned a part in the planning and in the execution of the project. Many of the small groups are discussion groups.[6] Sometimes these subgroups, or committees, work outside the school, making an investigation in the community, finding materials in the library, or preparing a visual aid or other exhibit.

In a small school, it is not unusual for the teacher to be assigned two small classes to teach in the same room or adjoining rooms, in the same class period. This works out better if a great deal of the work of one class is practice or supervised study, as in a typewriting class. Naturally, the instructor divides his time between the two groups, being certain that each understands what is to be done and employing silent study or a cooperative procedure within a group when he is engaged with another group.

**Teaching Large Classes.** Occasionally, a teacher is assigned a class of from thirty to forty students, and, indeed, sometimes two teachers combine sections of some class that meet during the same class period. A large class is not taught in exactly the same way as a smaller class. In a large class, there should be less oral discussion, a larger number of written quizzes and examinations, and, definitely, assistance for the teacher in reading and marking papers.

The following are useful procedures for management of large classes; the first ten of which are quoted from a book by Mills and Douglass[7]:

1. Identification of suitable alternative reference materials
2. Use of a seating chart and a permanent seating arrangement in the classroom
3. Following a certain routine for collecting and returning papers, perhaps involving the use of student assistants
4. Use of mimeographed instructions and assignments to save class time
5. Greater use of objective test exercises in order to avoid spending an excessive amount of time in reading papers
6. Planning of seat work and blackboard work so that all may participate in situations in which only a part of the class can go to the blackboard
7. Greater use of conferences with individuals about their work and their difficulties

---

[6] Discussion groups are described on pages 255–256.
[7] Hubert H. Mills and Harl R. Douglass, *Teaching in High School* (2d ed.) (New York: The Ronald Press Co., 1957), p. 441.

8. Greater use of data in regard to students in school records as a substitute for learning about them in class
9. Planning for rotation of learning activities when there are not enough tools, tables, or learning stations
10. Use of pretests to obtain a clearer picture of varying abilities of pupils and range involved
11. Much use of the blackboard, especially with lecturing and for summaries
12. More reliance upon carefully prepared telling and less upon recitation
13. More use of appropriate audio-visual materials

## PROBLEM-SOLVING AND PROJECT PROCEDURES

**Problem-solving Procedure.** There has been, in recent years, an increase in the extent to which problem-solving activities are employed with groups in class discussion, although most teachers do not use this procedure entirely. In the problem-solving procedure, various steps and aspects make demands upon the planning and the skill of the instructor, even if they are carried on as a specialized group activity by the class.

First and most important is the selection of a problem. In this connection, considerable guidance is needed by the teacher to see that a problem is selected that is significant, timely, of concern to the individual student, and of some importance to society. The problem, also, should be appropriate to the maturity and background of the students, should not require an excessive amount of time for its consideration, and should call for a solution for which the resources needed are available.

As a second step, the group needs to make effective plans for the attack of the problem, thinking through the materials that may be needed and perhaps assigning to various individuals or small groups responsibility for reporting back to class on the materials available.

**Teacher Leadership.** Group discussion of problem-solving procedure requires great skill of the teacher. The following points should be kept in mind:

1. The teacher must see that individuals in the class have definitely in mind the exact nature of the problem.

2. The instructor and the student leaders must assist the class in avoiding diversions from the problem, including digression and discussion of irrelevant data.

3. The instructor and/or the student leaders must encourage and, in fact, insist upon participation of all members of the class according to their potentialities. Monopoly of the discussion by the more extroverted pupils, particularly those who are likely to speak "off the cuff" and have little to offer, must be prevented.

4. The discussion must be kept moving toward the solution or solutions of the problem or the completion of the project.

5. The class must be led and assisted in the formulation of the conclusions and in the evaluation of the project.

**The Project Method.** The project method has been employed for many decades by teachers of shop, of industrial arts, and of home economics. It has many advantages. In the first place, it appears to the pupils to have more reality, and it has more definite goals. Projects may be individual projects or group projects. Both are used to advantage. Group projects may involve a few students or the entire class.

Ordinarily, work on a project is much more interesting to pupils than their ordinary study activities. The goals of the project give purpose to the study. Things are read, looked up, and thought about with a view to making progress toward the completion of the project rather than merely to recite them to a teacher or using them in passing an examination. The project approach is suitable for students at all levels of intellectual ability. It is a challenge to the initiative and the problem-solving ability of the more capable students, and it has valuable possibilities of interesting those who are not easily interested in strictly verbal and unapplied material in undertaking something more concrete and more immediately purposeful. The project approach is employed by many teachers as a means of adapting to differences among individual pupils as to intellectual ability, interest, vocabulary, and previous experience.

**Projects as Problem-solving Activity.** As is pointed out by Mills and Douglass, the project has the following characteristics:

1. The project is a learning unit. Its unity depends upon pupil purpose rather than upon the logical arrangement of subject matter.
2. The project is a self-imposed or willingly accepted task growing out of the pupil's awareness of its significance. Along with the acceptance of the challenge of the task goes the acceptance of resposibility for "following through" until its completion.
3. The project grows out of the pupil's experiential background, thus enabling him to discover clues for planning and organizing his own activities.
4. The project retains its identity only as long as the pupil has freedom to pursue his purpose unrestrained by the barriers of the subject-matter boundaries or teacher domination.
5. The project invokes a whole-hearted effort on the part of the pupil to achieve an attainable and desirable goal.
6. The project leads to goals which are recognizable by the pupil, thereby enabling him to evaluate his own progress in achieving his objectives.[8]

[8] *Ibid.,* p. 239.

Projects may be material projects such as have been used widely for many years in home economics, shop work, and agriculture, involving the preparation of diagrams, graphs, or illustrated materials, or the performance of some concrete service in the school or in the community. They also may be intellectual projects of the problem-solving type such as (1) Discover the relationship between population increase and climate. (2) In what fields has there been a very great increase in the amount of knowledge in recent years? (3) Prepare a monthly budget for a family of three children aged four, six, and eight living in a town of 25,000 in the Middle West, with the father with a yearly salary of $7,200. Compare it with a budget of a family of five in a similar town, with a girl in junior high school, a boy in senior high school, and a boy in college, and with an annual income of $9,200.

## GUIDING THINKING AND TESTING RETENTION BY QUESTIONING

The good teacher is somewhat expert in the matter of conducting recitation, discussion, or an oral or written quiz when it seems advisable to have students engaged in such an activity in the class period. Questions employed in oral and written quizzes may be of two types: thought questions or mere reproduction questions. It is necessary to use both, although, whenever possible, emphasis should be placed upon the thought questions.

**Purposes and Types of Questions.** The teacher should bear in mind the following principal purposes of questioning and plan questions and procedure accordingly:

1. To ascertain the degree to which the students individually and collectively have mastered the content of the lesson or unit, have developed correct understanding, and have developed methods of thinking
2. To provide practice and drill for retention
3. To focus the attention of the pupils on the more important points and bases of the work
4. To provide organization in the students' minds through the use of the blackboard and the material under study
5. To stimulate interest, perhaps by arousing curiosity and raising problems
6. To stimulate thinking on the part of the pupils in applying and evaluating subject matter
7. To discover the interests of the pupils
8. To relate student experiences to the material being studied

9. To check the degree to which the assignment or plans for study are clear

The principal useful types of questions that may be employed are shown below with examples. These include a number of types that stimulate thinking and initiative, as well as recall, and for that reason should be employed often.

1. *Selective recall, basis given:*
Name the presidents of the United States who had been in military life before their election.
2. *Evaluating recall, basis given:*
Which do you consider the three most important American inventions in the nineteenth century, from the standpoint of the expansion and growth of transportation?
3. *Comparison of two things on a single designated basis:*
Compare England and Russia with respect to social equality.
4. *Comparison of two things in general:*
Contrast the New Deal with laissez faire philosophies of government.
5. *Decision for or against:*
Are you in favor of a world government?
6. *Causes or effects:*
What were the causes (effects) of the French Revolution?
7. *Explanation:*
Tell how atomic energy is derived.
8. *Statement of relationships:*
In what ways are education and economic prosperity interrelated?
9. *Illustration or examples (the pupil's own) of principles in science, construction in language, etc.:*
Give one example of the application of Boyle's law to a practical situation.
10. *Classification* (usually the converse of No. 9):
What is the principle involved in the gears of an automobile?
11. *Application of rules and principles in new situations:*
Tell how the concept of evolution applies to social progress.
12. *Statement of aim:*
What do you think was the author's purpose in his selection and organization of these paragraphs?
13. *Criticism* (the adequacy, correctness, or relevancy of a printed statement, or a classmate's answer to a question on the lesson):
Was that statement only a half-truth or partial answer?
14. *Reorganization of facts* (the student is asked for a report in which facts from different sources are arranged on an entirely new basis):
Draw a parallel between World War I and World War II?

15. *Formulation of new questions* (problems and questions raised by the student):
    What questions would you want to have discussed as the result of reading the assigned chapter?

16. *New methods of procedure:*
    Suggest a plan for bringing about world peace. How would you change the plot in the play in order to produce a different effect?

17. *Analysis:*
    What are the most important characteristics of an economic depression?

**Techniques of Questioning in Class.** Following are good procedures for the effective use of questioning:

1. The wording of the questions should be clear.

2. The questions should be adapted to the age and the maturity of the pupils and their previous background in the subject.

3. The questions should be definite and should describe clearly what is expected of the pupil or the class of which they are asked.

4. A series of questions should be thought out in advance to give unity, to provide sequence, and to serve best the objectives of the instructor for the unit.

5. Questions should be informal and natural and should not follow too closely the wording and the organization of the textbook.

6. Questions should be fairly well distributed among the different members of the class over a period of time but not in any predetermined order, and the distribution should be such that a student who participated one day might not expect to be overlooked the following day.

7. The instructor should ask the question first and then, after the class has had ample time to think about it, an individual student should be designated to answer.

8. It is important to allow time for at least the great majority of students to think through to an answer.

9. The rate of questioning should be adjusted to the nature and the purpose of the questions and the relative familiarity of the class to the material covered.

10. Since there are great differences among individuals in a class with respect to their interests, background of experience, and capacity for learning, the teacher should assign questions in view of knowledge of his students, putting to the abler students the questions requiring the higher level of intellectual ability and to the less able students those making lesser requirements of this type.

11. Questions should occasionally be assigned to inattentive students. Repetition of a question, in most instances, is advisable only when the teacher has good reason to believe that it was not clear when originally stated.

12. A natural, interested, and conversational tone should be used by the teacher, rather than a demanding, formal, or officious manner.

13. The questions should be asked in a manner that indicates confidence in the students.

14. Pivotal questions, thought out in advance, should be employed in the development of the lesson.

Many very skilful teachers employ at least occasionally what has come to be known as the "Socratic" question procedure, so called because it was used by Socrates in his attempts to guide the thinking of the youths of Athens. "Socratic" questioning is a type of questioning that leads the mind of the students along a certain sequence in an effort to have them think for themselves and discover desired conclusions; in other words, it is a heuristic method.

**Handling Student Answers.** The most effective teacher is skillful and thoughtful in handling students' answers to his questions and in dealing with questions raised by the students. Among procedures that more effective teachers recommend are the following:

1. The pupils should be required to state their answers in good English and in complete thought units.
2. Haste should be avoided in questioning procedure, and deliberation and careful thinking should be not only encouraged but insisted upon.
3. The amount and nature of commendation or disapproval by the teacher should be determined somewhat on an individual basis.
4. All sincere questions by members of the class, if they are related to the discussion at hand, should be treated with appropriate consideration, but diversionary and irrelevant questions should be dismissed.

In situations where opinions differ on important matters the student should usually not be deprived of the privilege of stating his own opinion. Nevertheless, long drawn-out arguments should be avoided. Occasionally the student questioner should be referred to a reference rather than having his question answered.

At times, a good question may be asked that will be of little interest and help to the entire group. The instructor must remember that the welfare of at least the majority of the group must be kept in mind during the whole class procedure, and he should dismiss the question.

## OBTAINING COOPERATIVE STUDENT BEHAVIOR
## AND DISCIPLINE

One of the most difficult problems of teachers, success in the handling of which is a criterion by which teachers are largely judged by parents and, indeed, by many principals, is that of obtaining the cooperation of the students and thereby avoiding misbehavior, which latter not only interferes with the student's own learning but may constitute a serious distraction to others about him. Since most teachers now are much better acquainted with mental hygiene and child growth and development, there is less tendency to develop unfortunate attitudes than formerly. Interviews with dropouts, juvenile delinquents, and underachievers indicate, however, that a great deal of harm is done to students through their school experiences and that much of it might be avoided or at least kept to a minimum.

Into junior and senior high schools today come many students who by reason of unfortunate training in their homes have not attained sufficient psychological and social maturity to enable them to maintain self-discipline, that is, control of their own behavior in a way that is acceptable socially and that will cause them to be liked and respected. The following illustrates one method of dealing with this problem:

Late afternoon classes for disruptive pupils suspended from regular day attendance have been authorized in Washington, D.C. The school board waived its regulations pertaining to school hours and gave Superintendent Carl F. Hansen permission to try the scheme on an experimental basis.

"Twilight" students will begin school at 3:15 p.m. and continue to about 8 o'clock with a break for supper. During these hours students may use shops and gym facilities that are in continuous use prior to 3 p.m. The classes will be staffed by full-time teachers who show ability to work with hard-to-manage children.

Hansen said he plans to use these activities to lead the unruly students back into the regular academic program, and that he hopes the schools designated will become community-centered institutions to be used for a wide range of activities.[9]

Discipline in the classroom and elsewhere in the school has been complicated a great deal in recent years by the type of philosophy and the practices of discipline in the homes of many of the students. For one reason or another—working mothers, indulgent parents, bad peer associations, low-grade movies and television—many boys and girls develop undesirable habits of behavior, an unfortunate lack of regard for the

[9] "Keeping Abreast in Education," *Phi Delta Kappan* (June, 1963), Vol. 44, No. 9, p. 456.

rights of others, a propensity for defying or at least attempting to evade the authority of adults, and other unsocial attitudes and practices that create problems for the teacher and the school. On the other hand, a great many young people have arrived at a high degree of maturity as a result of good home experiences and influences and fit readily into the cooperative learning situations of the school.

**Fundamental Principles.** It has come to be rather generally acknowledged that *the first and major approach to the matter of discipline is the planning of worthwhile and interesting learning activities.* This does not suggest an emphasis on entertainment; it does, however, put a premium upon careful planning of assignments, of learning activities, and of the introduction of students to them, explanation on the part of the teacher, development of the feeling on the part of the pupils that the teacher is fair and impartial, an obvious enthusiasm of the teacher for the subject, and an obvious interest of the teacher in each individual boy and girl. In other words, the positive approach is much to be preferred to the negative approach. Nevertheless, situations develop with some pupils that make the negative approach indispensable.

Following is a list of fundamental principles that have been proved useful by superior teachers as a basis for maintaining good behavior:

1. Do not take too seriously slight irregularities of conduct; remember that high school students are young and somewhat immature and that they have a zest for what they regard as harmless fun.

2. Punishment should be primarily for the purpose of causing the individual punished to make a more satisfactory adjustment to the school situation rather than as an example and warning to other students.

3. Learn as much as possible about each individual in the class, and attempt to interpret his behavior in the light of full knowledge.

4. While definite standards of behavior apply to all students, do not treat all in a uniform manner, but, rather, each according to his needs.

5. In serious cases of misbehavior, make a very determined effort to discover the causes, for example, lack of interest in the subject matter, unfortunate home conditions and problems that cause the youngster to be somewhat upset or emotionally disturbed, desire to attract attention or to provide humor in the class, dislike for the teacher, ill health, lack of belief in the value of a learning activity, a feeling of frustration and failure to be appreciated, or desire to impress others that one is a person of some importance. The teacher should, naturally, have conferences with the parents of chronic offenders, in order to gather information. He should, of course, always first consult the records of the school, other teachers of the offending students, and the principal.

**Recommended Techniques.** Among practices that are recommended by principals and successful teachers for inspiring good student behavior are the following:

1. Learn the first name of each student as soon as possible.

2. Plan carefully a routine in the class, and follow it rather regularly, for example, for starting the class period or for collecting and distributing papers and materials.

3. Avoid expressions of anger and emotion and any evidence of nervousness or fear; give an impression of confidence in your ability to handle the situation.

4. Make careful assignments; see that they are well understood and that they are in line with the capacities of the pupils and the time that is available.

5. Discover who are the leaders in the class, and get on friendly terms with them.

6. Use sarcasm exceedingly sparingly and only with a smile.

7. Treat all pupils with equal consideration and as fairly as possible.

8. Refrain from assigning schoolwork as punishment.

9. Be consistent; correct minor rule infractions promptly.

10. Be firm, but not tough, at first; it is easier to relax control than to increase it.

11. Before any serious punishment, sharp scolding, or deprivation of privileges, for example, is administered, the instructor should carry on an investigation to discover, if possible, the causes of the individual's behavior.

12. Classroom activities should be planned 'and carried on in such a manner as to avoid monotony or a feeling that these activities are not worthwhile. Avoid long, dry lectures.

13. Never punish a group of students for the misbehavior of one or for anything short of misbehavior of a great majority of the students in the class, and then only rarely.

14. Almost invariably avoid rebuking individuals before other members of the class. Utilize instead a personal conference. Both the individual and other members of the class may be antagonized by unfortunate remarks by the instructor.

15. Endeavor to be as objective as possible. Avoid holding grudges against offenders.

16. Remember that the degree to which the students participate in the planning of the learning activities determines the freedom from conflict of teacher-pupil interest and resulting unsocial behavior.

17. Avoid posing or assuming an unnatural, hard-boiled attitude toward the class.

18. Avoid, as far as possible, making threats, in spite of the necessity for informing students occasionally as to what the effects will be of their failure to cooperate.

19. Avoid scolding.

20. Insist upon orderly and deliberate response to questions. Discourage excited waving of hands, and give time for thoughtfulness by slow thinkers.

21. Never force apologies.

22. Get acquainted with parents of problem youngsters with a view to obtaining more information about them, obtaining the cooperation and good will of the parents, and influencing these students' attitudes by acquaintance with their parents. Parent contacts should be as friendly as possible; in them, avoid, except as a last resort, any condemnation of the student or threat of punishment.

23. Avoid nagging.

24. Do not use corporal punishment in either junior or senior high school. If corporal punishment is needed for an individual child, it should be the result of a very special investigation by the principal, a counselor, and others, should follow a conference with the parents, and probably should be administered by the principal.

**Sending Offenders Out of the Classroom.** Good teachers send students to the principal's office only on rare occasions. Most schools have a rule that the student is not to be sent from the class to the principal's office for misbehavior. In cases of important insubordination and continued disruptions and misbehavior that distract the class, the more skilful teacher either sends for the principal to come to the classroom, if he is available, or sends the student to a study hall with a note to the study hall supervisor.

Some good teachers occasionally ask a misbehaving student to leave the room for a few minutes until he has been able to think the situation over and has himself under control and then to come back quietly into the classroom. This is best done quietly, privately and briefly. It should be resorted to rarely, as it constitutes in itself a distraction in the minds of the class that may last for several minutes, if not for the remainder of the period, and it sometimes enlists sympathy for the offender.

**Contributing to Personal and Social Adjustment.** Secondary school teachers should remember that adolescence is a period of unusual stresses, insecurities, exploration, and problems. It is a period of transition in which young people are forced to make, within a relatively short time, very important adjustments to themselves, with their increased appetite for independence, and their problems of changing from children to adults physically, physiologically, and socially, and of relating to their parents, to social peers of both sexes, and to the growing recognition of their approaching responsibility for leaving home, making a living, and choosing a vocation and a mate.

Teachers who are truly friends of young people in their classes will provide opportunity for experience in group activities and interpersonal cooperation. They will develop and direct cooperation of students in determining the principles for effective work conditions in the classroom— as may be related to rules, discipline, etc.—avoiding making mountains out of molehills, for example, by making disciplinary problems of gum chewing, peculiarities of hair style, dress, etc, concentrating instead upon the truly important things.

The wise teacher will use the individual conference with a boy or girl who shows signs of developing into a problem youngster distracting other students from their learning activities. Open rebuke before the class should be avoided, even though it may be necessary to ask the student to refrain from the disturbance.

Individual conferences should take the nature of counseling. Following are practical suggestions:

1. Arrange for privacy during the interview.
2. Set aside sufficient time for the interview to avoid superficial approach.
3. Plan the interview in advance by deciding what specific purposes and information are to be sought.
4. Analyze the student's cumulative record and identify specific items to be covered in the interview.
5. When the student appears for the interview, start on time, greet him cordially, ask him to sit down. In a brief "warm-up" period, make some casual remarks of a general nature concerning the student's achievements or school affairs. Frequently, these general comments will lead into the specific matter to be considered, such as a test score, and can then branch out to other matters.
6. Give the student opportunities to express his ideas. To keep the discussion going, raise questions which require more than a "yes" or "no" answer.
7. If there are several questions to be answered take them up one at a time. Do not confront the student with all of them at once.
8. Avoid the "probing" attitude in seeking answers to questions by picking up "conversational hooks" to get to the heart of the matter.
9. Avoid arguing with the student. Accept his statements at face value, and give him a chance to explain and elaborate his statements. Keep your biases and pet theories under control. Lectures should be reserved for the classroom.
10. Cover a few items well, rather than a number in a superficial manner.
11. End the interview within fixed time limits. Mutual agreement in regard to subsequent interviews should be reached by the student and teacher.
12. Analyze, summarize, and make a written record of the interview.[10]

10 Hubert H. Mills and Harl R. Douglass, *Teaching in High School* (2d ed.) (New York: The Ronald Press Co., 1957), p. 72.

Small-group work in science at Clay Junior High School, Syracuse, New York.

Concreteness in teaching a mathematics class—Albuquerque, New Mexico.

Student demonstration in a Chicago science class.

**Rebuke and Punishment of Offenders.** Following are effective suggestions for use in punishment in secondary school classes:

1. *Slight irregularities of conduct* should not be taken too seriously. Strict and unwavering adherence to arbitrary standards of behavior without consideration of the intentions of the individual or the causative factors in the situation provokes feelings of resentment on the part of pupils. The teacher thus destroys his chance to assist the student in making a satisfactory adjustment.

2. Punishment is for the purpose of *assisting the individual* to make a more satisfactory adjustment to the school situation. The practice of making the punishment an example and a warning to other pupils is psychologically and ethically unsound.

3. Before any punishment is administered, *investigate the causes of* the individual's misbehavior. There may be possibilities of adjusting the curricular materials or modifying instructional procedures to make them more significant and challenging to the student. *Get all the facts* relevant to the incident of misbehavior before disciplinary action is taken.

4. In the event that the student's misbehavior appears to be related to his failure to adjust to the regulations imposed by the school organization, *consider the need of modification of the regulation* in terms of whether it promotes or hinders the mental health of the pupils.

5. In considering possible courses of action, select the treatment or form of punishment which appears to have the *greatest long-range value* in preventing recurrence of the individual's misbehavior.

6. Remember that the agreement of rules aaginst inattention, whispering, and the like is a poor substitute for *classroom situations that are vital and interesting* to students.

7. Be certain that in punishing the individual you are not making him the victim of *a general unsatisfactory group attitude.*

8. Keep in mind the fact that *certainty of punishment* is a greater deterrent to wrongdoing than harshness.

9. The severity and the form of punishment should be in terms of the *seriousness of the offense* and the *needs of the offender.*

10. *The immediacy of the punishment* is important in assisting the child to establish the proper connection between misbehavior and punishment. However, a careful consideration of the causes and consequences of the misbehavior prior to the punishment is essential.

11. Punishment on the installment plan is usually undesirable. Once a difficulty has been adjusted satisfactorily, *avoid referring to the matter again.*

12. *Do not hold grudges* against pupils. The mental health of the child is not promoted by his belief that "the teacher has it in for me."

13. *Accept the facts* in a case of misbehavior and make the decision as to the best course of action without demonstration of anger or irritation.

14. *Methods of discipline should be consistent* within a given classroom, and also from one classroom to another.

15. *Punishment of individual violations* of good behavior should be the rule, not punishment of the entire group.

16. *Avoid attributing misbehavior* to an individual until you are certain that he committed the offense.

17. The form and method of punishment should *enable the individual to retain his self-respect*. The pupil's belief in his own integrity is basic to any effort of constructive self-improvement. Treatment of misconduct should seek to *inspire the pupil to right action* as well as to restrain him from misconduct.

High school teachers are expected to manage their classes and to call upon the principal for help only in unusual cases of student misbehavior. Teachers are not expected to send their students out of their class to the principal's office except as a last resort. However much relief it may give the teacher, it turns loose in the halls a pupil who is already a problem case, and he may prove a distraction to other pupils. If it seems necessary to good working conditions to have a pupil leave a classroom, the teacher should escort the pupil to the study hall or to the library, where he will be under supervision until the teacher can arrange a conference between the student, the principal, and himself. In these cases the teacher should be careful to be quite objective and to restrain his anger lest his judgment be influenced by emotion.[11]

**Class Attitude and Discipline.** The teacher should be on guard to see whether or not one or more students seem to be uncooperative and to exhibit unacceptable behavior in an effort to appeal to the approval of the class in opposition to the teacher. The teacher should think through carefully whether or not there is an undercurrent of hostility and unfriendliness and, if there is, should attempt to discover the causes. This may be done, perhaps, by a frank and friendly conference with some of the more reliable students of the class. It is not wise to attempt to meet the situation through intimidation of the offending individual or scolding of the class. It may be that the class feels that the teacher is not fair in making assignments, is exhibiting partiality, or is not doing an interesting type of teaching. It may be that the offending students assume a hostility that is not there, and that their play for approval falls on unfertile ground. Brief conferences with the offending individuals may be the way to handle the situation.

**Mental Health and Discipline.** Investigators of the causes of emotional disturbance among adolescents attach much significance to the manner of discipline in the school. Particularly beginning teachers, but many experienced teachers as well, must think through the effects on the individual student of any type of punishment or other treatment as a result of misbehavior. Each teacher should make it a point to learn much about each individual student as soon in the school semester as possible and should continue to learn more and more about the individual who seems to be developing into a problem case. The latter should be discussed with counselors and occasionally with the principal and with the

---

[11] Hubert H. Mills and Harl R. Douglass, *Teaching in High School* (2d ed.) (New York: The Ronald Press Co., 1957), pp. 135–136.

parents. Studies of juvenile delinquents have revealed that a definite contributing factor to juvenile delinquency is dissatisfaction with work in school and with what the offender believes to be unfair, embarrassing, or humiliating treatment at the hands of teachers. Above all, it must be remembered that each student is an individual with individual characteristics that must be kept in mind, and that the major purpose of discipline is to assist the individual to become more mature socially and psychologically.

## QUESTIONS, PROBLEMS, AND TOPICS FOR FURTHER STUDY

1. If you were ever a student in a class in which the assignment-recitation procedure was used regularly, give your evaluation of it as compared to the laboratory procedure.
2. What is your opinion about discussion of controversial issues in the classroom?
3. In teaching your major subject, how would you attempt to organize your class?
4. How much opportunity is there, in teaching your major subject, for the use of the problem-solving method?
5. How much opportunity is there, in teaching your major subject, for the use of the project method?
6. Be able to explain in class the characteristics of a teaching machine, its advantages and its limitations.
7. What opportunity is there for the use of recordings in the teaching of your major subject?
8. What are two projects and two problems that you could use in providing learning activities for students in classes in your major field? How would you go about getting the students in your class started on the projects?
9. For each of the types of questions listed in this chapter, try to think of an example that might be used in your major subject.
10. Read carefully the suggestions on questioning procedure, and pick out three or four that you doubt to be really good procedure.
11. State in a few words your ideas about how to handle student answers in the teaching of your major subject.
12. It is frequently claimed that the schools should be much more strict in discipline and that their failure to be so is responsible in part for juvenile delinquency. What do you think about that? Give reasons for your position.
13. What do you think are the most important things to be remembered by a classroom teacher if he is to maintain good behavior on the part of the students?

## SUPPLEMENTARY MATERIALS

### SELECTED READINGS

ANDERSON, STUART A. "Where Students Maintain Much of Their Own Discipline," *Nation's Schools*, LXVII (May, 1961), 70–74, 168–76.

ASUBIL, DAVID P. "A New Look at Classroom Discipline," *Phi Delta Kappan,* XLIII (October, 1961), 25–30.
BOWMAN, HERMAN J. "A Review of Discipline," *Bulletin of the N.A.S.S.P.,* No. 248 (September, 1959), 147–56.
CLARK, LEONARD H., and IRVING S. STARR. *Secondary School Teaching Methods.* New York: The Macmillan Co., 1959. Chapter 7, "Group Teaching Techniques."
COX, PHILIP W. L., and BLAINE E. MERCER. *Education in Democracy.* New York: McGraw-Hill Book Co., Inc., 1961. Chapter 8, "Group Process and the School."
GRAMBS, JEAN D., WILLIAM J. IVERSON, and FRANKLIN K. PATTERSON. *Modern Methods in Secondary Education.* New York: Holt, Rinehart & Winston, Inc., 1958. Chapter 5, "Democratic Behavior in the Classroom"; Chapter 9, "Discussion, Role Playing Related Techniques."
HANSON, EARL H., and MYRTLE M. BONN. "Controversial Issues in the Classroom." Washington, D.C.: National Educational Association of the United States, 1961.
HAVIGHURST, ROBERT J. "Dealing with Problem Youth," *Nation's Schools,* LXVII (May, 1958), 43–45.
HOCK, LOUISE E. *Using Committees in the Classroom.* New York: Holt, Rinehart & Winston, Inc., 1958.
KETTLEKAMP, GILBERT C. *Teaching Adolescents.* Boston: D. C. Heath & Co., 1954. Chapter 7, "The Class in Action"; Chapter 8, "Discipline."
MILLS, HUBERT H., and HARL R. DOUGLASS. *Teaching in High School* (2d ed.). New York: The Ronald Press Co., 1957. Chapter 8, "Discipline and Good Human Relations in the Classroom."
NOAR, GERTRUDE. *The Junior High School—Today and Tomorrow* (2d ed.). Englewood Cliffs, N.J.: Prentice-Hall, Inc., 1961. Chapter 14, "Discipline," pp. 302–13.
OLIVA, PETER I. Corrective Measures and Punishment," *Bulletin of the N.A.S.S.P.,* No. 220 (January, 1956), 73–84.
RISK, THOMAS M. *Principles and Practice of Teaching in Secondary Schools.* New York: American Book Co., 1958. Chapter 20, "Managing Classroom Activities"; Chapter 21, "Guidance Problems and Disciplinary Control."
RIVLIN, HARRY N. *Teaching Adolescents in Secondary Schools* (2d ed.). New York: Appleton-Century-Crofts, Inc., 1961. Chapter 6, "Discussing: A Way of Learning"; Chapter 13, "Managing a Classroom"; Chapter 14, "Contributing to the Adolescent's Personal and Social Development."
WATKINS, RALPH K. *Techniques of Secondary School Teaching.* New York: The Ronald Press Co., 1958. Chapter 8, "Problem-Solving Processes."

AUDIO-VISUAL MATERIALS

*Films*

*Broader Concert of Method: Part II—Pupils Planning and Working Together.* McGraw-Hill. 19 minutes.
*Discipline During Adolescence.* McGraw-Hill Text Films. 16 minutes.
*Discussion in Democracy.* Coronet, 1948. 10 minutes.
*Maintaining Classroom Discipline.* McGraw-Hill. 14 minutes.
*Practicing Democracy in the Classroom.* Encyclopedia Brittanica. 22 minutes.

*The Problem Method: Part I—Defining the Problem and Gathering Information.* McGraw-Hill. 18 minutes.

*The Problem Method: Part II—Using Information To Solve the Problem.* McGraw-Hill. 16 minutes.

*We Plan Together.* TC. 21 minutes.

*Filmstrip*

*Achieving Classroom Discipline.* Wayne University. 44 frames.

# 15

# Individualization in
# Secondary Education

## THE NECESSITY FOR INDIVIDUALIZATION

As was pointed out in Chapter 3, there are considerable and significant variations among high school students. It is obvious to every secondary school teacher, from contact with individuals in the classroom, especially by reading of examination papers and participation in other types of evaluation of the progress of the students, that individuals differ greatly.

**A Change in Underlying Educational Philosophy.** In earlier days, and still to some extent, teachers ascribed the differences in achievement to differences in such qualities of character as industry and responsibility, as well as to degree of interest in, and appreciation of, the materials and values of education, and secondarily to the difference in the ability of students to learn. While it is recognized today that these factors are important, there are also other factors such as the differences in (1) the present and future needs of the student, (2) the cultural and educational morale and facilities in the home, including the education of the parents, (3) the relative effectiveness of different procedures and types of teaching and learning, (4) previous preparation, particularly in the development of skills such as reading, computation, oral and written expression, and study, (5) interest in the particular subject, (6) the opportunities for study at home, (7) the amount of time spent in work, social life, and other types of non-school activities, and (8) the aspirations and plans for the future.

The problem was not such a difficult one in the days when it was generally expected that the majority of students would drop out before reaching the tenth grade. The attitude and philosophy of many teachers was "I'll lay it out for them, and they can take it or leave it. If they leave it, they can leave school." With universal attendance through the tenth grade and the general expectation that all students would complete high school or find themselves out of school and unemployed, a different philosophy has developed. However difficult and next to impossible it may seem, secondary school teachers must plan instructional materials and activities as well as they can for each student to learn as much as he can, and that means, of course, adaptation to interest, capacity, previous preparation, and other variations among the students.

**The "Individual" Pupils.** A teacher cannot teach a class; at any rate, a class cannot learn. It is the individual in the class who learns or fails to learn, and what is learned varies individually from student to student. The situation is something like an experiment in chemistry: Into each a number of test tubes arranged in a rack, a fluid is poured from a beaker—in each case causing formation of a precipitate of a different color. This interesting phenomenon results from the fact that, in the test tubes, there were different chemicals that combined with the common chemical poured from the beaker to form the precipitates of different colors. Similarly, what is learned by an individual student is the result of a combination of what is already in him with the learning materials and activities to which he has been exposed.

There should be individual standards in order to draw the most from each individual. If everyone in a class learns as much as he can, the whole class cannot move at the same rate. The teacher's job is to start the student where he is and take him just as far as he can possibly go.

**Recent and Current Trends Toward Individualization.** Accelerated by criticisms and the demand for better provisions for the exceptional student—the bright, the creative, the dull, the uninterested—as well as by the greatly increased concern relative to probable dropouts, new provisions for adapting secondary education to individuals have been developed and put into practice, and those already employed are being carefully investigated, evaluated, and modified. Among the types of adaptations of the learning materials and activities to the individual are the following:

1. Special courses for bright students
2. Adaptation of criticism and praise of students to the current needs of the temperament and disposition of the individual
3. Assignment of various questions and responsibilities for participation in discussion on the basis of the ability and background of the individual

4. Use of a dual marking system including both a mark for effort and one for actual achievement and cooperation
5. Vocational and educational guidance through exploratory courses
6. Student participation in planning the work of the class and managing learning activities
7. Separation of class sections into smaller groups working along the lines of special interests, experiences, and abilities
8. Special remedial sections, particularly in junior high school
9. Special coaching of slow pupils
10. Use of problem-project methods that furnish opportunity for different types of activities for different types of individuals
11. Differentiated assignments
12. Variation in the number of subjects a pupil may carry
13. Scientific study of problems of individuals by school psychologists, expert counselors, etc., particularly of important disciplinary and absentee cases.
14. Use of laboratory and large-unit plans of organization of learning activity, the more important of which will be discussed in this chapter

## LEARNING ABOUT THE INDIVIDUAL

All of those engaged in planning or implementing the adaptations of learning materials and activities for the individual student should first acquire as much information about each individual student as possible by consulting the school records, acquiring additional data through check lists of interests and of out-of-school occupations, analyzing biographies and oral and written material, holding conferences with the parents or using other sources of home data, and holding conferences with counselors about unusual cases.

**Types of Student Data.**[1] Following is a list of the types of information likely to be of use that shows the sources and means of attaining data:

| Areas of Information | Means of Obtaining Data |
|---|---|
| 1. General mental ability | Psychological-test scores—I.Q., M.A.—previous scholastic record |
| 2. Special aptitudes | Aptitude-test scores; observations; samples of student's work |
| 3. Educational status | Age-grade status; school marks; achievement tests |
| 4. Personal adjustment | Projective techniques; observations of personality; disciplinary record |

[1] See pages 364–365, for a list of appraisal instruments for gathering data about individual students.

| | |
|---|---|
| 5. Social adjustment | Sociometric devices; classroom and playground observations; interviews with student, parents, and other teachers and employees; autobiography; disciplinary record, activity participation record |
| 6. Recreational activities | Questionnaires; school activity records; travel experiences |
| 7. Work experience | Records of employment; employer reports; records of counselor; conversation with student; autobiography |
| 8. Home and family relationships | Home visitation; interviews with student and parents; school records; autobiography |
| 9. Community backgrounds | Observations; surveys; newspapers; official documents; publications of civic and educational groups; attendance at community functions |
| 10. Citizenship | School citizenship records; participation in service activities; student leadership positions; anectodal records; participation in community activities |
| 11. Health and mental status | Physical-examination records; observations; family consultation |
| 12. Special interests | Interest inventories; conversation and interviews with student; autobiography; school activity records; elective courses; hobbies |
| 13. Future educational and vocational plans | Questionnaires; interviews; courses taken; statements of student concerning future plans |

The following is a suggested outline for a student autobiography:

    I. Birth
       a. Place.
       b. Date.

   II. Family
       a. Ancestors.
          1. Nationality.
          2. Interesting experiences and background.
       b. Parents
          1. Names.
          2. Occupation.
          3. Interesting facts.
       c. Brothers and sisters.
          1. How many.
          2. Names
          3. Interesting facts.
       d. Outsiders living with the family.

  III. The Home
       a. How you get along in the home.
       b. What you like most about your home.
       c. What you would change if you could and why you would change
          it.

IV. Your Neighborhood
   a. Is it pleasant and friendly?
   b. Do you have congenial playmates?
   c. Have you moved a lot?

V. Experiences You Have Had
   a. Unusual experiences
      1. Pleasant.
      2. Frightening.
      3. Sad.

VI. People Who Have Helped You
   a. Ideas or help teachers have given you.
   b. Ideas or help others have given you.
      1. Parents.
      2. Friends.

VII. You, Yourself
   a. What kind of a person are you?
      1. Strong Points.
      2. Weak Points.

VIII. You and your Friends
   a. Do you make friends easily?
   b. Once you make them, do you keep them?
   c. What do you most like and look for in a friend?

IX. You and Your Life
   a. How you spend your leisure time.
   b. What do you sometimes worry about?
   c. Where do you go for help when you need it?
   d. If you could do exactly what you want to do now, what would you do?
   e. What do you think you would like to be doing ten years from now?

X. What would you like most to contribute to the world in which you live? Explain this:[2]

## EDUCATION OF MORE CREATIVE AND ABLER STUDENTS

**Plans and Proposals.** In recent years, practically all secondary schools have stepped up their programs for the better education of the bright and creative student. Among the plans used in a considerable number of schools are the following:

1. *Offering seminars, honors, and college courses to the abler seniors and very outstanding juniors.* These courses are ordinarily in academic subjects such as history, English, chemistry, analytical geometry and calculus, and philosophy. An increasing and considerable number of colleges and universities allow credit toward graduation for students

---

[2] Harold F. Cottingham and William E. Hopke, *Guidance in the Junior High School* (Bloomington, Ill.: McKnight & McKnight Publishing Co., 1961), pp. 118–119.

doing well in these courses. Sometimes passing of an examination formulated by the college or by the College Entrance Examination Board is required. Some colleges and universities do not give credit for work done in high school but permit the student to skip the beginning course and take a more advanced course. This latter procedure is referred to as advanced college placement.

2. *Permitting the bright student to carry five, and the brightest even six, "solids" and to complete the requirements for graduation in one year less than the normal time.* Ordinarily, students doing this are required to attend at least one summer school session. There is considerable opposition to this plan by senior high school principals and parents, on the assumption that the student should not enter college too soon. Practically all the careful investigations of the matter that have been made reveal that bright students who enter college at the age of sixteen or early seventeen make much better grades than the average college student, take greater part in social life than the average student, carry an average load and extracurricular activities, and furnish a disproportionately small number of disciplinary cases.[3]

3. *Providing special honors or college courses or sections for superior students.* Since the middle of the 1950's, there has been a very great increase in the number of schools employing what had formerly been somewhat inaccurately called "ability" or "homogeneous" grouping, which involves identifying as well as possible students with greater academic ability and teaching them in special classes.[4]

Unfortunately, there are very few textbooks available as yet for superior pupils and it is necessary for the teacher to plan learning activities and learning materials specially adapted to the more capable student. For this reason it is coming to be generally recognized that the teacher who is put in charge of a class of abler students should be specially qualified, preferably having had at least one course in teaching of the bright student.

Some teachers of such classes attempt to teach the bright student by employing without modification the materials used in college and university classes. This falls definitely short of the best provision for the bright student. It does not make adequate allowance for originality, initiative, and creativeness. This course is often organized as a sort of seminar or honors course in a particular field.

---

[3] S. L. Pressey, "Acceleration: Disgrace or Challenge?" *Science*, Vol. 104 (September 6, 1946), pages 215–219. See also "An Analysis of the Effects of Acceleration," *Educational Administration and Supervision*, September, 1944.

[4] In 1962, 90 per cent of the high school teachers queried who had taught with grouping and without it favored grouping in separate classes in such academic subjects as mathematics and foreign languages. *NEA Research Bulletin*, Vol. 40, No. 41 (December, 1962), p. 121.

It is very important to see that students who are admitted to honors or college courses in high school are those who are interested and capable of doing the kind of work that is expected of them. It is desirable to set up a set of criteria and to have counselors assist teachers concerned in selecting the personnel of such classes.

In the Niles Township four-year high schools at Skokie, Illinois, the following criteria are employed in selecting those who are invited to go on to take the college or honors courses.

1. An I.Q. of at least 125
2. Two years of acceleration on a reading test
3. A B average in allied courses in previous years
4. Evidence of physical and emotional ability to carry difficult advanced classes
5. Recommendation by previous teachers
6. Interest on the part of both the student and the student's parents

"Advanced placement—is it worth all the trouble?" Cincinnati schools asked this question of 208 students who took advanced placement examinations there and got replies that added up to enthusiastic indorsement of the program. Of the 208, replies were received from 196, of whom 189 were attending college. The college group had taken 265 advanced placement examinations, receiving college credit for 124 of these and advanced placement, without credit, for 23. Following are conclusions from this study:

College graduates were reported by 170 students. Nearly half were attending the U. of Cincinnati, where their grades averaged 3.00 or "B." Those enrolled in Eastern colleges reported grade averages of 2.58.

Asked if they would do it all over again, 97% of the students who responded said "yes." Asked how much benefit they thought they had gained, 73% said "a great deal"; 20% said "some" and 3% said "little."

Even without college credit or advanced standing, the students said, they regarded the advanced high school courses, involving a rather heavy work load, [as] helpful, particularly in their adjustment to college study. They thought these courses had aided them in developing good study habits and had provided helpful background for college work.

Often mentioned was that the students had found it intellectually stimulating to be in a high school class with other able, interested students. Many had high praise for their high school teachers of advanced courses. Some emphasized that participation in the program should be encouraged more for the sake of added learning and intellectual stimulus than for the possibility of earning college credit. Most reported no special problems in adjusting to college because they thought their high school preparation had served them well. The college problem mentioned most frequently was adjusting to the increased study load and planning for study time.

Parents tended to concur with the judgment of their offspring. A random sample were questioned and only one of the 15 from whom responses were received could see no advantage in advanced placement courses. "Challenging," "very worthwhile," and "of great benefit" were the common responses.

Students in the group were a capable lot, chosen on the basis of test scores, teacher recommendations, grades, and expressed interest. IQ's ranged from 111 to 160 with a median of 134. Nearly 2 out of 5 had received scholarship help during their freshman college year. All but 7 of the 189 included in the survey had entered college.[5]

4. *Providing opportunities for superior students to engage in independent study or research activities under the supervision of qualified teachers.* This may be done in the library, in the laboratory, or at various places outside the school, such as civic and government offices, or chemical and industrial plants, with the aid of resource persons in the community, the public library, and the home.

**Teaching the Bright Child.** In most heterogeneous classes, the secondary school teacher will find some bright students. There will not be many if grouping has been used in the school, but there will be a considerable number, usually somewhere between 10 and 30 per cent of the class, if ability grouping is not employed. Communities differ with respect to the percentage of able children and the percentage who are less able. Some communities are made up of well-educated parents in the upper economic class who send to the local secondary schools several times as many bright students as come from homes of subnormal cultural and economic levels.

**Saturday Classes.** The following account shows how Saturday classes for bright children may be set up:

Junior and senior high-school students of Lindenhurst (New York) registered this fall for their choice of eleven Saturday morning courses. Students registered at Lindenhurst Senior High School, Lindenhurst Junior High School, and Our Lady of Perpetual Help School. A total of 24 class sessions will be held for each course.

. . . Junior high-school students, in grades 7, 8, and 9, registered for Modern Mathematical Concepts, Famous Scientific Experiments, and Advanced Learning Techniques. Senior high-school students, in grades 10, 11, and 12, had their choice of Literary Criticism, The Communist Challenge, Music Appreciation, Electronic Theory and Practice, Independent Advanced Art, Advanced Learning Techniques, Typing for Personal Use, Classical Drama, and Science of Propaganda. The only charge for these courses is a $2.00 registration fee. Books, equipment, and supplies in most courses are furnished by the school. Non-residents are not admitted.[6]

[5] From "Report Card on Advanced Placement," *Education U.S.A.* (December 20, 1962), pp. 1–2.
[6] "Students Register for Saturday Classes" *The Bulletin, N.A.S.S.P.,* No. 278 (December, 1962), p. 140.

The "Ungraded" Secondary School. In recent years, some secondary schools have become what are called "ungraded" secondary schools. In most such schools, the more capable students may enrol for courses intended for more advanced classes while the less able students may enter and receive credit for work in classes intended for younger students, for example, seniors may be put in tenth-grade classes. In some junior high schools, the bright seventh- and eighth-grade students are allowed to carry one elective normally carried by ninth-grade students.

The principal characteristic of the ungraded school is that students may progress and take courses above their grade level or below their grade level as they need to be and as seen to be by the counselor and teacher. The principal, counselors, and teachers working for such a school at Melbourne, Florida, report great progress and unusual interest on the part of the students. It must be said in passing, however, that at Melbourne and at some of the other schools in which the idea has been most successful there are additional factors. Among them is the assignment of teachers who are unusually qualified to deal with youngsters on the ungraded basis and who are willing to devote the time and attention necessary to it. It is not a type of thing that can be done successfully by mediocre or even average teachers.

Teaching the Creative and Talented Child. Much of what has been said above applies also to teaching of the creative child. Efforts should be made to recognize the few students who have oustanding creative ability. From this type of individual will come some of the greatest contributions to our society. Among the creative students are a considerable proportion who are somewhat of a "one-track" mind. They are extremely interested in one field or two or three related fields, sometimes in only one small aspect of a field. Some of them are so keenly interested in this one area that they are definitely resentful of distractions and become aggressive to the point of constituting disciplinary problems. Some even become emotionally disturbed and need psychiatric help.

Not only should the bright pupil have more work to do, but it should be of a type to challenge his superior and special abilities. He should be required to locate and organize materials, to find and state relationships and generalizations, and to read more difficult technical material. He should be relieved of some of the easier routine tasks that may be necessary for the average or below-average youngster. He should be given larger units as well as tasks and problems with a greater number of steps. He should be freed of some of the repetitious and wasteful reciting of the class and permitted to work more on his own. For him, instruction may safely be individualized. He should be stimulated to undertake imaginative and creative tasks. Frequent diagnostic testing is unnecessary for him; he can be trained in self-diagnosis and in planning his own remedial work. The brighter the youngster is, the more these suggestions should be employed and the further they should be carried. They usually apply to youngsters with an I.Q. of 120 to 135. Those of definitely higher I.Q. (140 and up) should be treated as special cases.

**Discovering and Conserving Talent.** Since the problems of the nation have become not only greater but more clearly recognized by our leaders, an increased amount of attention has been given to the amount and quality of the waste of the most precious national resource, namely, human talent. While the use of various types of tests, many of which have been recently developed, has been quite effective in aiding careful students of the matter to discover talent, much talent is not identified in this way. For instance, alert teachers may identify in the classroom, at least tentatively, various kinds of talent, note them on the students' records, and take them into consideration in planning learning activities for the talented students. Certainly, students with "divine" gifts should be kept in school and every opportunity should be given them to develop their talents.

**The Underachiever.** While teachers have always recognized the problem created by youngsters who are not achieving in school up to their potentialities, this problem has come to the forefront only in recent years. It is being recognized as a very important and unnecessary waste of talent. The problem has been definitely increased during the period from 1940 to 1960 by the development of the peer-age club. Most youngsters wish not to be regarded by their peers as a "brain" or a "square." Many youngsters actually do not attempt to do their best on intelligence tests. They do not want to be put in bright sections. Many of them are not encouraged by their parents to attain academic stature. More recently, many young people have realized that, in order to support a family at anything but the lowest level and to achieve their goals in material possessions and status, it would be necessary for them to do better in their school work, and many have come to realize that they would not be accepted by a good college or university unless their grades went up and unless their scores on college entrance examinations were high; so the trend has been somewhat reversed. Nevertheless, many young people in high schools are not achieving up to their ability, and with some the discrepancy is particularly great. This is especially true among creative youngsters with unusually narrow interests but great imagination.

Today, in most secondary schools, there is conducted every year an investigation to identify those youngsters who may be definitely known as underachievers. Not only are test scores examined and compared with various types of work being done, but a look back over previous grades often throws light upon the possibilities of achievement, particularly in those cases where the youngster had obviously demonstrated much ability and has since suffered a definite deterioration.

Work with the conspicuous underachiever is a complicated matter involving careful case study, conferences with the underachiever by people who have a good chance of getting close to him, and conferences with the parents to guard against the possibility of unwise pressure from that source.

In an increasing number of schools, as at Stratford, Connecticut, classes of underachievers are taught by teachers who are specialists in teaching underachievers.

**Parental Acceptance and Academic Growth.** There seems to be a significant relationship between parental acceptance and the academic achievement of adolescents. High, average, and low achievers were identified among eighth-grade students, using a regression equation based on Otis Beta Group Intelligence Test scores and actual first-semester grades. The children's perception of parental acceptance was measured by Whitesel's Situation Questionnaire for Parent-Child Relationships, Gilmore's Sentence Completion Test, and the Thematic Apperception Test (TAT). Boys achieving at a higher level reported fathers as more accepting than did those achieving at a lower level. Both the average- and the low-achieving boys perceived their mothers as more accepting than did the high-achieving boys. Father acceptance and mother acceptance as perceived by the girls increased as the level of achievement became higher.

Barwick and Arbuckle draw the following conclusions from their findings:

> The results of this study would indicate that, in attempting to solve the problem of underachievement in our schools, it would be advisable for the teacher of the underachiever to discuss the problem with the student and his parents in order that all concerned may understand the dynamics of the problem. Furthermore, it is obvious that effective counseling services for both children and parents would assist greatly in preventing and solving the problem. All too often, the schools and the parents rely upon "warning" or "deficiency" notices, threats of withdrawal from athletic teams, band, and other extracurricular activities, in the belief that such steps will force the student to achieve to capacity. Many times, these very steps aimed at ameliorating the situation force the child deeper into a state of underachievement. It should be pointed out that a brief, perfunctory conversation between counselor and student, which in many schools is a ritual which follows the issuance of "warning" notices, may ease the conscience of the counselor but will in itself lend little to the solution of underachievement.

In conclusion, one must realize that the frequency of underachievement in our schools is great, and that the probability of successfully solving the problem at the secondary level is much less than during the first few years of school. Consequently, earlier identification of the underachieving student and the availability of counseling services at the lower grade levels for parents are most important.[7]

# EDUCATION OF THE HANDICAPPED

**The Slow, or Mentally Handicapped Child.** Fortunately, throughout the country provisions have been developed in recent years for special classes and special education for severely mentally handicapped children including those with I.Q.'s of less than 65 or 70. Nevertheless, there are in most schools some students who are so inferior in academic ability that they profit little in classes intended for average and superior students and, indeed, in many instances become disciplinary problems, dropouts, or juvenile delinquents.

Among the provisions made in an increasingly large number of secondary schools for the student of inferior academic ability are the following:

1. *Special classes for students who have been identified as definitely inferior, usually including students with I.Q.'s of less than 85.* To be sure, other criteria, which will be mentioned later in this chapter, are employed for identifying the mentally slow as well as those of superior academic ability.

2. *Remedial or lower-track sections.* Particularly in the field of mathematics and English, but also in all other subjects, special sections for remedial work have been established in a large and increasing number of secondary schools, for example, in mathematics, sections are offered on general mathematics and on remedial arithmetic.

3. *Reduced load.* Experiments permitting students to carry less than a normal number of courses have not proved that this is an effective approach, except in cases of students who are employed during a considerable proportion of their day. Students doing unsatisfactory work ordinarily do little if any better when carrying a smaller number of courses.

Among other provisions for the less able students are the following: (a) vocational and educational guidance through exploratory courses; (b) student participation in planning some of the details of the work of the class and in managing learning activities; (c) separation of classes into smaller groups working along the lines of special interests, experi-

---

[7] Janice Barwick and Dugald Arbuckle, "Parental Acceptance and Academic Growth," *Phi Delta Kappan,* Vol. 36, (February, 1963) pp. 233-234.

ences, and abilities; (d) other types of ability groupings; (e) special coaching of the slow pupils; (f) the use of problem-project methods that furnish opportunities for different types of activities for different types of individuals; (g) differentiated assignments; (h) scientific study of problems of individuals by school psychologists, expert counselors, etc., particularly in important disciplinary and absenteeism cases. In many schools there are special sections for those of less talent and special sections for those of more talent in physical-education, art, music, shop, and homemaking classes.

**Ability Grouping.** It has seemed to many careful students that, while a student may be somewhat embarrassed and his parents irritated by his place in a slow section, the effect upon his personality is likely to be better than that of all the failure, frustration, and embarrassment that results from his attempt to carry on his work in a heterogeneous class in which most of the students are superior to him not only in learning abilities but also in interest and previous educational progress, while each day he knows he has little chance of success and his friends about him observe his poor performance and deficiency.

The claim that the students in the bright section are likely to get exaggerated ideas of their abilities and become conceited has not stood up well. Students who are always at the top of their section are much more likely to become conceited and self-satisfied. When materials are adapted sufficiently to the abler students so that they constitute a real challenge and the student is in competition with his peers, there is much less opportunity for him to get an exaggerated opinion of his abilities and his importance.

**Conferences with Slow Learners and Underachievers.** Individual conferences may profitably be held with slow learners.

1. To talk with the pupil about his learning problems and outline procedures which may help him solve these problems
2. To suggest activities, projects, investigations, and other individual undertakings which may be more profitable to the learner than those which he has selected on his own or small group planning
3. To discuss experiences which the pupil has missed for illness or other reasons, and plan steps where he may undertake these or related experiences on his own
4. To explain concepts, processes, or information which the pupil has not understood in group work
5. To answer questions the pupil has raised in class that were not appropriate for group discussion, or questions that he has asked the teacher to answer in conference
6. To give specific direction to study procedures, and observe the pupil in use of these procedures

7. To lend a sympathetic ear to the pupil's problems, and give the security that comes from confidence in one's teacher

8. To go over specific pieces of work and test papers to help the pupil understand his difficulties, and praise him for improvement and achievement

9. To review the pupil's self-evaluation of his learning experiences, and plan next steps in the light of such evaluation

.    .    .    .    .    .    .    .    .    .    .    .

11. To plan learning experiences which will be related to the pupil's unique vocational interests or present work activities

12. To help the pupil plan for special roles he has in the class or school organization[8]

**Teaching the Slow-learning Pupil.** Following are principles and practices found to be usually effective in teaching the less able student:

1. Efforts should be made to discover fields of special interest on the part of individual learners and to utilize them.

2. The dull student must be kept conscious of progress at all times. He must be given reason to believe he is improving at least a little.

3. Real visual objects and other concrete and lifelike aids should be used.

4. Applications of the subject matter to life should be pointed out.

5. Daily assignments should be very specific, meaningful tasks.

6. The teacher must be satisfied with attempting what is possible and taking time to teach that well.

7. Slow pupils should be given things to do, not because they do things well, but because they learn better that way than otherwise.

8. An excessive vocabulary load should be avoided in favor of short and familiar words and simple sentences. A special effort should be made to see that the pupil understands adequately new terms that are essential to the meaning and that will come up later, writing them on the blackboard, defining them, and giving examples of their use.

9. Misunderstandings and relatively poor learning should be discovered immediately and remedial teaching undertaken at once.

10. Dull pupils should be helped to read better. Some time should be taken in class for oral reading, to develop comprehension and vocabulary.

11. The dull students should not be given meaningless routine tasks from which little progress in learning can be expected.

12. Frequent diagnostic devices, oral and written, should be employed to identify the dull student's weak spots, and approved remedial explanations and study assignments should be given to him.

[8] William M. Alexander and Paul Halverson, *Effective Teaching in Secondary Schools* (New York: Holt, Rinehart & Winston, Inc., 1956), pp. 361–362.

13. Belief in the student's ability to do acceptable work should be evidenced, but not ostentatiously, by the teacher.

14. Symptoms of tension, discouragement, mild disorder, or lack of interest on the part of the dull pupil should be taken in stride by the teacher.

15. Each student should feel that his teacher is interested in him as an individual.

### Relucant Slow Learners.

The California Association of Secondary-School Administrators has released a report of its *Study of Current Practices and Trends in Working with Slow Learners and Reluctant Learners in California Secondary Schools.* The introduction of this report states: "Many educators have expressed growing concern about meeting the needs and otherwise coping with the slow learners and the reluctant learners in our secondary schools. The combination of these slow learners and reluctant learners have changed teaching from joy to drudgery for many teachers; others have been driven from the teaching ranks rather than face the frustration of fruitless effort in the classroom; potential teachers find fields other than teaching more attractive and less exasperating.[9]

**The Socially Handicapped.** In recent years, much more importance has been attached to the handicaps that some young people seem to have in their social adjustments and contacts. Not only is it normal and desirable for young people to spend a substantial amount of time in the presence of other people and in participating normally in social situations, but investigations have revealed that the student who is socially withdrawn is far more likely to have mental ill health, to become emotionally disturbed, or to drop out of school and become a juvenile delinquent.

Teacher expectation has a surprising impact on pupil achievement. Indeed, one might even say that teacher expectation has a similar impact on pupil intelligence scores. The teacher who expects achievement, who has hope for the educability of his pupils, conveys this through every nuance of his behavior. The teacher who conveys hopelessness for the educability of his students usually does so without ever really verbalizing such an attitude—at least in front of his pupils.

In Detroit, there have recently been established after-school classes for various types of students needing special help to try to catch up or keep up to minimum standards of achievement for their age. Specially prepared teachers are given extra pay for teaching such classes. This promising provision is likely to be introduced in many places.[10]

[9] "News Notes," *The Bulletin of the N.A.S.S.P.,* No. 283 (May, 1963), pp. 167–168.

[10] Carl L. Marburger, *Basic Considerations for Educational Planning for Children in Depressed Urban Areas,* Detroit, Mich., Public School, 1962, pp. 13–14.

In every high school some children, and in a few high schools an alarming number of them, do not seem to "fit in." Not only are they deprived of educational values and educational contacts, they also tend to develop unfortunate personality traits that bring about unhealthy attitudes about people, social institutions, and themselves.

In many schools, principals, counselors, and teachers devote some time and attention to identifying socially handicapped young people and attempting to involve them in social situations, both in and out of class, that will be helpful for them.

Many secondary school teachers, as well as elementary school teachers, have learned to make use of a device for identifying the socially handicapped isolated—the sociogram. Shown below is a copy of an actual sociogram, which is quite revealing relative to social relationships, including the lack of social satisfaction and the social isolation of some members of the class.

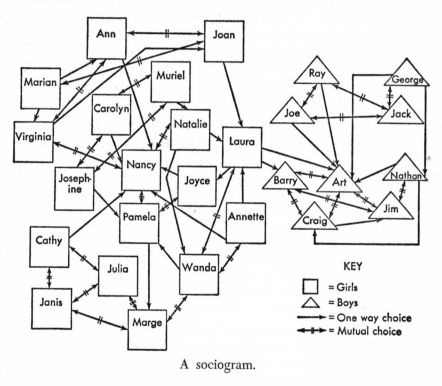

A sociogram.

**The Emotionally Handicapped.** Increased and improved means for identification of young people whose emotions and their control and direction have not developed normally have been devised. With developments in the fields of mental hygiene and psychiatry, the schools have felt an increased responsibility for identifying these young people and assisting them to receive appropriate counseling through school counselors, in some instances offering their parents the services of a psychiatrist. The extension and improvement of counseling services in secondary schools have made service along these lines more practical and effective than formerly.

**The Physically Handicapped.** In some schools, the very greatly physically handicapped children, particularly the spastics and those who also have mental and/or emotional handicaps, are provided for in special classes. Nevertheless, there are in most high schools at least a few definitely physically handicapped children who need individual attention. Among those are students with speech defects—stuttering, harelip, and others—who need special help by teachers trained in those areas.

Each teacher should make an effort at the beginning of the year to discover whether there are in his class students whose hearing is defective or whose eyesight is such that glasses are needed. By appropriate seating in the room, teachers may assist these youngsters. The cases of those with definitely defective eyesight and hearing should be called to the attention of the school nurse or health officer, and the parents should be informed.

The following is a description of one school district's method of handling temporarily home-bound students:

Students, with temporary illness, who will be absent from school for 3 months or more, may receive tutoring services. Teachers are assigned to individual students on a 4-hour-a-week basis.

The object of the program is to keep the student educationally apace with his classmates while he is ill, thus relieving tension and worry.

Subject: All academic courses
Grades: 1–12
Number of teachers: 10
Number of students: Maximum caseload 7 students per teacher
Average mental ability: Normal and up
Time: 4 hours per week
Equipment and materials: Regular adapted to bedside teaching
Observable by appointment: September through May
Written description: Available[11]

**Students from Low-cultural-Level Homes.** There have always been in secondary schools students from homes of low economic, cultural, and educational level, but more recently a higher percentage of them have been remaining through junior high school and into senior high school. Furthermore, they have tended to become congregated in certain sections of the cities called "slum" areas, many becoming juvenile

[11] From *An Inventory of Educational Innovation*, Tucson, Ariz., School District No. 1, p. 2.

delinquents. In recent years, this problem has received major attention in a considerable number of cities, particularly in Detroit and in New York City. However, most cities still have a slum element, and all secondary school teachers should attempt to identify such students in their classes and to take into consideration the handicap that these youngsters have, both in conferences with them and in marking their assignments. Indeed, conferences with parents of such children are highly desirable and are being held by an increasing number of teachers and counselors, often at the students' homes.

In a small but increasing number of schools, after-school tutoring is provided for students who need it to catch up and keep up with their classes. For Negro students, this aid is often provided by the National Association for the Advancement of Colored People or by the Urban League. The following is excerpted from a report of a 1962 Detroit experiment involving integration of underprivileged youngsters into a school student body:

The second primary focus of our attention is upon the parents and the community. Once again, this is a question of involvement. Parents who are not involved, who do not know what is taking place in the school, can certainly not reinforce what the school is doing with their children. We also see a need to involve parents and the community so that we may raise the aspirations of the parents and their children with regard to academic and social achievement. Parents in depressed urban areas typically stay away from schools. They stay away from school because their own experiences have been either unpleasant or short-lived or both. They are fearful of the institution of the school and they lack information about what is taking place in the school. They do not typically join organizations and therefore do not normally attend parent group meetings, do not participate in adult education classes—they generally avoid all school contacts.

Large numbers of parents were brought into contact with the school in a number of ways—as members of recreational and social groups and as students in adult education classes. Definite improvement was observable in the attitude of the students and the work in class of many.

The visiting teacher is the school social worker. This person has had specific training in the case-work methodology and operates primarily with children and the parents of children who have crucial school-adjustment problems. The visiting teacher is normally assigned in the Detroit schools; but she is usually assigned to six or more schools and spends perhaps a half a day a week in each school attempting to handle an unrealistic case load in this fragmented fashion.

The coaching teacher is actually a language arts teacher who is performing special remedial functions with children who are retarded in reading. She often conducts small classes ranging from five to fifteen children working on the particular skill deficiencies of children. Once again, the coaching teacher's role is changing. She often finds it more effective to work less specifically with small groups of children and more with total staff in helping all teachers gain the necessary skills to work with the reading deficiencies of children regardless of the subject matter area.

*Each* school has had to organize after-school and evening activities in terms of its own community and the needs of that community. Some of the schools have put a greater emphasis on the enrichment programs for youth in the afternoon, others on adult programs in the evening. The greatest difficulty in involvement of youth and adults has naturally come at the secondary level, where the ambivalence of youth toward their parents and the size of the school attendance area mitigate against parental participation in school functions.

In cooperation with the Neighborhood Service Organization and the Detroit Behavior Project, day camps were conducted at one of our schools during the summer of 1961 for 55 emotionally disturbed children from the project schools.

What are the "short term" forecasts for the Great Cities Project in Detroit? It is believed that a considerably larger number of children attending project schools will leave them with positive self-images, higher goals, greater scholastic achievement and improved citizenship; more adequately prepared for continuing school or going to work—independent rather than dependent citizens.[12]

### Minority Groups and Textbooks.

The Michigan Curriculum Committee for Better Human Relations has developed a policy guide, "The Treatment of Minority Groups in Textbooks," at the request of representatives from the approved textbook publishing companies. Lynn M. Barlett, State superintendent of education, has adopted the statement for the Michigan Department of Public Instruction and sent it to the American Textbook Publishers Institute, which is bringing it to the attention of all member publishers.

The committee functions under Michigan's Curriculum Program. Beginning in 1935 with one committee of 6 members as a cooperative effort of citizens in the State to improve education, the program has now grown to 31 committees with nearly 1,000 members. The State superintendent appoints committee members from all sections of the State to work independently in many subject fields, such as agricultural education of exceptional children, foreign language, guidance, family living, international understanding, mathematics, and science.[13]

# THE USE OF TEACHING MACHINES, PROGRAMED MATERIALS, AND PROJECTION MACHINES

**Teaching Machines.** Since the middle 1950's, there has been a greatly increased use of what have come to be called "teaching machines," although as yet their use is quite limited. More than a score of types of machines have been devised and put on the market. Since the price ranges from just a few dollars to more than $12,000, obviously only the cheaper machines could be employed where it would be necessary to have a machine available for each student for at least one period each day, and these are not very effective.

---

[12] Carl L. Marburger, *Basic Considerations for Educational Planning for Children in Depressed Urban Areas,* Detroit, Mich. Public Schools, 1962, p. 18.
[13] *School Life,* Vol. 45, No. 6 (April, 1963), pp. 22–23.

Common features of these teaching machines are as follows: (1) The individual student is permitted to proceed at a pace in harmony with his ability and interest. (2) The multiple-choice or the blank-filling technique is emphasized in testing the student's knowledge. (3) Little or no written work is required on the part of the student. (4) The machines are student-operated. (5) The student is immediately informed as to whether or not the answer is correct.

Some teaching machines provide explanations of mistakes; they provide a *feedback*, a technical name for reference to materials treating a particular type of mistake made by the student. Some require the student to write out an answer instead of selecting one or more alternative answers.

The teaching machine concept is not a new one. As far back as the 1920's, Dr. S. L. Pressey, of the Ohio State University, argued for a limited use of automatic teaching and developed a type of machine that could be used for testing. It was only, however, with the very great engrossment of the general public in technology and various types of new machines and with the increased prosperity of the country that serious consideration was given to widespread use of such machines. In recent years, one of the most widespread and intense campaigns known in the history of American education has been organized by their advocates and their manufacturers, to promote their adoption and use.

The devices used for automatic teaching range from fairly simple machines to highly complicated and very expensive electronic apparatus. They all, however, rely upon the same fundamental principles: (1) The learning materials are carefully arranged in advance and in sequence so that the student can proceed without the teacher's guidance. (2) The student is informed immediately of the correctness or the incorrectness of his answers to the questions set before him by the machine. (3) If the student's response is reported to be correct by the machine, he goes on to the next step; if his response is incorrect, he is referred back to the material that he should restudy.

Programed material consists largely of detailed facts to be learned and of subject-matter skills arranged, as far as possible, in sequence. To speak of the machines as "teaching machines" is, indeed, to use a misnomer; as a matter of fact, the machine is essentially a testing machine.

The principal arguments that have been advanced by proponents of the machine teaching are, firstly, that it enables each student to go on at his own rate and that, therefore, better results are achieved, and, secondly, that the teacher is freed from time-consuming duties of explaining things to the class or to each individual that the students can learn by themselves. Some have even claimed that the teaching machine will replace teachers.

On the other hand, teaching machines have been criticized rather vigorously, it being claimed that (1) they really do not teach, but only test; (2) since the same material is employed for all students, the provision for individual differences is only in terms of speed, which is not a very satisfactory adaptation; (3) they diminish very seriously the personal contact between teacher and student; (4) they tend to emphasize factual material, which is already overemphasized by most teachers; (5) the curriculum materials employed with the teaching machine are not sufficiently well developed and organized to be the equivalent of the excellent textbooks that are now available; (6) they do not give training in problem-solving procedure; and (7) they do not develop skills in discussion or in social contacts.

**Programed Materials.** To be used either with teaching machines or separately in the form of "scrambled books," programed materials for a considerable number of courses have been developed and published by some of the leading textbook publishers. In the "scrambled book" plan, the student is given a very small bit of learning material and then asked to make a response indicating his understanding or memory of it. The student progresses through the book by following directions that skip from page to page through various parts of the book for each exercise.

While the idea of the "scrambled" or other type of programed book is very intriguing, it is subject to some of the same limitations as the teaching machine. The quality of the materials in most programed books will have to be very materially improved before they will be widely used.

In "Some Practical Pointers on Programming," in the March, 1962, issue of *Education Screen and Audiovisual Guide*, William B. Sanborn reported his

. . . comprehensive experience actually using programmed materials in various realistic public school situations coupled with impressions and comments from observing programmed activities in many sections of the country, participating in conferences on the subject, plus careful examination of dozens of different programmed materials.

He noted that

. . . the absolute key to success is reading. Programming involves no reading panacea. It cannot eclipse the language level factor. If a student does not read well, his success will be impaired. . . . If programmed materials at present lack any basic element common to strong instructional materials, it is assuredly their almost uniform lack of color, illustrations, maps, diagrams, etc. In other words, they are quite unattractive. Page appeal should not be forgotten. Certainly all that we know about the values commensurate with fine, well-keyed, quality illustrations should not be discarded for the convenience of format. Dozens of frames, or even sequences of frames, have been studied that were not as efficient or effective as a possible illustration. It remains to be seen whether entire courses or shorter units within a subject area will be the most palatable via the programmed format. There is perhaps merit to both, but it would not be illogical to presume resentment on behalf of a high school young-ster taking five solids, four of which were via the programmed format. This appears to be a reasonable consideration which may lend strength to the value of shorter unit presentation. . . . Programmed materials (at least in their present stage of development) cannot (a) hold class discussions; (b) conduct a debate; (c) give a demonstration; (d) or diagnose a particular student's adjust-ment or learning problems. They should not be promoted on such a basis.

**Tape Recordings.** Much more widely used, and likely to remain so, are tape recordings. A great many of the institutions of higher education that prepare teachers notably Kent State University at Kent, Ohio, have already developed large collections of educational tapes for all grades and all subjects, which may be purchased at very low cost or rented very cheaply.

Tape recordings are useful and are used for instruction in practically every subject in the curriculum, but they are especially useful in the teaching of music, speech, and modern foreign languages. One of their major advantages lies in the fact that, by means of the tape, the student may hear his own voice, his pronunciation, and his enunciation.

**Modern Language Laboratories.** Another promising development in the use of new machines and equipment is the plan for providing indi-vidual stations in what have come to be called "modern language laboratories." Here students are furnished recorders and speakers that enable them to hear the pronunciation of a language by an expert, as well as their own, and to compare their own pronunciation and enunciation. In addition, in the modern language laboratories, the instructor may carry on conversations with individual students or the class as a whole.

## PROVIDING FOR DROPOUTS

**Extent and Importance of the Problem.** Recently, very greatly in-creased attention has been paid to the problem of students who do not remain to graduate from high school. While the proportion of dropouts has been steadily growing smaller, the plight of the students who do drop out before receiving a high school diploma, usually from 20 to 50 per cent, has become worse.

The problem of unemployment of dropouts has become very serious. Young people constitute a large percentage of those unemployed in normal times. The opportunities for boys and girls to obtain employment of any kind have decreased in recent decades, and the kind of employment that they do obtain is in the nature of "blind alley" jobs—jobs with no future.

Furthermore, with the disappearance of work about the home and on the farm for young people, there has been a great tendency for young people to develop a type of social life that is dangerous for them and for society. Indeed, a rather high percentage of juvenile delinquents are students who have dropped out from secondary school before graduating and have not found suitable employment. Many of them are frustrated and bitter and become antisocial and vicious, if not actually mentally ill.

The very great majority of employers have an aversion to employing a teen-ager who has not completed high school. This is not entirely because of his lack of education but because dropping out suggests the probability of a lack of such character qualities as reliability, cooperativeness, industry, and stick-to-itiveness, which makes him a poor employment risk.

People are divided in their opinions about what should be done about dropouts. Throughout the country, there have been increased efforts to retain all students in school unit graduation.

On the other hand, a great many people including educators, sociologists, and legislators doubt the advisability of keeping all boys and girls in school until graduation, not only because they believe that what little education some students are capable of receiving is not consequential, but also because they believe that problem students become a distracting and corrupting influence upon the other students of the school, as well as a burden upon the teachers, requiring as they do a disproportionate amount of teacher help and time. Among the proposals made for dealing with dropouts and potential dropouts are the following:

1. Identify the potential dropouts at the beginning of the junior high school or earlier and provide for them courses of study and guidance appropriate to their ability, interests, and home background.

2. Provide a work-study program in which the potential dropouts may find satisfying activities at work, earn some money, and spend from one-half to three-fourths of their time on school studies.[14]

3. Form special sections of the students of less than average ability, to be taught by specially trained teachers.

4. Identify each marked underachiever at any level of ability and make him the subject of a careful case study and guidance involving his parents.

5. The social agencies, employers, and others in the community should give careful attention to the problem and make every effort to provide

[14] See further discussion of work-study plans in Chapter 6. In many cities such as Chicago and Kansas City, they have proved very successful.

some form of employment, even with low pay, for those who do drop out. These youngsters constitute a community problem as much as, or even more than a school problem.

6. Establish for the most hopeless cases something like the Civilian Conservation Corps of the 1930's, which would involve work on various kinds of needed civic improvements and would provide the participating youths with the necessities of life, some amusement, and vocational training away from the school.

**The Factors in Early Leaving of School.** Many studies have been made in an effort to discover why some young people decide to drop out of school. While it is difficult to say that all of the factors involved are causes rather than being merely associated with dropping out, the following have been identified as related to early leaving of school:

1. Low I.Q. especially when less than 80—a factor in a large number of dropouts
2. Low economic status of parents, particularly in slum neighborhoods and bilingual homes
3. Retardation or excessive age—almost always a cause of dropping out before completion of high school
4. In many homes, apparent necessity for children to help support their family
5. Bad citizenship and disciplinary records—possibly because bad citizenship and dropping out are effects of the same cause or causes—inability to do, or lack of interest in doing, schoolwork
6. Failure on the part of adolescents to realize the value of going to school (Many dropouts insist that that was their main reason.)
7. Desire to be married
8. Access to family cars
9. Poor attendance
10. Lack of part-time jobs
11. Failure to participate in extracurricular activities—a very important indication of social maladjustment
12. Lack of interest and poor teaching—for many dropouts the major reason for withdrawal
13. Lack of education on the part of parents (Children of parents who have not completed elementary school drop out in large proportion, as to a lesser extent do those neither parent of whom has completed high school. Such parents are usually of lower economic status.)

Several studies have been made with respect to the types of occupations of parents of those who leave school early. Children whose wage-earning parents were farm laborers, unskilled laborers, tenant farmers, or domestic servants tend to drop out in much larger percentages, while children with parents engaged in professions or business tend to stay on until graduation. One of the apparent causes behind a considerable number of dropouts is financial inability to dress as well as the average student, to meet the incidental expenses of school life, and be accepted by fellow students.

Adolescent sons and daughters of fairly recent immigrants from Latin American countries tend to drop out in large proportion, particularly those living in congested slum areas.

Dropouts also occur in larger numbers in rural areas, especially where poor school facilities are provided, although this difference is disappearing. It is interesting to note that, among Negroes, the percentage of dropouts in rural areas of southern states is several times that of Negroes in urban areas of northern and western states.

Students who belong to three or all four of the above groups are almost certain not to complete high school, and those who do to constitute a serious disciplinary problem.

Developing in the 1940's and reaching a peak in the late 1950's there has been a material increase in the number of young people being married while still in school. Various actions have been taken by school boards relative to the place of married students, some boards going so far as to exclude them. More commonly, boards of education, upon the recommendation of the superintendent of schools, approve legislation barring married students from the usual extracurricular activities. Even this restriction has met with serious criticism, and there has been a slight trend away from it.

In the 1960's, there has been a decline in the percentage of young people being married while teen-agers. The glamor built up in the minds of adolescent boys and girls and stimulated and exaggerated unduly by conversations with young married students has given way sharply before the realization of the actual facts. Even though both boys and girls have been able to obtain employment enabling them to make a living, they have often found it exceedingly difficult to get permanent positions. Youngsters may begin to arrive, forcing the mother to give up work and become heavily burdened with household duties. These couples have been more or less forced to withdraw to a large extent from social life, and many of them have been able to manage financially only with the assistance of parents, which leads to misunderstandings and alienations; many have actually gone on relief and, in consequence, felt disgraced. Statistics show that the proportion of divorces is definitely higher among those who marry as teen-agers.

**Helping Potential Dropouts.** Using experimental and control groups of potential dropouts in a selected high school, Donald A. Davis, Associate Professor of Education, Western Michigan University, Kalamazoo, conducted a study in order to determine effects of special attention, establishment of friendly relations with students by teachers and counselors, invitation of consultants to discuss delinquency and dropout problems with staff and personnel, field trips, and holding of formal and informal counseling interviews with the students. He found that when these measures are implemented systematically in a school, students tend to be less likely to drop out, tend to get higher marks, and tend to be referred less often to the office for disciplinary reasons (usually of a less severe nature than those that would ordinarily occur). A report of this study appears in the May, 1962, issue of the *Personnel and Guidance Journal.*

**Suggestions for Senior High School.** Although a definitive statement on this point must await further evidence, it seems that continuous contact between school and out-of-school youths is one of the keys to increasing the number who eventually finish high school. In effect, continuous contact avoids closing the door and encourages those who leave to return.

An experimental model for the high school level should take account of the fact that many potential dropouts are alienated from the rest of the school population. Many high schools receive pupils from junior high and elementary schools in which there has been no special attempt to foster the social acceptance and participation of the potential dropout. A special program in the high school is also required to supply the curriculum content specifically needed by these youths.

The staff of a special program should be encouraged to create a new curriculum which would reject many of the conventional courses in order to include such content and such experience as are shown by experimentation to meet the special needs of potential dropouts. This new curriculum must span all years of possible enrolment, and it should incorporate day-by-day inventions as these occur. Essential provisions of this new curriculum, if its objectives are founded upon the major adult roles the youth will fill, include:

1. Continuous individual and small-group work with basic academic skills, particularly reading, writing, speaking, and in such fields as science, mathematics, and the social studies.
2. Vigorous attempts to adapt the materials developed by the outstanding curriculum-improvement projects to the needs and abilities of the potential dropouts (Possible materials to be adapted are the mathematics courses of the University of Illinois Committee on School Mathematics [UICSM] and those of the School of Mathematics Study Group [SMSG], as well as the science courses developed by the Physical Science Study Committee, the Chemical Bonds Approach Committee, and the Biological Sciences Curriculum Study. While most of these courses were originally planned for students with above-average academic aptitude, a few bold and creative teachers have taken advantage of the ways

in which these courses have been made understandable to boys and girls, and have used parts of the courses with average and below-average students. Thus, some evidence has been developed to indicate that being able to discover some of the basic content for himself may be extremely useful and valuable for the student with low academic aptitude.)

3. Work experience in the community, with emphasis on job responsibilities
4. Vocational training in those skills that occupational surveys indicate will be in national demand in the future, which may imply somewhat less attention to future local demands, though these must not be ignored
5. Preparation for family living

## QUESTIONS, PROBLEMS, AND TOPICS FOR FURTHER STUDY

1. In the teaching of your major subject, what type of individual difference among students do you think is the most important?
2. In teaching your major subject, would you be in favor of grouping students according to their ability? What are your arguments pro and con? How would you select the students to go in the bright group and those to go in the slow group? Where would you get your information?
3. Do you believe in allowing a bright student to finish high school a year or two younger? What are the arguments pro and con? Which arguments impress you most?
4. Do you think that a bright student should carry more subjects than the average student?
5. What do you think are the four most important things to keep in mind in teaching a bright student?
6. Do you believe that a bright student should be permitted to take classes ordinarily offered to students in higher grades?
7. Do you believe that a slow student is more seriously stigmatized and discouraged by being classified in a slow section or by being in a section with average and bright students?
8. Make six or seven of what you think are the best suggestions for teaching a dull student.
9. In recent years there has been much concern about dropouts. Do you think it is important that all students complete high school? Why or why not?
10. What do you think the school ought to do with respect to the students who are likely to leave school before finishing?
11. List in their order of importance five factors causing students to withdraw from school.

## SUPPLEMENTARY MATERIALS

### SELECTED READINGS

ANDERSON, LESTER W., J. E. FERGUSON, and STEWART B. ATKINSON. "How To Modify the Curriculum To Benefit the Academically Talented Student," *Bulletin of the N.A.S.S.P.*, No. 263 (April, 1961), 243–47.

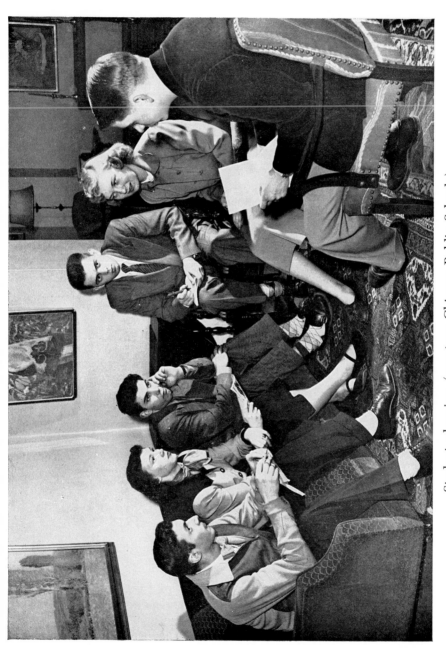

Student planning (courtesy Chicago Public Schools).

Tape recording for hard of hearing—Syracuse, New York.

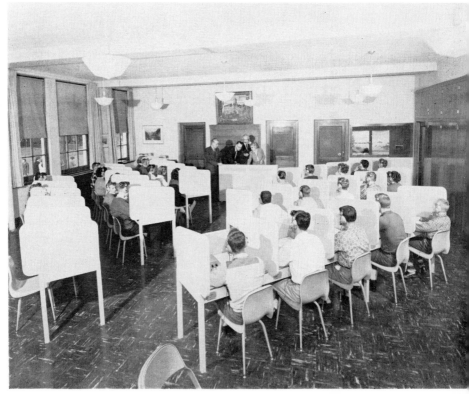

A modern language laboratory makes possible group or individual instruction and recitation (Dwight D. Eisenhower High School, Blue Island, Ill.).

ANDERSON, VERNON E., and WILLIAM T. GRUHN. *Principles and Practices of Secondary Education* (2d ed.). New York: The Ronald Press Co., 1962. Chapter 10, "Provision for Special Interests and Talents"; Chapter 11, "Quality Programs for the Individual."

APPLEBAUM, M. J. "A Survey of Special Provisions for the Education of Academically Superior Pupils," *Bulletin of the N.A.S.S.P.,* No. 249 (October, 1959), 26–43.

ARBOLINO, J. N. "What's Wrong with the Advanced Placement Program?" *Bulletin of the N.A.S.S.P.,* No. 261 (February, 1961), 28–31.

BAXTER, JOSEPH R., and REGINALD L. JONES. "Principals Comment on a Program for the Acceleration of Superior High-School Students," *Bulletin of the N.A.S.S.P.,* No. 267 (December, 1961), 1–9.

BISH, CHARLES E., and MINNIS GILLILAND. "A Program for the Academically Talented in Science," *Bulletin of the N.A.S.S.P.,* No. 259 (December, 1960), 138–44.

BONAWIT, DOROTHY, and IVINS WILSON. "How Can the Senior High School Best Provide for the Academically Talented Student?" *Bulletin of the N.A.S.S.P.,* No. 247 (April, 1959), 24–28.

BROCK, C. A., DAVE FITZPATRICK, A. W. MASTIN, and M. E. NORTHAN. "How Can the Junior High School Provide Quality Education for the Academically Talented Students?" *Bulletin of the N.A.S.S.P.,* No. 253 (February, 1960), 139–45.

BROWN, B. FRANK. "The Non-graded School," *Bulletin of the N.A.S.S.P.,* No. 280 (May, 1963), 64–72.

CHAFFEE, EVERETT. "Programs for the Gifted in California Secondary Schools," *Bulletin of the N.A.S.S.P.,* No. 253 (February, 1960), 110–14.

CONANT, JAMES B. "Development of Talent in Europe and the U.S.," *North Central Association Quarterly,* XXIV (April, 1962), 265–72.

CUONY, E. R. "Integration for Educable Mentally Retarded Pupils in the Junior High School," *Bulletin of the N.A.S.S.P.,* No. 258 (November, 1960), 87–90.

DOUGLASS, HARL R. *Trends and Issues in Secondary Education.* Washington, D.C.: The Center for Applied Research in Education, Inc., 1962. Chapter 7, "Adapting Instruction to the Individual."

*Education and the Disadvantaged American.* Washington, D.C.: Educational Policies Commission, 1962.

FAUNCE, ROLAND C., and MORREL J. CLUTE. *Teaching and Learning in the Junior High School.* San Francisco: Wadsworth Publishing Co., Inc., 1961. Chapter 8, "Learning Through Individual Exploration."

FRANSETH, JANE. "Does Grouping Make a Difference?" *The Educational Digest,* January, 1963, 15–17.

GRAMBS, JEAN D., WILLIAM J. IVERSON, and FRANKLIN K. PATTERSON. *Modern Methods in Secondary Education.* New York: Holt, Rinehart & Winston, Inc., 1958. Chapter 13, "Slow and Fast Learners."

HANSEN, KENNETH H. *High School Teaching.* Englewood Cliffs, N.J.: Prentice-Hall, Inc., 1957. Chapter 10, "Diagnosing Common Learning Difficulties."

HARNLY, PAUL W., and HARRY D. LOVELASS. "How Have Summer Schools Been Used To Enrich the Educational Program for the Academically Talented?" *Bulletin of the N.A.S.S.P.,* No. 247 (April, 1959), 182–86.

HARRIS, RAYMOND P. *American Education.* New York: Random House, Inc., 1962. Chapter 10, "The Happy Plight of the Gifted Child."

HOWELL, WALLACE J. "Grouping of Talented Students Leads to Better Achievement in the Secondary School," *Bulletin of the N.A.S.S.P.,* No. 270 (March, 1962), 67–73.

JONES, LEWIS WADE. "The Social Unreadiness of Negro Youth," *The Saturday Review,* October 20, 1962.

JONES, REGINALD L., and JOSEPH R. BAXTER. "Parent Views on the Acceleration of Superior High School Students," *Bulletin of the N.A.S.S.P.,* No. 270 (March, 1962), 24–28.

KEMENY, JOHN G. "The Mathematically Talented Student," *Bulletin of the N.A.S.S.P.,* No. 279 (April, 1963), 26–40.

KOHLER, MARY CONWAY, and ANDRE FONTAINE. "Drop-Outs: The Children Nobody Wants," *The Education Digest,* XXVIII (October, 1962), 35–38.

LEESE, JOSEPH. "Creativity and Academic Excellence—Incompatible?" *Bulletin of the N.A.S.S.P.,* No. 267 (December, 1961), 113–21.

LEESE, JOSEPH. "Individualizing Programs in the Junior High School," *Bulletin of the N.A.S.S.P.,* No. 267 (December, 1961), 113–21.

LORETAN, JOSEPH O. "Individualizing Programs in the Junior High School," *Bulletin of the N.A.S.S.P.,* No. 269 (February, 1962), 50–66.

MARTIN, HOWELL C. "A Defensible Plan for Promotion," *Bulletin of the N.A.S.S.P.,* No. 280 (March, 1962), 63–66.

MEADE, MARY E., H. C. CAMPBELL, and R. K. SORENSON, "The Case for and Against Multiple High-School Diplomas," *Bulletin of the N.A.S.S.P.,* No. 263 (April, 1961), 29–33.

MERSAND, JOSEPH. "Individualizing Instruction in Large and Small Classes," *Bulletin of the N.A.S.S.P.,* No. 254 (March, 1960), 111–23.

NEWTON, D. E. "Curricular and Instructional Practices for Superior Students," *Bulletin of the N.A.S.S.P.,* No. 261 (February, 1961), 23–27.

NOALL, MATTHEW F., and MAURICE NUTTALL. "Hurricane, Utah, High School Ungraded English Project," *Bulletin of the N.A.S.S.P.,* No. 258 (January, 1962), 185–93.

PUNKE, HAROLD H. "Ability Grouping as Individual-Group Relationship," *Phi Delta Kappan,* XLIII (June, 1962), 16–40.

SALARIO, MORRIS. "The Mentally Handicapped Child in High School," *The Education Digest,* XXVI (September, 1960), 45–47.

SCHREIBER, DANIEL. "The School Dropout: Fugitive from Failure," *Bulletin of the N.A.S.S.P.,* No. 272 (May, 1962), 233–41.

SHAW, M. C., and J. T. McCUEN. "Onset of Academic Underachievement in Bright Children," *Journal of Educational Psychology,* LI (June, 1960), 103–8.

SILVERMAN, HIRSCH LAZAAR. "Educational 'Unadaptives' and the Schools," *Bulletin of the N.A.S.S.P.,* No. 241 (October, 1958), 129–33.

STILES, LINDLEY, EARL McCLEARY, and ROY TURNBAUGH. *Secondary Education in the United States.* New York: Harcourt, Brace & World, Inc., 1962. Chapter 7, "Discovering and Developing Talent"; Chapter 17, "Challenging the Gifted Student"; Chapter 18, "Providing Educationally for the Handicapped."

STIMSON, PAUL, and PAUL PETRICH. "How Can Students Best Be Grouped for Teaching and Learning?" *Bulletin of the N.A.S.S.P.,* No. 275 (September, 1962), 78–90.

TOMPKINS, ELLSWORTH. "Individual Differences in the 1960's—Their Implications for School Administrators," *Bulletin of the N.A.S.S.P.,* No. 271 (April, 1962), 1–6.

WAKEFIELD, ROBERT. "Work Experience for the Mentally Retarded in Santa Monica," *Bulletin of the N.A.S.S.P.*, No. 271 (April, 1962), 217–21.
WATTS, MRS. Y. C. "A Study of High School Failure," *Bulletin of the N.A.S.S.P.*, No. 249 (October, 1959), 69–75.
ZENNER, E. A. "High School Honor Courses," *The Catholic School Journal*, LIX (May, 1958), 80–81.

## AUDIO-VISUAL MATERIALS

### Films

*Challenge of the Gifted.* McGraw-Hill Text-Film. 11 minutes.
*Grouping Students for Effective Learning.* Bel-Mort Films, Inc., Portland, Ore. 44 frames, color, captions.
*Individual Differences.* McGraw-Hill Text-Film. 23 minutes.
*Learning to Understand Children: A Diagnostic Approach.* McGraw-Hill. 21 minutes.
*Learning to Understand Children: Part II—A Remedial Program.* McGraw-Hill Text-Film. 23 minutes.
*Problem of Pupil Adjustment: Part I—The Dropout.* McGraw-Hill. 20 minutes.
*Problem of Pupil Adjustment: Part II—The Stay-in.* McGraw-Hill. 19 minutes.
*The Gifted Ones.* International Film Bureau. Chicago, Ill. 20 minutes.

### Recording

*Providing for Individual Differences in the Classroom,* #213. William C. Trow. Educational Growth Series. Educational Recording Services. Los Angeles, Calif. 36-44-minute discussion, 33⅓ rpm.

# 16

# Evaluating and Reporting Student Growth

## NATURE AND OBJECTIVES OF EVALUATING PROGRESS

**Evaluation and the Objectives of Teaching.** One of the very important and most difficult and hazardous responsibilities of the classroom teacher is the measurement and evaluation of the degree to which the students have grown toward the objectives of the teaching. The teacher needs to measure as far as possible the acquisition of the desired information, understanding, skills, habits, interests, attitudes, and ideals, and to evaluate what changes have taken place in the pupil with respect to the degree of attainment of the objectives of teaching. Evaluation includes not only measurement but also the process of judging the value of the growth that has taken place.

In selecting a standard test or constructing a test, the teacher should always use as the principal criterion the degree to which scores on the test will represent the growth or status of the pupils with respect to the principal objectives of the courses. Ideally and logically, the evaluation of student growth should start from the objectives of secondary education and move from there toward the ways by which data may be gathered and evaluated to reveal the progress made by the student toward those objectives. This must be done under any circumstances, but the teacher also needs to know what progress has been made toward the objectives of the particular course.

**Purposes of Measurement and Evaluation.** The major purposes of measurement and evaluation of student growth are to

1. Prepare a report to the student and the parents concerning the growth that has been made

2. Diagnose students' learning difficulties
3. Stimulate students' learning
4. Place students in grades or classes
5. Group students for better teaching
6. Predict students' future performance
7. Form a basis for marking and promotion
8. Diagnose teaching difficulties
9. Measure the results of teaching
10. Furnish a basis for guidance and counseling

**Types of Data Used in Evaluation.** The careful teacher employs a variety of types of data in determining what information, understanding, skills, habits, interests, ideals, and attitudes have been developed as the result of a student's learning experiences in the teacher's class. Among them are the following:

1. Observations of the student's performance in class and elsewhere
2. Evaluations of the student's written work in class or outside of class
3. Results of written tests the student has taken
4. Recorded observations of the quality of the student's responses in class in oral quizzes, discussions, reports, etc.
5. Quality of completed projects such as things made in the shop, things prepared in the home-economics laboratory, or typewritten exercises
6. Self-evaluation of the student through questionnaires, check lists, or interviews by the teacher

**Self-evaluation.** Among the techniques most commonly employed by teachers for obtaining self-evaluation by students is a check list prepared by the teacher and the class, with ratings of, let us say, A, B, C, D, and E, or 1, 2, 3, 4, and 5, or Excellent, Very Good, Good, Fair, and Poor on each of the points in the check list. These points have to do with various types of accomplishment and growth that the instructor considers worthwhile and likely to result from the teaching and learning activities for a given time.

A second type involves an essay to be written by the student and handed in to the teacher, containing a statement of what the student thinks he has gained from his learning activities—the growth that he thinks he has made in understanding, skills, ideals, etc.

Important values are attributed by many educators to the use of self-evaluations of students in secondary school classes. Among the more important of these are the following: (1) It reduces the degree to which evaluation is imposed from outside and, therefore, may be somewhat difficult to accept; consequently, it tends to improve both the relationship between the student and the teacher and the student's attitude toward evaluation. (2) Valuable training in self-analysis is given that will carry over into out-of-school life at present and in the future. (3) It develops useful attitudes and skills in evaluation.

## USE OF OBJECTIVE TESTS

"Objective" Tests. Most teachers employ what have come to be called "objective" tests, although no test is completely objective. Two or more competent people might disagree as to which is the correct answer to many so-called objective questions or exercises. The types of test exercises most commonly employed are the true-false, multiple-choice or best-answer, matching, completion, enumeration, and comparative enumeration exercises.

Following is an example of each of these types of test items:

(1) True-False
The Constitution of the United States sets forth the exact number of justices necessary for the Supreme Court...........Yes....No....

(2) Multiple-Choice, or Best-Answer
( ) A chief characteristic of the novel is (1) humorous passages, (2) portrayal of character, (3) historical facts, (4) fairy element.

(3) Matching

| | |
|---|---|
| 1. Tint | _____ Darker than normal color brightness |
| 2. Shade | |
| 3. Normal | _____ The strength of a color |
| 4. Intensity | _____ Lighter than normal color |
| 5. Value | _____ Color at full strength |
| 6. Hue | _____ The name of a color |
| 7. Triad | _____ Harmony based on one color |
| 8. Analogous Colors | _____ Degree of light or dark |
| 9. Monochromatic Colors | _____ Opposite colors |
| 10. Complementary Colors | _____ Three colors equally distant on color wheel |
| | _____ Three colors related with a common hue |
| | _____ The grayness of a color |

(4) Completion
Our national government derives its authority from the _____
_____ of the United States through our national _____.

(5) Enumeration
The names of the primary colors on the color chart are:
(a) _____, (b) _____, and (c) _____.

(6) Comparative Enumeration
What were the three most important reasons for the Confederacy to win the War Between the States?
1. _____
2. _____
3. _____

With the development of teachers' skill in test construction, there is less need to use "standard" tests prepared and distributed by outside agencies. However, they are still used in secondary school classrooms, principally to compare the achievements of the students with the achievements of students in other classes or other schools. A "standard" test is one to be used in many schools and for which are available data relative to the performance of a carefully selected nationwide sample of students. Such "norms" are usually in terms of the median or of percentiles of the group upon which the test was standardized.

**Standard Achievement Tests.** Standard achievement tests—tests for which standards have been established on a national basis—may, if properly interpreted, be of much value, though they possess the following serious limitations:

1. The achievement tests now available do not measure all the outcomes of teaching. They measure best factual knowledge and skill. They are least adapted to measuring more subtle outcomes such as appreciations or attitudes, though a few attempts have been made to devise tests for measuring these outcomes.

2. Standard achievement tests may not be well adapted to the objectives of the subject matter taught in a course, in which case they are not valid measures of pupil growth or teacher effectiveness.

3. If teachers coach classes so as to produce good results on a test, the results cannot be considered valid. Such instruction may lead to undue emphasis on certain material or outcomes in a course, especially upon factual materials.

4. Since standard achievement tests are based on present practices in curriculum content, too great emphasis upon the measurement by them of the work of students, teachers, or the school may lead to limiting of progress because of fear of lowering test results if new materials or methods are tried.

5. Maladministration of the tests, or errors in securing or computing the results, will lead to erroneous conclusions.

In interpreting standard test scores, it should be borne in mind that the scores are to some degree determined by:

1. Intelligence of the students
2. Socioeconomic-cultural environment of the students
3. Maturity of the students
4. Relative emphasis in teaching

It is especially important to keep these factors in mind when comparing the scores of different classes or schools.

**Procedures for Constructing Objective Tests.** The following are suggested procedures that teachers have found to be valuable in the construction of tests:

1. Decide first what types of growth you wish the test to measure.
2. Decide upon the amount of time the test should consume, and be certain that the test does not require time in excess of that amount.
3. Formulate, as far as possible, test items that will measure something more than memory—judgment and discrimination, comparison, evaluation, summarization, etc.
4. Include some items that all pupils might be expected to answer, as well as some that only few can answer, thus giving opportunity for the least able and the ablest students to register their growth.
5. Review the test items very carefully, reading them over several times to avoid ambiguous or misleading statements.
6. Arrange the remaining exercises into groups by types, that is, the true-false exercises together, the multiple-choice together, etc. Within this arrangement, put the items in order of difficulty.
7. Give special attention to where the answers should be placed, preferably along the right-hand margin so as to facilitate scoring.
8. Prepare a key of correct answers to be laid alongside the pupil's paper and thus permit rapid scoring. Cardboard is useful for this purpose. In preparing the key, some questions may arise that will result in changing some of the items.

**Administering Objective Tests.** Objective tests are usually mimeographed so that each pupil may have his own copy; to copy the exercise from the board requires too much time. In giving tests, the instructor should keep uppermost in mind that he wishes to get a good measure of the growth of his pupils toward the objectives of the course, not to measure ability to work under stress or to work rapidly. An atmosphere of quiet and relaxation should prevail as far as possible.

A number of suggestions for administration of tests are worthy of consideration. A spirit of confusion or hurry is to be avoided. Ordinarily, rate tests or time-basis tests are not advisable. Instructions should be very brief, in most instances consisting only of a few sentences, and should appear on the test sheets. Questions from the students while the examination is in progress should be answered individually and sparingly. Painstaking care should be taken to prevent cheating.

**Announced vs. Unannounced Tests.** One feature of the examination system in many high schools is the short unannounced quiz. Some teachers think this type of test is valuable in that it tends to ensure more careful preparation of the daily assignment. The results of the test can be used also as a check on the pupils' preparation. The unannounced quiz should be limited to the daily or other short-term assignment. In the event the teacher uses this type of test, he should inform the pupils that he intends to use it, at the beginning of the course. One of the chief disadvantages of the unannounced quiz is that the opportunity of systematic review is lost.

Ordinarily an announced quiz should require only a small part of the class period. The teaching value of this type of test can be enhanced by pupil participation in scoring of the papers and discussion of the results.

## USE OF ESSAY EXAMINATIONS

For many years there has been controversy about the relative merits of essay examinations. Following is an excellent statement of the claims, pro and con.

**Advantages.** Advantages of the essay test include the following:

1. The essay examination, if carefully prepared, can place emphasis upon the students' ability to use knowledge rather than merely to retain it. The examination questions provide situations wherein students may organize ideas, summarize data, identify the most important facts, apply knowledge to the solution of a problem, creatively combine ideas, and the like. Pupils are required to recall pertinent information and use it in writing their answers.

2. Teachers may secure insight into the thinking of the students, for the answer to a discussion question usually is a record of this thinking. Points at which the material is incorrectly understood, misinterpretations, and gaps in knowledge are examples of the sort of learning problems that are likely to be revealed.

3. The use of essay tests helps to promote a certain type of study habit. The best preparation for discussion questions requires intensive rather than extensive study. For most objective examinations, the students are likely to skim everything they have on the subject—lecture notes, papers, textbooks. Essay tests encourage the making of outlines, summaries, comparisons, contrasts, and lists of principles, as well as the identification of central ideas and concepts. They really constitute a particular approach to study.

4. The essay examination tends to eliminate guessing.

5. Essay examinations are easier to prepare, though really good essay tests require much time and careful planning. Any good test question is difficult to formulate, and, of course, essay tests include fewer questions than objective tests. The questions do not have to be duplicated, although the practice of writing the questions on the board might place

some handicap on students in the back of the room who must squint or possibly come forward to copy them down.

**Limitations.** Possible disadvantages include the following:

1. An essay examination is not usually a *comprehensive* test of subject matter. The practice in most high schools is to give the essay test in a single class period. This means that the teacher can only narrowly sample the classwork which was covered. Actually, six to ten questions, unless they are so broad that each would require the bulk of the period to answer, cannot sample the learning except to a limited degree.

2. Factors other than the actual test questions come into play in grading essay examinations. Spelling, handwriting, grammatical construction, and neatness often enhance the "halo" effect when teachers allow the appearance of the paper to influence the grade. The essay overemphasizes the importance of knowing how to say a thing, as opposed to having something to say. Both ability to distribute time wisely and skill in writing concisely are often very important to success. If a student does not complete an essay test because he spends his time on the first few questions and simply does not have time to answer the last ones, the grade, which presumably communicates something regarding achievement has been diluted to some degree; it may reflect ineptness in test taking rather than poor achievement.

3. Essay examinations are especially affected by subjective factors in grading. The teacher's physical and mental state, his attitudes toward the subject, and his conscious feelings toward the students all affect the way he grades. Teachers find, unless special precautions are taken, that they are inconsistent in their grading. The grade for one paper may be affected by the grade of an immediately preceding paper. A C paper may be given a B, if it follows an F paper; if it follows an A+ paper, it may receive a D. Moreover, as teachers read down through a pile of papers, the standards for the grades they give tend to rise as time passes.

4. The time factor in scoring essay examinations is an important disadvantage. In fact, the additional expenditure of time and energy over that needed for scoring objective tests is so serious a limitation that the use of essay examinations can be justified only if it can be shown that the values realized are commensurate with this investment. Nevertheless, if essay questions are used because of their real advantages and with proper recognition of their limitations, the time required for grading may be worthwhile.[1]

---

[1] This discussion of the advantages and disadvantages of essay tests has been adapted from Robert C. McKean, *Principles and Methods in Secondary Education* (Columbus, Ohio: Charles E. Merrill Books, Inc., 1962), pp. 189–191.

**Types of Essay Questions.** There are several types of essay-test items. They vary principally with respect to the type of reaction the instructor wishes to test. Among the question types are the following:

1. Discussion: "Discuss the early settlements in Virginia."
2. Description: "Describe the physical characteristics of New England."
3. Explanation: "Explain the process involved in preparing diphtheria serum."
4. Narration: "Trace the course of the explorations of the American continent."
5. Evaluation (including criticism): "Point out the weak points and strong points in the Articles of Confederation."

**Preparation.** The quality of an essay examination is largely dependent upon the amount of attention and skill devoted to the following principles and suggestions in devising the exercises:

1. Select topics that, when together, constitute a good sample of the more important sections of the course area the examination is intended to cover.

2. In stating the topic and the instructions for dealing with it, be specific and clear; for example, if pupils are asked to "criticize," they should be told upon what basis or with respect to what. Frequently, there should be subordinate or supplementary instructions. Rarely if ever should students be asked to "Tell what you know about . . ."

3. State each question or make each statement so as to measure something besides recall of information, such as understanding of the information, its importance, its implications, etc.

4. Word each question or topic so that the students will be likely to write their answers in sections or parts in response to the different points to be discussed.

5. Estimate the time required by a slow student to write out an excellent answer to the question, and indicate that amount of time in parentheses after the question.

6. Try the questions out on some disinterested person to see if they will be clearly and accurately understood.

7. Attempt to keep at a minimum the time required for writing answers. It is of great value in essay examinations to call for concise answers so that more questions may be asked. Skilled test makers do this well.

8. The questions should be such as will permit objective scoring as far as possible. This is achieved by planning questions in the manner suggested in item 4 above. Questions so planned can be scored against an inventory of the parts required in a perfect answer.

## MEASUREMENT OF UNDERSTANDING AND ATTITUDES

One of the great improvements in measurement and evaluation in recent years has been along the lines of better techniques and ideas for the measurement of understanding.

**Types of Data for Evaluating Understandings, Interests, and Attitude.** In discussions by specialists of measurement of understanding in various subject fields, not only are the more conventional types of tests—true-false, multiple-choice, completion, enumeration, matching, essay, etc.—discussed and illustrated as instruments for measuring undestanding, but others not so commonly used are also discussed and illustrated. Among the latter may be mentioned:

Class opinions of work done by fellow pupils
Systematic and recorded observations of pupil attitudes and behavior
Records showing extent and choice of reading and music listening
Self-appraisals
Check lists of interests and activities
Interviews with pupils and parents
Health-examination records and reports from physicians, dentists, and
    nurses
Diaries
Samples of creative work
Records of participation in out-of-school activities
Ratings by self and by fellows, often involving score cards
Observation of pupils at work, at play, and at study
Pupils' comments on plays, fiction, music, and clothing
Analysis of family situations
Examination of laboratory notes, records, and reports
Watching pupils operate machines requiring judgment and understanding
    of principles
Having students draw and explain diagrams or graphs
Having students make explanations, describe operations, and demonstrate
    principles in class and on paper
Use of diagrams in prepared tests

**Measurement of Attitude.** The simplest form of attitude test is a list of stimulus words. The pupil is asked to underline each word that he does not like or that bothers or disturbs him.

| | |
|---|---|
| Sunday School | Communist |
| Germany | War |
| Cigarette | Soldier |
| Republican | Invasion |
| Alcohol | Strike |
| Democrat | Peace |
| Russia | Mob |
| Capitalist | Negro |
| Labor union | Black market |
| Socialist | OPA |

On attitude scales used at the upper-grade levels, the pupil often is asked to check for each item or statement the one of five responses that states most accurately how he himself feels about it: Strongly agree. Agree. Undecided. Disagree. Strongly disagree.

No group should be ridiculed because of its religious practices. (Tolerance)
A school strike would be a good way to protest against an undesirable school regulation (School rules)
A student should pick up another student's waste paper without being asked by the teacher. (School responsibility)
No one should be expected to pay attention in class to anything that is uninteresting. (Courtesy)
A difficult task should be worked out by a group of students. (Cooperation)
The chance to attend a school party thrills me. (Social participation)

**Test To Measure Ability To Interpret Relationships.**

Example: The students in a health class were studying the number of hours of sleep needed by boys and girls. One student brought in the table below, showing the number of hours of sleep needed at several different ages. The students noticed some definite relationships between pairs of numbers.

| Age | 6 | 8 | 10 | 12 | 14 | 16 |
|-----|---|---|----|----|----|----|
| No. of Hours | 14 | 13 | 12 | 11 | 10 | 9 |

Directions: Study the table and the statements below. Suppose the facts stated in the table are true. If you agree with a statement that follows, put A on the line by the statement. If you disagree with a statement, put D on the line. If you can neither agree nor disagree but are uncertain, put U on the line by the statement.

_____ (1) As the age increases from 6 to 16, the number of hours of sleep needed decreases.
_____ (2) The number of hours of sleep needed at any age is greater than the age.
_____ (3) In this table the ratio of the number of hours of sleep to the age is constant.
_____ (4) A 4-year-old should have 15 hours of sleep.
_____ (5) A 12-year-old only needs about half as much sleep as a 6-year-old.
_____ (6) From age 6 to age 16, for every 2 years that your age increases you need one hour less sleep.
_____ (7) A person 30 years old needs very few hours of sleep.
_____ (8) If the number of hours of sleep needed is subtracted from 17, the result is half the age.

**Comprehensive Measurement.** It should be emphasized that the teacher is obligated not only to measure the acquisition of facts, ideas, and concepts but also to attempt to evaluate the extent to which growth has taken place in all areas of objectives, including skills, appreciations, attitudes, interests, etc. Too often, teachers begin and end their evaluation of students by testing for memory of factual information and thus base the students' grades on but a portion of the learning sought by the teacher and achieved by the students.

In addition to devices and procedures already described in this chapter, check lists and rating scales may be employed to advantage, especially in connection with evaluating oral reports, term papers, objects constructed, musical performances, or works of art or creative writing.[2]

## DIAGNOSTIC TESTING

**Devising Diagnostic Tests.** Since there are relatively few standard diagnostic tests available and really useful for high school use, it is necessary that teachers learn to construct diagnostic tests for their own use. The steps in constructing a diagnostic test are

1. Analyze the ability, skill, or other learning to be tested into its smallest component units or parts.
2. Devise test items to measure the learning in each of these subordinate units.
3. Select a sufficient number of items for each of the subordinate units to measure accurately the students' ability to perform correctly in each of these units, in order to be sure that errors on each item are recurring errors due to faulty learning and not chance errors due to inattention, accidents, or a similar cause.
4. Combine the items into a test, keeping together those items that measure each subordinate unit.

**Use of Diagnostic-Test Data.** Failure to know how to recognize the causes of students' difficulties in learning is often the cause of teachers' inability to use diagnostic tests satisfactorily. There are many causes of failure to learn, among them being deficiency in some fundamental knowledge or skill, insufficient practice, improper methods of work, physical defects, special disability in a particular subject, lack of interest, and factors in the home background or environment. Diagnostic subject-matter tests will reveal only those causes of failure to learn that are related to subject matter.

Teachers must be taught to supplement their diagnostic subject-matter tests by information from other sources. Intelligence-test scores will furnish evidence of the students' intellectual level, and the school records will contain a large amount of valuable data concerning home back-

[2] See Hubert H. Mills and Harl R. Douglass, *Teaching in High School* (2d ed.) (New York: The Ronald Press Co., 1957), Chapter 21.

ground and physical characteristics. Observation of students by the teachers, to obtain information concerning study habits, sensory or motor defects, attitudes, interests, environmental influences, and similar factors affecting performance, will provide additional data valuable for diagnosis.

Teachers should not fail to recognize that, while good diagnosis of the weaknesses of groups of twenty to thirty students may be made on the basis of a single item in a test, and while good diagnosis of the general weakness of an individual may be made from his total score on a unit of ten or more test times, a diagnosis of a single individual on the basis of less than ten test items is more than likely to be unreliable and misleading.

## CURRENT MARKING PRACTICES

In assigning marks to examination papers, many teachers employ a numerical system in which a certain number of points are allowed for each correct answer and the score on a particular paper is the total of those points, which may be one hundred or more or less, depending on the test. The numerical scores are then converted into letter marks. Thinking of a numerical mark as a percentage of perfection has all but disappeared. Many teachers assign a number of points for the most satisfactory answer to a particular exercise or question and partial scores for answers that have merit but fall somewhat short of the most satisfactory answer.

After a considerable amount of experimentation, secondary school teachers rather generally employ a point marking system, such as A, B, C, D, and E or F, for marks to be recorded on reports to parents instead of the numerical percentage system or the plan of using only two marks, S for satisfactory and U for unsatisfactory, while received considerable attention.

In making up a final mark to be entered on the report cards for a given subject, the teacher very frequently employs a variety of data, as was indicated earlier in this chapter, and rarely bases the report on written examinations alone.

**Assigning Marks in Accord with the Normal Probability Phenomenon.** After a period of rather unintelligent and mechanical following and, indeed, often misinterpretation of what was called the "normal probability," or "curve," system of marking, many teachers abandoned it. But in recent years there has been a slight trend toward a return to that practice.

The theory of probability is based upon the results of observations of the traits of large numbers of unselected human beings. These observations reveal that, in the measurement of any trait, when many cases are involved, the scores are distributed much as in the figure below.

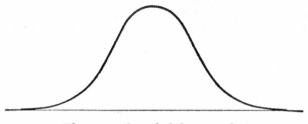

The normal probability graph.

It will be observed that a large number of cases cluster around the average and that a steadily decreasing number are found as the extremes are approached. Since the results of accurate measures of the school achievement of unselected groups of children tend to be distributed according to the normal probability curve, it seemed logical to make a somewhat comparable distribution of marks. But it should always be borne in mind that, in a small group, achievement is unlikely to be distributed in a manner closely resembling normal probability. The teacher should use considered judgment in deciding in what way and to what extent the group achievements being marked are "normal" or "abnormal." Teachers who consistently give a preponderance of high marks, and those who give a large percentage of low marks, are usually regarded with suspicion, and both parents and students are misled by the reports from such teachers.

**Rewarding Effort.** Much has been said in recent years in favor of evaluating students' progress in terms of their estimated potentialities rather than by comparison of their achievement with that of other students in the class. It is impossible for some children, no matter how hard they try, to do as well as the abler students or even as well as the average student in the class. A great amount of effort on their part is often rewarded by a grade that is relative to the achievement of other youngsters but that is no better than a C or some corresponding mark of mediocre achievement. Furthermore, bright youngsters are able to achieve a high mark with relatively less effort and, what is also important, without using their full potentialities.

As a means of rewarding effort and informing parents of the degree of effort expended by the student, a dual marking system in one form or another is employed in a large and increasing number of schools. In some instances, sets of marks are given in each subject, one for absolute achievement or achievement relative to other youngsters in the class, and the other in terms of the degree of the student's achievement in proportion to his estimated potentialities. For example, a student of average intelligence who achieves slightly better than the average student in the class might receive a B for achievement and a A for effort, whereas a youngster of outstanding scholastic ability with the same achievement should probably receive a mark of C or even D for effort.

## REPORTING TO STUDENTS AND PARENTS

The practice has developed of sending reports to the homes of pupils at less frequent intervals, for example, at the end of semesters and at mid-semesters. Monthly report cards have all but disappeared. There has been developing in recent years a feeling that parents are entitled to a much more comprehensive report about the progress of their sons and daughters in school than a report "card" on which has been entered a grade for each subject. To bring this about there have been several trends:

1. Use of report forms with a considerable number of places for marks, rather than just one or two for each subject
2. A place on the form for written comments
3. Sending home from time to time short notes about the student
4. Conferences with the parents at school, at home, or on the telephone, which may cover a great many things including exchange of information between the parent and the teacher that may be very useful to both
5. A report form or slip from each teacher
6. Conferences with groups of interested parents, in which explanations are made relative to standards for marks, questions of parents are discussed, and an effort is made to cause parents to attach less importance to grades

The parent or student, or both, might well read into a conventional, old-fashioned report a variety of things that might correspond very poorly to what the teacher had in mind when assigning the marks. Good teachers tell the students in advance on what the marks will be based, but this is rarely reported accurately to the parents. There is an increasing use of reports that explain what the marks are intended to measure and that may provide space for several marks to report on different aspects of progress within a given subject.

**Conferences with Parents.** The following suggestions pertain primarily to parent-initiated conferences for the discussion of various problems, but they are also of value for conferences with parents in which reports of progress are given:

1. Point out the student's strengths and virtues before mentioning his weaknesses. Parents always feel better when they know that their child is doing well in something and has some strong points.

2. Reflect the parents' feeling in your remarks to them. If a parent says, "Jimmy isn't doing as well in school as he should," reply with "You think that Jimmy is not doing as well as he should" or a similar statement reflecting the parent's feeling. Do not say, for example, "I think that Jimmy is doing fine" or "Jimmy is a slow learner."

3. Use the parents' remarks and the feeling they express as a lead for your own remarks and questions. A parent who says, "Jimmy is not interested, but I want him to become an engineer" might be answered with "Do you think that you can interest him in engineering?" or "Do you think it wise for his teachers to continue trying to get Jimmy interested in engineering?" Avoid such responses as "I feel certain that Jimmy cannot become an engineer" or "Jimmy should make this decision himself."

4. Explain fully how progress or comparative achievement is assessed. Here samples of the student's work can be used to good advantage. As was pointed out in earlier chapters, results on the same test administered at two different times, the student's actual work, recordings of him speaking or giving a musical performance, and the like are useful.

5. As needed, summarize the main points that are brought out, for example, "Jimmy is doing well in English and social studies. His work in geometry and chemistry has not shown much improvement. His attitudes toward the teachers and school are good" or "Jimmy seems not to try in subjects he has no interest in, and as yet we have not found out how to get him interested in geometry and chemistry."

In recent years, a great many children have suffered some degree of emotional disturbance as a result of pressures from parents and from themselves to obtain high marks. In one township high school district near Chicago, it was estimated that between 40 and 60 boys and girls in an enrolment of approximately 2,400 were receiving psychiatric treatment in an attempt to repair the damage done by such unfortunate pressures, stresses, and frustrations, and that as many more were equally disturbed emotionally. Teachers should assist parents to assume a more practical attitude toward the grades of their children.

Interviews by the author of this volume with inmates of penal and correctional institutions for adolescents and young adults reveal that, in the majority of instances, these young people disliked school, developed truancy, dropped out of school early, and got into difficulties with law-enforcement officers as an indirect outcome of marks assigned, grade reports sent home, resultant reprimands and removal of privileges, and, indeed, in many instances, physical abuse by parents.

One of the unfortunate things about marking and grade reports is the ill feeling that arises between the teacher and at least some of the students in almost every class. Furthermore, the parents' interpretations of marks and their resulting relations with their sons and daughters in connection with the marks in most cases leave something to be desired and in many cases are very unfortunate. Parents are ambitious and proud and, in most instances, wish their offspring to make at least average marks, and some are satisfied with nothing short of A, or whatever the top mark may be. The pressure put on students does more harm than good, in a great many instances. Indeed, students have often reported that their relationships with their parents deteriorated greatly as the result of conversations they had about the grades brought home on their reports.

**New Types of Progress Reports.** An example of a modern student progress report form follows:

STUDENT PROGRESS REPORT

University High School          Mathematics _____

Student _____ Grade Period Ending _____

Teacher _____ Adviser _____

Note: The statements checked below are descriptions of the student's achievement with respect to the objectives of this class. His achievement is judged in terms of what is usually expected of high school students in his grade. The part of any statement which does not apply has been crossed out.

Participation
    Needs to enter into discussion more actively
    Occasionally volunteers, speaks willingly when asked to do so
    Takes active part in discussion, often shows leadership

Effort
    Needs to complete work and turn it in on time
    Sometimes fails to complete assignments on time
    Does required work on time
    Exceeds required work, shows interest and initiative

Use of Class Time
    Needs to bring necessary materials more consistently
    Needs to make better use of study time provided in class
    Usually works efficiently, occasionally needs reminding
    Is self-reliant, requires minimum of supervision

Principles
 Can state principles; sometimes fails to apply them
 Understands principles, can apply them in problems previously studied
 Can select and apply principles to new situations

General Accuracy of Results
 Often inaccurate; needs to correct:
  misreading problems _____
  forming judgment before sufficient consideration _____
  faulty use of process _____
  wrong meaning of words _____
  wrong meaning of symbols _____
 Occasionally inaccurate
 Is usually accurate
 Is highly accurate

Arithmetic Skills
 Student needs to build: Speed _____ Accuracy _____
 Computational skill satisfactory
 Can compute accurately and rapidly

Checking Results
 Checks answers only when required
 Usually checks
 Consistently checks

Credit Granted toward Graduation (semester only) Yes_____ No_____[3]

On this report form, each teacher is required to report the number of A's, B's, etc., assigned in the class section. Additional comments may be made on the reverse side of the sheet.

Another and a more promising trend in practice is to send home from time to time a non-technical report—merely an informal statement in regard to the progress of the student, usually some praise and often some suggestions for improvement of his schoolwork, personality, or character. In some schools, these reports are sent to all parents at regular intervals. In others, they are sent as there seems to be occasion or need. In some schools, reports are made largely by home visits and telephone calls.

While, in general, modern teachers are frank with parents, they find good things to say about youngsters as well as pointing out shortcomings. The teacher should also use good judgment with respect to what to tell the parent. The new type of reporting is relatively free from the worst evils of the formal report card and has much to recommend it. The greatest obstacles to the spread of its use are (1) parents' conservatism and unwarranted faith in the old-fashioned report card and (2) opposition of inferior teachers who fear they cannot motivate their pupils without "telling on them" and of those who wish to punish lazy or uninterested

[3] Reproduced with permission of the University of Iowa High School.

pupils by giving them poor reports. It should be understood that the most intelligent use of this type of reporting does not in the slightest diminish the need for careful, accurate testing and reporting of educational growth and status, and regular recording of marks for diagnosis, guidance, and other purposes.

The most important changes made in the forms of reporting are (1) the breaking up of achievement in a a particular subject into a number of subdivisions of outcomes or types of growth and (2) the inclusion of estimates or marks for a number of traits not closely related to the specific objective of the particular subject. The first is of value because it specifically points out strengths as well as weaknesses. The second informs students and parents of the teacher's estimate of the pupils' growth in several lines.

Pupil progress should be evaluated, marked, and reported in terms of the total objectives of the school and the objectives in each subject area. The child's progress toward educational objectives should be evaluated and reported to his parents. This means that evaluation practices, the marking system, and the procedure for reporting to parents must all be based on the educational objectives of the school. Certain objectives obtain throughout the entire school program, such as personality, character, and citizenship objectives. Others are achieved primarily in certain subject areas. Pupil progress toward schoolwide objectives and subject objectives should be evaluated and reported to the pupil and to his parents.

There should be some record of the pupil's achievement and effort as compared with his fellows as a basis for guidance, graduation from high school, admission to college, and recommendation for employment. College admission boards and prospective employers may be interested in knowing how the applicant stands in comparison with his classmates. Such information should be accumulated and become a part of the permanent records of the school.

A subject-matter mark alone gives little information. The pupil and his parents should have as much information as possible about his progress toward all the objectives that form a part of the school's educational program. They should be kept informed about his progress at all times, instead of just at report-card time. The shock of report-card day is educationally unsound and unjustifiable. The child should know day by day how well he is doing, with any formal report at the end of a marking period merely making this information a matter of record. Furthermore, there should be some provision for informing parents immediately if there is any serious change in the child's progress between formal periodic reports.

## QUESTIONS, PROBLEMS, AND TOPICS FOR FURTHER STUDY

1. Can you think of ways of evaluating student growth toward the objectives of secondary education, other than by written tests?
2. What do you think of self-evaluation by students? How would you go about organizing it in teaching your major subject?
3. Which of the so-called objective tests would you employ in teaching your major subject?
4. There are those who claim that the use of objective tests is bad because it encourages guesswork and because students do not receive training in written composition. What do you think of those criticisms?
5. Devise some essay questions for use in teaching your major subject that would not require a great deal of time and that might be graded somewhat objectively.
6. What would be the more important suggestions to keep in mind in constructing an essay examination?
7. How could you go about teaching understanding in the subject that you are likely to teach?
8. How could you go about teaching attitudes in the subject that you are likely to teach?
9. Be able to discuss in class the use of diagnostic tests in the teaching of your major subject.
10. Would you ever use unannounced tests in your class? Give reasons for your position.
11. What are your ideas about a marking system?
12. How do you think you might best report to parents about the growth and the difficulties of their children in your classes?
13. Do you think that marks are too much emphasized? If so, how would you persuade parents not to attach too much importance to marks?

## SUPPLEMENTARY MATERIALS

### SELECTED READINGS

ALEXANDER, WILLIAM M. "Reporting to Parents: Why? What? How?" *The Education Digest,* XXV (February, 1960), 21–23.
"Are Americans Over-testing?" *Overview,* August, 1961, 31–33.
BATES, G. S. "A Two-Way Reporting System," *Bulletin of the N.A.S.S.P.,* No. 224 (September, 1956), 68–71.
BRIMM, R. P., ALBERT F. MERZ, JR., and JAMES M. PEBBLES. "Thorny Problem—How Weigh Student Marks in Honor Courses?" *Bulletin of the N.A.S.S.P.,* No. 253 (April, 1961), 43–48.
DOUGLASS, HARL R. *Trends and Issues in Secondary Education.* Washington, D.C.: The Center for Applied Research in Education, Inc., 1962. Chapter 8, "Evaluating and Reporting Learner Status and Growth."
FOSTER, E. C. "The Use of Evaluative Instruments," *Bulletin of the N.A.S.S.P.,* No. 254 (March, 1960), 15–18.
GRAMBS, JEAN D., WILLIAM J. IVERSON, and FRANKLIN K. PATTERSON. *Modern Methods in Secondary Education.* New York: Holt, Rinehart & Winston, Inc., 1958. Chapter 17, "Testing Instruments"; Chapter 18, "Grading Student Progress."

KLAUSMEIER, HERBERT J. *Teaching in the Secondary School.* New York: Harper & Row, 1958. Chapter 9, "Evaluating Progressive Learning"; Chapter 17, "Reporting Pupil Progress."

McKEAN, ROBERT C. *Principles and Methods in Secondary Education.* Columbus, Ohio: Charles E. Merrill Books, Inc., 1962. Chapter 7, "The Evaluation of Teaching and Learning"; Chapter 8, "Grading and Reporting Pupil Progress."

MORRELL, RADCLIFFE. "Are Your Parent-Teacher Conferences Worthwhile?" *School Management,* III (November, 1959), 52–62.

MOULY, GEORGE J. *Psychology for Effective Teaching.* New York: Holt, Rinehart & Winston, Inc., 1960. Chapter 14, "Measuring Academic Achievement," pp. 365–406.

MURRAY, THOMAS R. *Judging Student Progress.* New York: Longmans, Green & Co., Inc., 1954. Chapter 10, "Charting Student Participation."

PHILLIPS, B. N. "Characteristics of High School Report Cards," *Bulletin of the N.A.S.S.P.,* No. 224 (September, 1956), 63.

RISK, THOMAS M. *Principles and Practices of Teaching in Secondary Schools.* New York: American Book Co., 1958. Chapter 19, "Evaluating and Reporting Student Progress."

RIVLIN, HARRY N. *Teaching Adolescents in Secondary Schools* (2d ed.). New York: Appleton-Century-Crofts, Inc., 1961. Chapter 11, "Evaluating the Results of Teaching and Learning."

WARNER, FRANK B. Pros and Cons of External Testing Programs," *The North Central Association Quarterly,* Fall, 1961, 201–10.

WATKINS, RALPH K. *Techniques of Secondary School Teaching.* New York: The Ronald Press Co., 1958. Chapter 13, "Evaluation of Learning"; Chapter 14, "Formulation of Marks, Records, and Reports."

WEIR, EDWARD C. *Bulletin of the N.A.S.S.P.,* No. 275 (December, 1962), 23–29.

WOOD, DOROTHY ADKINS. *Test Construction-Development and Interpretation of Achievement Tests.* Columbus, Ohio: Charles E. Merrill Books, Inc., 1961. Chapter 6, "Planning an Objective Test."

# 17

# Extrasubject Learning Activities

## MODERN ATTITUDES TOWARD EXTRASUBJECT LEARNING ACTIVITIES

**Participation in Extrasubject Activities as Learning.** In recent years, increased attention has been given to organizing, sponsoring, and managing extrasubject activities so as to achieve greater educational values—to contribute to desirable educational growth in skills, attitudes, ideals, etc. In order that this might be done most completely and effectively, there have been for several decades now a considerable number of educators holding the view that extrasubject learning activities should be absorbed into the regular subjects rather than being kept separate. However, this view has not gained much ground. Vigorous opponents to it hold that there are special values inherent in the separate activities that are largely managed by the students—under conditions where there is little in the way of daily assignments, book reading, testing, teacher authoritarianism, and grades.

Theory and practice have developed along the lines of carefully analyzing the educational potentialities of each activity, obtaining a well-trained sponsor, and holding that individual responsible for seeing that the activities are conducted in a way that will result in substantial educational growth. To be sure, in some instances, such activities have actually been incorporated into the curriculum or have replaced a subject in the curriculum. This has been true particularly of secondary school bands, orchestras, choral groups, and, to some extent, journalistic activities.

The following is a diagram indicating the possible contributions of participation in extrasubject activities to the ultimate objectives of secondary education:

CONTRIBUTIONS OF EXTRASUBJECT-ACTIVITY PARTICIPATION TO ULTIMATE
OBJECTIVES OF SECONDARY EDUCATION

| Objective | Type of Outcome | Contributing Activity |
|---|---|---|
| Health and safety | Information about sports, games, animals, flowers, plants, scientific basis of health and sanitation, first aid, fire and accident prevention<br>Habits and skills in games, sports, outdoor activities, dancing, first aid, avoiding accident, general bodily skill and strength<br>Ideals of sound, healthy bodies and proficiency in physical activities<br>Tastes and interests in sports, the outdoors, and health | Athletic teams of all sorts, hiking, outdoor clubs, biology clubs, nursing club, dancing, Junior Red Cross |
| Vocation | Information concerning occupations (nature of work, rewards, chance for advancement, etc.) and concerning pupils' abilities in differing pursuits—information underlying choice of vocation<br>Habits and skills: those general habits (honesty, industry, and ambition) that make for vocational success; skills in one or more vocations or activities common to several vocations (salesmanship, accounting, writing)<br>Ideals of success, influence, independence, fair dealing, cooperation, and service<br>Tastes and interests in explorations of the above ideals as a basis for vocational choice | Sports and games, musical and other fine-arts clubs, journalistic and forensic clubs, household-arts clubs, semiscientific clubs (radio, photography, automotive, aeronautic), semivocational clubs (printing, millinery, cartooning, agricultural and commercial clubs) |
| Leisure | Information about culture (art, music, drama, current and classical literature and authors), current social problems and events, games and sports, nature, scientific phenomena and laws<br>Habits and skills in fine arts, games and sports, reading<br>Ideals of culture, dignity, self-respect, approval of others in such matters; tastes and interests in fine arts, sports, games, hobbies of various sorts | Athletic and other sports; chess, checkers, and other games; musical and other fine-arts clubs; foreign-language clubs; mathematics clubs; drama clubs; reading clubs; history clubs; sewing and basketry clubs; short-story clubs; radio, motion-picture, and television clubs<br><br>(continued on next page) |

| Objective | Type of Outcome | Contributing Activity |
|---|---|---|
| Command of fundamentals | Information on how to read, study, write, speak, solve problems<br>Habits and skills in application of computation, study methods; skills in written and oral communication, getting on with other people<br>Ideals, tastes, and interests; continuation of desirable types begun in elementary school | Practically every activity, particularly those involving reading books, writing reports, keeping accounts, giving oral reports, or participating in discussions (journalistic and forensic activity) |
| Home living | Information about culture, human nature and character, biology, sanitation, household decoration, purchasing, budgeting, diet and nursing, preparation of foods, making and repairing clothing, household machines, children's reading<br>Habits and skills in fields mentioned above<br>Ideals of culture, monogamy, fair play, courtesy, cooperation, happy home lives, beautiful homes<br>Tastes and interests in fields named above, in artistic things, in games and sports | All sorts of fine-arts clubs, household-arts clubs, and semiscientific clubs<br>All clubs, insofar as they develop an understanding of human nature and psychology and how to get on in close contact with others |
| Citizenship | Information about government (national, state, local), public utilities, community organizations, results of unsocial acts or neglect<br>Habits and siklls in getting along in group activities as followers and as leaders, respecting feelings and rights of others, suppressing unsocial impulses, thinking through consequences of behavior<br>Ideals and attitudes: "the group above the individual," fair play, service, patriotism, favorable social attitudes, attitudes toward self resulting from "belonging" and participation<br>Tastes and interests in local and other social institutions, justice and fair play, welfare of others; antagonism toward unsocial ideas and acts | All organizations involving group efforts—student government, teams, civic clubs, letter clubs, traditions clubs or committees, Girl Reserves, Girl Scouts and Boy Scouts, Hi-Y clubs, service clubs, religious clubs |

There is great variation in the percentages of students who participate in one or more clubs or other organizations. While in most schools from two-thirds to three-fourths of the full-time students do, in a few schools more than nine-tenths, and in some schools less than one-half, do. In Evanston (Illinois) Township High School, generally regarded as one of the most outstanding high schools in the United States and one where the students score very high on National Merit Scholarship and other national academic examinations, more than 90 per cent of the students participate in at least one club or organization, whereas in several neighboring schools with great concentration on subject-matter test scores smaller numbers participate and fewer obtain National Merit Scholarships.

**Dangers and Limitations of Participation.** It has been very frequently claimed that participation in extracurricular learning activities is likely to decrease the amount of time spent on the subjects themselves and, therefore, to interfere with scholarship. Apparently most students have time to spare, however: The results of practically all of the many studies of this problem that have been made indicate that, with few exceptions, participation in extracurricular learning activities has little effect upon the quality of work done, or at least upon the grades made in subject learning activities. As a matter of fact, it has been shown that, while in a few instances excessive participation seems to result in lower grades, in many instances participation seems to improve the morale of students who have not previously been participants.

One of the characteristics of those students who withdraw from high school before graduation is that most of them have not been participants in extracurricular learning activities. With few exceptions, students participating in extracurricular activities seem to make as good grades as those not doing so.

Investigations have shown that, other things being equal, high school students who have participated in extracurricular activities, particularly those who have been organizers and leaders, achieve more in later life than students who have made the same average grades in secondary school; a larger percentage of the former have gotten advanced university degrees and special honors, have made outstanding accomplishments, published research and other materials, and served in positions of community leadership. Many employers definitely favor applicants, other things being equal, who have been very active participants or leaders in student organizations.

The objection is also raised that if he is to do well in coaching, sponsoring, or otherwise working with student organizations or other extracurricular learning activities, the teacher's load must be increased unwisely. In recent years, however, secondary school teachers teaching as many as five long periods daily have been relieved of study halls, which compensates at least in great part, if not entirely, for the extra load in connection with extracurricular activities. Furthermore, in many instances, teachers who are required to spend an unusual amount of time in an activity over and above an ordinary teaching load are given extra pay.

Emphasis upon competition in certain activities, particularly athletics, has become so great as to cause considerable comment and alarm and to invite both investigation and efforts to reduce unfortunate effects of excessive interscholastic competition. Pressures have been brought to bear on teachers to give passing grades for very inferior achievement by athletes, while schools have been disrupted by hysterical pregame rallies, drunkenness, and automobile accidents, and vandalism has occurred with increasing frequency as compared to twenty or thirty years ago, especially on the eves of interscholastic athletic contests. Trips to witness games played at other schools are often made by students, sometimes the entire student body, frequently involve leaving school early, automobile accidents, and disreputable behavior. Star athletes are frequently given a false impression of their importance that proves to be costly to them later in adjusting to human beings on the job and in other social relationships.

## NUMBER AND TYPES OF EXTRASUBJECT ORGANIZATIONS AND ACTIVITIES

In the very small schools there may be no more than eight or ten clubs, teams, and other organizations, while in a considerable number of large four-year schools there are at least fifty. In junior high schools there usually are from twenty to thirty. The Niles Township (Illinois) High School has sixty-two, in addition to special events such as homecoming, commencement, talent shows, play productions, and the junior-senior prom. The organizations found in American secondary schools, classified according to their purposes and nature, include the following:

*Subject-study clubs:* foreign-language conversation, science, mathematics, art
*Forensic:* debate, dramatics, discusion, stagecraft
*Journalistic:* reporting, short-story writing, yearbook
*Sports:* fencing, football, swimming, golf, tennis, modern dance, skiing, hiking, baseball, soccer, basketball
*Civic, social, and character:* Boy Scouts, Girl Reserves, Allied Youth, Junior Red Cross, Hi-Y
*Hobby and leisure:* candy making, marionettes, model-airplane flying, photography, chess, radio, space travel
*Musical:* orchestras, choruses, modern-music clubs, bands, orchesis

*Vocational:* printing, commercial art, Future Farmers of America, Future Teachers of America, 4-H

*Service:* library assistants, student secretaries, safety patrol, cheerleaders, pep clubs, audio-visual aids, projection clubs

*Domestic:* interior decorating, cooking, gardening, Future Homemakers of America

*Honor societies:* including national honor societies such as those sponsored by The National Association of Secondary School Principals

While some educators wonder if there are not too many clubs, there is a growing feeling that perhaps there cannot be too many if there are students who want them and if competent and willing sponsors can be found on the faculty. Adolescents vary a great deal with respect to their interests and talents, and there is a real need for a sufficient variety of clubs to enable them to explore possible interests and possible talents.

It is quite likely that, even in the small schools, there should be an organization for educational experiences in each of the following categories: student association and student council, class organizations, public speaking, dramatics, school news department or paper, glee or choral club, orchestra or band, semiscientific clubs (such as camera, radio, and aeronautics clubs), subject-matter clubs (such as Spanish, local-history, business, and home-economics clubs), plus at least one character club for each sex (for example, Girl Scouts, Girl Reserves, and Campfire organizations for girls, and Boy Scouts, Hi-Y, and a civic improvement club for boys), at least one exercise or sport club for each sex or for both sexes (for instance, for golf, tenis, or hiking), and at least one interscholastic team (for example, for football, basketball, or baseball in the senior high school, or for basketball, baseball, or track in the junior high school).

**Assemblies.** In practically every school, assemblies are held from time to time, usually once a week in the larger schools. These assemblies serve very valuable purposes, including providing an opportunity to make announcements, to hear reports of student committees, to present musical and other talents, to hear unusual speakers from outside the school, to permit expression of opinions, to vote on approval or disapproval of various proposals for the school that affect the student body, to acquaint students with the principal and other members of the faculty of the school other than their own teachers, to publicize the achievements of the faculty, the students, and the school in general, and to develop school spirit and school loyalty.

**Homerooms.** The type of homeroom organization varies greatly from school to school. In some schools, homeroom groups meet each day for a very short period. They are not really homerooms but are "roll" rooms, where attendance is checked, announcements are made, and supplies are distributed, although often these rooms do elect representatives for the student council.

In many other schools the homeroom is a longer period of from thirty to fifty minutes, during which discussions of problems that interest young people and about which discussion would constitute group guidance constitute a major part of the program.

In many schools, a sequence of problems has been worked out for each grade, giving the teacher definite guidance and preventing excessive overlapping of discussions. Also in many schools, there has been obtained for the library a rather large collection of pamphlets and small books about various problems of concern to adolescents, which they can read in preparation for following up the discussions in the homeroom.

Where homerooms exist, every student belongs to a homeroom group and is expected to attend. Homeroom groups are usually made up of students of the same grade and are usually coeducational. Various methods of dividing the enrolment into homeroom groups are employed. Where the longer period is used, the homeroom usually meets only twice a week, clubs and activities meeting two other days at the same period, an assembly or study period usually being held on the fifth day.

Many senior high school teachers have not had courses in group guidance or other preparation for homeroom leadership. These people have usually been uneasy, unhappy, and very ineffective in giving leadership to students in their groups. Quite frequently, they are permissive in letting students study for a class during the homeroom period. Because of this situation and because of the decrease in the number of periods a day as a result of lengthening the class periods, homerooms have not gained ground in secondary schools in recent years, particularly in senior high schools.

Functions of Homerooms. Complete and well-organized homerooms serve four principal functions: (1) administration, (2) curriculum supplementation, (3) guidance, and (4) promotion of extracurricular activities.

In practically all homeroom organizations, administration is one of the functions. In schools where homeroom periods are short, it is the principal function. At this time attendance is checked, excuses for absence and tardiness are administered, announcements are made, and textbooks, supplies, and other things are distributed.

Where the homeroom period is thirty minutes or longer and where there are two or more meetings a week, there is an excellent opportunity for learning about certain problems and topics not adequately treated in the subjects of the regular curriculum or about subjects which can be better studied by the informal procedure of the homeroom, for example, safety education, personality development, occupations, home relationships, social conventions, current events, and study habits and techniques.

The homeroom in many schools serves splendidly as an organization and opportunity for group guidance in such fields as health, selection of courses, personal appearance, making friends, obtaining, holding, and getting ahead on a job, boy-girl relationships, matters of ethics and sportsmanship, use of leisure time, orientation to the school, and school citizenship. If the homeroom sponsor is adequately trained, he may render excellent guidance service to the individual student, and, under any circumstances, the homeroom adviser may render at least the non-technical type of guidance service.

The homeroom organization may assist in promoting extracurricular activities by contributing to the all-school program of activities and by its own program of activities. In homeroom periods there may be discussed such things as the types of clubs and extracurricular activities available, their values, and how to participate in them. Certain types of administrative routines pertaining to extracurricular activities may also be taken care of in the homeroom period, including making of announcements, election of homeroom representatives to various all-school organizations, rally programs, and so forth. The homeroom may have its own program of activity; it may once a year contribute a program to the all-school assembly; and it may occasionally have a period for a homeroom program including musical numbers, debates, reading of an unprinted homeroom newspaper, and guest speakers and entertainers.

**Homeroom Programs.** In recent years, the practice has been adapted of developing programs for homerooms so that overlapping may be held to a minimum and so that teachers may have some sort of an outline to follow. Usually homeroom membership is on the basis of grades, there being several homeroom groups for each grade, with the membership being more or less a random sample of both boys and girls in the grade. More recently, a few schools have shifted to a plan of membership in which each group has members of each grade in proportion to the number in each grade in the school. Principal Harold B. Brooks, of the Benjamin Franklin Junior High School of Long Beach, California, where this plan is used with boys and girls in separate homeroom groups, believes that the system there has several advantages including valuable leadership by the older pupils and franker and more sincere discussions than when pupils of both sexes are present.

**Social Events and Organizations.** In practically all secondary schools in the United States there has been, in recent decades, a steady increase in the attention given to organized social life for the students. It is fairly generally believed by secondary school principals and other authorities on adolescents that this is a very desirable development, since so many students come to secondary schools today from homes with very inadequate opportunities for training in social behavior. Furthermore, they believe that a great deal of the social life of adolescents outside the school is undemocratic or otherwise of an undesirable type.

In many schools there are picnics, parties, dances, and other types of social events sponsored by the school, for which members of the faculty serve as counselors and supervisors. These add quite a bit to the burden of some secondary school teachers; in addition, many secondary school teachers are not suited by their personality, views, background, and experience for this type of work. Administrators, however, are usually able to identify those who would be more successful and to see that they are selected as sponsors. In some schools, sponsors are given extra pay. Furthermore, in recent years, parents have been invited, in fact drafted, to take over a great deal of the responsibility for supervising student affairs.

These affairs are usually on a strictly democratic basis, although racial problems exist in some schools, often owing to the snobbishness of parents. The social activities are usually held after school, often in the evening, and in the school building. The types of social activities and the ways in which they are carried out differ from the junior to the senior high school and from grade to grade, being organized on the basis of the maturity of the young people involved.

For several decades, a serious problem has existed in some schools in the form of undemocratic social organizations—snobbish, select groups of adolescents attempting to imitate the worst aspects of college and university fraternities and sororities, which through their national organizations, have gone on record as opposing high school fraternities and sororities, on the basis that they give the students and the people in the community the wrong idea of college fraternities and sororities. In very few schools are fraternal organizations permitted to meet in the school building; nor are announcements made about them in most schools. They are not considered a part of the school social life.

A number of states prohibit high school fraternities and sororities by law. This law is difficult to enforce, but, in a great many schools, members of these organizations are not permitted to represent the school in any interscholastic contest or exhibition or to hold any class or school office. In many schools, no student may represent the school or become a candidate for any office in the school until he has signed a statement that he is not a member of any such organization.

**Interscholastic Athletics.** Interscholastic competitive athletic events were originally attended only by students and a small number of other spectators. Over the years, particularly with the development of night games in the last quarter-century, attendance of the public has grown rapidly, and, in many communities, interscholastic athletic competition is one of the major interests of a considerable portion of the population.

Because of this, there has been great and unwise pressure on the part of aggressive and emotional people in the communities, sometimes very large groups, upon the principal and the coach of the local high school to produce winning teams, especially where there are traditional rivalries from nearby schools. Because of this pressure, many coaches have defied the principal and superintendent of the school in their coaching activities, in recruitment, and with respect to eligibility. Rather generally among educators, interscholastic athletics is thought to have developed in very unfortunate directions.

Greatly stimulated by these developments, there has been formed in every state a State Interscholastic Association, which sets up standards and rules and attempts to enforce them. This has been a great help to administrators.

The American Association for Health, Physical Education and Recreation has from time to time made excellent recommendations for interscholastic athletics. Below is an excerpt from a report published by this association.

The "ten cardinal athletic principles" are accepted as expressing the policies of our organizations, and it is urged that these be displayed in the literature of our organizations. To be of maximum effectiveness, the athletic program will

a. Be closely co-ordinated with the general instructional program, and properly articulated with the other departments of the school.
b. Be such that the number of students accommodated and the educational aims achieved justify the use of tax funds for its support, and also warrant the use of other sources of income.
c. Justify the time and attention which is given to the collection of "other sources of income" which will not interfere with the efficiency of the athletic program or of any other departments of the school.
d. Confine the school athletic activity to events which are sponsored and supervised by the proper school authorities so that any exploitation or improper use of prestige built up by school teams or members of such teams may be avoided.
e. Be planned in such a way as to result in opportunity for many individuals to explore a wide variety of sports and to set reasonable season limits for each listed sport.
f. Be controlled in such a way as to avoid the elements of professionalism and commercialism which tend to grow up in connection with widely publicized "bowl" contests, barnstorming trips, and interstate or intersectional contests which require excessive travel expense or loss of school time, or which are claimed to be justified by educational travel values.

g. Be kept free from the type of contest which involves a gathering of so-called "all-stars" from different schools to participate in contests which may be used as a gathering place for representatives of certain colleges or professional organizations who are interested in soliciting athletic talent for their teams.

h. Include educative exercises to reach all nonparticipating students and community followers of the school teams in order to insure a proper understanding and appreciation of the sports skills and of the need for adherence to principles of game ethics.

i. Encourage a balanced program of intramural activity in grades below the ninth to make it unnecessary to sponsor contests of a championship nature in these grades.

j. Engender respect for the rules and policies under which the school conducts its program.

All schools shall use reasonable care in avoiding any participation in a contact sport between participants of normal high-school age and participants who are appreciably above or below normal high-school age.

No basketball tournament which is purported to be for interstate high-school championship shall be sanctioned, and no basketball tournament involving schools of more than one state shall be sanctioned unless the tournament is purely community in character.

No contest which is purported to be for a national high-school championship in any sport shall be sanctioned.

**Athletic Competition for Girls.** Interscholastic athletic competition for girls is a subject of very intense debate. For a number of years, it was frowned upon and lost ground in the secondary schools, particularly in the 1930's and 1940's. However, in recent years, there has been an increase in interscholastic competition between teams of girls. The following is excerpted from a statement of principles that should govern girls' interscholastic activities. It is taken from the *Handbook of the New York State Athletic Association,* 1961.

*Supervision and conduct.* All extra-mural athletic activities for girls shall be conducted under girls' rules sanctioned by the Division for Girls' and Women's Sports and under standards established by that organization. (See appropriate D.G.W.S. Guide.) Women shall act as referees, umpires, and officials.

*Types of participation.*

a. *Sports day:* A day when pupils from two or more schools meet and engage in a *variety* of competitive sports events.

   *Type 1.* Two schools competing in more than one sport, but with each girl participating in only one sport.

   *Type 2.* More than two schools competing in more than one sport, but with each girl participating in only one sport.

   *Type 3.* Two or more schools competing in more than one sport, but with each girl participating in more than one sport. In all of these, both team and school identity are retained.

b. *Invitation activities:* Those games or other events dealing with one sport, arranged by invitation of one school to one or more other schools, without leading to any formal schedule or championship.

*Type 1.* Two schools competing in one sport.

*Type 2.* More than two schools competing in one sport. In all of these, both team and school identity are retained.

.      .      .      .      .      .      .      .      .      .      .

*Amount of participation.*

a. *Per day.* Maximum participation of any one girl in any of these activities shall not exceed one full-length game or its equivalent for one day.

b. *Per time division.* The maximum total of sports days and invitation activities shall be 6 *per girl* in a given time division and may not exceed 6 per girl in a given sport in adjacent time divisions; in either case, only 4 of these may be type 1 sports days and/or type 1 invitation activities.

**Intramural Athletics.** The intramural program offers an opportunity for many who may not have the time or ability to compete in interschool contests to gain educational experiences through games and sports. Because these participants may lack the skill, natural ability, experience, or training of the varsity athlete, as good or in some respects even better teaching or coaching ability is required to direct these activities.

In many junior high schools, either there is no interscholastic athletic competition or it is limited to very few games with other junior high schools in the same district. In these schools, an intramural program has an excellent opportunity to develop the values that derive from participation in athletics.

The intramural program provides an opportunity for academic teachers in the school system to direct sports activities. The academic teacher who is qualified may find a refreshing outlet for his athletic interests through the direction of intramural activitites that do not involve the pressures of interscholastic competition. Instructors in physical education who are not involved in coaching teams in interscholastic competition usually make excellent leaders for intramural groups.

An intramural program needs to be very carefully organized, supervised, and supported. There must be adequate playing fields, gymnasium space, and equipment, particularly first-class protective equipment in football. Adequate provision must be made for first aid and for immediate examination of any injuries that seem at all serious.

The type of classification used in composing intramural teams varies greatly from school to school, but, ordinarily, teams are composed on the basis of one or two of the following criteria: by weight, by age, by grade. If it is carefully planned, the intramural program presents an excellent opportunity to teach the student rules and sports appreciation.

**Essay Contests.** One of the sources of vexation of high school principals and teachers has been the pressures exerted by various groups interested in influencing opinions, even of adolescents, by promoting essay contests. They have become such a nuisance that the National Association of Secondary School Principals has for a number of years drawn up a list of the national essay contests it approves. It has also drawn up a list of suggested criteria for the approval of state and local essay contests.

In general, secondary school principals are opposed to such contests imposed from outside, although some principals are eager to gain personal favor by cooperation with an influential group. It is a rather general rule, though not observed by many schools, that local essay contests should not be participated in by students. Faculty members, in general, are opposed to all esasy contests and probably with good cause, since they tend to divert the students from the normal and probably more valuable learning activities.

**Basic Principles for Engaging in Contests.** A committee of the National Association of Secondary School Principals, appointed for the purpose, drew up a basic set of principles that ought to govern participants in contests.

1. *Primary Objective*
   The first purpose of a national contest or activity is to benefit high-school youth in educational, civic, social, and ethical development.

2. *Types of Contests Preferred*
   Contests that make it possible for individual students to work out contributions, solutions, and creations by their own efforts are preferred. Essay contests may invite dishonest collaboration; therefore, they are not considered desirable. Scholarship and achievement tests and contests involving original work by the contestant are preferred.

3. *Purposes*
   The contest or activity must be educationally sound, worthy, and timely. It should be stimulating to student and school and be a desirable activity for both.

4. *Values*
   a. The contest or activity should be well planned and have adequate, objective evaluation.
   b. The contest must emphasize a potentiality for good citizenship, high moral standards, and intellectual competence.
   c. The subject of the contest or activity must not be commercial, controversial, sectarian, or concerned with propaganda.

5. *Restrictions*
   a. No contestant may be excluded because of race, color, or creed.
   b. The activity must not place undue burdens on students, teachers, or the school.

    c. The student or school should not be required to pay an entry fee or to purchase products or materials to participate.

    d. Teachers should not judge or select contestants in any stage of a contest.

    e. The contest or activity must not require frequent absence of participants from school.

    f. Ordinarily, out-of-state travel should be limited to one student. Exceptions may be made if scholarships are substantial.

    g. Contests or activities should not duplicate those sponsored by other organizations.

    h. An organization should not conduct more than one national contest or activity in the same school year.

6. *Awards and Prizes*

    a. The contest or activity should be philanthropic.

    b. Awards and prizes must be adequate in number and amount.

    c. Scholarships and well-chaperoned educational trips during out-of-school periods are regarded as the most desirable types of awards.

7. *Sponsorship*

    a. The organization sponsoring the contest or activity must be engaged in a creditable or acceptable enterprise regardless of the kind and amount of prize offered and must not use the contest or activity as a "front" for advertising a company name or product.[1]

## STUDENT PARTICIPATION IN SCHOOL GOVERNMENT

**The Student-Government Movement.** All but a very few secondary schools in the United States now have some kind of "student government." There is great variation as to its form, powers, and fields of activity. In most instances, it should be thought of as student participation in government and management. This is particularly true at the junior high school level.

In spite of favorable publicity given a considerable number of schools that attempted to introduce student government, it almost invariably became within a few years a failure or a very limited success. Today, very little responsibility for government is given to the student officers or representatives. Nevertheless, the students, through their homerooms and their student-council officers, do, in the majority of schools, play an invaluable part in influencing and, in effect, legislating the conduct of students. While their recommendations are advisory, subject to modification and veto by the faculty, more and more secondary school administrators and faculty members attach much importance to the student recommendations and, in many instances, go along with them even though they may not seem to represent the best way to handle the situation.

[1] *The Bulletin of the N.A.S.S.P.*, No. 274 (May, 1962), pp. 317–318.

**The Student Council.**[2] The student council participates along with the faculty in selecting the activities for the year, scheduling times and places for the activities, and chartering new student clubs or revoking charters of those that seem unwilling to conform to the standards of the school or that are no longer active or effective educationally.

The student council, usually through its committees or officers, is, in many schools, active in the control of the student activity funds, their apportionment, and the overseeing of collections and expenditures. In a great many schools, there is only one student activity fund, which includes the funds for all student organizations including athletics, dramatics, publications, and musical presentations. Each organization has a divisional budget as a means of encouraging economy.

Student councils and their committees, as well as homeroom groups, promote and perform a great many types of services in the school, including drives for funds for charity, cleanup and paintup campaigns, management of honor study halls, assistance in regulation of traffic, guiding of visitors through the school, assistance to the librarian, studying and recommending and managing car safety measures, and, in many schools, planning of the school assemblies.

The following is a list of principles that have been found to be sound relative to working with student participation in government through a student council:

1. The principal and the majority of the teachers must be thoroughly in sympathy with the fundamental philosophy of the idea.

2. The principal and those to be associated with the council as sponsors or advisers must be well read in the theory and practice of student participation in management and administration, as organized in a secondary school.

3. There must be a desire on the part of the great majority of the students for student participation.

4. Both students and faculty must have a clear idea of the plan, its scope, and its limitations. This is especially true with respect to the degree to which the control of the students and their representatives is complete but cooperative.

5. The development and extension of student participation, particularly in organized form, must be practiced; the students participating must be prepared in advance by discussions and, perhaps, by reading materials before each successive step in the development and expansion of participation, and before the initial organization for participation.

[2] See Chapter 15 of Harl R. Douglass, *Modern Administration of Secondary Schools* (Boston: Ginn & Co., 1963), for descriptions of student councils and their functions, activities, and management.

6. The faculty advisers must be carefully selected on the basis of their sympathy, understanding, and training and the reading they have done in the field of student government and management; as far as possible, they should have personalities that are attractive to young people and will cause them to be readily liked, accepted, and respected.

7. A carefully worked out constitution should be adopted as the result of a great deal of deliberation by various groups specially appointed for the purpose. Its various drafts should be discussed by small groups of the students and later by the entire student body at the time of its adoption.

8. It is necessary that the students have confidence in the council, its operations, and its officers, and in the attitudes of the faculty in the matter of non-interference.

9. From the outset there should be cordial cooperation and constructive criticism on the part of members of the faculty.

10. As far as is practical, considerable numbers of students must be given responsibilities of some importance, though not onerous ones, in connection with the activities of the council.

11. The principal should retain a veto power, which he should exercise in a very limited way, permitting the students to move ahead even along lines that may be somewhat doubtful but not definitely disastrous.

12. There should be definite business-like organization for the collection, expenditure, and supervision of the finances. Usually the assistant principal or a member of the faculty of the business department is appointed as the supervisor of student funds with whom the student council and other student organizations work.

13. There should be an annual audit; indeed, many schools have a semiannual audit.

14. The plan of organization must provide for adequate representation of all the students, regardless of grade, sex, etc.

15. The student government should be developed gradually, in proportion to the developing maturity and sense of responsibility of the students.

While in only a few schools do members of the faculty participate as members of the council, practically every council has at least one faculty advisor, chosen principally on the basis of such criteria as the degree of competence of the students, the degree to which the faculty member will use his judgment in avoiding domination of the council, and the degree to which he may be counted upon to steer the students away from definitely unfortunate or unethical actions. The members of the student council are usually elected annually, although sometimes semiannually. Ordinarily, the only qualifications for office are that the student be carrying a full program of work in the school and that he be in good standing in the school and passing in all subjects.

**Student-Council Committees.** Among the most commonly employed types of student-council committees are the following:

1. Assembly committee—responsible for planning and coordinating the school's weekly assembly programs
2. Grounds committee—responsible for landscaping and for traffic in the schoolyard
3. Hall committee—charged with the duty of studying hall traffic conditions and making recommendations for their improvement
4. Study-hall committee—responsible for making weekly ratings of the (student-governed) study halls
5. Noon-hour committee—takes complete charge of the lunchroom and of other rooms used for noon-hour recreation programs
6. Budget committee—drafts the budget for disposition of all activity ticket revenues
7. Club committee—responsible for chartering new clubs or discontinuing those which have become inactive
8. Athletic board—responsible for schedules, equipment, participation, conduct, and awards connected with athletic activities
9. Forensic board—similarly responsible for speech activities
10. Publications board—selects staffs for the school newspaper and annual
11. Committee on committees

Committees 1–10 should be appointed by the "committee on committees," which in turn should be appointed by the student-council chairman with the advice of the faculty student-council sponsor and the principal. In general, these committees should consist of from five to seven members, the majority of whom are members of the student council, who should serve for one semester. At least two or three new members should be appointed to each committee each semester. In the junior high school, each committee should have a faculty sponsor.

## ORGANIZATION AND ADMINISTRATION OF EXTRACURRICULAR ACTIVITIES

**Initiating and Chartering Clubs.** It is a very common practice in secondary schools today to put the burden of proof upon a group of interested students to show that a particular club being proposed is needed and has a chance of being effective in operation.

Nevertheless, the formation of a club is frequently suggested to groups of students by members of the faculty, particularly in the case of clubs that are closely related to the subject the member of the faculty is teaching. Ordinarily, it is necessary for those proposing to organize a club to draw up a petition to be signed by a member of the faculty and to submit it to the student council through the principal of the school. In most schools, a club or organization is not recognized unless it has been approved by the student council and the principal.

**Membership.** There are two important problems of membership. One of them is that of seeing that all, or practically all, students participate in at least one student organization. The other is to make sure that some students do not participate in so many organizations as to deprive others of opportunity, particularly with reference to holding office, or to endanger the quality of the students' scholarship.

Various methods are employed for promoting membership, including announcements and other publicity in assemblies, homerooms, and sections, as well as materials in student handbooks. In some instances, counselors, members of the staff, the principal, or the assistant principal may advise students who are not participating in any activity to become participants and may counsel as to what activities or what organization might be most appropriate for the individual concerned.

In controlling participation, ordinarily one of the following two methods is employed:

1. *The major-minor system,* in which the participation is limited to, for example, two types of major participation such as serving as the president of the student body and captain of the football team, or a major and two minor types of participation—what are major and what are minor types are determined, listed, and publicized by the student council with approval by the principal.

2. *The point system,* in which a student is limited to participation according to a specified maximum number of points—different kinds of participation are given different numbers of points; the allocation of points to each of the various activities and positions as officers is determined by the student council and approved by the principal.

It is a fundamental and important rule of practice in almost all secondary schools today that membership in student organizations must be absolutely democratic. This means that there can be no black list or selection of members by the students already in the group. To be sure, membership in certain groups may be democratically limited to those who can meet certain specified qualifications such as ability to play football, ability in dramatics, etc., but limitation even on that basis is usually not too strict.

**Student-Organization Meetings.** Originally, student organizations met after school at the time at which the officers, the members, or the faculty sponsor wished to have a meeting. This practice has proved usually to be unsatisfactory for a number of reasons, among them being the fact that, in schools where this plan is employed, the percentage of students participating in activities is definitely too small.

In the very great majority of secondary schools, today, clubs and activities meet during the regular school day, at some specified period. Usually they have definite dates for meeting, such as every other Wednesday, every Tuesday, or Tuesdays and Thursdays of every week. It is the duty of the faculty sponsor to see that there is not an excessive number of meetings at which students find little to do.

Practically every school has an activity calendar, and each activity must obtain an approved place on this calendar for any meeting of any activity to which the public might be invited. This prevents conflicts and possible reduction of the size of the audience. Usually, a schedule is worked out several months in advance for all such meetings and also for the school assembly.

The following is an excerpt from a school calendar followed for the month of February at Central High School, Evansville, Indiana:

| Date | Activity |
|---|---|
| Mon., Feb. 3 | Meeting of Councils |
| Tues., Feb. 4 | Club Schedule B |
| Wed., Feb. 5 | Guidance |
| Thurs., Feb. 6 | College Week Assembly |
| | Lunch Hour Movies |
| Fri., Feb. 7 | College Week Assembly |
| | Basketball—Bloomington (There) |
| Sat., Feb. 8 | Basketball—Jaspers (Here) |
| Mon., Feb. 10 | Meeting of Girl Reserves and Hi-Y |
| | Big Broadcast Practice—7:00–9:30 P.M. |
| Tues., Feb. 11 | Club Schedule A |
| | Big Broadcast Practice—7:00–9:30 P.M. |
| | P.T.A. Meeting—3:15 P.M. |
| Wed., Feb. 12 | Guidance |
| | Big Broadcast Practice—7:00–9:30 P.M. |
| Thurs., Feb. 13 | Scholarship E Assembly |
| | Lunch Hour Movies |
| Fri., Feb. 14 | Pep Assembly for Bosse Game |
| | Basketball—Bosse (Here) |
| Sat. Feb. 15 | Senior Open Dance (Away) |
| Mon., Feb. 17 | Meeting of Councils |
| | Big Broadcast Practice—7:00–9:30 P.M. |
| | Stage Crew Practice—3:00–5:00 P.M. |
| Tues., Feb. 18 | Club Schedule B |
| | Big Broadcast Practice—7:00–9:30 P.M. |
| | Stage Crew Practice—3:00–5:00 P.M. |

| Wed., Feb. 19 | Guidance |
| | Student Council Assembly |
| | Faculty Meeting |
| | Big Broadcast—8:00 P.M. |
| Thurs., Feb. 20 | Student Council Assembly |
| | (In Front of Curtain) |
| | Lunch Hour Movies |
| | Big Broadcast—8:00 P.M. |
| Fri., Feb. 21 | Student Council Assembly |
| | Basketball—Bedford (Here) |

**Encouraging Student Participation.** In most secondary schools, effort is made to have every student participate in at least one organization. Following is a statement issued to all students by the administration of the Niles Township (Illinois) High School:

The best high school program is the balanced high school program, with time for activities as well as for studies.

. . . . . . . . . . .

The student who does not join any activity, deprives himself of an important part of his self-development, and passes over some of the most vital experiences he can have in high school. He may miss knowing the spirit and team-loyalty of competing in athletics, or the thrill of taking part in producing a play or a musicale, or the satisfaction of helping the school in some service such as getting out a student newspaper or operating film projection equipment, or seeing his artistic, literary, scientific, or hobby interest grow and expand to new undreamed-of horizons. Most serious of all, he will miss the important life-lesson of learning to get along with others and how to work together with them on common purposes and goals.

No student—freshman, sophomore, junior, or senior—can afford to ignore the advantages of becoming part of at least one school activity.

All of the extracurricular activities at Niles are sponsored and supervised by well-qualified members of the faculty. Some of the activities are seasonal—sports for example—but most of them have a September to June schedule. Meeting time is after school, and, occasionally, on Saturdays.

Caution: It is just as bad to get involved in too many activities as to neglect them altogether. The student who has an excessive number of extracurricular outlets spreads himself too thin . . .

## ROLE OF THE CLASSROOM TEACHER

The degree to which an extracurricular activity is really educational depends largely on the educational philosophy, the competence, the industry, and the imagination of the sponsor or coach. The same activity that in one school is of little educational value other than as a sop to the students and as a sort of busy work for them may in another school be managed so as to constitute very valuable educational experience contributing materially to the development of important ideals, attitudes, interests, skills, habits, information, and understanding.

**General Principles of Supervision of Extrasubject Activities.** Each school should set up general principles that the adviser should translate into specific practice in the light of the particular activity, the local situation, and the personnel of the organization. Among such principles are the following:

1. The supervision of activities should not amount to domination. Opportunity must be provided for the development and exercise of pupil initiative, leadership, imagination, and thinking through of consequences. Pupils must be permitted to make some mistakes as a part of their training. The educational value derived from an activity depends largely upon its incidental training value, and by no means entirely upon success in the ostensible purpose of the organization.

2. Supervision must circumvent the influence of immoral and unsocial practices, for example, mismanagement of funds, domination by social cliques, undemocratic selection of members and officials, and unethical business and competitive practices.

3. Supervision should be, as far as possible, by suggestion rather than by authoritative direction.

4. Supervision must involve cooperation with the central administration and the general activity program, especially in accounting (records and reports) and in management of activities in such a way as to ensure loyalty to administrative policies.

5. Supervision must include recognition of the exploratory value of activities as a factor in guidance. Advisers should be constantly on the lookout for evidence of special talent, and should advise pupils concerning the possibilities of training and employing such talent.

6. Supervision should have as one of its primary objectives the integration of curricular studies and extracurricular activities.

## QUESTIONS, PROBLEMS, AND TOPICS FOR FURTHER STUDY

1. Select some extracurricular student activity that you might sponsor, and be able to describe thoroughly the types of desirable educational growth to which that activity might contribute.
2. Examine the chart of the contributions of extrasubject-activity participation to ultimate objectives of secondary education (pages 331–332), and estimate the degree to which those potentialities for educational growth can be realized.
3. Do you have any information about the degree to which participation in extracurricular activities interferes with scholarship?
4. If you had to decide what extracurricular activities would be sponsored in a school of 200 to 400 students, which ones would you suggest?
5. What good purposes do you think well-organized homerooms might serve? Why are homerooms so often a failure?

6. Be able to discuss in class your position on the school being responsible for social events. What do you think should be the policy of the school in managing them?
7. Be able to give in class your position on essay contests.
8. What do you think ought to be done to curb the evils of excessive emphasis on interscholastic athletic competition?
9. Do you think there should be any interscholastic athletic competition between junior high schools?
10. Do you think there should be any interscholastic athletic competition between girls?
11. Think through carefully your attitudes about student participation in school government and about student councils.
12. What is your idea about the handling of the high school sorority and fraternity situation?
13. What do you believe are the best methods of dealing with the problems of membership in extrasubject student activities?
14. Be able to give in class your ideas and suggestions about who should sponsor extrasubject student organizations.

## SUPPLEMENTARY MATERIALS

### SELECTED READINGS

ANDERSON, VERNON E., and WILLIAM T. GRUHN. *Principles and Practices of Secondary Education* (2d ed.). New York: The Ronald Press Co., 1962. Chapter 12, "Experiences in Extraclass Activities."

ARCHER, JOHN K. "Summary of the presentation of Athletics for Girls," *Bulletin of the N.A.S.S.P.*, No. 231 (April, 1956), 125–26.

BICK, KENNETH F., NELSON F. HURLEY, and C. P. WRIGHT. "The Student Council—Partner or Plaything?" *Bulletin of the N.A.S.S.P.*, No. 263 (April, 1961), 259–63.

DALY, C. A. "Social Clubs at Southwestern," *Bulletin of the N.A.S.S.P.*, No. 233 (September, 1956), 142–45.

DOUGLASS, HARL R. *Trends and Issues in Secondary Education.* Washington, D.C.: The Center for Applied Research in Education, Inc., 1962. Chapter 9, "Guidance and Extracurricular Organizations."

FAUNCE, ROLAND C., and MORREL J. CLUTE. *Teaching and Learning in the Junior High School.* San Francisco: Wadsworth Publishing Co., Inc., 1961. Chapter 6, "The Program of Student Activities."

MAYBEE, G. D., and OLIVER McCRACKER, JR. "Do Interscholastic Athletics in the Junior High School Aid or Retard a Desirable Educational Program?" *Bulletin of the N.A.S.S.P.*, No. 255 (April, 1960), 96–100.

MILLS, HUBERT H., and HARL R. DOUGLASS. *Teaching High School* (2d ed.). New York: The Ronald Press Co., 1957. Chapter 25, "Teacher Leadership in Home Room and Student Organizations."

PEAKE, FRANK A., GEORGE W. JANKE, and C. H. ORTT. "Developing Tomorrow's Leaders Today Through the National Honor Society," *Bulletin of the N.A.S.S.P.*, No. 263 (April, 1961), 238–42.

PUNKE, HAROLD H. "Cost to High School Seniors," *Bulletin of the N.A.S.S.P.*, No. 192 (February, 1954), 41–226.

VAN POOL, GERALD M. "The Home Room," *Bulletin of the N.A.S.S.P.*, No. 176 (February, 1952), 150–56.

VAN POOL, GERALD M. "The Case Against High School Secret Societies," *Bulletin of the N.A.S.S.P.*, No. 264 (May, 1961), 5–20.

XAVIER, MARY. "Some Educational Trends in School Activities," *Catholic Journal of Education*, January, 1957, 15–26.

### AUDIO-VISUAL MATERIALS

### Recording

*Improving the Services of Extra Class Activities*, #235. J. Lloyd Trump. Educational Growth Series. Educational Recording Services. Los Angeles, Calif. 36-44-minute discussion, 33⅓ rpm.

# 18

# Guidance and Counseling

## NATURE AND EXPANSION OF MODERN GUIDANCE SERVICES

**Increased Need for Guidance.** Over the years of the past century, the importance of counseling and guidance in secondary education has grown steadily. Particularly in recent years, the need for guidance has increased considerably for the following reasons, among others:

1. The wise choice of a vocation has become more difficult. Because of technological, economic, and industrial development in the United States in recent years, the employment opportunities have shifted very significantly among different occupations. For example, there is much less need for workers in many types of unskilled labor, and the number of people engaged in personal service has increased very greatly, for instance, in the fields of beauticians, food servers, and laundry and dry-cleaning workers. Furthermore, many new occupations have developed in a variety of fields, for example, in the fields of electronics and automation. The activities involved in some occupations have changed greatly, and the preparation has changed accordingly.

2. There is greater need for guidance for those students who are likely to drop out before graduating from high school. Their problems are different from those of other adolescents and are more immediately pressing.

3. College admissions problems have become more serious. With the greatly increased number of students applying for admission to college, it is much more difficult to obtain admission to many colleges. With the greatly increased number of graduates from high school in the 1970's, the colleges will not be able to admit all of those who would like to come, and it will then become difficult to get into any college. Because

of the stepping up of standards in many colleges and universities, greater degrees of academic interest and ability are necessary for success as well as for admission, and it has, therefore, become more important for the college-bound student not only to select the college or university appropriate for his abilities, interests, and vocational ambitions but also to select an appropriate curriculum and division of the college or university.

4. With the increase in the number of schools offering sections for the slow and less able academic student and sections for the abler ones, effective educational guidance in these areas has been becoming of much more importance, as it has in the area of the wise choice of elective courses.

5. Guidance in matters of social life has also become more important, if for no other reason, because of the age stratification of social life and the great increase in the tendency of adolescents to want to participate in a more sophisticated social life involving such things as the use of the automobile, drinking of intoxicating liquors, and visiting of questionable amusement places. Similar guidance needs arise from ideas of adolescents about sex relationships and from the variety of standards and degrees of control by parents.

6. The requirement of a period of military training for all young men creates problems not experienced by previous generations. The necessity of military service makes it necessary for young men to plan a coordinated program of school attendance and military service, as well to select a type of military service and a division of the armed forces. The aggressive competition of the military services for recruitment adds further to the desirability for guidance by informed individuals whose only consideration is sound advice to the youngster.

7. In recent years, there have been several developments that have increased the possibilities of, and the need for, guidance in the area of health. In the first place, many schools have increased their program of health education, immunization, and health counseling. Furthermore, far more is known about preservation of good health, both physical and mental.

Not only have a surprisingly large number of cases of mental ill health and emotional disturbance been recognized among young people, but, with developments in psychiatry, the resources available for arresting or correcting mental ill health have increased greatly. The out-of-school life of adolescents, particularly senior high school boys and girls, involving as it does for many of them late hours, unfortunate diet, excessive smoking, and lack of exercise, has contributed to the greater need for health guidance.

8. The drift away from religious ideals on the part of a large share of the population has created in many youngsters conflicts between religion

and non-religious life that call for guidance in setting up a personal philosophy of life.

9. There is an increased necessity for guidance and counseling relative to the matter of socially acceptable behavior. Counselors are coming to play a larger role in chronic and critical disciplinary cases among youngsters, particularly with respect to the discovery of reasons for the unacceptable behavior and to the suggesting of constructive approaches to the problem. Teachers and principals have also increased their use of this type of approach to the problem of misbehavior. Problems of social relationships both within and outside of the home, including matters of acceptance by one's peers and of relationships with other members of the home challenge the school to be of service to young people.[1]

It is unfortunate that, while the needs for guidance and the importance of good counseling service have increased so much, the amount and quality of counseling by parents have not increased proportionately, but perhaps in the majority of families they have actually diminished by reason of the following facts:

1. Parents are often preoccupied with their jobs and social lives, particularly in those homes where both the mother and father are working.

2. Life has become more complex and apparently lacking in appropriate standards.

3. Many parents fail to understand the problems of adolescents today or the changes in American life that impinge upon adolescent development. There is also a tendency for many parents to indulge their sons and daughters, even to the extent of bringing about rivalry between the parents themselves, either intentionally or as a result of trying to obtain the good will of the youngsters or to impress them.

The opportunities of valuable guidance service have been heightened by the increased amount of knowledge that is available today relative to the psychology of learning and maturation and to mental hygiene of people in general and adolescents in particular.

**Changes in the Philosophy of Guidance.** In recent years, new ideas about guidance have been developed by experts and careful students in the field, along with new information about healthy growth and development. The more important elements in a modern philosophy of guidance may be summarized as follows:

1. Effective guidance does not necessarily mean making decisions for young people or pushing them toward any particular solution of their problem. The best service is to assist the counselee to think effectively

[1] See pages 43–53 for a listing of some of these important problems.

about his problem. In many situations, the problem is not one that can be solved once and for all at the time but is more or less constantly recurring or chronic.

2. In many cases, the problem of the counselee cannot be solved immediately or directly. For example, the problem may have to do with the face, figure, or height of a girl or the size and appearance of a boy, or it may be a problem in the home about which nothing can be done immediately. In many such instances, the solution to the problem involves enabling the youngster to develop a sound philosophy of living with the situation and developing compensatory interests and satisfactions.

In recent years, counselors and school administrators in many communities have established contacts with, and cooperated with, local community agencies such as state, national, and local social welfare personnel; juvenile courts; Kiwanis and other service clubs; state employment agencies; and health and recreational agencies.

In addition to individual counseling in personal conferences, group guidance has become increasingly recognized as very promising. Group guidance is conducted in homerooms, core classes, and, indeed, in regular classes, through dissemination of useful information and discussion of life problems.

## EDUCATIONAL GUIDANCE

Adolescents in junior and senior high schools need information and counseling with respect to a number of very important problems in connection with decisions that they must make about schoolwork. In this section will be described some of the major enterprises of the better schools along these lines.

**Orienting New Students to the School.** The very great majority of secondary schools now have functioning programs for orienting new students to the new school. Information is given to them concerning the courses available in the curriculum and how they might make the best decisions with respect to election of these courses or curriculums. This, of course, is closely tied in with vocational decisions and vocational counseling, since courses taken and curriculums followed should be selected with a view to preparation for one or two vocations or a vocational field the student has tentatively chosen.

In this orientation program, information also is given concerning the opportunities and conditions for participation in clubs, as well as the rules and procedures relative to attendance, tardiness, behavior in the building, driving and parking of cars, lockers, the daily bell schedule, marking systems, study-hall regulations, etc. In addition, the new students are encouraged to raise their own questions.

Almost all but the smallest schools now prepare and distribute handbooks with information of these types and with respect to many other matters. (See next chapter for description and discussion of student handbooks.)

**Guidance in the Lower Schools.** In a considerable number of school systems, the representatives of the higher schools go to the lower schools contributing students, give information about the new school, and answer the questions students ask about it. The representatives of junior high schools will probably go to several elementary schools, and the representative of senior high schools will go to two or more junior high schools. The representatives are usually two carefully coached students, a boy and a girl, who explain student life in the new school, including opportunities in the various clubs and other student organizations.

**Registration for Courses.** Much more attention is being given in better secondary schools to registration of students for courses than was the case in years past. In many schools, registration takes place in the spring, preceded by a period of several weeks in which students may consider the problem and receive counseling and during which a bulletin is sent to the parents. In some schools, conferences are held with parents. Also, many use a form for obtaining the parents' signatures as approval of the student's selection of courses for the coming semester.

Many schools appoint as registration advisers specialists with better-than-average training for that type of work. Past experience has shown that counseling by unselected and relatively uninformed teachers is likely to be quite misleading and to consist largely of recruiting students for courses in departments in which the teacher has a special interest. In many schools, all student registrations are examined finally by representatives of the principal, usually specialized counselors, who may refer some of the registrations back to the students and counselors for further study.

**New Students and Their Progress.** In a great many secondary schools, new students are given special attention, particularly during the first semester. At the close of the first month or six weeks, particularly when the first report cards are issued, the marks given to each new student are examined and compared with previous marks, measures of academic ability, and other data that may be available about the student and should give some idea of his academic capacity.

Conferences between the student and the counselor are arranged immediately in cases in which the student is obviously an underachiever, in other words, where he is not getting as good marks as are expected of him. At this conference, the counselor attempts to discover why the student is an underachiever, exploring with one or more teachers such matters as personality maladjustment, excessive time spent out of school at work and in social life, or the possibility of the student having enrolled for a subject that is too difficult or uninteresting for him.

After this initial conference, the counselor attempts to work out some adjustment with the student, in some cases confers with the student's parents, usually with the student present, and arranges for future conferences over the rest of the semester, spaced at intervals of about three weeks.

**Guidance for College.** Much more attention is being given in most secondary schools, particularly senior high schools, to guidance of students for college. In recent years, guidance and counseling services have extended not only down into the tenth grade but even into the eighth and ninth grades, as it has come to be believed that students give some thought as early as in the seventh or eighth grade to the matter of attending college and should be given information concerning how to choose a college and how to select a college curriculum. Students intending to visit one or more colleges should be given special briefing on what to see, hear, and otherwise find out.[2]

In recent years, a great many colleges and universities have made it much more difficult to enter, by becoming more selective and raising their entrance requirements. While in 1964 there are still many good colleges and universities that can take more students, by 1970 it will be difficult for any but superior students to obtain admission to a good four-year institution. This has very greatly increased the interest of students and their parents in good counseling and preparation for college. In many senior high schools, there are counselors given the specific responsibility of becoming specialists in guiding students with respect to the selection of a college, to obtaining admission to college, to selecting a curriculum, and to the factors related to success and congenial life in college.[3]

Causing much surprise on the part of many parents are the facts being disseminated widely concerning the differences among colleges and universities with respect to the pattern and degree of intellectual ability required for success. There are some colleges in the United States in which the lowest fourth of the students corresponds to the upper fourth

---

[2] See *How To Visit Colleges,* by the National Vocational Guidance Association, Washington, D.C., 1960.

[3] High school seniors may well be referred to such books as *Introduction to College Life,* by Norman I. Bell (Boston: Houghton Mifflin Co., 1962), and *Complete Planning for College,* by Sidney Sulkin (New York: McGraw-Hill Book Co., Inc., 1962).

in other colleges. It follows naturally that students of less-than-average academic ability should select a college the requirements of which are not too great for them. Likewise, students of superior ability should enter a college in which there is ample stimulation and opportunity for the exploitation of superior talent.

Although a great many colleges and universities require some set pattern of credit in high school subjects, particularly English, mathematics, science, and foreign languages, there has been repeated and ample proof that grades made in college have practically no relationship to subjects taken in high school. That students who had certain subjects such as foreign languages and advanced mathematics do better in college has been definitely shown to be attributable to the fact that the students who select courses in these fields have superior academic ability and interest. Nevertheless, students need to know the pattern of subjects required for entrance to the college or colleges they would like to attend. There is great variation in these patterns.

Students may be well advised to write to one of the following centers established to assist students to obtain admission to an appropriate college or university:[4]

Association of College Admissions Counselor, Northbrook, Ill.
College Admissions Center, Evanston, Ill.
College Admissions Assistance Center, New York, N.Y.
Catholic College Admissions Center, Worcester, Mass.

**Available Loans.** For students of superior promise, substantial loans are available if they are needed for college attendance. Between February 1, 1959, and February 1, 1964, approximately $200,000,000 will have been loaned to more than 300,000 students.[5]

**Factors Associated with College Marks.** A great many investigations have shown that perhaps the datum most closely related to marks in college is the average high school mark or rank in the graduating class. Closely behind that are scores made on college entrance examinations. From neither can grades made in college be predicted with great accuracy.

The average mark made in any particular high school subject is also correlated with the average mark made in that subject in college. The relationship between the number of units taken in foreign languages, in mathematics, or in any particular subject with grades made in college in general or grades in a particular field, when academic aptitude is held

[4] Catholic students would find useful the *Official Guide to Catholic Universities and Colleges* (New York: Doubleday & Co., Inc., 1962).

[5] Current information may be obtained free from the Division of Higher Education of the National Education Association, Washington, D.C. Quite frequently, indebtedness is canceled for students entering the teaching profession.

constant, is almost negligible and affords little basis for prophecy of the degree of success in college.[6] If the high school average and the intelligence, college aptitude, or college entrance examination score are combined, a somewhat better prediction can be made. Neverthelss, it is impossible to predict at all accurately from any combination of data the marks that will be made in college by high school students. Sometimes those with the best prognosis do not survive the freshman year, and some of those who are thought to be average students turn out to be very superior. This is because among the important factors are the student's interest and industry and the amount of time he spent outside in work, in social life, and in athletics.

## VOCATIONAL GUIDANCE

**Information About Vocations.** Guidance in secondary schools originally was very largely vocational guidance, and this still is a major field. The majority of secondary schools offer a course on occupations, usually for a semester, sometimes in both the junior high school and the senior high school. In this course, students read a great deal of material on various occupations. They are lead by the instructor to discover criteria by which one should select a vocation. Students are taught how to study themselves and to make appropriate interpretations. They are given information concerning a great many occupations, including, of course, how to prepare for one, what the financial rewards are, what the conditions of work are, what security is attached, how soon one is forced to retire, and what fringe benefits there usually are in that field. There may be obtained from the Superintendent of Documents, Washington, D.C., copies of *The Occupational Handbook*, with up-to-date information about occupations in the United States.

As approximately half the students entering the tenth grade have narrowed their choice, tentatively at least, to one or two vocations, there is great need to assist boys and girls in learning how to choose a vocation by the time they reach the ninth grade. In many junior high schools, vocational-guidance service has been increased and improved in recent years.

A student should study carefully the entrance requirements of the colleges he is thinking of attending. It is desirable to make a vocational choice before the twelfth grade, and nearly three-fourths of secondary school students were doing that in 1962.

For use by students taking the courses in occupations there is usually provided a large collection of pamphlets and bulletins containing infor-

[6] See the results of the Eight-Year Study described in Chapter 10.

mation about occupations. Because of the important changes taking place in American vocational life, these materials are usually kept up to date. This collection is also very desirable and valuable to students who have had the occupation class and have discovered how to obtain and interpret vocational information and how to approach a vocational decision.

In vocational guidance, of course, there is the necessity of having appropriate counseling data such as scores on aptitude tests in those fields in which they are available, the Strong Vocational Interest Inventory, and the Kuder Vocational Interest Check List.[7]

Some schools still arrange a series of talks in assemblies on different occupations by a representative of each occupation. This procedure has not proved to be very successful and has been discontinued in many schools. Also of limited value but employed in a number of schools are what are called "career nights," in which the student goes at night to a room in the school building where the vocation of his choice will be discussed by one or more of its representatives in the community.

**Placement Service.** In an increasing number of senior high schools, a placement bureau is operated that will assist students in obtaining work during the school year and during the summer. The placement bureau is usually under the management of an individual who is well versed in vocational guidance and who, therefore, can see that the experience of the student on the job during school and in the summer is, wherever possible, of a nature that will assist the student to learn more about the vocation he might want to follow.

In fairly recent years, placement bureaus have also been serving former students—dropouts and graduates. In many senior high schools, one or two counselors are specially designated as vocational counselors and become very efficient specialists in this particular field. Sometimes one counselor deals with boys and the other with girls. To an increasing degree, vocational counselors are making contact and exchanging information with personnel specialists in various industries and other concerns.

## OTHER FIELDS OF GUIDANCE

**Guidance Relative to Military Service.** This recently developed field is forging to the front as an important area of guidance service in secondary schools and colleges. It has been increasingly apparent that, while representatives and recruiting officers of the armed forces and the advertising employed by them provide a great deal of information, they do so from the point of view of the particular service involved and not

[7] See Donald E. Super and J. O. Crites, *Appraising Vocational Fitness by Psychological Tests* (New York: Harper & Row, 1962).

primarily for the benefit of the advisee. For this reason as well as because plans for military service should differ for different students, depending upon a considerable number of factors, secondary schools are moving rapidly these years to improve their programs of military guidance, which must, of course, be tied in with educational, vocational, and, in many instances, health and character and personality guidance.

**Health Guidance.** With the expansion of programs of health education and health examinations and service, there has come a greater opportunity for guidance in connection with health. It centers largely, to be sure, around the counseling of students on the basis of physical and health examinations, conferring with parents in many instances, but it also includes counseling with students about health problems not brought into relief by examinations. The student may bring a problem to the health counselor, or some teacher or other counselor may report to the health counselor his suspicion that the student's health may call for some study or a conference with his parents.

With the greatly increased attention being given to mental and emotional health, and with the recognition of the fact that many more young people than was formerly supposed are suffering from at least a mild form of mental illness or emotional disturbance, health counseling and guidance in this area have been markedly improved in a great many secondary schools in recent years.

**Social Guidance.** Increased attention has been given in recent years to what is called by many "social guidance." Boys and girls seem to be getting into junior and senior high schools without having developed nearly as much as is desired in the realm of social life and contacts with other people. Some have become somewhat withdrawn and isolated; others, aggressive and unpopular; others, shy and awkward in social contacts; and still others, lacking in the social graces.

While, without question, giving youngsters opportunity to improve in this area should not in any way displace any part of the regular subject curriculum, it can be and is being provided for to a greater extent in a number of ways including group discussion, individual counseling along lines of individual needs, and provision of opportunities for practice in extracurricular activities, in the classroom, and in social events that are part of the school program.

**Character and Personality Guidance.** Since the beginning of secondary schools, principals and teachers have attempted to counsel and guide young people in matters of character and personality, particularly in the days when schools had a strong religious orientation. This type of service has continued, and, since World War II, the rise in juvenile delinquency has stimulated secondary school principals and counselors to seek to improve counseling service, and, indeed, the whole educational program, with respect to the development of a healthy character and personality. In many instances, the guidance situation develops out of a case of discipline. In an effort to discover why a student is continually a disciplinary problem or why a student has committed some very serious crime, a very careful case study is made and a number of conferences with individuals carefully selected for the purpose are provided. All this is undertaken in order to help the student.

Often, school counselors have attempted to work with juvenile courts in connection with the juvenile delinquency of their counselees. In many schools, a system of procedure has been developed that usually includes the following:

1. The local courts and police inform the principal of all arrests and impending arrests involving students in the school.
2. The counselor promptly interviews the student involved, with a view to getting his side of the case and seeing to what extent the counselor could be of service.
3. The counselor cooperates with parents and others in making certain that reasons for the student's behavior may be ascertained, as a means to seeing that treatment or punishment is adapted to suit the individual child.
4. The counselor arranges to be present at court hearings and to keep informed concerning the case.
5. If the student is sent to jail or reform school, he is assisted in working out a program of rehabilitation, and the counselor works in confidence with the student in an effort to reduce to the minimum the harmful effects of conviction and confinement.

## COUNSELEE DATA[8]

If counseling is to be at all effective, it must be based on a considerable amount of accurate and valid knowledge concerning the counselee. In the great majority of good secondary schools, data on all students are available to teachers as well as counselors. Throughout each student's school career, data about him are steadily accumulated. A representative list of the contents of the files, after a period of time might include the following data:

1. Vital data: age, birthplace, home, number and sex of siblings, age and occupation of parents, educational level of parents, etc.
2. Health records: height, weight, history of disease, history of inoculations and vaccinations, dental conditions, eyes and ears, etc.

[8] See Chapter 15, for additional information and suggestions relative to learning about the individual student by teachers.

3. School record: academic marks, achievement test scores, attendance and punctuality record.
4. Intelligence-test scores.
5. Personal-social adjustment: to peers, to older persons, in home, school, community.
6. Personal problems, fears.
7. Aptitude test results.
8. Personality test results.
9. Interests and hobbies.
10. Student activities: record of participation and leadership.
11. Vocational goals and plans for college attendance.
12. Employment record.
13. Image of self: personal goals, values, standards.
14. Anecdotal records.
15. Pupil- and parent-conference reports.
16. Record of participation in church and other community activities.
17. Samples of writing, art, etc., from various years.
18. Autobiography.
19. Insights about social or civic problems.
20. Special achievements.
21. Time budgets.

Some of these data need to be collected by the classroom teacher for the students in his classes, for example, data relative to interests and hobbies, image of self, vocational and college plans, conference records, personal problems, and employment activities.

**Testing Programs.** Particularly for the purpose of guidance, but also for other purposes, most schools today have definite testing programs similar to that in the Niles Township (Illinois) High Schools (grades nine to twelve), shown below.

| Test | What It Measures | When Given and to Whom |
| --- | --- | --- |
| *8th Grade and Entrance* | | |
| 1. Otis Quick-Scoring Test of Mental Ability* | Intelligence (gives an I.Q.) | Second semester, 8th grade—to all students |
| *Freshman Year* | | |
| 2. Kuder Preference Record—Vocational | Ten areas of possible vocational interest | First semester— to all freshmen |

* Test scores obtained by the high schools are supplemented by various test scores from the public elementary schools of the township. The Iowa Tests of Basic Skills, measuring vocabulary, reading comprehension, language skills, work-study skills, and arithmetic skills, are given in the second semester of the eighth grade. Students transferring into grades ten, eleven, and twelve are given the Iowa Silent Reading Test, Advanced Form.

| Test | What It Measures | When Given and to Whom |
|---|---|---|
| 3. Differential Aptitude Tests (Verbal and Numerical) | Verbal reasoning ability, numerical ability, and composite of verbal reasoning and numerical ability | First semester— to all freshmen |
| *Sophomore Year* | | |
| 4. Sequential Tests of Educational Program | Five areas of general educational growth: mathematics, science, social science, reading, and writing | Second semester— to all sophomores |
| *Junior Year* | | |
| 5. Preliminary Scholastic Aptitude Test of College Board Examinations (PSAT) | Mental ability—appraises capacity to undertake college study Includes both verbal and mathematical sections | In October—to juniors who register |
| 6. National Merit Scholarship Qualifying Test | First screening test in process of qualifying for certain scholarships Consists of five divisions: English usage, mathematics usage, social-studies reading, natural-science reading, and word usage Gives a composite score | In March—to juniors who register |
| *Senior Year* | | |
| 7. Johnson Temperament Analysis | Degree of personal-social maturity and adjustment Nine behavior patterns or tendencies included | Any time—to family-living classes |
| 8. Scholarship Qualifying Test— Preliminary Scholastic Aptitude Test | First screening test in the process of qualification for certain scholarships Two sections: verbal and mathematical | In October—to seniors who register |
| 9. College Entrance Examination Board Tests | Potential for doing college work Two divisions: a. Scholastic aptitude testing in verbal and mathematical areas b. Achievement testing in eleven different subject fields | On four scheduled dates in December, January, March, and May—to seniors who register |
| 10. American College Testing Program (ACT) | Potential for doing college work Four divisions: English, mathematics, social studies, and natural sciences Gives a composite score | On three scheduled dates in November, February, and April —to seniors who register |
| 11. General Aptitude Test Battery of Illinois State Employment Service | Aptitudes and interests in a variety of occupations, primarily those not requiring college training | non-college-bound First semester—to seniors who register |

The test score of each individual is available to all teachers, counselors, and, under certain circumstances and to an increasing extent in recent years, parents.

**Case Studies.** It is very desirable to make a careful investigation of the individual youngster who seems to constitute an unusual problem of lack of cooperation, chronic or severe misbehavior, or conspicuous under-achievement. This should involve a variety of sources of data and conferences with a number of people who know the student, including his counselors, former teachers, principal or assistant principal, and parents. Quite frequently, conferences with several of these people prove to be very profitable.

Case studies of individuals who are failing may bring into relief factors that can be remedied but that will make further unaided efforts by the pupil seem useless. Case studies may include any combination of the following types of data:

1. Reasons for dislike of school
2. Conditions at home: mental, emotional, and hygienic
3. Outside employment: nature and hours
4. Health records and medical-examination data
5. Temperament and moral character
6. Vocational plans or interests
7. General mental ability
8. Reading ability and study habits
9. Extracurricular participation

In every school, there should be someone to consult all the available data of these types, gather other needed data by visitation or conference with the pupil, his parents, his teachers, or his associates, and determine as far as possible why the pupil is failing. In small schools, the principal may carry on this work alone or assisted by the members of his staff who are interested in various individual cases; in larger schools, trained counselors should be employed in this work. With proper organization for guidance, the head of the guidance program should include this work as one of his major responsibilities. The visiting teacher, if there be one, should be utilized as an important agent for obtaining useful data.

Perhaps the most usable organization for such guidance is that of having each homeroom or group counselor handle his own group of pupils. Failing work or deficiencies likely to lead to failures should be reported directly to the counselor or to the office, from which the reports will be sent to the advisers concerned.

Careful analysis of data will locate the remediable causes for a considerable percentage of failures, many of which are otherwise not readily discernible. The following cases are illustrative of both the causes of poor work and the remedial treatment prescribed:

Pupil A. Inability to read effectively. Remedy: Training in reading.

Pupil B. General poor health and lack of vitality. Remedy: Light program, tactful management.

Pupil C. Imaginary illness. Remedy: Enlightenment of parents and pupil on point.

Pupil D. Stomach disorder causing nervousness. Remedy: Medical treatment.

Pupil E. Works in army store from 7:00 p.m. to midnight. Remedy: Lighter program, consult parents about more sleep.

Pupil F. Engaged in milking and delivering milk from 5:00 to 8:00 a.m. Remedy: Shorten pupil's work schedule to from 6:30 to 8:30 a.m.

Pupil G. Dreaming in class—never pays attention. Remedy: Train to check self, take notes on trend of recitation, influence largely by inspiration of adviser.

Pupil H. General lack of interest in, or taste for, school. Remedy: Personal interest of teachers.

Pupil I. Speech disability and emotional complications. Remedy: Special speech instruction, diplomatic handling by teachers.

Pupil J. Interested only in drawing. Remedy: Change program—drop most distasteful subject, employ talent in all school affairs.

Pupil K. Eyesight poor—consequent headaches, dislike of study, nervousness. Remedy: Provide glasses through loan from available fund.

Pupil L. General lack of interest; parents, both employed, frequently quarrel; no check on boy, who spends time in pool halls and around depot. Remedy: Urge parents to give more attention to boy and his interests, more companionship during leisure time at home.

**Counseling and Discipline.** Following is the report of a typical case that was an apparent problem of discipline that actually proved to be one of citizenship guidance:

A Discipline Case Which Really Is a Guidance Case

(Girl. Age 16. Sophomore in High School)

California mental maturity test—93 I.Q.

Wechsler-Bellevue:

Verbal Scale—93 I.Q.

Performance Scale—122 I.Q.

Co-op Reading—20 per cent (sophomore norms).

Orthorator (Vision Test)—Normal vision.

My own check tests:

Vocabulary—very weak.

Information—weak.

Grades—0.23 (D average).

Student is a severe behavioral problem in school. She is a leader of sorts, but is unable to retain friends. Discipline is ineffective. She responded temporarily to encouragement in a counseling situation.

Student shows severe anxiety reactions. Is a remedial case—has high potential ability, but low achievement. We have an interview, reading diagnosis, and reading progress report on her.

Student's difficulty is not entirely due to academic causes. Her low self-concept seems to be the primary problem at the present time.

## GUIDANCE PERSONNEL

In recent years, not only has the number of counselors with definite training in counseling and guidance increased very greatly, perhaps more than doubling between 1950 and 1963, but various types of specialists including the following have been added:

1. *Psychometrists.* These are well trained, at least with a master's degree, many with a doctor's degree, in the field of tests, measurements, and the interpretation of measurements.

2. *Directors of guidance.* These are usually people wtih successful experience as counselors and a doctor's degree in that field who have the responsibility for selecting and supervising the counselors and for leadership in the guidance program. They maintain contacts with individuals and agencies in the community. In some places, they are also in charge of the psychometric program.

3. *Psychologists.* Many of the larger schools have added to their staff in recent years a full-time psychologist whose principal responsibility is to confer with teachers about problem youngsters, to confer with problem youngsters themselves, and, in some instances, to recommend psychiatric treatment and to confer with parents about the unusually difficult cases. In some schools he also has charge of the psychometric program.

4. *Psychiatrists.* It still is a rare school that has a full-time psychiatrist; nevertheless, in recent years, the number of schools able to provide at least a little psychiatric service to their students has increased very greatly. Usually, half-time service of a psychiatrist is available, and to him youngsters definitely in need of psychiatric diagnosis and treatment are sent. Ordinarily, he is not able to give psychiatric treatment, but he may make various types of recommendations for home treatment or for special treatment by the school psychologist or the student's teachers.

5. *Home visitors.* On the staff of the larger and better-supported schools is at least one home visitor, perhaps a social worker. The responsibilities of the home visitor are largely those of liaison, passing back and forth of information needed by parents and by teachers, and of advising parents and teachers in connection with the difficulties of problem youngsters. The results of the work of home visitors have been so obviously useful

that many secondary schools with only one home visitor are now adding a second and some schools with two are adding a third.

It should be clear that the work and responsibility of counseling and guidance are distributed among various types and levels of workers—classroom teachers, class counselors, and specialized counselors in such fields as vocational guidance, educational guidance, and health guidance, as well as those mentioned in the foregoing paragraphs.

**The Counselor's Proper Functions.** An excellent statement of the proper functions of the professional counselor specified that he should

1. *Engage in professional counseling* with individuals and groups of students (limit of eight) who are involved in emotional problems which inhibit their ability to learn. The school counselor would provide a counseling atmosphere in which the student could mature emotionally and more actively involve himself in the process of learning.
2. *Motivate students to seek counseling* of their own volition through a creative and continuous program involving orientation to counseling. For students to make use of the counseling service, the counselor must offer a significant helping relationship and develop an image of the professional counselor among students.
3. *Conduct research* designed to measure the effectiveness of individual and group counseling in promoting the emotional maturity of students.
4. Conduct group-centered *in-service programs* with teachers, administrators, and parents whereby they can become acquainted with the philosophical and empirical considerations which influence the work of the counselor.
5. Provide *informational services* to students, parents, teachers, and administrators to meet the informational needs of each group.
6. Function as a *resource consultant;* that is, develop a reciprocal relationship between the school and community resources to develop fully the individual student.
7. Provide *testing services* which would enable the student to appraise his actual and potential capabilities.
8. Assist in the *grouping of students* to provide a learning situation of maximum benefit to students.[9]

**Qualifications of Professional Counselors.** An outstanding publication, sponsored jointly by the American Personnel and Guidance Association, *Identification and Guidance of Able Students,* contains the following recommendations regarding the training and personal qualifications for people entering the guidance field:

The following items cover the skills and knowledge that education at the graduate level must develop for the counselor.

1. Skill in the use of various kinds of educational and psychological tests and measurements and in interpretation of the results. This is not the

[9] Angelo V. Boy and Henry Isaksen, "The Secondary School Counselors Determine Their Role," *Bulletin of the N.A.S.S.P.,* No. 276 (October, 1962), pp. 98–101.

technical skill of the test builder or psychometrist, but rather the know-how of the test-user.

2. Skill, developed under supervision, in the use of the interview.
3. Knowledge of referral resources and how to use them, including both those within the school itself and those in the surrounding community.
4. Knowledge about sources of vocational information, methods of evaluating such data, and ways of utilizing them in occupational counseling situations.
5. Special understanding of personality development and adjustment, with competence in dealing with problems of adjustment which students present.
6. An understanding of society and of social trends, including especially the social institutions in the fields of education and industry.
7. Competence in dealing with students and their problems of learning and an understanding of educational and occupational choice and planning.
8. A broad background in the behavioral and social sciences, particularly as·applied to the age levels and job settings in which the counselor works.
9. An understanding of American educational philosophy as it affects the the schools, including administrative structure, policy, and procedures and the roles of administrators, teachers, special staff, and pupils.
10. Philosophical and psychological understanding and appreciation of the counseling function which give him: (a) confidence in adapting techniques and procedures to the needs of the student being counseled; (b) appreciation and acceptance of the ethical implications and obligations of the counseling relationship; (c) knowledge about the various roles he may legitimately assume effectively in counseling; (d) understanding of personal limitations as well as potentialities; and (e) appreciation of the value of continuing study and experimentation in adapting new methods and techniques, together with a willingness to conduct ongoing scientific evaluation of his efforts.[10]

## THE TEACHER AS COUNSELOR

**Opportunities and Limitations.** It has been repeatedly pointed out that the teacher has unusual opportunities for guidance, since he is in the physical presence of many students each day and may easily arrange conferences with them. Furthermore, the student has at least an acquaintance with the teacher, if not a friendly feeling favorable for counseling and cooperation. The teacher also has acquired information about the student from working with him in the class.

Nevertheless, it is equally, if not more, obvious that the typical classroom teacher has only a small part of the knowledge that a counselor

[10] *Identification and Guidance of Able Students,* American Association for the Advancement of Science, Report of Conferences on Testing and Counseling, University of Michigan, Ann Arbor, 1958.

must have about the student to render high-grade service, and the teacher has, indeed, a very limited amount of information relative to such things as college life, university entrance requirements, vocational life, and many other subjects about which the student must be counseled.

Every teacher should be alert to the possibilities of employing teaching subjects or extracurricular activities assigned to him as means of contributing to one or more of the following:

1. Exploration of students' potential interest in the various
   a. Fields of learning
   b. Types of vocational activities
   c. Types of non-vocational activities and leisure interests and activities
2. Exploration of the students' abilities in various types of
   a. Academic learning
   b. Motor learning and activities
   c. Vocational activities
3. Orientation of the students with respect to such aspects of various vocations as
   a. Kinds of activities performed
   b. Opportunities and rewards—financial and social, initial and ultimate
   c. Conditions of work with respect to safety, health, permanence of home, and hours of work
   d. Demands in the way of education, qualities of personality, etc., as prerequisites to entrance and advancement
4. Orientation of the students with respect to the high school and its program and opportunities, and to higher institutions, especially with regard to
   a. Opportunities and types of education provided through both curricular and extracurricular avenues
   b. Expenses and opportunities for self-support in higher institutions
   c. Demands of various types of curriculums and subjects for general and special ability
   d. Entrance requirements of the higher institutions
5. Self-analysis by students to determine personality and character growth along such lines as
   a. Cooperativeness
   b. Fair-mindedness
   c. Appearance and adjustment to social conventions
   d. Initiative
   e. Originality
   f. Leadership

**Division of Functions between Teachers and Counselors.** The following diagram is indicative of the differentiation in the responsibilities and activities of specialists and non-specialists in guidance and suggests good working relationships:

FUNCTIONS OF TEACHERS AND SPECIALISTS IN GUIDANCE SERVICES

(Principal [or designated representative] coordinates administration of services.)

| Special Services to Individual Youth | Functions of Classroom (and Homeroom) Teachers | Functions of the Guidance Specialists |
|---|---|---|
| 1. Choosing a vocation | Provides learning situations Collects data about interests Confers with youth on interests Plans studies related to choice | Maintains occupational materials, files, records Observes youth at work Gives aptitude tests Helps teachers prepare resource units on vocations |
| 2. Finding a job | Maintains records for specialists Helps youth with applications and interview preparation Helps youth with work habits and techniques | Maintains records for prospective employers Makes opportunity analyses Places youth in jobs Helps in adjustment on job Maintains records of follow-up studies |
| 3. Planning an educational program | Collects data about interests Maintains records for specialists Confers with youth about needs Studies school's total curriculum | Maintains records of college requirements Gives intelligence and other tests Studies success in school and college Advises faculty on curriculum changes |
| 4. Solving personal problems | Studies youth's total activities Maintains personal histories Confers with youth regarding problems and refers to specialists | Maintains contact with non-school sources of help Confers with individuals Arranges for special help |
| 5. Overcoming academic difficulties | Observes difficulties in skills Administers diagnostic tests Confers with youth and recommends sources of help Gives remedial instruction Advises other teachers of needs | Recommends or gives tests Refers to clinical agencies Confers with youth and teacher Advises teachers on remedial instruction |

SOURCE: William M. Alexander and J. Galen Saylor, *Modern Secondary Education* (New York: Holt, Rinehart & Winston, Inc., 1957), p. 176.

Good teacher-counselor relationships involve the following:

1. Bringing teachers into active participation in guidance program.
   a. Teachers devise personal inventory forms for student use.
   b. Teachers prepare student survey forms to be considered for use in parent conferences.
   c. Teachers express opinion on courses or sections students should take.
   d. Conferences held with new teachers by counselor to introduce guidance facilities.
   e. Pre-school workshop and in-service training of teachers includes the unit on guidance services.
   f. Individual conferences of teacher and counselor on special cases.
   g. Case conferences include teacher, special service staff, and administrator with counselor as chairman.
   h. Teachers participate in identification of gifted students with counselor.
2. Standardized test results and resumé of student's cumulative record is distributed to all teachers.
3. Guidance handbook is provided for teachers.
4. Emphasis on teachers' understanding of testing program in faculty and in-service training meetings.
5. Potential drop-out lists with factors needing the most attention are provided for each teacher.
6. Emphasis on every teacher having course work in guidance.
7. Counselor supplies information on all new pupils to teachers.
8. In order to cut clerical work on part of teachers and counselor in guidance activities to a minimum, administrators assign clerical personnel to the guidance office or arrange for the work to be done in other offices.[11]

**The Teacher and Student Data.** In an increasing number of schools, many of the data concerning students are provided to the teacher of each student's classes. This is a relatively recent but long-overdue development. Teachers should know far more about the individual student than they do.

A number of types of data about the students that are of much importance in counseling are gathered and recorded by the classroom teachers themselves for their own use and for the use of the counselors. Among these types of data, the following are increasingly employed:

1. An autobiography written by the student, which may throw light on many things including his interests, his personality and other characteristics, the sources of some of his emotional disturbance and worry, his ambitions, his social adjustment at home and among his peers, etc.

[11] Harold F. Cottingham and William E. Hopke, *Guidance in the Junior High School* (Bloomington, Ill.: McKnight & McKnight Publishing Co., 1961), pp. 349–350.

2. Data concerning interests of the individual student, which may grow out of an interest-inventory check list that the teacher has administered, or out of the recording of the interests of the student as he has revealed them in class discussion, in the field, or in conference

3. Data concerning the student's social behavior and social adjustment, obtained from observations by the teacher of the student in his relations with other students—including observation of his leadership qualities and his negative qualities.

4. Sociometric data, which may be obtained by use of either formal sociograms or ordinary informal observations of the teacher, who notes the number, nature, and pattern of the student's social relations with his classmates

**The Superior Teacher-Counselor.** The teacher who is best equipped to do superior counseling has had courses or has done much careful reading in the following fields: intelligence and aptitude tests and their interpretation, theory and principles of counseling and guidance, adolescent and social psychology, mental hygiene, and elementary statistical methods. The specialized counselor will, of course, have had these and also courses in social psychology, vocational information, special aptitudes and their measurement, school achievement testing, the psychology of personality—its measurement and diagnosis, and techniques of counseling.

The superior counselor usually has had a great deal of experience in association with young people in their play and social activities; has worked with youth clubs and organizations such as the Scouts, Camp Fire Girls, YMCA, and youth church groups; has had work experience outside of the classroom; and has had experience in interviewing.

Characteristics of the superior teacher-counselor include the following: He maintains a cheerful and thoughtful objectivity; avoids excessive sympathizing or condemnation; avoids backslapping superficiality in meeting young people; recognizes that the withdrawing, daydreaming child is as much in need of individual help as the aggressive one; makes it a point to consult a great quantity of data about the individual before attempting to give advice; keeps teacher-student conferences confidential; is slow in arriving at conclusions; is not too free with positive advice; is a good listener; realizes that the problems that the boy or girl mentions first are usually not the major ones and that at times the counselee either does not recognize the real problem or is reluctant to mention it if he does; realizes that most frequently the first conference is but the beginning and that there must be a series of conferences if help is to be given in connection with a serious problem; realizes the frequent necessity for referral to someone who is better able to assist the student by reason of greater experience, training, and specialization; recognizes the type of problem that calls for referral; quite frequently does considerable reading or talking with specialists about the student's problem when it has been identified; always encourages the student to come back for additional conferences if the student wants them; and does not pry too quickly or aggressively into private matters.

**Conferences with Parents.** In conferences with parents, the superior teacher-counselor, particularly in matters of discipline,

1. Avoids early discussion of the misbehavior of the student
2. Avoids insincerity, especially in the form of grossly exaggerated complimentary remarks
3. Permits the parent to save face but, nevertheless, eventually causes the parent to see where he or she may have been at fault and attempt to lead the parent to think of the proper procedure under the circumstances
4. Is quite receptive to a parent's suggestions, avoiding early rejection or acceptance of what the parent proposes
5. Avoids attempting to advise the parent too quickly or too much about what apparently needs to be done
6. Realizes that a second and third conference may be necessary and that some things, particularly those that may prove very embarrassing to discuss, might well be left until then

## QUESTIONS, PROBLEMS, AND TOPICS FOR FURTHER STUDY

1. Can you add to the reasons for the current need for better guidance services one not mentioned in the textbook?
2. What responsibility, if any, do you think the school should have for guidance and counseling in connection with military service?
3. Should most guidance be left to parents? Give your reasons.
4. In what fields can parents be relied upon to give good guidance service?
5. In what ways should the school and the parents cooperate?
6. What purpose can counseling serve if the counselor is not able to solve the student's problem?
7. Work out in your mind, and make notes for a talk, the guidance of high school students for college.
8. Is there anything that you can do in teaching your major subject to contribute to the vocational guidance of students?
9. What are your opinions about the place of the school in connection with adult guidance? In connection with operating a placement service?
10. What in your opinion is the part the school should play with juvenile offenders who get into trouble with the law?
11. There are those who insist that teachers should not attempt to do any guidance at all, others who insist that the teacher should do practically all of the guidance, and still others who believe that guidance services should be distributed among different kinds of staff members. What is

your opinion? If you choose the alternative, what do you think the place of each type of staff member should be?

12. What types of data about each student should a teacher have? Where would the teacher get these data?

13. Write out a list of suggestions for teachers in connection with their guidance services.

14. A boy is fifteen years of age, in the tenth grade, and has an I.Q. of 118. He made better-than-average grades throughout elementary school. He is tall, skinny, and non-athletic and his interests are in music and literature, much to the disappointment of his father. He is doing failing work in mathematics, is barely passing in science, and will not take a foreign language. He likes to spend time in school arranging music and dreaming up compositions. He does not like history. His parents say they cannot do anything about him. What if anything, would you do to help him if he were your student?

## SUPPLEMENTARY MATERIALS

### Selected Readings

Austin, David B. *"External Tests and the Junior High School,"* Bulletin of the N.A.S.S.P., XLVI (February, 1962), 42–47.

Bennett, Margaret C. *"Guidance and Counseling in Groups"* (2d ed.). New York: McGraw-Hill Book Co., Inc., 1963.

Douglass, Harl R. *Modern Administration of Secondary Schools* (2d ed.). Boston: Ginn & Co., 1963, Chapters 12 and 13, "Organizing and Improving Guidance," 260–317.

Frymier, J. R. *"Acceptance and Rejection of New Students,"* Progressive Education, XXXIV (January, 1957), 30–32. These are positive suggestions about the ways new students can be helped to become a part of the established group.

Goldman, Lev. "Group Guidance: Content and Process," *Personnel and Guidance Journal,* XL (February, 1962), 518–24.

Harvey, C. C. "Most Serious Problems of Seniors," *Bulletin of the N.A.S.S.P.,* September, 1956, 52–57.

Hill, George E. "Evaluation of Guidance Services," *The Education Digest,* XXVIII (May, 1963), 22–25.

Johnson, Mauritz, Jr., William E. Busacker, and Fred Q. Bowman. "Junior High School Guidance." New York: Harper & Row, 1961. Pp. x–275.

McLean, Paul E. "A Study of Guidance Programs in Selected Texas Junior High Schools and a Recommended Junior High School Guidance Program," *Bulletin of the N.A.S.S.P.,* February, 1962, 316–17.

"Should Parents Know Results of IQ Tests?" *The Education Digest,* XXVII (April, 1962), 19–21.

Van Til, William, Gordon F. Vars, and John H. Lounsbury. *Modern Education for the Junior High School Years.* Indianapolis: The Bobbs-Merrill Co., Inc., 1961. Chapter 21, "Evaluation and Reporting," pp. 470–93.

Warner, Frank B. "Pros and Cons of External Testing Programs," *The North Central Association Quarterly,* Fall, 1961, 201–10.

Watkins, Ralph K. *Techniques of Secondary School Teaching.* New York: The Ronald Press Co., 1958. Chapter 13, "The Evaluation of Learning"; Chapter 14, "Formulation of Marks, Records, and Reports."

Weir, Edward C. *Bulletin of the N.A.S.S.P.*, December, 1962, 23–29.
Wood, Dorothy Adkins. *Test Construction-Development and Interpretation of Achievement Tests.* Columbus, Ohio: Charles E. Merrill Books, Inc., 1961. Chapter 6, "Planning an Objective Test."

## Audio-Visual Materials

### Films

*Counselor's Day.* McGraw-Hill Text-Film. 11 minutes.
*Diagnosis and Planning Adjustments in Counseling.* McGraw-Hill Text-Film. 18 minutes.

### Filmstrip

*Personal Problems of Adolescent Youth.* Ohio State University, 1953. 43 frames, silent, black and white.

# 19

# Articulation of Secondary with Elementary and with Higher Education

## CONTINUITY BETWEEN THE ELEMENTARY SCHOOL AND THE JUNIOR HIGH SCHOOL

**Sixth Grade–Seventh Grade Gap.** When the seventh and eighth grades were in the elementary school and the ninth grade was in the high school, there was good articulation between the sixth grade and the seventh and eighth grades and between the ninth grade and the other grades in the high school, but there existed an unfortunate gap between the eighth grade and the ninth grade. Today, in the school systems where there are junior high schools, the situation has definitely changed. There is a serious gap between the sixth grade and the seventh grade, and there remains a need for improving articulation between the eighth grade and the ninth grade and even more so between the ninth grade and the tenth grade.

In the school systems of practically every other important country, the situation is quite different; somewhat resembling that which existed in the United States a century ago: Secondary education overlaps elementary education, there being a dual system of parallel schools, and the problem of articulation is not a particularly important one, especially since only abler students attend the secondary schools.

**Nature of the Gap.** When students transfer from the sixth grade to the junior high school, they

1. Shift from some seven or eight different elementary school subjects in the academic field, for example, the student no longer has classes in spelling, penmanship, and language and literature but has one class in English
2. Come into contact with teachers who are somewhat different in their training and philosophy of education; being, in every large part, graduates of colleges and universities who have majored in a subject field and minored in one or two others, rather than having majored in education and minored in several fields, many of them have what is commonly referred to as the "subject-centered point of view," as opposed to the "child-centered point of view"
3. Come into contact with the departmentalized assignment of teachers, that is, instead of having one teacher for all or practically all subjects—one teacher who gets well acquainted with each student, providing individual guidance—each student now has at least five or six teachers, and in some schools seven or eight
4. Encounter new standards of discipline and ways of behaving that differ from those to which they had been accustomed in the previous six grades
5. Are taught by methods definitely different from those in the elementary schools, placing much more emphasis upon problem solving, independent effort, and home study
6. Find themselves in a school in which there are new, or at least broadened, facilities which had not been available in their previous years, such as specialized counseling rooms, a large library, an auditorium, and a cafeteria
7. Find an expanded curriculum and a more diversified program of clubs and other extracurricular activities

**Improving Continuity.** Much has been done to bring about articulation between elementary education and secondary education and thus remove unnecessary obstacles to the educational growth of the student. On the other hand, there have been some developments that have impaired articulation.

The junior high school is intended to be a transitional school—to bring about gradual transition from elementary school subjects, standards, and methods to those of secondary education.

Leading educators have wielded a strong influence against overdepartmentalization, recommending that the student have three of his subjects in the seventh grade and two of his subjects in the eighth grade with the same teacher. This practice is successfully followed in a large number, perhaps the majority, of junior high schools.

Furthermore, there has been a great increase in the practice of having the committees that plan the curriculum and other aspects of the educational program made up of representatives of both the elementary school and the junior high school. This operates to reduce undesirable duplication in the subject matter and to bring about subject sequence that tends to make learning less difficult.

In many school systems, the teachers employed in the junior high school have had some special training for that level or else have had some elementary school training in addition to experience in the upper grades of the elementary school, preferably grades seven and eight. With the improvements in the testing program, record systems, and counseling in the schools, there has been a very great increase in the practice of having elementary school records follow the student to the junior high school and become a part of his cumulative records there. This contributes to the better acquaintance of the teachers, counselors, and administrators in the junior high school with the students.

Many schools have a student handbook, frequently prepared with the assistance of student representatives, that is distributed to all new students.[1] The following is an outline of the contents of a typically good student handbook:

A. Introduction
   1. Students' creed
   2. Location, how to reach school
   3. Flag salute
   4. Picture of school
   5. Names and assignments of faculty members
   6. School emblems, colors, mottoes
   7. Aims of the school and accreditation
   8. Greetings: Principal and president of Student Council
B. School Organization
   1. Attendance laws
   2. Excuses
      Absences
      Tardiness
      Leaving class
   3. Building plan
   4. Grounds plan
   5. Calendar of school year
   6. Examinations
   7. Fire and traffic rules
   8. Library information
   9. Transfers, procedures for
  10. Daily bell schedule
  11. Marks
  12. Registration

[1] See pages 356–357, for a description of guidance for students new to the school.

13. Admission
14. Books; bookstore
15. Air-raid shelters
16. Placement bureau
17. School bank
18. Cafeteria
19. Activity tickets
20. School parties
21. Lost and found
22. Reports to parents
23. Study-hall regulations
24. Advisers
25. Assemblies
26. Lockers
27. Parking
28. Nurse, doctor, hospital
29. Offices

C. Program of Studies
   1. Classification, promotion
   2. College admission requirements
   3. Graduation requirements
   4. Curricula
   5. Required and elective courses
   6. Guidance program

D. Student Organizations and Activities
   1. Clubs and organizations
   2. Alumni association
   3. Athletic records and schedules
   4. Names of club, class, and school officers
   5. Letters and numerals
   6. Scholarships
   7. Band, orchestra, glee clubs
   8. Student council
      Description of plan
      Names of officers
      Roster of past presidents
   9. Debating
  10. Dramatics
  11. Constitution of school
  12. Regulations for clubs
  13. Rules—office holders
  14. Awards
  15. Home-room plan
  16. Elections
  17. School publications
  18. Noon-hour program
  19. Ushers
  20. Court
  21. Commissions and committees

E. General Customs and Traditions
   1. Care of personal property
   2. Care of school

3. Dress, appearance
4. Manners and courtesy
5. Use of telephone
6. Obtaining working permits
7. Yells
8. School songs
9. Book exchange
10. Bulletin boards
11. Homework
12. Study suggestions
13. Trophies
14. Visitors
15. Citizenship marks
16. "Did you know"
17. Good sportsmanship
18. History of school
19. Parent-teacher-student association
20. Fees and other costs[2]

## CONTINUITY BETWEEN JUNIOR AND SENIOR HIGH SCHOOLS

When a student enters a senior high school from a junior high school, not only has he more elective subjects from which to choose and a larger number of teachers to whom he must become adjusted, but he is in an atmosphere that places greater stress upon independent study. The school is usually larger; the pupil-teacher relationships are more impersonal, and the number and variety of opportunities for participation in clubs and other student organizations are greater.

**Improving Continuity.** In an increasing number of school systems, more attention is given to articulation than formerly. Teachers of both schools serve on committees, for example, senior high school English teachers might constitute a committee on the curriculum, with at least one teacher from the junior high school working with them, and junior high school committees include one or more teachers from the senior high school.

To bring about articulation up and down the line, there has been a pronounced trend in recent years for the appointment of directors of curriculum or directors of instruction who serve elementary schools, junior high schools, and senior high schools. Likewise, a specialist may be appointed in a special field such as the English language arts whose responsibility is for all grades from kindergarten through the twelfth grade.

[2] Harl R. Douglass, *Administration of Modern Secondary Schools* (Boston: Ginn & Co., 1963), pp. 273–274.

# ARTICULATION BETWEEN SENIOR HIGH SCHOOL AND COLLEGE

**Subject-Matter Overlap.** Examination of the content of courses taught in institutions of higher education, particularly in colleges of arts and sciences, reveals very questionable overlapping between some of the courses for lower-division students, especially freshmen and those offered in the upper years of the senior high school. This is particularly true in physics, biology, chemistry, trigonometry, English literature, and American history. The amount of overlapping varies a great deal from college to college—in some amounting to very little, while in others the practice is to include in the first-year college course practically everything taught in the high school course in that field, and sometimes little else.

Many college professors have claimed that it would be very difficult to bring about articulation, since secondary school courses vary from school to school. Some of them have excused their failure to bring about articulation by stating that students who have had the course in high school do no better in the first-year college course in the subject than those who have not had it in high school. This conclusion is not accepted by many, who point out that it would not be difficult for students who have not had the course in high school to do as well as those who have had it, if the content of the course were not based upon the content of the high school course, and also that those who have not had a high school course in the field would be stimulated by the fear that they need to work hard in order to do as well as those who have had it, while the latter would be inclined to rest on their oars.

In recent years, progress has been made in reducing the amount of overlapping. In a considerable number of colleges and universities, courses for beginning students have been stepped up with respect to both content and standards of attainment by the students. In many colleges, students who have had a high school course in a subject enter special sections on that subject, where the content of the course presumably is based upon the high school content. Furthermore, many high schools now offer what are called "college-placement" courses in a number of subjects. These courses presumably are very similar to those offered in college for students who have not had previous work in the subject.

**Need for Better Preparation for College.** A considerable proportion of the students entering a four-year college or university do not remain to graduate. Indeed, more than one in four do not complete more than a year in college, many withdrawing before the end of the first year. While a considerable proportion of these withdraw for financial and other personal reasons, many more than half of the withdrawals are students who have not done satisfactory work in their courses. No one knows what proportion of these could have done better work had they not been distracted by social and other activities that left too little time for study. At any rate, the problem has been sufficiently serious so that, in recent years, much more attention has been given to the improvement of articulation between secondary school and college by such means as the following:

1. Better preparation of students for college
2. Better guidance of students in secondary schools in selecting a college and a curriculum
3. Better orientation, guidance, and placement programs for the beginning students in college
4. The junior college

**Articulation Functions of the Junior College.** The number and percentage of high school graduates going to junior colleges instead of four-year institutions have very greatly increased in recent years. Among the students going to junior college are many who do not believe that they are ready for the four-year college or university and who prefer to attend first a college in which the classes are smaller and more attention can be given to individual students by instructors and counselors. Furthermore, it is rather generally believed that the standards for passing grades are not quite as high in the typical junior college as they are in the typical four-year college or university.

Investigations have shown that students entering a four-year college or university after completing two years of junior college make approximately as high an average mark in the college or university they attend later as do students of the same college aptitude, ability, and average high school marks who have attended the university as freshmen and sophomores. It has been argued that many students going to a junior college where there are no fraternities and sororities and where the social life is not so highly developed are less likely to be distracted seriously from their studies.

**Growth of the Junior College.** There were few junior colleges before 1920, and some of these were really small, weak institutions grafted onto four-year high schools. The number of junior colleges and the enrolments of students in them multiplied until there were in 1963, more than 1,200 junior colleges enrolling approximately 500,000 students, more than double the number in 1945. New junior colleges are being established every year, and, with the greatly increased number of high school graduates and the shortage of facilities for freshman at four-year institutions, it is quite likely that many more junior colleges will be established in future years.

**Other Features of the Junior College.** Among the splendid features of many junior colleges are their services as community institutes offering courses that are useful not only to their students but to others in the community as well. Some of these courses are of such a nature that institutions of higher education will not give credit for them.

In many communities, the local junior college makes it possible for a great many high school graduates who could not afford to attend college away from home to continue their formal education for at least two years.

The junior college is at one and the same time an institution of higher education, an institution of adult extension education, and a continuation of secondary education. Indeed, the academic instruction in junior college corresponds very much to what is offered in the upper years of the better secondary schools in Europe. For example, in European colleges and universities, work is not offered in trigonometry, analytic geometry, beginning physics, beginning chemistry, the first two years of a foreign language, etc. These are taught in the *Gymnasium* and the *Realgymnasium* in Germany and Sweden, and in the *lycée* and the *collège* in France.

For many students the junior college serves largely as a transitional school between high school and college. High school counselors advise many graduating students not to go at once to a college or university, particularly the latter, but to try out their wings first in a junior college where the classes are small, there is a good deal of opportunity for personal contact between the student and the teacher, and the athletic and social sideshows are not so distracting as in the four-year college or university.

## ADMISSION TO COLLEGE

**College Entrance Examinations.** For more than 100 years, the colleges and universities in the United States examined personally each applicant for entrance, usually giving both oral and written examinations. Early in the nineteenth century, colleges began to delegate the examination responsibility reciprocally so as to reduce the amount of time and expense involved in travel by many students to the college of their choice in order to be examined.

In 1871, the University of Michigan adopted a revolutionary plan which was to affect college admissions methods materially from then on. On the theory that the university was a part of the public school system of the state, it began to admit graduates of approved Michigan high schools without requiring them to take college entrance examinations, provided they had credit in the courses specified for entrance to the particular university division they wished to enter.

The University of Michigan then set up a system of inspection of the high schools in order that it might identify the better college-preparatory schools for placement on their approved list of schools, the graduates of which would be admitted without college entrance examinations, if they had credits in the courses required for entrance.

In 1873, Indiana University set up the same system, and, before the end of the century, 44 state universities and colleges and nearly 200 other institutions of higher education had adopted the accrediting system in some form. Many colleges and universities did not inspect schools and did not have their own list of approved schools, and these would admit students from secondary schools on the approved list of a state department of education that had an inspection system. There also was reciprocity among institutions that did have approved lists of schools.

**The College Entrance Examination Board (C.E.E.B.).** Many colleges and universities, particularly those in New England and the Middle Atlantic States, have been reluctant to admit students without college entrance examinations. Such a testing program, however, was quite expensive, because the student had to present himself at the college or university to take examinations. But, in 1900, a group of colleges in the United States agreed to cooperate in a program of examining applicants. Beginning in 1901, some ninety colleges and universities cooperated to set up a college examination board[3] and prepared examinations in all fields in which credit would be accepted for entrance. Examinations were given in a number of selected cities in the United States. Applicants who wished to enter college by this method would report to the designated place and take the examination in such subjects as were required for entrance by the college the applicant wished to enter.

The number of students taking the College Entrance Board examinations at its 1,700 centers in the United States and twenty foreign countries was more than 800,000 in 1962.

Under the C.E.E.B. system the student does not unequivocally either pass or fail an examination. He is given a score on each examination, and this is reported to the authorities of the college designated by the student, who decide whether or not he will be admitted. Not all colleges have the same standards, and some take into consideration other criteria such as high school marks, recommendation of the high school principal, and the student's record of leadership. Even geographical distribution is taken into consideration by some of the universities that wish to serve as national institutions. Investigations have shown that the scores

---

[3] Central offices of the College Entrance Examination Board are in New York, N.Y.; Evanston, Ill.; Sewanee, Tenn.; and Palo Alto, Calif. The construction, administration, and scoring of the examinations are managed by Educational Testing Services, Princeton, N.J.

made on these examinations are only very loosely in proportion to the subsequent grades made in college, so that, as a predictive or selective device, they leave very much to be desired.

There has been much controversy as to the desirability of the effects of these college entrance and similar statewide or nationwide testing programs upon secondary schools. There are those, particularly those who are primarily interested in having the student learn what can be tested on a written examination, who believe that examinations are quite stimulating. Indeed, for a considerable number of non-public secondary schools, the primary function and objective are to coach and prepare their students to pass the College Entrance Examination Board examinations.

A great many students of secondary education, on the other hand, are convinced that the effects are not good, since the system tends to distort the teacher's concept of the true objectives of education and to motivate the teachers to become coaches stressing the subject matter likely to prepare students for examinations and neglecting the broad education of students, including such things as ideals, attitudes, interests, habits, and skills which cannot be tested as easily by means of written tests. Recently, there has been a widespread protest against nationwide testing programs, developing increasing vigor as it has become more evident that scores on such tests by themselves are little value in predicting academic achievement in college.

**Modern Procedure.** While there are very important differences in the criteria and procedures of different colleges and universities for selecting students to be admitted, very important changes have been made in recent years. Realizing that the test scores are not a very valid or reliable method of selecting good college students, authorities of many institutions have set up college entrance committees who study the examination scores and other data about the applicants, which data are much more abundant in recent years, with the improvement of the guidance and record systems in American secondary schools. Many institutions of higher education now admit readily students with only average C.E.E.B. test scores, or other academic achievement records, who give evidence of unusual qualities of leadership and character and who seem to be possessed of unusually creative talents. Even the National Merit Scholarship Award Committee soon began to realize that it was not identifying many students of very unusual talents and possibilities and has recently modified its procedure with a view to better selection. Some colleges, for example, Williams College, are admitting experimentally as part of each freshman class a number of students who have not demonstrated academic achievement but who seem to possess other qualities to an unusual degree.

**Recommendations.** The following nine recommendations relative to college entrance were made in 1962 by a committee of the North Central Association of Colleges and Secondary Schools (NCA):

1. The development and use of a standardized secondary school record form
2. The development and use of reliable tables of test equivalences, and persuasion of colleges to accept an equivalence score in lieu of the tests they administer externally
3. That test publishers develop a common test for admission and scholarship purposes, and insist that only these be used—even by the Merit Scholarship Testing Program
4. That colleges must accept greater responsibility for the success of the students whom they admit
5. That the secondary schools should develop profiles to be furnished to colleges, and that colleges, in turn, should provide the high school principals with profiles of their graduates
6. That more emphasis be placed upon the schools' recommendations by the colleges for admissions purposes
7. That college admissions policies be kept sufficiently flexible for the college to be able to admit members of groups whose low test scores are caused by deprived background or minority status
8. That studies be made among the high schools of the NCA to determine whether changes have been made in the curriculum owing to external testing pressures in the past several years
9. That much closer relationships be developed between colleges and secondary schools at the state level in each of the nineteen states of NCA, and that NCA take the initiative in bringing this about

**College Entrance Requirements.** From the beginning, the great majority of colleges and universities have required for entrance specific subjects, particularly English, mathematics, foreign languages, and, in many cases, science and history. Hundreds of investigations have been made to check the validity of such criteria. Almost without exception, these studies have shown that the grades made in universities and colleges have practically no relationship at all to what subjects were taken in high school. Students who have taken many units in a foreign language, English, mathematics, and science make no better grades in college than those who have done much less work in these fields but who have the same intelligence quotient or college-aptitude-test score. Some of the investigations show that abler students tend to do more work in mathematics, science, and foreign languages, particularly the last, and that, therefore, they make somewhat higher grades.

Many institutions of higher education still cling to the old theory that good college students may be selected on the basis of subjects they have studied in high school. On the other hand, some institutions of higher education have abandoned the practice and content themselves with requiring the minimum of credit in the academic subjects, usually ten or eleven year units after the eighth grade, which must include three units of English.

In recent years, the public schools have been sending an increased percentage of students to colleges and universities that previously got the majority of their students from non-public schools. For example, in a recent study, it was discovered that, in 1960, 72 per cent of the students in Mount Holyoke came from public schools, as did 69 per cent of those at Barnard, 59 per cent at Smith, 58 per cent at Wellesley, 55 per cent at Vassar, and 53 per cent at Radcliffe.

A number of institutions of higher education, for example, Harvard, Yale, and Princeton, that previously required all students to enter on the basis of college entrance examinations now admit without examinations those ranking toward the top of their high school graduating class in grades received, provided they have credits in the required subjects.

Tens of thousands of high school seniors each year find it impossible to obtain admission to one of the better colleges or universities, and this situation will grow worse. The Association of College Admission Counsellors has established at Evanston, Illinois, the College Admissions Center, a non-profit organization to assist students in obtaining admission to an appropriate college.

**The Famous Eight-Year Study.** In order to discover the relative effectiveness of a modern program of secondary education developed without reference to college entrance requirements, as compared to a conventional program including college entrance requirements, thirty selected secondary schools carried on an investigation of the post-high school achievements of 1,475 students who were admitted to college regardless of the pattern of subjects taken in high school. The achievements of these students were compared to achievements of a control group made up of individuals who were selected to be equivalent, on the average, in intellectual capacity, age, and average school marks and who had taken the subjects designed for entrance to the college they attended. The ratio of males to females were the same in both groups. Cooperating colleges and universities agreed to accept the experimental students. In 1942, after eight years of study, the Commission on Relations Between High School and College, of the Progressive Education Association, reported that the experimental students:

(1) earned a slightly higher total grade average in college;
(2) earned higher grade averages in all subject fields except foreign languages;

(3) received slightly more academic honors each year;

(4) were more often judged to possess a high degree of intellectual curiosity and drive;

(5) were more often judged to be precise, systematic, and objective in their thinking;

(6) were more often judged to have developed clear or well-formulated ideas concerning the meaning of education—especially in the first two years of college;

(7) more often demonstrated a high degree of resourcefulness in meeting new situations;

(8) had about the same problems of adjustment as the comparison group, but approached their solution with greater effectiveness;

(9) participated somewhat more frequently, and more often enjoyed appreciative experiences, in the arts;

(10) participated more in all organized student groups except religious and "service" activities;

(11) earned in each college year a higher percentage of nonacademic honors (officership in organizations, election to managerial societies, athletic insignia, leading roles in dramatic and musical activities;

(12) had a somewhat better orientation toward the choice of vocation;

(13) demonstrated a more active concern for what was going on in the world.[4]

**A Follow-up Twenty Years Later.** As a result of a follow-up investigation of the fifty-five students in the Eight-Year Study who had graduated from the Ohio State University High School in 1938 and who were still alive and could be located, the following facts were revealed:

These students were taught definitely on the basis of progressive education including core programs, pupil participation in planning, parent-teacher interviews, parent-teacher conferences, individualized reading programs and no report cards. In their school they were nourished on a strict diet of democratic living and working.

More than 50 of the 55 are now successful people. All of them are useful members of society. They contribute to their communities at a higher level than others. Sixteen members of the class have publications, another had a novel now in the hands of a publisher. They all read more than the national average; they all earn more than the national average. Thirty-four of the 55 graduated from college; 17 received one or more honors in college; 12 took master's degrees and 4 took doctor's degrees. Seventy-three per cent entered the army as privates during World War II and one only remained at that rank at the time of discharge. Forty per cent became commisisoned officers and more than one-half of them became non-commissioned officers. Among those successful in business and professional life there doesn't seem to be a single "Babbitt."[5]

[4] Wilford M. Aikin, *The Story of the Eight-Year Study* (New York: Harper & Row, 1942), pp. 111–112.

[5] Margaret Willis and Lou LaBrant, "The Guinea Pigs After Twenty Years: A Follow-up Study of the Class of 1938 of the University School at Ohio State" (Columbus: Ohio State University Press, 1962), pp. 32–36.

# THE REGIONAL ACCREDITING ASSOCIATIONS

Of great importance relative to the college–secondary school relationship are four regional associations of colleges and secondary schools. The largest is the North Central Association, whch comprises nineteen states from Montana to West Virginia. Others are the Middle States (eastern), Southern (Virginia to Texas), and Northwest (Oregon, Idaho, and Washington) associations.

Each association designates a considerable percentage of the high schools in its region as "Accredited Schools." Graduates of these schools who have taken the subjects specifically required for entrance to a given college are admitted without being required to take examinations in high school subjects. To be listed and to maintain standing as an accredited institution, a school first must be inspected thoroughly and from then on must return detailed annual reports that are especially concerned with the educational qualifications of its staff.

Following is an outline of the scope of inspection, taken from "The Evaluative Criteria" employed by the North Central Association:

### CRITERION I.   Philosophy and Objectives

The degree to which the statement of the objectives seem[s] to be sound and conform to the situation in the local schools.

### CRITERION II.   The Educational Program

This school . . . shall include at least 26 units of course work with some in each of the following fields: English, science, mathematics, social studies, foreign languages, fine arts, practical arts including business, home economics, agriculture and industrial arts, health and physical education.

This criterion also applies to the conditions and functional procedures in classroom instruction, the program and management of extra-classroom activities, and guidance service, and health and safety services.

### CRITERION III.   Organization, Support, and Control

The member secondary school must include grades 10, 11, and 12. The school must enroll a number of students sufficient to justify employing a faculty which can offer a comprehensive and balanced program. Also in this criterion are administrative policies and procedures and the relationship between the Board and the professional staff which must be set forth in a statement of Board Policies of the Board of Education.

### CRITERION IV.   The School Staff

. . . The chief administrator must have earned a master's degrée, including 18 semester hours' work in education emphasizing administration and supervision. Schools of more than 250 students must have a full time person who devotes most of his time to administration and supervision.

There shall be . . . not more than 27 students for every teacher. The teaching load must not be in excess of seven shorter periods daily or six longer periods. It is recommended that each teacher be free for one period daily for conferences and preparation. The total pupil load per teacher is not to exceed 170 pupils per day. Every teacher must hold a baccalaureate degree from an accredited college or university and must have 30 semester hours in general education, including such fields as English, history, social science, science, mathematics, fine arts, languages, philosophy, religion, and psychology.

In the field of specialization taught each teacher must have at least 18 semester hours of work. Towards this 18 semester hours one hour may be credited for each unit of work taken in the high school in foreign languages and also in mathematics.

In business the teacher shall have at least 5 semester hours in each division in which the teacher teaches a subject.

Teachers of English shall have at least 5 semester hours of work in speech but not more than 5 of the 18 semester hours may be in speech and journalism.

Social studies includes history, government, economics, sociology, geography and psychology. Teacher[s] shall have at least 5 semester hours in each specific course to which they are assigned. They shall also have at least 5 semester hours in World and European History, 5 semester hours in Modern or Contemporary Problems and Citizenship.

.    .    .    .    .    .    .    .    .    .    .    .    .

General science teachers must have at least one course in a biological science and one course in a physical science. Teachers in physical science must have at least 10 semester hours in at least one of the physical sciences.

Teachers in driver training must have a valid state certificate in the field.

Core or large block-of-time teachers shall have at least 24 semester hours appropriately distributed among the subjects included in the core or large block-of-time field.

All teachers must have or earn a master's degree or thirty semester hours of graduate credit within a period of ten years of service in a North Central high school. This graduate work must include some course work in the teacher's major teaching field. The teacher must have at least eighteen semester hours of professional teacher education.

Requirements and criteria are also set forth for counselors; librarians; the clerical and custodial staffs; administrative and supervisory services; the school plant; the school year, day, and week; requirements for graduation; pupil load and credit; and library and laboratory equipment.

## OTHER COLLEGE INFLUENCES ON SECONDARY EDUCATION

Since it has become clear that students may not be prepared well for college merely because they have taken high school courses in designated fields, attention has been given to improving the preparation of students for college. Interest in this field has been greatly accelerated in recent years by the increased number of students wanting to go to college and the difficulties of obtaining admission to, and doing well in, the colleges, which have become increasingly selective in their admissions policies. Among ways in which students are being better prepared for college than formerly are the following:

1. Teachers of all subjects are assisting the students to increase the size and, above all, the precision of their vocabulary. In other words, teachers are giving more attention to seeing that students understand the precise meaning of words, especially those likely to be employed by college teachers and found in college textbooks.

2. Students are being given training in habits and skills of study both in general and in particular subjects, it being realized that, for each subject, there are at least some skills that are peculiarly useful.

3. In many schools, students are being given special training in techniques and skills of locating materials in the library and organizing them for oral or written reports, and in preparing for comprehensive written subject-matter examinations.

4. Increased attention is being given to accuracy and fluency in oral and written expression. It is realized that one of the major factors in grades made in college is the ability of the student to express himself well both orally in class and in writing in papers, examinations, and exercises.

5. Special attention is being given to seeing that college-bound students have reasonable accuracy in computational skills, it being recognized that, in many courses in college, it is necessary for the successful student to make accurate and quick numerical computations involving whole numbers and decimal and common fractions, in connection with evaluation of formulas in particular.

6. Most secondary school teachers are giving more attention to the development of students' interests in their subject matter fields. College and university professors almost uniformly complain bitterly that most of their students today seem to have little interest in learning in the academic fields but to be concerned almost entirely with working for a grade.

7. The counseling system in most secondary schools operates in a manner calculated to orient the students with respect to the problems of succeeding in courses in college, of selecting a college curriculum and courses, and of making an effective adjustment so as to get the most out of their college life intellectually and socially.

**Education of Secondary School Teachers.** Colleges and universities have very considerable influence upon a number of facets of secondary education, prominent among which is the education of the secondary school teachers. The quality of the work done by secondary school teachers is conditioned by the extent to which they have acquired mastery in broad fields in which they teach. Because of the failure of the colleges to prepare many of the students going into teaching in some aspects of their field, for example, to prepare general-science teachers in all the fields of science included in the course, English teachers in speech or dramatics, history and social studies teachers in sociology or political science, the quality of instruction by many teachers is unfortunately limited.

Secondary school teachers are likely to be influenced by the philosophy of education taught to them by professors of education, to the degree to which they have absorbed that philosophy. The nature and quality of the instruction by many secondary school teachers are also conditioned to some extent by how well they have been prepared to select instructional materials, to plan and motivate learning activities, to counsel and guide, to measure and evaluate student progress, to cooperate in public-relations activities in the community, and to adapt materials and methods of instruction to various groups of students with different potentialities.

College and university professors also influence teacher education by their participation in the writing of textbooks in subject-matter fields and on education. In recent years, many textbooks and other books read by teachers in service, both on their subject field and on education, particularly the former, have been written by teams of co-authors from secondary schools, colleges, and universities.

Secondary school teachers and administrators, and therefore secondary education, are also influenced by college professors through the media of summer-school courses, institutes for teachers, consultant and advisory work, and articles in pamphlets and bulletins prepared for teachers.

## QUESTIONS, PROBLEMS, AND TOPICS FOR FURTHER STUDY

1. What do you think are the more effective things that can be done to bring about articulation between the elementary school and the secondary school?
2. Can you give some examples of overlapping of your college courses with your high school courses? To what extent do you think it was necessary or desirable?
3. Why do you think students drop out of college before finishing?
4. What do you think are the place, functions, and future of the junior college in American education?
5. Do you think that colleges should require students to take entrance examinations? If so, in what fields?
6. Be able to give in class a talk of some six or eight minutes on the nature and procedures of accrediting associations and their influence on secondary schools.

## SUPPLEMENTARY MATERIALS

### Selected Readings

ANDERSON, VERNON E., and WILLIAM T. GRUHN. *Principles and Practices of Secondary Education.* (2d ed.). New York: The Ronald Press Co., 1962. Chapter 18, "Relation to Elementary School and College."

BENT, RUDYARD K., and HENRY H. KRONENBERG. *Principles of Secondary Education* (4th ed.). New York: McGraw-Hill Book Co., Inc., 1961. Chapter 8, "Relation of Elementary to Secondary Education."

DIAMOND, ESTHER, and MILDRED FOX. *Preparing Students for College.* Chicago: Science Research Associates, Inc., 1959.

DOUGLASS, HARL R. *Secondary Education.* New York: The Ronald Press Co., 1952. Chapter 22, "Relationships and Articulation with Elementary and with Higher Education."

FOX, RAYMOND B. "Improving Relations between High Schools and Colleges," *The Education Digest,* XXVII (May, 1962), 49–51.

FRENCH, WILLIAM M. *American Secondary Education.* New York: Odyssey Press, Inc., 1957. Chapter 10, "The Articulation Problem."

GRUHN, WILLIAM T., and HARL R. DOUGLASS. *The Modern Junior High School* (2d ed.). New York: The Ronald Press Co., 1956. Pp. 352–57.

KRUG, EDWARD A. *The Secondary School Curriculum.* New York: Harper & Row, 1960. Chapter 5, "The High School and the Colleges," pp. 130–67.

*Michigan Secondary School–College Agreement: Analysis of 1960 Reports.* Bulletin No. 43. Lansing, Mich.: State Department of Public Instruction, 1960. Report on the progress of this most significant plan of cooperation of secondary schools and colleges with regard to college admissions.

"Next Year's Bright Freshmen—Too Good for Ordinary Colleges, Too Numerous for the Best?" *Time,* May 11, 1962, 71.

SEYFERT, WARREN C. "Do Colleges Determine What the High Schools Teach?" *The Clearing House,* XXXIV (May, 1960), 515–20.

TELFER, HAROLD E. "Curriculum Development Under the Michigan Secondary School Agreement," *Bulletin of the N.A.S.S.P.,* No. 253 (February, 1960), 98–102.

# V

## ORGANIZATION, COMMUNITY RELATIONS, AND STAFF PROBLEMS

# 20

# Types of Secondary Schools

## DECLINE OF THE 8-4 PLAN

**Origin of the 8-4 Plan.** The first secondary schools in the United States were not uniform with respect to the number of years included or the ages of their students. Some Latin grammar schools, particularly the earlier ones, admitted students as young as eight years of age and, therefore, overlapped elementary schools, which, in the first century and a half of American education, were very poorly organized and articulated. In the early Latin grammar school, the students might study as long as nine or ten years. Later on, as the elementary schools began to be organized better, students were admitted to the Latin grammar schools at the age of eleven or twelve, after they had spent some five or six years studying the "three R's."

The academy, which came on the scene in the latter half of the eighteenth century and flourished throughout the nineteenth century, was at first a three-, five-, or six-year school and later a four-year school. By the time of the academy, the elementary school had begun to be of the graded-school type, that is, with first grade, second grade, and so on. A considerable amount of articulation was developed during the nineteenth century between the academy and the elementary schools, although the elementary schools were largely public schools, that is, supported by local taxation and governed by local school boards, while the academies were not.

By the middle of the nineteenth century, the public high school had begun to replace the academy. Almost from the start, it was a four-year school based on an eight-year elementary school (a nine-year elementary school in some New England districts and a seven-year one in many southern districts). It was usually governed by the board of education that governed the elementary school. Toward the end of the nineteenth century, the goal of an 8-4 school system was being attained throughout the United States, although, of course, the great majority of rural and village districts had only elementary schools.

**Dissatisfaction with the 8-4 Plan.** No sooner had the 8-4 plan become established and spread throughout the United States than serious dissatisfaction developed with it. The types and sources of dissatisfaction varied. The most serious complaints came from college faculties and presidents, though some complaints also were registered by teachers and administrators of the secondary schools.

As early as 1873, the very energetic President Charles W. Eliot of Harvard University began to voice criticism of the 8-4 plan of organization, primarily on the basis that the typical freshman entering Harvard was more than eighteen years of age. He took the position that too much time was being spent on elementary and secondary education, particularly the former. To the National Education Association, in 1888, he made a rousing plea for a study of the situation with a view to bringing about a correction of what he thought was a bad plan of organization. As a result of his talk, what came to be called a "Committee of Ten on Secondary School Studies" was appointed and authorized to hold conferences with school and college teachers throughout the country and to make recommendations to the meeting of the National Education Association. In 1893, the Committee gave its report, which included the following statement:

In the opinion of the committee, several subjects previously reserved for high school—such as algebra, geometry, and foreign languages—should be begun earlier than now and therefore within the schools classified as elementary, and the secondary school period in general should be made to begin two years earlier than at present leaving six years instead of eight for the elementary school period.

This startling recommendation attracted very much attention, but educators generally were divided in their opinions on the matter, and not much was done about it. Nevertheless, the idea of earlier introduction of secondary school subjects and methods persisted and influenced the thinking of leading educators.

At the 1895 meeting of the National Education Association, a committee was appointed to study college entrance requirements. This committee also recommended the earlier introduction of some of the secondary school subjects, and the 6-6 plan of organization.

Even more startling and subsequently more influential were the recommendations in 1903 by the Committee on Six-year Courses of six years of secondary education, and the recommendation by the Committee on

Economy of Time, in 1915, of a 6-3-3 plan of organization. The intermediate three-year school was to be a transition school.

In the first quarter of this century, national attention was drawn to the results of investigations of the withdrawal of students from school, which led to the definite conclusion that the lack of articulation between the eighth grade and the ninth grade was responsible for a large percentage of withdrawals from school. Together with the opposition to the plan of shortening elementary education to six years, the idea of the transition school found more followers and came to be the prevailing idea.

**Arguments for Reorganization.** Among the arguments advanced for reorganization were the following:

1. The need for earlier introduction of secondary school subjects and, consequently, better preparation for college
2. The need for a safe transition period from elementary to secondary education
3. The need for better-trained teachers in grades seven and eight, where they were principally graduates of two-year courses in normal schools
4. The need for better articulation of the courses of study and for reduction of the amount of overlapping, particularly in English and history
5. The advisability of the departmentalized assignment of teachers instead of assignment of teachers to all of the subjects taught in a particular grade
6. The need for the separation of pubescent youngsters from immature elementary school children, if for no other reason, for the protection of the elementary school children, and, likewise, the separation of ninth-grade children from the more mature and sophisticated boys and girls of grades ten, eleven, and twelve
7. Enrichment of the curriculum for grades seven and eight with home economics for girls and manual training (shop work) for boys, which would be very expensive in all but very large elementary schools
8. The need for provision for social experiences for seven- and eighth-grade boys and girls through student clubs and organizations, which might be better provided in the junior high schools than in the elementary schools
9. Shortening of the elementary-secondary school period for many students to eleven years
10. The better articulation that would result from a larger percentage of students being likely to be retained at least through the ninth grade, eliminating the sharp break between the eighth-grade and ninth-grade curriculums, methods, and types of teaching
11. In the junior high school with larger enrolments in grades seven and eight than would be possible in the typical elementary

school, better provision for individual variation among the students with respect to their ability, interests, and needs, particularly through a wider offering of courses of study
12. In the junior high school, the better provision that might be made for guidance and counseling
13. Improvement of discipline by separation of youngsters in grades seven, eight, and nine from the elementary school and from grades ten, eleven, and twelve

## THE "REORGANIZED" SCHOOLS

Beginning in 1910 and spreading slowly for a few years and then more rapidly, junior high schools of the two- or the three-year type began to be established throughout the United States. By 1920, the spread was rather rapid and there was a distinct trend toward the three-year school. Nevertheless, in many districts, for reasons that will be explained later in this chapter, reorganization was of a 6-6 type. By 1925, it was obvious that secondary education was headed toward a new type of grade organization.

**Achievements of the Junior High School.** Not all of the claims made for the junior high school were realized, and some were realized only in part and in varying degrees in different schools. Nevertheless, in spite of continued opposition by some of the elementary school teachers and principals and of the parents who wanted their children to attend schools closer to home, the advantages of reorganization became increasingly apparent. Following is a statement of the conclusions that can be safely made on the advantages and disadvantages of the junior high school as compared to the schools of the 8-4 plan:

I. Conclusions relative to instruction
1. The curriculum of the junior high school is broader and provides for more enriched learning experiences than does the 8-4 system, especially for pupils in grades seven and eight.
2. It is easier to introduce changes in the curriculum, especially when the junior high school is first introduced.
3. A broader program of extraclass activities can be provided. This is possible for ninth-grade pupils as well as those in grades seven and eight.
4. Teachers with better preparation, particularly in the special subject fields, can be attracted.
5. It is easier to attract men teachers than in grades seven and eight of the elementary school.
6. The supply of well-qualified administrators, supervisors, and teachers for the junior high school has been increasing in recent years.

II. Conclusion relative to pupil achievement

    7. Pupils in junior high schools do as well in the fundamentals as pupils in schools under the 8-4 plan, even though they spend less time on these subjects because they take a number of new subjects and participate in extraclass activities.

    8. Pupils from junior high schools do as well as those from other schools when they enter the senior high school.

III. Conclusions relative to guidance, meeting pupil needs, and retention of pupils

    9. Better guidance personnel, facilities, and activities are provided.

    10. It is easier to make provision for individual differences in the junior high school because the number of pupils in grades seven and eight is larger than in an elementary school.

    11. There are usually more opportunities in both the curricular and the extraclass programs for pupils to explore their interests, abilities, and talents.

    12. Pupils tend to remain in school longer, usually through the ninth grade.

    13. There are fewer failures and less retardation in the junior high school, especially in the ninth grade.

    14. Articulation between the elementary and the secondary school has been introduced. However, much still needs to be done to achieve satisfactory articulation.

    15. Although evidence is lacking on this point, many educators believe that the disciplinary situation, both in the elementary school and in grades seven and eight of the junior high school, is better when the older pupils are separated from the younger ones.

    16. Ninth-grade pupils are less likely to develop early sophistication because they do not have contact with older high school pupils. Furthermore, they can usually participate more fully in pupil activities in the junior high school than in the four-year high school.

IV. Conclusions relative to housing and costs

    17. Better building facilities, equipment, and athletic fields can be provided, especially for seventh- and eighth-grade pupils.

    18. The cost of providing an adequate educational program for young adolescents is less in the junior high school. If comparable facilities were provided for grades seven and eight in the elementary school they would need to be duplicated in every school.[1]

In 1962, 70 per cent of the secondary school teachers in the United States querried by the Research Division of the N.E.A. favored the 6-3-3 plan.

**The Six-Year Secondary School.** The majority of school districts in the United States do not enrol enough students to warrant the establishment of separate junior and senior high schools. The enrolments in each would

---

[1] William T. Gruhn and Harl R. Douglass, *The Modern Junior High School* (2d ed.) (New York: The Ronald Press Co., 1956), pp. 57–58.

be too small to permit the offering of suitable curriculums and economical use of the school plant. For this reason, a large number of school districts established six-year secondary schools including grades seven through twelve.

Among the advantages of the six-year school for districts with less than 500 or 600 students above the sixth-grade level are the following:

1. Common use may be made of expensive housing and equipment such as the gymnasium, the swimming pool, the auditorium, the library, and the cafeteria.

2. Common use may be made of the equipment of special departments, which would be employed only during a portion of the day if separate junior and senior high schools were maintained, including household-arts kitchens and sewing rooms and related equipment, and rooms and equipment for instruction in music, art, science, typewriting, and various types of shop work.

3. One well-trained and well-paid principal may be employed who will be able to devote all of his time to administrative and supervisory duties, rather than two less well-trained and less well-paid principals.

4. More complete departmentalization of the teaching staff is possible.

5. Better curriculum articulation between junior and senior high school grades may be achieved as the result of the fact that many of the teachers would teach at both levels.

6. Training from one school to another at the end of the ninth grade may be avoided, resulting most probably in reducing the number of students leaving the school at the end of the ninth grade.

7. There are greater possibilities of enabling the more capable students to reduce to five years the time spent in secondary school.

**Current Trends in Reorganization.** From 1920 on, there has been a very steady increase in the number of school districts organized on the 6-3-3 or the 6-6 plan, but, since 1955, the movement has been greatly accelerated. As a result of greatly increased enrolments of students born in the late 1940's and the consequent necessity for constructing many new buildings, local school authorities were given flexibility in planning; therefore, many districts previously organized on the 8-4 or the 6-6 plan shifted to the 6-3-3 plan.

As the enrolments in six-year secondary schools became large enough to warrant separation into junior and senior high schools, many districts with crowded buildings constructed a new one to house a three-year senior high school. By the autumn of 1963, only one in four school systems still employed the 8-4 plan of organization. More than 40 per cent were organized on the 6-6 plan, and more than 30 per cent on the 6-3-3 plan. Of the students enrolled in school beyond the sixth grade, approximately half were enrolled in junior or senior high schools, 20 per cent in six-year secondary schools, and only 30 per cent in conventional secondary schools. Four-year schools existed in largest numbers in Illinois, California, and Arizona, where many secondary school districts and elementary school districts are not coterminous and have separate boards of education.

Investigations[2] by Wood and Menozzi have shown a preference of educational leaders for the 6-3-3 organization wherever possible and for the 6-6 plan in the smaller districts. Many prospective teachers being prepared in colleges and universities to teach in secondary schools prefer to teach junior high school students. Furthermore, the widespread adoption of single salary schedules, according to which teachers in the junior high school are paid as much as teachers in the senior high school with the same training and experience, has gone far to encourage college and university graduates to become junior high school teachers.

## SMALL AND LARGE SECONDARY SCHOOLS

**The Why of the Small School.** After the middle of the nineteenth century, schools were established in small towns, even though such schools might have less than 100 students. The small school is obviously subject to severe limitations, and, in recent decades, there has been a very pronounced movement toward the consolidation of schools and the bringing together at one central school of secondary school students from a much larger area. The extension and improvement of the highways and transportation to school have encouraged and accelerated consolidation.

Whereas in 1930 the median enrolment of high schools in the United States was approximately 130 students, in the autumn of 1963 approximately half of the secondary schools in the United States had more than 265 students and the proportion with less than 100 students had shrunk to less than one in five. The trend has been further stimulated by the publicity given the recommendation of Dr. James B. Conant that, as far as possible, all secondary schools be organized to have at least 100 students in the twelfth grade. Nevertheless, there will be for many years a great many small secondary schools in sparsely settled districts in areas where weather conditions hinder transportation in winter months.

**Limitations of the Small School.** In the opinions of many investigators, the small school usually has an inadequate library, a lack of laboratory and shop facilities and of audiovisual equipment, excessive teacher turnover,

[2] W. C. Wood. Unpublished doctor's dissertation, University of Colorado, 1952.
John C. Menozzi. Unpublished doctor's dissertation, University of Denver, 1959.

inadequate health service, a large percentage of inexperienced teachers, inadequate supervision, a restricted extracurricular program, relatively inexperienced or incompetent administrators, community pressure for retention of outmoded materials and methods, too few teachers, restricted curriculum offerings, and inferior and restricted guidance service. In recent years, increased attention has been given to improving the small-school curriculum by having teachers teach two classes in the same room and during the same class period, by correspondence courses, by use of shared teachers and supervisors (specialized teachers who teach in more than one school), and by offering some subjects such as physics and chemistry only in alternate years. In New York State, legislation has encouraged the establishment of non-profit organizations to supply nearby districts with the services of specialized teachers, counselors, psychometrists, etc., which they could not afford as individual districts.

**The Large School.** There has also been opposition to the very large high school because of the impersonal contacts between the members of the faculty and administration and the individual students. The huge high schools that existed twenty or twenty-five years ago in some of our large cities have been replaced, but, nevertheless, a considerable number of schools have more than 2,000 students. As was revealed in studies made by Oliver and Menozzi, experts in the field believe that the optimum number of students in the senior high school is somewhere between 500 and 800, for a four-year high school 600 to 1,000, and for a three-year junior high school between 400 and 600.

**Schools Within a School.** An increasing number of the very large schools are organized into units with somewhat separate faculty, housing, extracurricular programs, and administration, in an attempt to bring about more personal contact and closer interstudent associations. Excellent examples are the Niles Township North High School at Skokie, Illinois, and the Evanston, Illinois Township High School.

## OTHER TYPES OF PUBLIC SECONDARY SCHOOLS

**Summer Schools.** Since the middle 1950's, there has been a very great increase in the number of secondary schools offering summer programs, and a very great expansion of the curriculums and other activities offered during the summer school session.[3]

The following are characteristics of typical secondary school summer sessions:

1. The large majority of the staff members are members of the regular school-year staff.

[3] In California, the number of secondary school students enrolled in summer school in 1962 was almost as great as in the previous school year.

2. Teachers are usually paid an additional salary, the ratio of which to the school-year salary is a little less than the ratio of the length of the summer session to the length of the regular session.

3. Students receive credits at about the rate of one unit for each six weeks or one and one-half units for eight or nine weeks, if they carry a full and intensive program.

4. Most classes meet in the morning, beginning not later than 8:00 and sometimes as early as 7:30.

5. There is a trend toward giving driver training during the summer session; aparently it can be given more cheaply then and without interfering with other subjects.

6. Class periods are usually approximately two hours in length, with a break between classes of five to ten minutes.

7. The length of the summer term is almost always between six and ten weeks, usually eight weeks.

8. Little or no tuition is charged.

9. Various kinds of classes are offered in summer schools, including the following: (a) makeup classes for students whose work was failing or at least highly unsatisfactory in one class during the previous semester or year, (b) classes for bright students who wish to graduate from high school in three years, and (c) courses taken not for credit but as recreation and interesting summer activities.

Summer-school offerings also include vocational agriculture projects, programs of distributive occupations, reading in the school library, musical groups practicing in the music studios, swimming, and games in the gymnasium and on the playgrounds. Also, many schools are annually converted to day camps for boys and girls. In some schools, during the summer, experimental work is done by teachers with volunteer students.

**Evening Schools.** There has also been an increase in the number of secondary schools offering courses in the evening, and, consequently, a greater variety of courses and services are offered. The courses in the evening schools are usually taught by day-school teachers as a means of supplementing their income. The students in the evening-school classes are very largely adults, though they include many teen-agers who wish to complete high school or to prepare for some vocation. The variety of courses offered for adults is very great, since adult interests spread into such areas as cultural lectures and studies and hobbies. Many of these courses are taken without credit.

**The Specialized vs. the Comprehensive High School.** For many years, some educators have advocated the establishment of specialized high schools that would concentrate upon some particular field of preparation, such as the Needle Trades High School, the High School of Science, and the High School of Commerce, all New York City public secondary schools. Some high schools are essentially college-preparatory schools, and some are largely of the vocational type, the latter being for students who do not fit into the regular secondary school programs. There has been, in recent years, a demand, not popularly received, on the part of some educators that secondary schools be established for outstandingly superior students and vocational schools for others.

The great majority of educators are opposed to specialized vocational high schools and believe strongly in the comprehensive high school, averring that the specialized school

1. Tends to break down the spirit and practice of democracy and the melting-pot function in American secondary education
2. Tends to lessen the value of cultural training by concentrating on narrow, technical, bread-and-butter types of training
3. Does not serve the needs of pupils as represented, because students usually attend the nearest high school without reference to its adaptability to their needs
4. Develops economic class-consciousness
5. Emphasizes vocational education disproportionately and prepares more workers in certain vocational pursuits than industry and commerce will absorb
6. Hastens a premature choice of vocation and the decision as to education beyond the high school
7. Weakens the vocational departments in the comprehensive, general, or academic high schools

Somewhat plausible arguments have been offered in favor of the specialized vocational high school. Among them are the following:

1. Students electing vocational curriculums in the comprehensive high schools become class-conscious and are often discriminated against socially by students electing college-preparatory curriculums.
2. Because the foregoing is true, many students elect general or college-preparatory curriculums though their real interests and needs demand vocational curriculums.
3. The administration of most comprehensive schools is neither sympathetic toward programs of vocational education nor informed concerning them; as a result, the realization of the most effective programs of vocational education is extremely difficult to achieve.
4. It is much eaiser to develop a desirable vocational morale in the specialized high school.
5. By concentrating vocational preparation for a city in specialized high schools, it is possible to provide better, if not exceptional, equipment and instruction, with less duplication and at no excessive cost.

**Segregation by Sex.** For a great many years, students were segregated in different schools according to sex, and a few schools now continue that practice. Boys and girls have so many needs in common, and they so strongly prefer coeducation, especially in the senior high school, that segregation has lost ground even in the southern states, in some of which it was maintained until recently. Segregation by sex is impractical in smaller high schools where there is only one section in many classes and in schools where ability grouping is employed. In recent years, some schools have been experimenting with class grouping by sex and report most favorably about it. Apparently, both boys and girls, particularly boys, do much better in sections made up only of one sex, and the discipline problems are much simpler. Furthermore, the teachers say that they may adapt the materials better to the interests and needs of each sex, and many of the teachers believe that boys and girls can profit by somewhat differentiated course-of-study materials.

**Segregation by Color.** Segregation of students on the basis of racial origins continues despite the constitutional provision for equality and the Supreme Court Decision in 1954 declaring segregation to be unconstitutional. Nevertheless, in the border states, segregation is disappearing very rapidly and considerable progress is being made in many districts in the Deep South, for example, at Atlanta, Georgia, and Charlotte, North Carolina. It is clear that, regardless of the merits of some white people's wishes to not have their children attend school with children of Negroes, the die-hard approach to segregation is waging a losing battle, and the sympathy of the majority of the people of the United States is not with the segregationists.

In a considerable number of districts in the South, schools for the Negroes have been greatly improved. In recent decades in North Carolina, for example, Negro and white teachers are on the same salary schedule, although classes assigned to Negro teachers are larger, and the buildings and equipment provided are usually very poor. Except in Arkansas, Mississippi, Louisiana, Alabama, and South Carolina, a great many splendid new buildings have been built for the Negro students.

In the past few years strong arguments have been advanced by Professor Robert J. Havighurst, of the University of Chicago, and others in favor of the establishment of high schools in underprivileged communities, for students who are typical of that sort of district, offering appropriate subjects and guidance, particularly in vocational fields.

## NON-PUBLIC SECONDARY SCHOOLS

**Enrolments.** In the United States, until recently, approximately 90 per cent of all secondary school students attended public secondary schools. However, since 1950, the percentage attending non-public schools has markedly increased, particularly that of those attending Catholic parochial secondary schools. In 1963, there were more than 5,000 non-public secondary schools, 70 per cent of them under religious control, more than 2,500 being Catholic, enrolling more than 1.25 million, or approximately 15 per cent of all secondary school pupils. The apparent reason for this is that, with increased prosperity, parents are able to spare more money for the erection of additional schools and to pay the tuition for their sons and daughters to attend such schools. Furthermore, the percentage of the population in the United States that is Catholic has been steadily and materially increasing.

Added to this is the desire on the part of many parents to have their boys and girls attend college-preparatory schools, boarding schools, and schools with small classes. Furthermore, the criticisms of the public secondary schools have motivated many parents to send their children to what they believed were better schools with more individual instruction.

Not negligible factors in the decision of many parents to send their sons and daughters to the more exclusive secondary school are the desire for social status and the wish to have their children form friendships with the children of parents of superior economic and social status.

Perhaps still another reason is that, since it is becoming increasingly difficult for students to get into the more selective institutions of higher education, it seems desirable to attend a school that will coach students to pass the College Entrance Board examinations. Non-church-affiliated non-public schools are freer to conduct reliable experiments on curriculums and methods of instruction, and much of our knowledge about secondary education has come from such experimentation. But, with the growth of non-public schools in recent years, the amount of experimentation has increased greatly.[4]

Many non-public secondary schools are operated without adequate financial support and are able to obtain only poorly paid teachers, who, heavily loaded, work in inferior plants with inadequate libraries, laboratories, and other equipment.

Three-fourths of the non-public secondary schools, with 90 per cent of their students, are religious institutions, chiefly Catholic, to which children are sent to be indoctrinated in the faith of their parents. Most of them are located in the northeastern quarter of the United States—east of the Mississippi and north of the Deep South—and in Louisiana. The independent (non-public and non-religious) schools are located principally in nine states: New York, Massachusetts, Pennsylvania, California, Texas, Connecticut, Michigan, Maryland, and Florida.

[4] See David Mallery, *New Approaches in Education: A Study of Experimental Programs in Independent Schools* (Boston: National Council of Independent Schools, 1961).

**Religion in the Public High School and the Parochial School.** One of the most prominent questions in public education in recent years has been that of the place of religion in the schools. The matter has been before the Supreme Court several times, and decisions have been made that are not favorable to teaching religion or having in the schools religious ceremonies that favor any one type of religion. It is becoming apparent that the schools can offer both the study of religion in general and the comparative study of the various types of religions and of the philosophies of life of great religious leaders such as Mohammed, Buddha, and Jesus Christ. Nevertheless, in secondary schools in general, in order to avoid local controversy, there has been a tendency for the teachers and principals to avoid teaching about religion at all, particularly to avoid mentioning names of any particular religions or religious leaders or discussing the philosophy peculiar to any one religion or sect.

There has been, in recent years, a very great increase in the number of schools operating what is called the "shared plan." In each of several hundred school systems in the United States, many students, particularly Catholics, go to a parochial school part of the day and to a public school part of the day. The most common pattern is for the students to spend a half-day in each type school—studying mathematics, shop work, home economics, physical education, and foreign languages in the public school, and the social studies, English, and science in the parochial school. In some school systems, however, the foreign languages are taught in the parochial school and the sciences in the public school.

An extension of this plan would probably have four important results:

1. An increase in the number of youngsters who spend at least part of their time in a parochial school
2. A decrease in the cost of parochial secondary education to the church organizations involved
3. A large increase in the number of students who have half-day contacts with young people of other religions, to that extent serving the "melting pot," or the "we-ness," function of secondary education
4. An increased financial burden upon public school districts

**"Quality" Schools.** A considerable number of non-public secondary schools have been established or revamped for the purpose of providing "quality" education. Although *quality* has been variously defined and, indeed, has been adopted by a great many as a catchword for all sorts of proposals, a very large number of schools not essentially college-preparatory or religious are offering what may be fairly designated as quality education. They are offering new curriculum materials, employing better staffs, and stressing guidance, small class size, and other quality features.

There are also a considerable number of non-public secondary schools that exist for the purpose of providing education for exceptional young-sters, for example, many schools offer programs for adolescents of one or more of the following types: juvenile delinquents, the emotionally disturbed, the physically crippled, the blind, the hard of hearing, the very bright.

**Vocational Schools.** Some non-public schools for adolescents concen-trate upon preparation for a particular vocation. These schools include business, auto repair, radio and television installation and repair, elec-tronics, nursing, barbering, and cosmetics schools.

## TYPES OF SECONDARY SCHOOLS IN OTHER COUNTRIES

In most other countries, young people enter upon their secondary education at an earlier age than in the United States, ordinarily at the age of eleven or twelve, although in some instances they start secondary school two or three years later than that. They are graduated usually at the age of eighteen or nineteen, after having been in the secondary school six or seven years.

Also, in most other countries, secondary education—as in the case of the *lycée* and the *collège* in France; the *Gymnasium*, the *Realgymnasium*, and the *Oberrealschule* in West Germany; the "public" and other second-ary schools in England; and the secondary schools of Japan—is made up of two divisions corresponding somewhat to our junior high school and senior high school.

Admission to these secondary schools is on the basis of examination and ability to pay tuition, although, in many countries, especially Eng-land, tuition scholarships are available for abler students.

Since the schools are usually highly selective with respect to the intel-lectual ability of the students and the secoial and financial standing of their parents, the curriculum is neither broad nor modern. Indeed, if the student wishes to take a somewhat different curriculum, he must enter another school. For instance, in the German *Gymnasium* the stu-dents take a classical curriculum emphasizing classical foreign languages, while in the *Realgymnasium* less attention is given to classical languages and more is given to modern languages and somewhat more to mathe-matics and science, and in the *Oberrealschule* still less attention is given to classical languages and much more is given to the humanities and science.

Except in England and, to some extent, the Scandinavian countries, the curriculums of the secondary schools of other countries are largely detached from the more practical needs and problems of modern life.

In England, France, Germany, Japan, and many newer countries, particularly in Latin America and in Africa, there is a definite trend toward more definitely functional curriculums that will prepare students to assist in developing their nation's natural resources, economy, government, and participation in modern life in general.

## QUESTIONS, PROBLEMS, AND TOPICS FOR FURTHER STUDY

1. What is your opinion about having secondary school subjects begin earlier, for instance, algebra and foreign languages in the seventh grade?
2. From the standpoint of the associations of students with each other, do you think it is better to have schools organized on the 8-4 plan, the 6-3-3 plan, or the 6-6 plan?
3. What advantages do you think the junior high schools have? What disadvantages?
4. What do you think is the chief disadvantage of the six-year high school? Does it have any advantages other than economy?
5. There are those who believe that the small school is, by virtue of its smallness, a good school. What do you think about that? What do you think can be done to improve the small school?
6. What is your opinion concerning the maximum size of a high school? What are the advantages and disadvantages of a large high school?
7. There has been much talk, in recent years, of setting up specialized high schools for bright students, for students following vocational curriculums, and for students who have bad disciplinary histories. But, in general, educators seem to be in favor of the comprehensive high school. What are the principal arguments pro and con?
8. Enrolments in non-public secondary schools have been materially increasing since World War II. Do you think this is good or bad? Give reasons for your answer.
9. What are the different types of non-public secondary schools, and what is the particular purpose of schools of each of the types?

## SUPPLEMENTARY MATERIALS

### SELECTED READINGS

BOHRSON, RALPH G. "The Small High School—Its Strengths and Limitations," *Bulletin of the N.A.S.S.P.*, No. 279 (April, 1963), 106–17.

BULLOCK, ROBERT S. "Some Cultural Implications of Year-round Schools," *The Education Digest*, XXVIII (November, 1962), 26–28.

CAMPBELL, W. H. "Summer High School Survey," *Bulletin of the N.A.S.S.P.*, No. 254 (March, 1960), 44–49.

DE LA FLEUR, FREDERICK J. *Shared Services Boards*. Albany: New York State School Boards Association, Inc. March, 1961. For small schools.

DEGOOD, K. C. "Profile of the Small High School," *Educational Leadership*, XVIII (December, 1960), 170–72, 182.

DIAMOND, HUGH J. "In Niskayuna a House Fits into an Existing School," *Nation's Schools*, LXVII (June, 1961), 68–69, 94.

DOUGLASS, HARL R. *Trends and Issues in Secondary Education*. Washington, D.C.: The Center for Applied Research in Education, Inc., 1962. Chapter 10, "Secondary School Organization."

DULSTEAD, WILLIAM M. "How Can Summer Schools Improve the Total School Program?" *Bulletin of the N.A.S.S.P.*, No. 239 (April, 1958), 31–36.

FITTS, DANIEL B. "The House Plan as a New Concept in Secondary School Organization," *Bulletin of the N.A.S.S.P.*, No. 238 (March, 1958), 155–63.

FOGG, WALTER. "Scarsdale Plan Is Flexible and Relaxed," *Nation's Schools*, LXVII (June, 1961), 66–68.

GAUMITZ, WALTER H., and DAN HULL. "Junior High School Versus the Traditional (8–4) High School Organization," *Bulletin of the N.A.S.S.P.*, No. 206 (March, 1954), 112–21.

GRUHN, W. T., ELLSWORTH TOMPKINS, J. L. TRUMP, and VIRGINIA ROE. "The Junior High School Grades in the Six-Year High School," *Bulletin of the N.A.S.S.P.*, No. 259 (November, 1960), 46–48.

HAMILTON, DEFOREST, and ROBERT N. ROWE. "Academic Achievement of Students in Reorganized and Non-reorganized Districts," *Phi Delta Kappan*, XLIII (June, 1962).

LATHROP, IRVIN T., and THOMAS J. KIEFFER. "College Achievement of Public Versus Private High School Graduates," *The Clearing House*, XXXIII (January, 1959), 299–302.

LOWE, ALTON D. "Three Schools Within a School," *Bulletin of the N.A.S.S.P.*, No. 271 (February, 1962), 47–52.

McCOMB, STUART F. "Why Pasadena Dropped 6-4-4 Plan," *Nation's Schools*, LIV (November, 1954), 60–61.

"Place of the Private and Church Related Schools in American Education," *Progressive Education*, September, 1956, 152–67.

PRICE, NELSON B. "An Evaluation of the 'School-Within-a-School' Plan of Secondary-School Organization," *Bulletin of the N.A.S.S.P.*, No. 275 (September, 1962), 185–91.

"San Diego's Year-round School Camps," *School Management*, XIX (September, 1949), 6, 10, 11.

SHUEY, AUDREY M. "Academic Success of Public and Private School Students in Randolph-Macon Women's College: 1. The Freshman Year," *Journal of Educational Research*, XLIX (March, 1956), 481–92.

SHUNK, WILLIAM R. "Shared Time—New Light on an Old Problem?" *Phi Delta Kappan*, LIII (June, 1962), 31–42.

"Small Schools Needn't Be Weak Schools," *School Management*, IV (March, 1960), 64–66.

STILES, LINDLEY, EARL McCLEARY, and ROY TURNBAUGH. *Secondary Education in the United States*. New York: Harcourt, Brace & World, Inc., 1962. Chapter 20, "Nonpublic Secondary Schools."

TAYLOR, L. O., DON R. McMAHILL, and BOB L. TAYLOR. *The American Secondary School*. New York: Appleton-Century-Crofts, Inc., 1960. Chapter 4, "Reorganization of the High School To Serve All Youth"; Chapter 20, "Equalization of Educational Opportunities."

WHITCOMB, MILDRED. "Small High Schools Are Worth Retaining," *Nation's Schools*, XIII (April, 1959), 63–66.

## AUDIO-VISUAL MATERIALS

### Recording

*The Effective Junior High School,* #228. Myron S. Olson. Educational Growth Series. Educational Recording Services. Los Angeles, Calif. 36-44-minute discussion, 33⅓ rpm.

# 21

# Secondary Education and the Community

## IMPORTANCE OF SCHOOL-COMMUNITY RELATIONS

**Dependence of the School upon the Local Community.** As was pointed out in Chapter 1, public schools in the United States are dependent on local taxes for most, in some states practically all, of their financial support. If they are to have the funds to function effectively, and if their programs are to be successfully continued, the schools must be understood, appreciated, and supported by the people of the local community. In this way they are unlike the schools of any other country, and, therefore, their relations with the people of the community are more important than in any other country. Furthermore, the control of the schools and the approval of their educational programs are largely in the hands of a local board of education elected by the voters in the school district.

**Recent Criticisms.** While the schools have, from the beginning, been subject to criticism, constructive and otherwise, by people in the community, this criticism has in recent years been unprecedented in amount and vigor. Fortunately, criticism in most communities has apparently not destroyed or seriously weakened the faith of the people in their schools. It is difficult, however, to know what might have happened had the schools not always given attention to good public relations and had they not put more time and effort into improving their public-relations work in recent years.

## PUBLIC-RELATIONS PROCEDURES

**Developing Understanding, Interest, and Favorable Attitudes.** In recent years, the schools, through their personnel and through other agencies, have improved their facilities for effectively disseminating information about their work. This has been done not only through the local press but also by means of school publications, individuals connected with the schools, radio announcements and programs, and social contacts.

It has become evident among educators, as well as among businessmen, politicians, and the military, that good will and favorable interests are not obtained merely through information, no matter how abundant and convincing it may be, but much may be done through face-to-face contacts.

**The Student as an Avenue of Contact.** The most effective contact with the public is through the student. Parents are much more influenced by the information and misinformation received from their own children than they are from what they read or hear about the schools from other people. For this reason, educational administrators have increased their activities along the lines of keeping the young people informed about the work of the schools.

Furthermore, the increased participation of young people in planning their own learning activities has improved their attitudes as well as their knowledge about the school program. In addition, supervisors have urged teachers to avoid as far as possible unnecessary incidents of personal conflict with the students, particularly those in which the student is unnecessarily embarrassed and has the basis for feeling that he has been unfairly treated.

One of the most effective of the influences upon the student is the development of courses of study and programs of learning activities in the value of which he has confidence. The student must consider his school experiences to be useful to himself. For this reason, they must be neither unnecessarily distasteful nor discouraging, and, to this end, they must offer him a chance to achieve some degree of success.

**Contacts with Parents.** In the very large majority of schools, there has been a definite increase in the amount of contact of secondary school teachers with parents, the principal purposes of which are the dissemination of information about the school and its program and the development of good personal and school relations.

Many types of contact have been utilized more extensively in recent years. In many schools, teachers have designated office hours, usually once a week or every other week, after school, at which time parents are welcome to come, to get acquainted with the teacher, and to discuss school matters, their children's progress, and school-related problems of their children and themselves.

In many schools, the teachers have been given some in-service training, or at least some suggestions, on how to capitalize on their contact with parents to great advantage. Among other things, teachers who have been unusually successful in parent contacts are asked to make suggestions to new teachers. For example, among the suggestions most commonly made is to avoid having interviews with parents center on or emphasize complaints of the teacher about the student, rather than being concerned largely with intents to discover what are the difficulties of the particular child and to exchange and pool knowledge and ideas in an effort to improve the situation.

With some thought and practice, and perhaps a little training, many teachers who were not too skilful in interviews have greatly improved their effectiveness in making friends and developing good attitudes, without sacrificing standards. Among other things, teachers have learned to be good listeners and to avoid monopolizing their interviews.

In many schools, not only the teachers but also the secretaries, custodians, and other employees of the school are kept informed about appropriate aspects of the program and needs of the school and are given suggestions on how to contribute to better public relations.

**Conferences with Parents.** Currently, teachers have many more conferences with parents at home and at school than they had in the past. These relate chiefly to the progress in school of the parents' children or to questions parents wish to ask about the school, especially with respect to "rumors I have heard."

Conferences between teachers and parents should not be conducted in an impromptu manner. They should be planned carefully. The beginning teacher should talk with older teachers about procedures and should be constantly attempting to improve his effectiveness.[1]

The answers to many of the questions and problems of teacher-parent conferences are given in *Conference Time*, a sixty-four-page publication of the National Education Association, as is shown in the following, its Table of Contents:

Chapter 1 Why Confer?
Times, teaching, and the understanding of pupil progress have changed from Grandpa's day . . . parents want more than report cards . . . teachers need more from a parent than his signature on a report card . . . the youngster's education is improved when teachers and parents are partners.

[1] General principles of procedure are discussed elsewhere.

Chapter 2    What Parents Want to Know

And how the classroom teacher can answer questions parents ask . . . lists of questions which are most likely to be asked by parents with children in primary, intermediate, and upper grades . . . tips on conference language and vocabulary.

Chapter 3    The Group Conference

How individual teachers can provide ready relief for anxious parents . . . the "get acquainted" and preview of what's to come type . . . roles for the teacher, parents, and the pupils . . . essential steps to assure valuable accomplishments.

Chapter 4    Individual Conferences

How individual conferences can represent the ultimate in cooperative planning by the teacher and parent . . . preparing the child, the parents, and yourself . . . successful techniques and basic rules for conferring with parents . . . checklist for a good conference.

Chapter 5    Evaluation and Follow-up

Why evaluate? . . . how to evaluate . . . tips about the written follow-up record . . . how successful evaluation can affect attitudes of the pupil, the parents, the school, and the entire community . . . how to eliminate the mysteries of the conference.

Chapter 6    Bright Ideas

Tested ideas to make conferences more productive, more interesting, and more lively . . . demonstrations to illustrate conference techniques . . . new ways to work together with parents . . . letters, notes, and introductions.

**School Visitation.** For many years, parents have been encouraged to attend their children's classes. But, being occupied through much of the day and, in most instances, being discouraged by their children from the practice, parents do not visit the schools very often, even though a great many schools have for years scheduled a school-visitation day. However, many schools have inaugurated a school-visitation night, during which the teachers follow the regular daily schedule abridged to short periods, and parents are encouraged to attend to follow the schedule of their child. This at least enables the teacher to meet and become acquainted with the parents which, in the opinion of specialists in school public relations, goes a long way as a first step in improving personal relations.

At those occasions, students act as ushers and guides. In the library or cafeteria, light refreshments are served and the principal or assistant principal and the counselors are available to meet the parents and to exchange a few words about the students. This type of school visitation, which involves fathers as well as mothers, seems to be rather successful.

**Home Visitation.** In some districts, particularly in recent years, a few home-visitation teachers are employed, whose responsibility is almost entirely if not completely in connection with the visitation of homes, particularly those of problem children and of parents who have never visited, and are not likely to visit, the school. In areas where low-level economic groups live, this has proved to be particularly successful.

Notable examples are to be found in Chicago, Detroit, and Milwaukee. Where the parents are not only visited but encouraged to come to the schools for recreational, social, and educational activities, reports indicate a greatly improved attitude of parents, a much improved attitude of students, better schoolwork by students, and fewer disciplinary problems.

**Attitudes of Teachers.** Some secondary school teachers have felt that public relations was not their responsibility. This proportion of teachers has become definitely smaller in recent years, as the necessity for good public relations has been increasingly recognized and as teachers have come to enjoy their associations with other adults. Consequently, there has developed the feeling that teachers who are unwilling to do their part in the program of public relations are somewhat unprofessional, or at least somewhat unfair, in that they usually do not hesitate to accept the increased salaries, better equipment, and other benefits that result from good public relations.

**Increasing Parent-Teacher Social Contact.** In recent years, more and more school people have come to believe that it is good, not only for the school but also for the teacher, to have more teacher contacts with adults and adult interests, particularly social interests, and that it is somewhat hazardous for teachers to spend practically all of their time in association with young people and schoolbooks. Because of this, administrators and school leaders in the community have cooperated in assisting teachers to make social contacts and to increase their participation in social life. Not only are public relations likely to be improved by such efforts, but the teacher is likely to understand more about life outside of the school as it really is and what its problems are, as well as to become better acquainted with the thinking and the interests of non-school adults. It is believed by many administrators that increased social contacts with adults are good mental hygiene for teachers.

The Parent-Teacher Association affords opportunities for teachers to meet parents. At this organization's meetings teachers are encouraged to greet, and to get acquainted with, the parents of their students engage in social conversation with them. Teachers in non-public schools have exploited this and other types of opportunities for meeting parents of their students. A parent is to them a VIP.

**Education Week.** Each year, usually early in November, a week is proclaimed by the National Education Association as American Education Week. It is also sponsored by the National Congress of Parents and Teachers and the American Legion. At this time there are made available, by the National Education Association in particular, suggestions and materials for public-relations programs of various kinds, many involving various types of community participation, including having speakers address churches, schools, services clubs, and other organizations, and usually including the showing of short films in the local motion-picture theater.

**News Stories.** In recent years, teachers have been encouraged more and more to prepare appropriate news stories to inform the public about the work of the school, to increase public interest, and to improve public attitudes. The following is a list of the types of stories that are usually acceptable for local publication and that are likely to be read with interest:

1. Stories relating to contests of all sorts: athletics, debating, typing, and dramatics.
2. Unusual occurrences or situations; for example, achievements in spite of handicaps, records broken, superlatives, the youngest pupil or the tallest; queer, odd, and freakish occurrences.
3. Contrasts and comparisons; past and present; the local school test scores with state or national averages or norms.
4. Human-interest stories: achievements of the blind, the crippled, the self-supporting; marriages, deaths, serious illnesses, accidents; pretty girls and athletic boys.
5. Things that appeal to community pride; results of standard tests; distinctions or honors of pupils or faculty, particularly of individuals; comments on the school and its work by persons at a distance, particularly officials, eminent individuals, or persons well known to the community.
6. Stories about individuals or pupils or teachers related to individuals already in the public eye and stories about events related in some way to peculiar interests of the moment or of the locality; for example, relatives of famous aviators, athletes, public officials, and men or women prominent in industry, finance, or business, or events related in some way to a forthcoming community celebration or to "drives."
7. Stories that permit of interesting illustration with pictures.
8. Stories that are "live"; that is, those that are still fresh news.
9. Stories that affect the interests of large numbers of individuals in the community: proposed changes in tax rates, new buildings, the transfer of units or grades from one building to another, changes in the time of opening or closing school and in the school day.
10. Stories that center about and include the names of individuals are preferable, especially if individuals are prominent in the community or are related to those who are.[2]

## THE CURRICULUM AND THE COMMUNITY

**Adaptation of the Curriculum to the Community.** Until the present century, there was thought to be a definite need for adapting the curriculum of the schools to the local community. The need for such adapta-

---

[2] Harl R. Douglass, *Organization and Administration of Secondary Schools* (Boston: Ginn & Co., 1963), p. 575.

tion has greatly decreased, but, nevertheless, there are important considerations along this line that the effective schoolteacher, the supervisor, the administrator, and the board of education must bear in mind.

It was once thought by many to be necessary to emphasize teaching of those things that would be most useful to the people in the particular community, although, actually, not much was done to implement this. Beginning, however, in the latter part of the nineteenth century, subjects were aided not only for the purpose of providing electives but also for the purpose of providing training of boys and girls for life in the particular community, by means of courses in such fields as home economics, manual training, and agriculture in agricultural communities.

However, before a great deal of adaptation of details of courses of study to the needs and conditions of the local community were made, the communities began to be more and more alike. Textbooks were not differentiated according to the characteristics or needs of different communities, and secondary school teachers were too busy, too inexperienced, and too little acquainted with the communities' educational needs and with methods of adapting courses of study. Consequently, however sound the theory may have been, it was implemented only on a small scale.

The idea of adapting the curriculum to the community life has, however, become increasingly accepted, although interpreted in a variety of ways. Rather than attempting to adapt the materials of instruction and the learning activities to the peculiar conditions and needs of the community in which the school is located, experienced secondary school teachers are endeavoring to teach the subjects in relation to the applications of the subject matter in communities in general, with only a little special emphasis on uses that are unique in the local community. Not only vocational uses, but uses in the home, in leisure life, in health problems, and in other areas of life are stressed.

**The Community School.**[3] In the 1920's and 1930's, a number of very interesting secondary schools attempted to organize most of their materials of instruction and learning activities around the adult community's activities. Certain local communities, particularly rural and somewhat backward ones, were especially fitted for this type of approach, although even in those it was difficult to teach all of the things that were important.

Naturally, much learning that ought to take place has its application in areas broader than the local community, for example, state, national, and international problems, learning relevant to literature, college-pre-

[3] See Edward G. Olsen, "The High School in the Community," in *The American Secondary School* (Paul B. Jacobson, ed.) (Englewood Cliffs, N.J.: Prentice-Hall, Inc., 1952), for an excellent description.

paratory mathematics, and foreign languages. Nevertheless, the idea of relating learning to life applications has continued to find favor, and teachers have become more conscious of the need for this approach to ensure that instruction is understood and retained for a long time.

**Community Personnel and Educational Resources.** It is obvious that the materials and standards of instruction and other learning activities must be planned in the light of the abilities, interests, and backgrounds of the individual students. For that reason, in some communities, for example, those in which the population is largely of upper economic and cultural levels and in which the very great majority of students go on to college, specially adapted types of learning materials and activities may be employed to excellent advantage.

Likewise, in communities where low economic and cultural levels exist and where the majority of the students have limited abilities and limited academic interests and where possibilities of going on to college are not great, appropriate selection and adaptation of materials and learning activities in the various subjects are called for.

To a lesser degree, but, nevertheless, to some extent, the program must be planned in view of the financial ability of the community to support it. In communities of less financial ability, classes of very small numbers of students, for example, in Latin IV, solid geometry, and journalism, should not be maintained, desirable as they might be if sufficient funds were available. For that reason, electives must be somewhat curtailed in some communities; likewise, instruction in certain fields that call for very expensive equipment cannot be offered in less favored communities without unfortunate and unwise sacrifice of instruction in other areas. For example, this applies to instruction involving local television broadcasting or use of expensive business machines or electronic equipment.

**Community Instructional Resources.** There are in every community many resources that may be employed for purposes of instruction. Visits to various places in the community should be employed in a great many subjects. Likewise, there are in every community some people who, if identified and given appropriate briefing, can be used as research persons in instruction. The possibilities along this line were discussed in Chapter 8.

The more important educational values of using community resources are as follows:

1. Study of community life gives a realistic understanding of modern society and social processes.
2. Relating the curriculum to community activities develops an increasing awareness of, and sensitivity to, social issues and problems.

3. Utilizing the personal interests of the student in his immediate environment makes learning more meaningful to him.
4. Study of community conditions provides training in the scientific method of studying society.
5. Community study contributes to the student's sense of responsibility to society.
6. Community study serves to vitalize and enrich the curriculum by practical application to actual situations.
7. Community study contributes to the realization of one of the school's major responsibilities, namely, that of introducing youths to the life of their communities.
8. Study of community problems may lead to subsequent action to improve the quality of community life.
9. Community study counteracts isolation of the school from the realities of life, thereby enabling it to become a more effective agency for human welfare.
10. Community study fosters cooperation of individuals and agencies interested in making community life more wholesome.

## THE TEACHER AND THE COMMUNITY

**Learning About the Community.** It is important for every teacher to learn as soon as possible, to some extent before school starts, a great many pertinent points about the local community. Among things that instructors should learn as early as possible about the local community are data relative to the following:

1. Racial, religious, and economic composition of the population of the district
2. Industries and occupations of the people of the district
3. Financial ability of the district to support the public schools
4. Special attitudes and biases—political, religious, and otherwise—about which the public is very much concerned and emotional, especially where there are sharp differences of opinion within the community
5. Potential community resources for learning activities

Usually, the principal of the high school and the superintendent of schools furnish the teacher with very valuable information along these lines, much of it in printed or mimeographed form.

**Academic Freedom.** One of the limitations of local controlled schools is the danger of undue influence upon the teachers, administrators, and supervisors in connection with the learning materials, and instructional procedures, and learning activities. In general, at the college level, where the institution is somewhat removed from excessive local control, there exists what is known as academic freedom—the freedom of the teacher to select for instructional purposes the materials he considers most useful for instruction in his subject, regardless of the opinions of various groups in the community.

In the secondary school, however, academic freedom is not so complete. Indeed, the teacher should avoid provoking the anger, indignation, or opposition of influential groups and individuals, except in matters of unusual importance to the education of his students. This does not mean, however, teaching things that are not true and avoiding discussion of controversial issues. But it does mean that relative values must be considered and that the antagonism of a considerable proportion of the community or very influential organizations or individuals should not be risked, except where very important benefits can be gained, in the choice of subject matter and teaching methods. In important matters where students have much to gain by his doing so, no true professional teacher will fail to stand his ground. Under no circumstances should be stoop to teach what he does not believe, in order to gain favor or to appease biased or ignorant people or organizations, no matter how influential they may be.

In general, the National Education Association, the state educational associations, and, in particular, the American Federation of Teachers stand ready to protect teachers who are unduly attacked when exercising academic freedom. Unfortunately, some teachers seem to enjoy being the center of controversy and consider it more important to be publicized and regarded as martyrs than to make the greatest possible contribution to their avowed educational objectives. Many boards of education have adopted a definite policy to govern teaching about controversial matters and to protect teachers.

Teachers in a given school or school system need to know exactly where they stand with respect to permitting or encouraging discussion of controversial issues in their classrooms. For this reason, it is desirable that the local board of education adopt an explicit policy with respect to the handling of controversial issues. If the board of education has not already done so, the administration and teachers should submit to the board a policy similar to the following:

### CRITERIA FOR DETERMINING APPROPRIATENESS OF CONTROVERSIAL ISSUES FOR THE SCHOOL CURRICULUM

(1) The issue must not involve the indoctrination of religious beliefs.

(2) The treatment of the issue in question should be within the range of the knowledge, maturity, and competence of the students.

(3) There should be study materials and other learning aids available, from which a reasonable amount of data pertaining to all aspects of the issue may be obtained.

(4) The issue should be given only as much time as is needed for a satisfactory study by the class; but sufficient time should be provided to cover the issue adequately.

(5) The issue should be current, significant, real, and important to student and teacher. Significant issues are those which, in general, pertain to basic principles, concern considerable numbers of people, or are at the moment under consideration by the public and the press.

### Responsibility of the Teacher

(1) A teacher in a free society has the obligation to uphold, protect, and defend the fundamental freedoms as documented in the history of our American democracy.

(2) The teacher is responsible for establishing in the classroom an atmosphere of freedom for students to raise questions dealing with critical issues and for maintaining an atmosphere conducive to the free, spirited, and friendly interplay of ideas.

(3) It shall be the duty of teachers to see that all facts, evidence, and aspects of an issue are presented honestly.

(4) The teacher should acquaint students with books, newspapers, and other materials which present data on all aspects of a controversial issue under discussion.

(5) Statements presented and opinions expressed during discussion of controversial issues are to be carefully scrutinized by the teacher to make sure they are based on substantiated facts or reliable evidence. The teacher should exercise special care to avoid misunderstanding.

(6) The importance of the authenticity of facts and the purpose for which they were gathered must be stressed. Propaganda, in any form, should be clearly identified as such by teachers and students, and its intent should be clearly understood.

(7) Although it is the teacher's responsibility to bring out the facts concerning a controversial question, he has the right to express his opinion, provided his students understand that it is his own opinion and that it is not to be accepted by them as the authoritative answer He should, however, do this rarely on questions about which the community is divided sharply.

### Responsibility of the Administration

(1) The following assumptions are basic to the administration of a policy which provides for the inclusion of controversial issues in the school curriculum:

(a) That the teacher will consider controversial issues in the classroom only within the fields of his preparation and training;
(b) That the principal, as the administrator of his building, will bear a major responsibility for the administration and supervision of the curriculum, selection of materials, and methods of instruction, and, therefore, that he will be alert to and constantly aware of what is being taught in his school;
(c) That citizens have the right to trust that controversial issues are being presented fairly, and to protest to the Board of Education if they become convinced that unfair, biased, or prejudiced presentations are being made.

(2) A teacher who is in doubt concerning the advisability of discussing certain issues in the classroom should confer with his principal as to the appropriateness of the issue. If the principal and the teacher are unable to establish agreement, the issue shall be referred to the Division of Instruction. The Division shall refer the matter to the Superintendent of Schools if necessary.

(3) No outside individual or group may claim the right to present arguments directly to students in the schools. Such a "right" to present arguments directly would make the schools battlegrounds for all kinds of controversies. The teacher, with the approval of the principal and/or the Superintendent of Schools, should feel free to invite, on rare occasions, representatives of various viewpoints to discuss issues with his classes, in order to inform the students on all aspects of controversial questions.[4]

**The Teacher as a Public Servant.** Although at times it is embarrassing and objectionable, the teacher cannot escape being cast in the role of a public servant. The teacher is an employee of a public institution that is publicly controlled and supported by public taxation. An embarrassing, and in some cases a most irritating, aspect of this role is the necessity for at least an outward conformity to the accepted mores and customs of the people constituting the local community. For example, in some communities the consumption of alcoholic beverages operates to decrease the influence and effectiveness of the teacher, and, indeed, in many communities, to shorten the stay of the teacher in the community.

The same sort of taboos are encountered with respect to behavior in a considerable number of other areas. Indeed, some of them go so far as to affect the dress and the cosmetic beautification of the teachers, although in this area the situation has been changed considerably in the great majority of communities.

Some of the taboos are rather general and quite important, for example, the dating of high school students by teachers is generally frowned upon and inadvisable, and, of course, dating by a married teacher is, in most communities, very likely to ensure the dismissal of the teacher, or at least the failure to renew his contract.

Teachers greatly weaken their influence if they are known to participate in gambling, reckless automobile driving, or other similar types of activities that are thought to constitute unfortunate examples for the young people of the community. In addition, in practically all communities, but especially the smaller ones, teachers who spend all of their vacations and most of their weekends away from the community are subject to criticism and often find it difficult to develop good public relations and personal good will.

In a great many communities, especially the smaller ones, the teacher who attends some church in the community is rather certain to strengthen

---

[4] Adapted from a list of criteria that was drawn up by the Board of Education of Elizabeth, New Jersey.

his position, although this is not as important as it once was, and in many communities, especially large ones, it is not important at all. Teachers who exhibit good taste with respect to literature, art, and music also strengthen their positions and influence, as do teachers who participate in civic activities, if not to the extent of neglecting their schoolwork, unless controversial situations and conflicts develop. In smaller communities teachers who patronize local merchants and support local civic activities are looked upon favorably.

Among suggestions that have been made for good community relations are the following:

1. Be reluctant to criticize any individuals in your community, even in conferences. It is amazing how quickly and surely such remarks get back to persons criticized or to their friends.

2. Be sparing in outstanding praise of individuals, lest you be considered insincere or opposed to the interests of their enemies.

3. Discuss with your principal or superintendent any school-community relations that trouble you.

4. Never criticize and rarely discuss other teachers, your administrative school officials, or the board of education, except with your very close confidants and then most cautiously.

5. Be careful at all times to avoid being thought of as belonging to a faction.

6. Remember at all times that you yourself may be provincial and that you may have to learn to be tolerant and understanding.

7. Do not speak disparagingly of your community or of the state or section of the state in which it is located.

8. Do not engage in vocational, household, or civic activities that occupy more than ten or twelve hours a week.

## OTHER WAYS OF RELATING THE SCHOOL
## TO THE COMMUNITY

**Youth Serving the Community.** Many secondary school students receive valuable educational training by participating in various sorts of activities that have a community-service value, including the following:

Preparing and publishing recreational directories
Assisting in community cleanup campaigns
Producing music festivals for schools and churches
Entertaining shut-in children
Supervising playgrounds for younger children
Planning gifts of food, clothing, and furniture for needy families
Assisting in drives for social agencies

Entertaining at old people's homes
Renovating and making toys for younger children
Assisting in nursery schools
Arranging public exhibits
Conducting surveys for community agencies
Assisting in home demonstrations with regard to food
Producing community carnivals
Helping in nuisance-elimination campaigns (for example, campaigns against rats)
Assisting in hospitals

**Work Experience.** As is pointed out in Chapter 11 of this volume, the opportunities and stimulus for work experience for young people have been for a great many years on the way to disappearance. A large number of schools each year are making provision for work experience in the community. This work experience is of two types: (1) assistance in community enterprises for the common good without monetary compensation and (2) experience on the job as a part of vocational training and as part-time employment. Among the objectives and values of work experience are some which have to do with school-community relations. Work experience may provide a type of vocational education that is tied in with the practical activities in the community. In addition, it interests a considerable number of employers in cooperating in the educational program of the school, and it brings the youngsters into closer contact with the adult life of the community, thereby not only giving them orientation with respect to community life but also predisposing them to the acquisition of the ideals, attitudes, and concepts of adults in the community. Work experience should be developed in all secondary schools and should be under the careful supervision of someone well qualified in that field.

**Camping.** Another way of taking the high school into the community is provision for camping. Summer camps and school camps provide an opportunity for young people to profit educationally by experiences of living together and making the necessary interindividual and group-individual adjustments. A considerable and increasing number of schools already own camp properties that are used for school camping purposes. Among the purposes, philosophy, and educational activities of camps are the following:

I. The school camp should have as its central objective helping young people to understand the democratic way of life and to practice it in their relationships with others.

    1. The school camp should treat each youngster as an individual. It should guide him, help him to face his problems, help him develop his potentialities, and open up new interests to him.

     2. The school camp should help youngsters to live with others, giving and taking, sharing and accepting responsibilities, constantly learning to widen the area of shared interests through partaking in enterprises with others for objectives commonly agreed upon by the participants.

     3. The school camp should stress problem solving involving the process of critical thinking.

     4. The school camp should teach youngsters to be concerned for human welfare, inside and outside the camp.

II. Plans should be made to ensure that the pupils may participate effectively in such camp experiences as the following:

     1. Getting acquainted with the camp area and the other campers
     2. Observing trees, flowers, rocks, and birds in the area
     3. Making things to be used in the area
     4. Sharing responsibility for camp chores
     5. Offering programs of an inspirational nature
     6. Taking special exploratory trips
     7. Holding evening get-togethers
       a. Campfires
       b. Songfests
       c. Storytelling sessions
       d. Games
     8. Carrying on leisure-time activities
       a. Hobbies
       b. Crafts
       c. Swimming
       d. Reading
       e. Hiking
       f. Dramatics

**Bringing the Community into the School.** Various methods are available for utilizing community resources for educational purposes, and these include the following:

     1. Use of visual aids of various sorts, such as pictures, charts, films, slides, and specimens, prepared by pupils or committees of pupils and teachers or borrowed from firms or individuals in the community

     2. Providing in the classroom, homeroom, or assembly, discussion by individuals in the community who are well informed concerning some aspects of community conditions, community life, or community needs, such as the recreational facilities, chamber of commerce and service organizations, religious life, principal industries, and sources of income in the community

     3. Use of the printed material and other documents available from the chamber of commerce and from the various offices of the city and county government

4. Reports in class by individual pupils and groups of pupils who have undertaken to carry on investigations about some institution, conditions, problem, or operation in the community

## QUESTIONS, PROBLEMS, AND TOPICS FOR FURTHER STUDY

1. Do you believe it is better for the local school to be controlled by, and dependent upon, people of the local community, as compared to state and national control as it exists in other countries?
2. Do you believe that teachers ought to participate in maintaining good public relations, as opposed to leaving it to administrators?
3. What could be gained by visitation of homes by high school teachers?
4. To what extent and in what ways do you believe the curriculum should be adapted to the local community?
5. What do you think are the more important things for the teacher to know about the community in which he is teaching? How is the teacher to get that information?
6. Be ready to give a talk of some seven or eight minutes on the teacher's private life in the community.

## SUPPLEMENTARY MATERIALS

### SELECTED READINGS

ANDERSON, VERNON E., and WILLIAM T. GRUHN. *Principles and Practices of Secondary Education* (2d ed.). New York: The Ronald Press Co., 1962. Chapter 13, "A Community Institution."

AREND, PAUL. "The Supervisor, the School Newspaper, and Public Relations," *Bulletin of the N.A.S.S.P.*, No. 267 (December, 1961), 101–5.

BRIDGES, BERNICE, et al. "Voluntary Work Experience," *The American Child*, XLIV (March, 1962), 20–22.

BRUCE, WILLIAM F., and A. JOHN HOLDEN, JR. *The Teacher's Personal Development*. New York: Holt, Rinehart & Winston, Inc., 1957. Chapter 14, "Living in the Community."

BRYAN, ROY C., and MILDRED BEISEL. "Vitalize Your High School P.T.A.," *Bulletin of the N.A.S.S.P.*, No. 224 (May, 1956), 139–45.

CONANT, JAMES B. *Slums and Suburbs*. McGraw-Hill Book Co., Inc., 1961.

COX, PHILIP W. L., and BLAINE E. MERCER. *Education in Democracy*. New York: McGraw-Hill Book Co., Inc., 1961. Chapter 21, "The Community and the Pioneering School."

COZZO, JOYCE R. "Evaluation of Parent Group Meetings," *Bulletin of the N.A.S.S.P.*, No. 273 (April, 1962), 205–9.

DOUGLASS, HARL R. *Trends and Issues in Secondary Education*. Washington, D.C.: The Center for Applied Research in Education, Inc., 1962. Chapter 12, "School-Community Relationships."

FAUNCE, ROLAND C., and MORREL J. CLUTE. *Teaching and Learning in the Junior High School*. San Francisco: Wadsworth Publishing Co., Inc., 1961. Chapter 11, "School-Parent Relationships"; Chapter 12, "Serving the Community."

GRAMBS, JEAN D., WILLIAM J. IVERSON, and FRANKLIN K. PATTERSON. *Modern Methods in Secondary Education.* New York: Holt, Rinehart & Winston, Inc., 1958. Chapter 22, "The Teacher in the School and Community."

HINES, VYNCE A., and HULDA GROSSMAN. *"What Parents Think of Their Schools and What They Know About Them,"* Bulletin of the N.A.S.S.P., No. 229 (February, 1957), 15–20.

HUGGETT, ALBERT. *Professional Problems of Teachers.* New York: The Macmillan Co., 1956. Chapter 13, "The Role of Teachers in Community and Public Relations."

LEE, GORDON C. *Education in Modern America.* New York: Holt, Rinehart & Winston, Inc., 1957. Chapter 27, "Freedom To Teach and To Learn: Academic Freedom and Academic Responsibility."

LUND, S. E. TORSTEN. "Community Life and the Curriculum." Chapter 11 in *The High School Curriculum* (2d ed.). (HARL R. DOUGLASS, ed.). New York: The Ronald Press Co., 1956.

"Should Parents Know the Results of I.Q. Tests?" *The Education Digest,* XXVII (April, 1962), 19–21.

"Situational Factors and Negro Leadership Activity in Medium Sized Communities," *The Journal of Negro Education,* Winter, 1960, 85.

AUDIO-VISUAL MATERIALS

*Filmstrip*

*The Teacher and Public Relations.* NEA, 1952. 50 frames, silent with captions.

# 22

# Professional Relationships and Problems

## RECENT EXPANSIONS OF PERSONNEL

Until well into the twentieth century, the high school staff was, with few exceptions, made up of only the principal, secretary or a clerk or both, the teachers, and the librarians. In a few large schools there were assistant principals and/or an assistant called the dean of girls. However, beginning generally in the 1920's, earlier in some schools, specialists were added to the staff, particularly counselors and school nurses, though these were on part time only, except in the large high schools. Since that time, additional types and larger numbers of specialists other than teachers have been added to school staffs, particularly directors of health and physical education, of athletics, of activities, and of testing and research. Likewise, the secretarial staff has expanded, particularly since the secretary not only has additional paper work to do, involving correspondence, records, etc., but also, in many schools, acts as an administrative assistant to the principal.

Today, in the average or better secondary schools, the staffs ordinarily to be found are very similar to those represented in the table on page 433.

## EDUCATION AND CERTIFICATION OF TEACHERS

There has been much controversy over the education of teachers, particularly between extremist intellectuals who do not believe in much professional education and administrators who desire to have teachers

SUGGESTED STAFFING OF HIGH SCHOOLS*

| Position | Schools of 1,500 to 3,000 | Schools of 800 to 1,500 | Schools of 300 to 800 | Schools of 100 to 300 | Schools of Less than 100 |
|---|---|---|---|---|---|
| Principal | 1 | 1 | $\frac{2}{3}$–1 | $\frac{1}{3}$–$\frac{2}{3}$ | – |
| Vice-principal or coordinator of instruction | 1 | $\frac{1}{2}$–$\frac{3}{4}$ | $\frac{1}{3}$–$\frac{1}{2}$ | – | – |
| Vice-principal or director of activities | 1 | $\frac{1}{2}$–$\frac{3}{4}$ | $\frac{1}{3}$–$\frac{1}{2}$ | – | – |
| Vice-principal or director of guidance | 1 | $\frac{1}{2}$–$\frac{2}{3}$ | $\frac{1}{6}$–$\frac{1}{3}$ | – | – |
| Psychologist | $\frac{1}{2}$–1 | $\frac{1}{3}$–$\frac{1}{2}$ | $\frac{1}{6}$–$\frac{1}{3}$ | – | – |
| Counselors | 6–10 | 3–6 | 1–3 | $\frac{1}{3}$–1 | $\frac{1}{3}$ |
| Director of health and physical education | $\frac{1}{2}$–1 | $\frac{1}{4}$–$\frac{1}{2}$ | $\frac{1}{6}$–$\frac{1}{3}$ | – | – |
| Librarian | 2–4 | 1–2 | $\frac{1}{2}$–1 | $\frac{1}{3}$–$\frac{2}{3}$ | $\frac{1}{6}$ |
| Psychiatrist | $\frac{1}{2}$–1 | $\frac{1}{4}$–$\frac{1}{2}$ | $\frac{1}{8}$–$\frac{1}{4}$ | – | – |
| Director of athletics | $\frac{1}{2}$–1 | $\frac{1}{3}$–$\frac{1}{2}$ | $\frac{1}{6}$–$\frac{1}{3}$ | $\frac{1}{6}$ | – |
| Heads of departments or special supervisor | 4–6 | 2–3 | 1–2 | $\frac{1}{2}$–1 | – |
| Attendance supervisor | 1–2 | $\frac{2}{5}$–$\frac{4}{5}$ | $\frac{1}{5}$ | – | – |
| Physician | 1 | $\frac{1}{2}$–1 | $\frac{1}{6}$–$\frac{1}{2}$ | – | – |
| Nurses | 2–5 | 1–2 | $\frac{2}{5}$–1 | $\frac{1}{5}$–$\frac{2}{5}$ | $\frac{1}{4}$ |
| Dentist | 1–2 | $\frac{1}{2}$–1 | $\frac{1}{6}$–$\frac{1}{2}$ | – | – |
| Director of testing and research | 1 | $\frac{1}{3}$–$\frac{1}{2}$ | $\frac{1}{6}$–$\frac{1}{3}$ | – | – |
| Office secretary and clerks | 5–8 | 3–5 | 1–3 | $\frac{1}{2}$–1 | $\frac{1}{2}$ |
| Director of audio-visual education | 1 | $\frac{1}{2}$–$\frac{3}{4}$ | $\frac{1}{4}$–$\frac{1}{2}$ | $\frac{1}{4}$ | – |

* Entries denote the proportion of the time of a full-time official that should be available for the position in question. In schools of small or medium size, various combinations of duties may be centered in one individual, for example, psychologist and director of guidance, director of health and director of athletics.

SOURCE: Harl R. Douglass, *Administration of Modern Secondary Schools* (Boston: Ginn & Co., 1963), p. 56.

better prepared to do the job expected of them. It seems impossible in a four-year course to give the prospective secondary school teacher more than a "lick and a promise" and hope that he will continue to study, through either formal courses or independent reading, to improve the mastery of his subject, his general education, and his skills and techniques of performing the various duties of secondary school teachers.

**General Education.** The field in which perhaps the greatest progress has been made in recent years has been that of general education. Previously it was a neglected area, because the subject-matter specialists on college faculties, as well as professional educators and school administrators, pushed for the giving of more time to subject-matter and professional preparation of teachers.

The North Central Association of Colleges and Secondary Schools has strongly recommended that every secondary school teacher have a considerable amount of general education, so selected and planned as to produce a broadly educated secondary school teacher. There has been considerable confusion about the meaning of the term *general education*, many using it as a synonym of *liberal education*. Today, many employing officers look very carefully at the pattern and the manner of the general education of individuals whom they are considering for positions.

General education means broad, non-specialized education including various areas of culture and knowledge that should be common to all truly educated persons as individuals and as citizens in a free society. It is that part of education that is concerned with knowledge, skills, attitudes, interests, and ideals needed by each individual to be effective as a citizen, a worker, and a member of a family who understands the more important aspects of the world in which he lives. A broadly educated person has some knowledge of history, economics, political science, sociology, geography, physics, chemistry, biology, grammar, literature, speech, philosophy, psychology, and the fine arts.

General education not only consists of knowledge and understanding but it also covers important personal disciplines. Among those are the various intellectual skills in reading, thinking, problem solving, and appropriate habits of behavior. An important measure of the degree to which one is an educated person is one's behavior—one's speech and actions. Some believe that general education consists of training that will ensure that one behaves as an educated person with respect to leisure interests, cooperation and regard for the rights of others, and maintaining one's own mental and physical health.

General education is no longer thought of as the possession of information that may be exhibited to others without regard to the part that it plays in the behavior of the individual. Many decide whether or not any particular individual is educated on the basis of his interests, his speech, and his behavior in contacts with other individuals.

There is a growing belief in the great importance of general education for teachers, many today believing that, above all, the teacher must be an educated person. Today, on the average, prospective teachers spend more than a third of their time in college in general-education studies.

Partly because of recent criticism of secondary education, there has been a growing concern relative to the subject-matter preparation of teachers. This concern is felt with respect to the amount, pattern, and comprehensiveness of course work in the field in which the teacher expects to teach, particularly in such fields as general science, social studies, and literature. For example, a teacher may have a major in history and not be well prepared to teach social studies or, indeed, the history of several nations. Likewise, one who has majored in physics and chemistry but has taken little other science is poorly prepared to teach courses in general science, and one who has majored in literature may not be well prepared to teach speech, dramatics, journalism, or composition.

Increasingly, the prospective teacher is expected to have broader knowledge of, and familiarity with, his field. High school principals and superintendents are much less likely now than formerly to assign a teacher to a subject in which he is not well and broadly prepared.

**Professional Education.** Probably no aspect of education has been under greater criticism or received stouter defense than the professional education of teachers. It is vigorously protested by many college professors that time should not be taken away from subject-matter preparation and general education of teachers to be devoted to many courses in "methods." This frequently made assertion indicates either a considerable lack of information or, perhaps more often, of intellectual discipline or intellectual dishonesty in referring to all courses in education as "methods" courses.

The responsibilities of secondary school teachers today call for broad professional preparation. The secondary school teacher is not merely one who assigns lessons with threats and promises to motivate preparation and then checks up with oral or written quizzes or papers to be handed in. Even in the classroom, the responsibilities of the teacher and the possible superior techniques are far broader.

Beyond this, the secondary school teacher today almost always has responsibility incident to his acting as a sponsor of a club or some other extracurricular activity, to selection and arrangement of learning materials and provision of the motivation for the use of them, to evaluation of the progress of his students in various types of growth, involving knowledge of tests and other forms of measurement, and to effective counseling of young people. As the concept of the teaching profession has changed over the years there has come to be a greater necessity for more complete professional preparation.

It is a very common experience for an undergraduate student with a keen interest in his major field to find it difficult in preparing for teaching to become quickly equally interested in courses in professional preparation. This is a fairly common difficulty and quite understandable, as is the fact that, after a year or more of teaching, the very large majority of teachers begin to realize the inadequacy of their professional training and to spend substantial sums of money and time to improve it by attending summer schools and professional conventions.

**Five-Year Plans.** In a small but increasing number of states, a certificate to teach in high school may not be obtained by one with less than five years of preparation beyond high school. Regional associations have stepped up the requirements for accreditation to five years. In some states not requiring five years of preparation, a teacher must get a fifth year or credits amounting to thirty semester hours of advanced preparation in his subject and in education in order to get his certificate renewed. Furthermore, there has been, in spite of the shortage of secondary school teachers, a substantial increase each year in the number of boards of education requiring five years of appropriate preparation. It seems rather certain that the five-year plan will become very general. It will do much to solve the problem of too limited preparation in general education, in the subject field, and in professional preparation.

**Certification.** As is indicated elsewhere in this volume, there is a definite trend toward tightening up the requirements for certification of teachers so that it will be impossible to obtain a teaching certificate without a reasonable minimum of preparation in the subject field and in professional courses. It also will be very difficult for secondary schools desiring accreditation by one of the regional associations to be successful if they employ teachers lacking in either general, specialized, or professional education.

## SELECTION OF TEACHERS

Administrators have developed much more complicated and efficient procedures for the selection of secondary school teachers. Indeed, in a great many large cities, there is an assistant superintendent with assistants and a clerical staff who devotes his entire time to that important responsibility.

**Procedures.** Employing officials rather generally ask for recommendations from the institutions of higher education engaged in the preparation of teachers. The papers received from the placement bureaus of such institutions are examined very carefully, and the employing official usually interviews the prospective teacher either on the campus or in the city where he is to be employed. If both the employing official and the prospective teacher are interested, the latter is asked to submit an application furnishing certain types of data that may not be otherwise available.

**Criteria.** The most frequently desired and most useful information regarding prospective candidates may be summarized as follows:

1. Education: amount, subjects of specialization, professional certificate, participation in extracurricular activities.

2. Experience: amount, nature, character of success, dates and places, supervision or coaching of "activities."
3. Scholarship.
4. Ability to maintain orderly classroom conditions.
5. Teaching ability.
6. Tact and ability to get along with pupils and parents.
7. Special weaknesses likely to affect teaching efficiency.
8. Enthusiasm and interest in work.
9. Character.
10. Personal appearance.
11. General success in school and community.
12. Co-operation and loyalty.
13. Social qualities.
14. Probability of professional growth.
15. General culture, including reading tastes and habits.
16. Age.
17. Health and freedom from physical defects.
18. Marital status.
19. Height and weight.
20. Salary desired.
21. Intelligence.

Some of these items merit special consideration in the selection of teachers with superior qualifications.

SOURCES OF DATA. The most commonly employed sources of information concerning prospective teachers are listed below.

*Application Blanks:* education, experience, age, health, marital status, height and weight, salary desired, subjects of specialization, teaching and other vocational experience, activity experience, appearance (photographs), certificate.

*References:* (1) previous instructors: scholarship, character, personal appearance, personality traits, social qualities, intelligence; (2) school officials: experience, ability to maintain order, teaching ability, character, personal appearance, co-operation and loyalty, health, traits of personality, defects, social qualities, probability of professional growth, enthusiasm, interest in work.

*Interviews:* personality, appearance, salary desired, health, physical defects, general culture.

*Classroom Visitation:* scholarship, ability to maintain order, teaching ability, teaching personality, enthusiasm, interest in work.

*Credentials of Agencies and Bureaus:* items listed under application blanks and references.

*Transcripts of Credits:* indication of pattern of preparation in some detail and also of quality of scholarship (occasionally candidates have been known to misrepresent the courses taken and the grades received).[1]

Many employing officers insist that the prospective teacher submit scores on National Teachers' Examinations. These examinations, which

[1] Harl R. Douglass, *Administration of Modern Secondary Schools* (2d ed.) (Boston: Ginn & Co., 1963), pp. 67–68.

are given in a very large number of cities throughout the country, include tests covering the following fields:

1. Professional information in the areas of guidance, methods, curriculum, community relationships, and psychology of learning.
2. General culture, including knowledge of contemporary events and developments.
3. English expression.
4. Nonverbal reasoning.
5. Knowledge in one or two of the thirteen teaching fields in which there are examinations.

Upon payment of a small fee, the teacher or prospective teacher may take as many of these examinations as he wishes and have the papers scored, recorded, and sent to any designated administrator or board of education. There is no failing or passing mark. The score and its percentile rank among the scores of all taking the particular examination are recorded and forwarded to the employing person or board designated by the teacher. The employing agency may evaluate the score in any manner it chooses.

The National Teachers' Examinations are usually given in the second week in February. Applications must be received and approved by an announced date, usually before the end of the second week in January.[2]

**Philosophy of Education and Knowledge of Recent Trends.** In the past few years, employing officers in school systems where better-than-average salaries are paid make a definite effort to find out:

1. What is the basic philosophy of education of the teacher? What kind of objectives will he work for? What does he believe to be important in education?
2. What knowledge does he have of recent new developments, trends, and practices involving such things as teaching the bright child, teaching the slow child, the use of audio-visual equipment, the use of teaching machines, team teaching, the use of tape recorders, and community relations?

**Supply and Demand.** While the number of secondary school teachers increases materially each year, the supply of qualified teachers cannot keep up with the demand. This will certainly be true for many years to come, as it is certain that enrolments in the secondary schools will increase. Nevertheless, the supply will not fall far behind the demand, since many teachers are staying in the profession longer.

With salaries increasing materially every year, and inflation having slowed down, teaching becomes more attractive. With the five-year requirement, not only will salaries continue to increase and more men go into teaching, but those who put five years into training will be more likely to make it a life occupation.

[2] Harl R. Douglass, *Administration of Modern Secondary Schools* (Boston: Ginn & Co., 1963), p. 68.

## PROFESSIONAL LOAD OF TEACHERS

In spite of the fact that, with but very few exceptions, teachers teach no more than five classes a day rather than six or seven as they did formerly, the teacher has a full day and a full week. It has been variously estimated that the typical work week of the secondary school teacher is somewhere between forty-five and fifty hours.

Following is a statement on the load of a high school teacher in Rochester, New York:

### A Full Day for the Teacher

So you think a teacher spends all of her time in the classroom teaching? A Rochester, New York, newspaper reporter found out when he interviewed teachers that they devote a lot of time to non-teaching duties. . . .

A high-school teacher told the reporter she did those things and a few more, besides. This was her list: checking absences; writing admissions to classes, reading office notices; sending from classes pupils requested by the school nurse or other school personnel; issuing notices on overdue library books; helping with school census; preparing monthly attendance reports; issuing bus badges and locker numbers; handling money in fund-raising projects such as candy, periodical, and yearbook sales; taking tickets at interschool games; serving on faculty committees; chaperoning class parties; putting in appearances at school plays and concerts; helping at parents' nights; attending faculty, department, and test committee meetings; ordering books; conferring with specialists about students; and working with cadet teachers. . . .[3]

In recent years there has been a possibly unethical trend toward "moonlighting," accepting a second job, usually on part time, in addition to the job of teaching. In instances where the second job takes more than ten or twelve hours a week, the usefulness and effectiveness of the teacher are limited and the possibilities of his promotion and advancement are decreased. About one-fifth of the teachers in Texas in all districts—large, medium, and small—have second jobs, besides teaching, during the school year.[4]

City teachers work at teaching nearly 1.6 weeks longer each year than others, but they work fewer hours a week—43.5, compared with 47.3 for all teachers. The city teacher has more pupils—33 in the average elementary school classroom, 191 in secondary school classes. For all teachers, the average in elementary school is 29 pupils, while in secondary schools the average is 156 pupils.

A careful investigation has shown that English teachers spend, on the average, about 15 per cent more time on a class of twenty-five students

---

[3] "News Notes," *The Bulletin, N.A.S.S.P.*, No. 269 (December, 1961), p. 170.

[4] "Supplementary Earnings by Teachers in 199 Texas High Schools," Research Study No. 35, Study of Secondary Education, Austin, Texas, October, 1962, *NEA Journal*, Vol. 51, No. 9 (December, 1962), pp. 4–5.

than do teachers of most other subjects and that about 10 per cent more time is spent by teachers of science and social studies than by teachers of most other subjects. There has been a recent tendency toward giving English teachers lighter loads so that they can devote more time to their students' papers.

**Factors in the Teacher's Load.** The following are recognized as principal factors in teaching load. They are listed somewhat in the order of their importance:

*a*) The number of class periods taught; this is by far the most important factor in the teaching load.
*b*) The number of co-curricular activities sponsored and study halls kept.
*c*) The number of pupils taught.
*d*) The number of faculty study groups, committees, and conferences the teacher serves on or works with.
*e*) The extra administrative duties the teacher has, such as keeping accounts, doing secretarial work, especially in small high schools, or helping with attendance or cumulative records.
*f*) The length of the class period.
*g*) The number of different preparations or the number of duplicate sections.
*h*) The number of different subject fields in which the classes fall.
*i*) The relative maturity of the students (the senior requires more time than the freshman, for example).

Perhaps more important than any of the above (except the first) in the teaching load of some teachers is the nature of the class taught. For example, a class composed only of bright students or one composed only of dull students constitutes an unusually heavy load, with special planning of learning activity and the looking up of material to a degree far greater than for a normal heterogeneous class.[5]

A careful investigation has shown that English teachers spend, on the average, about 15 per cent more time on a class of twenty-five students than do teachers of most other subjects and that about 10 per cent more time is spent by teachers of science and social studies than by teachers of most other subjects. There has been a recent tendency toward giving English teachers lighter loads so that they can devote more time to their students' papers.

Another factor is the character of the pupils taught, their tractability, the ease or difficulty of motivating them, the proportion of outstandingly able or outstandingly less able students, and the extent to which special curriculum materials and methods must be planned for special sections of slow, abler, underachieving or low-cultural level students.

[5] Harl R. Douglass, *Administration of Modern Secondary Schools* (Boston: Ginn & Co., 1963), p. 79.

In recognition of the increased responsibilities of secondary school teachers, there has been, in recent years, a tendency to devise ways to provide teachers with assistance and to reduce the load. In a considerable and increasing number of schools, teachers' aides are provided, for some teachers at least, who will relieve the teacher of part of his work in connection with such duties as marking of papers, assisting of individual students, and assisting with laboratory and shop equipment and materials. Furthermore, in most secondary schools the teacher is relieved of practically all of the chores related to use of the mimeograph or other duplicating machines, copying of records, and other clerical work.

**Class Size.** Much variation exists with respect to the sizes of the classes assigned to teachers. In general, in secondary schools between twenty-four and twenty-eight students is the average; nevertheless, in most schools, some, if not all, classes are larger, and, consequently, teachers are likely to be overloaded. It would be very desirable to reduce the size of class to not more than twenty students, as is done in many independent schools that charge substantial tuition, but, in view of the shortages of teachers and funds and because of the necessity for raising teachers' salaries, this desirable situation will not be realized in many schools for several decades. The trend is, rather, toward the use of teachers' aides in large classes.

**Extra Pay for Extra Work.** While it is controversial, there has, nevertheless, been introduced in many schools in the United States a practice of giving extra pay to teachers who have extra loads of certain types. This applies most frequently to coaches of athletic teams, directors of musical organizations, and teachers who perform extra services such as sponsoring of student government and other extracurricular activities of a time-consuming nature and taking on of special assignments in the administrator's office.

The large majority of teachers receiving extra pay have families to support, and for that reason the practice, which might not otherwise be approved, is condoned. Nevertheless, there is opposition from those who do not receive extra pay for work done over the normal load. The normal or average load for secondary school teachers in most schools is five classes meeting five times a week with an average of about twenty-six students per class, plus an extra assignment for supervising a study hall or some club or other student activity, which will require from three to five hours a week. The amount of extra pay usually ranges from $100 to $400 a semester, the largest amounts going to head coaches of interscholastic sports and to directors of bands.

**Teachers' Aides.** To reduce the demands on the time and energy of teachers, non-certified assistants are being provided in a large and increasing number of schools. Serving as aides to teachers, the following types of personnel are employed:

1. Student teachers for teacher-training programs
2. College students other than teacher trainees
3. Clerical workers
4. College-trained adults from the community
5. Other adults (not college-trained or clerks)

Among other things, aides serve as

1. Laboratory supervisors
2. Lay readers of some written work
3. Objective-test graders
4. Teachers for makeup or remedial work by individuals or small groups
5. Hall or playground supervisors
6. Study-hall supervisors
7. Library assistants
8. Shop supervisors
9. Clerks
10. Field-trip assistants

## TEAM TEACHING LOAD

**Responsibilities Under the Trump Plan.** In recent years, several hundred secondary schools in the United States have employed, at least on an experimental basis, what has come to be termed *the Trump plan of team teaching* (developed by a committee headed by Professor Lloyd Trump, of the University of Illinois, now the associate executive secretary of the National Association of Secondary School Principals). Under this plan, teachers specialize somewhat in what are thought to be their strong points, and several teachers will cooperate in teaching several sections of each course.

It is recommended by Professor Trump's Committee on the Utilization of Secondary School Staff that (1) student would spend 40 per cent of their class time in hearing lectures; (2) students would spend 20 per cent of their class time participating in discussion in small groups of some twelve to fifteen students; and (3) students would spend 40 per cent of their class time in independent study in the library, in the laboratory, or in other special stations provided. It is customary that, wherever the plan is employed, that teachers' aides of several types are provided.

**Assignments.** In the Lakeview High School of Decatur, Illinois, the staff organization and respective duties are as follows:

Teacher Presenter

    Function and Role: Directs program; plans methods of instruction; gives large groups instruction; supervises evaluation.

    Training: Master's degree (certified teacher).

    Fields of Use: Business Education, Driver Education, English, Foreign Language, Mathematics, Health (P.E.), Science, Social Studies.

    Distribution of Time: Fifteen hours of student contact; twenty-five hours of planning, preparing, and supervising.

Teacher Instructor

    Function and Role: Works with small group instruction; assists with general instruction; works on student projects and individual learning problems.

    Training: Bachelor's or Master's degree (certified teacher).

    Fields of Use: Art, Business Education, English, Industrial Arts, Foreign Language, Homemaking, Mathematics, Music, P.E., Science, Social Studies.

    Distribution of Time: Thirty-six hours of student contact; four hours of preparation.

Instructional Aide

    Function and Role: Responsible for paper correcting; helps draft outside-of-class learning instruments.

    Training: Bachelor's degree (may or may not be certified).

    Fields of Use: English, Social Studies, Foreign Language, Science.

    Distribution of Time: Forty hours of work.

Clerk

    Function and Role: Types; duplicates materials; prepares reports; takes attendance; performs clerical chores, etc.

    Training: High-school graduate in Business Education (not certified).

    Fields of Use: Business Education, Driver Education, English, Foreign Language, Library, Mathematics, Social Studies.

    Distribution of Time: Forty hours of activity.

General Aide

    Function and Role: Responsible for student control in halls; co-curricular activities.

    Training: High-school graduate (not certified).

    Fields of Use: Study hall; co-curricular activities.

    Distribution of Time: Forty hours of work.

One of the teachers is selected by the principal, the head of the department, or the teacher coordinating the course, in many cases, as the main lecturer, although this is not always true; often, each member of the group of teachers lectures in his own special field of competence.

**Merits and Limitations of the Trump Plan.** Professor Trump and members of his committee, as well as many others, believe that the lecture plan would improve teaching and save time to be used in small discussion groups. It is also believed that, particularly when many of them are going on to college, more training in individual study should be given to high school students.

There have been objections to team teaching. Many teachers and administrators have found fault with the Trump plan, mentioning, among others, the following serious limitations:

1. The work of the course is fragmentized, while what is needed is more teaching in more comprehensive fields.
2. There is less personal contact between individual teachers and individual students.
3. It is very difficult to provide for as much independent study as is contemplated under the plan.

The following are advantages mentioned by proponents of team teaching:

Practical and effective in-service education through frequent team meetings.

Marked success in inducting new teachers into school systems by using interns as team teachers.

The use of aides to release teachers from routine duties.

Teacher involvement in planning and developing curriculum because of team structure.

Recognition for outstanding teachers through selection as team leaders.

Ability to form large and small groups for instruction, from one teacher to one student to one teacher for 200 students.

Improved guidance from the planned exchange of information about students and the atmosphere of fellowship within the team.

Increased interest and involvement of parents because of their children's common experience.

Improved climate of motivation because of the accent on individual identity and team spirit.

Greater student interest, due to varied groupings and presentations.

The best use of teacher talent, which should yield the highest quality of instruction.

Improved correlation of subject matter because of cooperative planning in team meetings. And, because teams can be kept together for more than one school year, the organization to develop sequences of content.

Through team leaders and team meetings, the identification and use of talented citizens and other educational resources of the community.[6]

## RELATIONSHIPS AMONG ADMINISTRATORS, SUPERVISORS, AND STAFF

Unlike college professors, secondary school teachers are supervised by a principal or superintendent or both and, in some instances, assistant principals and subject supervisors. The relationships between the

[6] Malcolm R. Douglass, "Team Teaching: Fundamental Change or Passing Fancy?" *The Education Digest*, Vol. 28 (May, 1963), pp. 50–51.

teachers and the administrators and supervisors are usually friendly and characterized by mutual respect. Gone are the close inspection and supervision of teachers that existed when teachers were poorly prepared, were overloaded, belonged to few if any educational organizations, read few if any educational journals and books, and in reality were not members of a profession but, rather, members of a skilled trade, and not too skilled at that.

The teacher of the present is much better trained, generally has a larger amount of experience, reads much more widely, belongs to several professional organizations, attends summer school occasionally, takes part in workshops, and needs less help in basic matters from the supervisor or administrator. Furthermore, with the increasing number of men going into secondary school teaching (in 1960, for the first time, the percentage proportionately exceeded 50 per cent) and the larger and increasing number of teachers having put five years into preparation, a larger percentage expect to make teaching a permanent career and, therefore, are alert to the need for self-improvement, getting help from a variety of sources.

Modern supervisors and administrators are cognizant of the improved status of teachers and give teachers leadership instead of directive supervision. The visiting of classrooms by supervisors and the holding of conferences with teachers are built upon this principle. With the very great changes taking place in education, and the many proposals and criticisms and resulting confusion, there is a distinct need for encouragement and professional assistance by supervisors and administrators.

**Cooperative Approaches.** Most administrators and supervisors believe that better results may be obtained by cooperative approach. In other words, stimulated and helped by the supervisors, teachers work together, do cooperative planning, assist each other, and approach the problems of their own teaching and those of the school in a cooperative fashion. The supervisor of today does not wish the teacher to believe him to know all the answers; he knows quite well that he does not, and, furthermore, he knows that for a good many of the problems there are no definite, permanent, and general answers. The correct answer varies from teacher to teacher, from school to school, and from situation to situation. Consequently, the modern approach is a cooperative study of the situation in order to work out what seems the best thing to do at the time.

Each beginning teacher should have at least one conference with the principal and each supervisor before school starts and another shortly after it starts. These should be continued through the first year and probably through the second and third years.

# QUESTIONS, PROBLEMS, AND TOPICS FOR FURTHER STUDY

1. There are those who are very much opposed to the addition to the secondary school staff of various types of specialized workers. What is your opinion?
2. Do you believe that all college graduates should be entitled to a certificate to teach in the schools?
3. What do you think should make up the general education of a teacher?
4. Do you believe that high school teachers should be required to do five years of college work before receiving a certificate to teach in high schools?
5. What courses in education do you think should be required of prospective teachers?
6. What things other than education should be taken into consideration in the selection of teachers?
7. Can you make some suggestions for reducing the load of teachers?
8. What do you think about the ethics of "moonlighting"?
9. What do you think supervisors and administrators can do to help weak teachers?
10. Be able to give a seven- or eight-minute talk on how a teacher may improve himself while in service.
11. Do you believe that evidence of professional growth should be required from every teacher every four or five years as a means to keeping his certificate in force?

## SUPPLEMENTARY MATERIALS
### Selected Readings

BRUE, WILLIAM F., and HOLDEN, JOHN, JR. *The Teacher's Personal Development.* New York: Holt, Rinehart & Winston, Inc., 1957. Part IV: "The Maturing Teacher"—Chapter 13, "Cooperating with Professional Associates."

CAROL, JOSEPH P. "Teacher Selection," *Bulletin of the N.A.S.S.P.,* No. 248 (September, 1959), 183–88.

CLEMENT, STANLEY L. "More Time for Teaching," *Bulletin of the N.A.S.S.P.,* No. 278 (December, 1962), 54–59.

DOUGLASS, HARL R. *Modern Administration of Secondary Schools.* Boston: Ginn & Co., 1963. Chapter 4, "Staffing the Schools," pp. 53–74; Chapter 5, "Arranging Staff Assignments," pp. 75–94.

HUGGETT, ALBERT. *Professional Problems of Teachers.* New York: The Macmillan Co., 1956. Part II, "Professional Personnel Policies and Working Conditions."

JOHNSON, CURTIS, and KARL VANDERHORCK. "Non-certified Laboratory Assistants," *Bulletin of the N.A.S.S.P.,* No. 244 (January, 1959), 13–48.

NORTON, MONTE S. "Extra Duties for Teachers," *Bulletin of the N.A.S.S.P.,* No. 269 (December, 1961), 105–10.

RICHLEY, R. W. *Planning for Teaching.* New York: McGraw-Hill Book Co., Inc., 1959. Chapter 1, "Aspects of Planning," Subdivision 5, "Professional Education and Certification of Teachers."

SMITH, VERNON H. "Team Teaching Has Advantages," *English Journal,* XLIX (April, 1960), 242–44.

SPIVAK, M. L. "Effectiveness of Departmental and Self-contained Seventh and Eighth-Grade Classrooms," *School Review*, LXIV (December, 1956), 391–96.

SPIVAK, M. L. "Junior High—Departmentalized or Self-contained?" *Phi Delta Kappan*, XXXVIII (January, 1957), 134–35.

"Team Teaching: A Review," *The Education Digest*, XXVII (December, 1961), 21–24.

TRUMP, J. LLOYD. "New Directions to Quality Education: The Secondary School Tomorrow." Washington, D.C.: National Association of Secondary School Principals Commission on the Experimental Study of the Utilization of the Staff in the Secondary School, 1960.

TURNEY, DAVID R. "Secretarial Help for Classroom Teachers," *The Education Digest*, XXVIII (December, 1962), 24–26.

WEISS, T. M. "Critique of the Team Approach," *Education Forum*, XXIV (January, 1960), 207–8.

WHERRY, JOSEPH E. "Staggered Schedule in Penn Hills," *Bulletin of the N.A.S.S.P.*, No. 275 (September, 1962), 51–53.

# 23

# The Secondary School Teacher and His Profession

## CHARACTERISTICS OF GOOD AND WEAK TEACHERS

**Criteria for Good Teachers.** The teachers who get the greatest satisfaction, recognition, and financial rewards are those who continue to improve themselves throughout their professional lives. Among the characteristics of superior teachers most commonly specified by the late Professor Arvil Barr, of the University of Wisconsin, and other investigators are the following: A good teacher

1. Plans assignments carefully and explains them clearly
2. Is helpful with students who have difficulties in the work
3. Obtains cooperation of students in planning learning activities
4. Is cheerful; has a pleasant disposition and manner and a sense of humor
5. Exhibits friendliness and interest both in the students as a group and in individual students
6. Frequently employs audio-visual aids and, particularly, visual aids
7. Sets reasonable standards for students—not too strict and not too easy
8. Maintains the same type of standards consistently and does not vary widely from day to day
9. Possesses a fair depth of knowledge of the subject matter, not only in textbook form but also in its applications
10. Is fair in marking papers and tests
11. Makes allowances for students of lesser abilities and requires more of bright students

12. Provides opportunities for creative students with narrow interests to engage in satisfying activities
13. Is fair and courteous in handling students' questions and differences of opinion but does not waste class time on those not worthy of much consideration
14. Possesses emotional stability, rarely losing his temper or seeming depressed or discouraged
15. Avoids favoritism or any indication of dislike for individual students
16. Rarely is sarcastic or emotionally critical, and then only with students who seem to respond well to that type of approach
17. Maintains good working conditions in the class while not being too strict in petty details of discipline
18. Does not talk too fast and speaks clearly in giving information, assignments, and explanations
19. Is of good appearance and wears good clothing that is modern though not ultrastylish or gaudy
20. Maintains good relations with students' parents

In evaluating teachers, it is very disconcerting and somewhat confusing to discover that there is very little direct relationship (1) between the measures of intelligence in the upper half of the range of intelligence or (2) between the grades made in subject-matter or educational courses and ratings of success by supervisors. It is exceedingly difficult to set up a means of measuring the effectiveness of teachers that is correlated closely with anything. Without question, teaching success is dependent upon many different factors, and it probably is correlated highly with the total of those factors and only loosely with any one.

**Characteristics of Weak Teachers.** It is unfortunate that the very large majority of ineffective teachers do not realize that they are really weak. They tend to overwork the natural, effective devices of rationalization and projection. They then think that the fault lies with the supervisor or the principal who does not back them up in an attempt to force their students to study harder and behave better. Some of them blame the parents for failing to imbue their children with the desire to learn, and, of course, many of them blame the children themselves.

Some good supervisors are able to assist the teachers in discovering where their weaknesses are through self-analysis, without discouraging them too much and without antagonizing them, and this can bring about an improvement in teaching quality. In some instances, it becomes obvious that the teacher is unsuited by disposition or temperament—as evidenced by lack of industry, ingenuity, or understanding of other people, particularly adolescents—to be successful in his profession. This is true even of some outstanding scholars.

Teachers who are unwilling or unable to improve should leave the teaching profession at the earliest opportunity in order that they may find a vocation in which they will be happy and will be rewarded adequately and in order that students will not suffer from weaknesses of an inadequate teacher. Among the teachers who are relatively unsuccessful are the following types:

1. Those *lacking in health and vitality.*

2. Those *who are overly conservative and old-fashioned.* Included in this group are very many young teachers who have a very narrow concept of responsibilites and opportunities and who attempt to justify their unwillingness or lack of ability to plan effective programs by the assumption that the newer methods are not effective but are merely passing fads.

3. Those *who are emotionally unstable.* These are inclined to excessive worrying, obsessed by fears, or unable to control their temper and excitability. In a considerable number of instances of this type, there is some degree of mental illness, and teachers who find themselves fairly frequently lacking in control of emotions such as anger and fear should seek medical or even psychiatric advice.

4. Those *with a discipline complex.* In many schools, there are at least several teachers who, for one reason or another—possibly the desire to satisfy their egos and appetites for respect, forced or voluntary—make very much of discipline, attempting to exert far greater control over the actions of the students than is necessary or wise, and who, as a matter of fact, often wind up with a relative lack of control of the class because of the antagonism of the students who oppose them.

5. Those *with defects of voice or speech.* Indistinct, scolding, whining, or condescending tone and inflection; lack of energy and color; too rapid speech; and lack of evidence of a sense of humor are examples of such defects.

6. Those *with defects in appearance or care of person.* These defects include flashy or gaudy dress, untidiness of dress or person, unchanging facial expression, lack of vivaciousness, and body odors.

7. Those *with defects in character or personality.* Irritability, overseriousness, insincerity, oversensitiveness, lack of confidence, drabness, lack of understanding of youthful points of view, abnormal activity, and emotional instability are numbered among such defects.

**Rating of Teachers.** From the beginning, it has been necessary for someone to make recommendations to the board of education with respect to the retention, dismissal, promotion, advancement of salary, and reassignment of teachers. This, of course, can only be done on the basis of some kind of rating, and the rating cannot be done well unless it is based on some observation of the teacher's work in the classroom.

Supervisors and administrators need to gather information about teachers that will lead to identification of those who, in order to protect the interest of the students, should not be retained, as well as those who should be promoted to be department heads, supervisors, assistant principals, and directors of instruction.

**Merit Rating and Salaries.** Originating early in the 1950's there has spread throughout the country, although it is still practiced in only a minority of schools, what is known as the *merit system of salary increases*. This movement developed out of the recognition by administrators and boards of education that there was a distinct shortage of superior teachers. There was a conviction on the part of some, and suspicion by many, that the best way to meet the situation for a local school system would be to identify the outstanding teachers and give them raises above those called for in the salary schedule obtaining in the school system at the time. This would enable the local school system to attract and retain the more effective and desirable teachers.

The plan of awarding extra pay increases on the basis of merit is favored particularly by individuals and taxpayer groups who believe that, if merit rating becomes general, it will not be necessary to raise teachers' salaries except for a small group of really superior teachers. Teachers are sharply divided on the issue.

Testimony with respect to the success of the idea varies from district to district. In many districts, particularly where there has been an active chapter of the American Federation of Teachers, merit rating has been vigorously opposed by the majority of teachers. Nevertheless, in a considerable proportion of school districts where the method is used, there has been very favorable testimony by administrators, the majority of teachers, and members of the board of education. Indeed, in some places it has served not to decrease the salaries of teachers but to improve them.

**Self-rating.** One of the recent trends in practice is that toward self-rating by teachers. Under the stimulation and guidance of supervisors, many teachers attempt to analyze their weak and strong points, which they may or may not discuss with supervisors and administrators. It is generally thought that the principal value of self-rating is what typically comes from situations where individuals attempt to analyze themselves with a view to self-improvement. It usually leads to a knowledge, on the part of the individual teacher who rates himself, of the qualities most desirable for teachers and to an idea of the degree to which he possesses those qualities.

**Rating by Students.** There have always been some schools in which teachers were formally rated, confidentially or otherwise, by their students. With respect to results of this practice, Bryan reported the findings shown in the tables below.

RESPONSES OF 75 TEACHERS TO THE QUESTION
"DO YOU THINK THAT OBTAINING STUDENT REACTIONS HAD ANY
FAVORABLE OR UNFAVORABLE EFFECT ON THE ATTITUDE OF PUPILS?"

|  | Teachers Responding | |
| --- | --- | --- |
| Possible Answers | Number | Per Cent |
| 1. Made pupils more critical................. | 4 | 5 |
| 2. Made pupils harder to discipline............ | 1 | 1 |
| 3. Seemed to have a desirable effect............ | 22 | 29 |
| 4. No observable effect one way or another...... | 48 | 64 |

SOURCE: Roy C. Bryan, *Student Relations and Merit Salary Schedules.* Kalamazoo: School of Graduate Studies, Western Michigan University, *Faculty Contributions,* Series IV, No. 2 (July, 1958), p. 50.

"DO YOU FEEL THAT INFORMATION CONCERNING YOUR STUDENTS'
REACTIONS BENEFITED YOU IN ANY WAY?"

|  | Response | | |
| --- | --- | --- | --- |
| Occasion | Yes | No | Total |
| First Response | 80 | 6 | 86 |
| Second Response | 69 | 6 | 75* |

* Only 75 teachers responded the second year, because eleven who had participated the previous year had transferred to other school systems.

SOURCE: Roy C. Bryan, *Student Reactions and Merit Salary Schedules.* Kalamazoo: School of Graduate Studies, Western Michigan University, *Faculty Contributions,* Series IV, No. 2 (July, 1958), p. 56.

## THE TEACHER'S PROFESSIONAL ETHICS

Doctors, dentists, lawyers, and even nurses seem to acquire quite early an understanding of, and a high regard for, what is known as professional ethics. The fact that this has been not too well developed in many teachers has caused many people to fail to think of teaching as a real profession. There is, however, in the teaching profession, a system of ethics covering a considerable number of points, particularly the relations of teachers to students, which has been approved by professional organizations, notably the National Education Association.

Professional ethics for teachers includes such matters as moral behavior outside of school and legal obligations, particularly to the board of education. There are teachers, for example, who think nothing of canceling in midsummer a commitment previously given to teach the following year, with little concern about the effect upon the school and its students. There has been developing recently very strong professional opposition to such irresponsible behavior.

An important aspect of professional ethics is the responsibility of teachers to cooperate with each other, with the parents, and with supervisors and administrators in planning and in teaching. Following is a statement of professional ethics that was prepared by the National Education Association:

We the members of the National Education Association of the United States, hold these truths to be self-evident—
—that the primary purpose of education in the United States is to develop citizens who will safeguard, strengthen, and improve the democracy obtained through a representative government;
—that the achievement of effective democracy in all aspects of American life and the maintenance of our national ideals depend upon making acceptable educational opportunities available to all;
—that the quality of education reflects the ideals, motives, preparation, and conduct of the members of the teaching profession;
—that whoever chooses teaching as a career assumes the obligation to conduct himself in accordance with the ideals of the profession.
As a guide for the teaching profession, the members of the National Education Association have adopted this code of professional ethics. Since all teachers should be members of a united profession, the basic principles herein enumerated apply to all persons engaged in the professional aspects of education—elementary, secondary, and collegiate.

FIRST PRINCIPLE. The primary obligation of the teaching profession is to guide children, youth, and adults in the pursuit of knowledge and skills, to prepare them in the ways of democracy, and to help them to become happy, useful, self-supporting citizens. The ultimate strength of the nation lies in the social responsibility, economic competence, and moral strength of the individual American.
In fulfilling the obligations of this first principle the teacher will—

1. Deal justly and impartially with students regardless of their physical, mental, emotional, political, economic, social, racial, or religious characteristics.
2. Recognize the differences among students and seek to meet their individual needs.
3. Encourage students to formulate and work for high individual goals in the development of their physical, intellectual, creative, and spiritual endowments.
4. Aid students to develop an understanding and appreciation not only of the opportunities and benefits of American democracy but also of their obligations to it.
5. Respect the right of every student to have confidential information about himself withheld except when its release is to authorized agencies or is required by law.
6. Accept no remuneration for tutoring except in accordance with approved policies of the governing board.

SECOND PRINCIPLE. The members of the teaching profession share with parents the task of shaping each student's purposes and acts towards socially acceptable ends. The effectiveness of many methods of teaching is dependent upon cooperative relationships with the home.

In fulfilling the obligations of this second principle the teacher will—

1. Respect the basic responsibility of parents for their children.
2. Seek to establish friendly and cooperative relationships with the home.
3. Help to increase the student's confidence in his own home and avoid disparaging remarks which might undermine that confidence.
4. Provide parents with information that will serve the best interests of their children, and be discreet with information received from parents.
5. Keep parents informed about the progress of their children as interpreted in terms of the purposes of the school.

THIRD PRINCIPLE. The teaching profession occupies a position of public trust involving not only the individual teacher's personal conduct, but also the interaction of the school and the community. Education is most effective when these many relationships operate in a friendly, cooperative, and constructive manner.

In fulfilling the obligations of this third principle the teacher will—

1. Adhere to any reasonable pattern of behavior accepted by the community for professional persons.
2. Perform the duties of citizenship, and participate in community activities, with due consideration for his obligations to his students, his family and himself.
3. Discuss controversial issues from an objective point of view, thereby keeping his class free from partisan opinions.
4. Recognize that the public schools belong to the people of the community, encourage lay participation in shaping the purposes of the school, and strive to keep the public informed of the educational program which is being provided.
5. Respect the community in which he is employed and be loyal to the school system, community, state, and nation.
6. Work to improve education in the community and to strengthen the community's moral, spiritual, and intellectual life.

FOURTH PRINCIPLE. The members of the teaching profession have inescapable obligations with respect to employment. These obligations are nearly always shared employer-employee responsibilities based upon mutual respect and good faith.

In fulfilling the obligations of this fourth principle the teacher will—

1. Conduct professional business through the proper channels.
2. Refrain from discussing confidential and official information with unauthorized persons.
3. Apply for employment on the basis of competence only, and avoid asking for a specific position known to be filled by another teacher.
4. Seek employment in a professional manner, avoiding such practices as the indiscriminate distribution of applications.

5. Refuse to accept a position when the vacancy has been created through unprofessional activity or pending controversy over professional policy or the application of unjust personnel practices and procedures.
6. Adhere to the conditions of a contract until service thereunder has been performed, the contract has been terminated by mutual consent, or the contract has otherwise been legally terminated.
7. Give and expect due notice before a change of position is to be made.
8. Be fair in all recommendations that are given concerning the work of other teachers.
9. Accept no recommendations from producers of instructional supplies when one's recommendations affect the local purchases or use of such teaching aids.
10. Engage in no gainful employment, outside of his contract, where the employment affects adversely his professional status or impairs his standing with students, associates, and the community.
11. Cooperate in the development of school policies and assume one's professional obligations thereby incurred.
12. Accept one's obligation to the employing board for maintaining a professional level of service.

FIFTH PRINCIPLE. The teaching profession is distinguished from many other occupations by the uniqueness and quality of the professional relationships among all teachers. Community support and respect are influenced by the standards of teachers and their attitudes toward teaching and other teachers. In fulfilling the obligations of this fifth principle the teacher will—

1. Deal with other members of the profession in the same manner as he himself wishes to be treated.
2. Stand by other teachers who have acted on his behalf and at his request.
3. Speak constructively of other teachers, but report honestly to responsible persons in matters involving the welfare of students, the school system, and the profession.
4. Maintain active membership in professional organizations and, through participation, strive to attain the objectives that justify such organized groups.
5. Seek to make professional growth continuous by such procedures as study, research, travel, conferences, and attendance at professional meetings.
6. Make the teaching profession so attractive in ideals and practices that sincere and able young people will want to enter it.

## THE TEACHER'S IN-SERVICE GROWTH

**Necessity for in-Service Growth.** Conditions of life are changing so fast and new knowledge is developing so rapidly that it is necessary for people in all professions and most vocations, including medicine, dentistry, business, engineering, and architecture, to continue study of their problems, responsibilities, procedures, techniques, and materials. This is true to a greater extent in the teaching profession than in most others, because, unlike the doctor, lawyer, dentist, nurse, or engineer, the teacher is only partly prepared when he begins teaching as a career. Even with five years of training, there will be the necessity for in-service growth. Former president of the University of California Sproul once said,

Nothing has handicapped the American educational plan more than the tendency of American citizens to think of schooling as a kind of vaccination against ignorance, and to consider that a concentrated dose of it in youth makes one immune for a lifetime. Actually, the immunity lasts only a few years, and unless it is renewed by periodic inoculations in study and thinking, one falls victim to a chronic type of ignorance which is often more dangerous than the acute form, because a patient, incompetent to recognize the symptoms, doesn't know he has the disease. We meet such chronic sufferers from ignorance everywhere. They look all right on the outside. . . . But inside, their minds are suffering from atrophy. Instead of thinking through problems in the light of all available facts, they merely supply a pattern of opinions based on facts that went out of date along with their yellowing diplomas, and liberally garnished with prejudices that have accumulated in their minds like broken furniture in an attic.

**Good in-Service Education Programs.** Some elements important in a good in-service education program may be listed as follows:

1. Teachers have an integral part in the planning and administering of the program.
2. Curriculum planning is carried on cooperatively by teachers, administrators, and supervisors.
3. Research and experimentation by teachers and teachers' groups are encouraged.
4. New teachers are well oriented to their position.
5. There is teacher-parent-community cooperation.
6. Sufficient time is available to carry on group activities without injury to the teacher's health and morale.
7. The administration is fair and open-minded. Suggestions of teachers carry weight and are given careful consideration.
8. All activities are carried on by administrators, supervisors, and teachers working as a team toward their fulfilment.

Among the types of teachers' in-service education activities that have been found most useful are the following:

1. Participating in curriculum planning.
2. Doing professional reading, writing, and speaking.
3. Planning and carrying out a series of faculty meetings dealing with the improvement of the instructional program.
4. Assuming responsibilities in professional education organizations.
5. Visiting schools to observe other members of the profession at work.

6. Continuing with an advanced-degree program.
7. Participating in institutes, workshops, and conferences in terms of special interests and needs.
8. Traveling for specific purposes.
9. Serving as an exchange teacher.
10. Participating in civic activities in the community.
11. Conducting research and applying research findings to local situations.

**Growth Through Research and Experimentation.** Increasingly, in recent years, classroom teachers have participated in planning and, indeed, in carrying on active research, which means, of course, trying a thing out but not on a very mathematically exact controlled situation.

**Growth Through Participation in Workshops.** One of the most effective types of organization for in-service education is the workshop, which is usually a cooperative study of specific problems of the school and staff, under the leadership of a workshop director. It is frequently conducted in the community in which the school is located, before the schools open in the fall or after they close in the spring. Practically all institutions of higher education provide workshops for teachers, primarily to study new developments in education.

**In-Service Growth Through Membership in Professional Organizations.** Practically all superior and professionally minded teachers belong to two or three professional organizations, including the state educational association, the National Education Association, or the Catholic Education Association, and certainly at least one of the national associations with specialized interests, such as the National Council of Teachers of English, the Music Educators National Conference, and the American Association for Health, Physical Education, and Recreation.[2]

## STUDENT TEACHING

In recent years, much attention has been given to improving the value of student-teaching experiences. In very few colleges and universities is it of the "hit-and-run" variety—leaving the campus to teach one course daily in the subject field and then returning to the college campus. More and more student teaching is taking the form of part-time internship with the very close cooperation of the school administration and the director or supervisor of student teaching of the college. In many places, experience is given the student teacher in some responsibilities and activities other than classroom teaching, such as assisting in the coaching

[2] See pages 151–152, for a list of such organizations, all with offices in Washington, D.C.

or sponsoring of an activity, assisting in the construction of a course-of-study unit, or assisting in the counseling of students. In many cases, the student is given an opportunity to observe a secondary school teacher other than the one to whom he is assigned.

## QUESTIONS, PROBLEMS, AND TOPICS FOR FURTHER STUDY

1. How could team teaching best be used in your major field?
2. What do you think about extra pay for extra work?
3. Do you think that teachers should be given tenure so that they may not be discharged from their positions except for very important reasons?
4. What are the pros and cons relative to the advisability of merit rating for salary increases?
5. Make a list of what you think are the twelve most important characteristics of a superior, effective teacher.
6. Examine carefully, the National Education Association Code of Ethics for the Teaching Profession (pages 453–455), and list any items with which you would take issue.
7. What do you think are the more important distinguishing characteristics of weak teachers?
8. In what ways do you think that the task of a student teacher differs from that of a beginning teacher?
9. List, in the order of their importance, ten points for the rating of teachers.

## SUPPLEMENTARY MATERIALS

### Selected Readings

BARR, A. S. "The Assessment of the Teacher's Personality," *The School Review*, LXVIII (Winter, 1960), 400–408.

BRUCE, WILLIAM F., and A. JOHN HOLDEN, JR. *The Teacher's Personal Development*. New York: Holt, Rinehart & Winston, Inc., 1957. Chapter 11, "Entering the Teaching Profession"; Chapter 14, "Living in the Community."

CASSEL, R. N., and W. L. JOHNS. "The Critical Characteristics of an Effective Teacher," *Bulletin of the N.A.S.S.P.*, November, 1960, 119–24.

DOUGLASS, HARL R. *Trends and Issues in Secondary Education*. Washington, D.C.: The Center for Applied Research in Education, Inc., 1962. Chapter 13, "The Education and Growth of Teachers."

FAUNCE, ROLAND C., and MORREL J. CLUTE. *Teaching and Learning in the Junior High School*. San Francisco: Wadsworth Publishing Co., Inc., 1961. Chapter 14, "Preparing Teachers for Junior High Schools."

GILCHRIST, ROBERT S., WILBUR H. DUTTON, and WILLIAM WRINKLE. *Secondary Education for American Democracy*. New York: Holt, Rinehart & Winston, Inc., 1957. Chapter 5, "What Makes a Successful Teacher?"

GRAMBS, JEAN D., WILLIAM J. IVERSON, and FRANKLIN K. PATTERSON. *Modern Methods in Secondary Education*. New York: Holt, Rinehart & Winston, Inc., 1958. Chapter 23, "Becoming a Teacher."

KETTELKAMP, GILBERT C. *Teaching Adolescents*. Boston: D. C. Heath & Co., 1954. Chapter 12, "Growing on the Job."

NOVAK, GAIL (ed.). *Your Career Opportunities in Teaching.* New York: Rowman and Littlefield, Inc., 1962. Contains information on many aspects of this profession—separate and related areas of the field, the nature of the work, employment prospects, institutions offering accredited instruction, etc.

POUNDS, RALPH L., and ROBERT L. GARRETSON. *Principles of Modern Education.* New York: The Macmillan Co., 1962. Chapter 3, "The Teacher Studying Himself," pp. 44–70.

ROSS, WILLIMIK. "In-Service Training of Junior High School Teachers," *Bulletin of the N.A.S.S.P.,* No. 251 (December, 1959), 13–17.

STILES, LINDLEY, ROY McCLEARY, and ROY TURNBAUGH. *Secondary Education in the United States.* New York: Harcourt, Brace & World, Inc., 1962. Chapter 15, "The Secondary School Teacher."

AUDIO-VISUAL MATERIALS

*Film*

*Planning for Personal and Professional Growth.* McGraw-Hill Text-Film. 18 minutes.

# Index

461